ENCOUNTERS WITH GODARD

THE SUNY SERIES
HORIZONS OF CINEMA
MURRAY POMERANCE | EDITOR

Also in the series

William Rothman, editor, *Cavell on Film*

J. David Slocum, editor, *Rebel Without a Cause*

Joe McElhaney, *The Death of Classical Cinema*

Kirsten Moana Thompson, *Apocalyptic Dread*

Frances Gateward, editor, *Seoul Searching*

Michael Atkinson, editor, *Exile Cinema*

Paul S. Moore, *Now Playing*

Robin L. Murray and Joseph K. Heumann, *Ecology and Popular Film*

William Rothman, editor, *Three Documentary Filmmakers*

Sean Griffin, editor, *Hetero*

Jean-Michel Frodon, editor, *Cinema and the Shoah*

Carolyn Jess-Cooke and Constantine Verevis, editors, *Second Takes*

Matthew Solomon, editor, *Fantastic Voyages of the Cinematic Imagination*

R. Barton Palmer and David Boyd, editors, *Hitchcock at the Source*

William Rothman, *Hitchcock: The Murderous Gaze, Second Edition*

Joanna Hearne, *Native Recognition*

Marc Raymond, *Hollywood's New Yorker*

Steven Rybin and Will Scheibel, editors, *Lonely Places, Dangerous Ground*

Claire Perkins and Constantine Verevis, editors, *B Is for Bad Cinema*

Dominic Lennard, *Bad Seeds and Holy Terrors*

Rosie Thomas, *Bombay before Bollywood*

Scott M. MacDonald, *Binghamton Babylon*

Sudhir Mahadevan, *A Very Old Machine*

David Greven, *Ghost Faces*

ENCOUNTERS WITH GODARD

Ethics, Aesthetics, Politics

JAMES S. WILLIAMS

Cover image: A still from *Éloge de l'amour* (2001) by Jean-Luc Godard featuring Edgar (Bruno Putzulu) and "Elle" (Berthe) (Cécile Camp). We have exercised due diligence in attempt to secure rights for the cover image from *Éloge de l'amour*. If you are the rights holder, kindly contact SUNY Press.

Published by State University of New York Press, Albany

© 2016 State University of New York

All rights reserved

Printed in the United States of America

No part of this book may be used or reproduced in any manner whatsoever without written permission. No part of this book may be stored in a retrieval system or transmitted in any form or by any means including electronic, electrostatic, magnetic tape, mechanical, photocopying, recording, or otherwise without the prior permission in writing of the publisher.

For information, contact State University of New York Press, Albany, NY
www.sunypress.edu

Production, Eileen Nizer
Marketing, Kate R. Seburyamo

Library of Congress Cataloging-in-Publication Data

Williams, James S., 1963–
 Encounters with Godard : ethics, aesthetics, politics / James S. Williams.
     pages cm. — (SUNY series, horizons of cinema)
 Includes bibliographical references and index.
 Includes filmography/discography.
 ISBN 978-1-4384-6063-5 (hc : alk. paper) — 978-1-4384-6062-8 (pb : alk. paper)
 ISBN 978-1-4384-6064-2 (e-book)
 1. Godard, Jean-Luc, 1930– —Criticism and interpretation. I. Title.

PN1998.3.G63W55 2016
791.4302'33092—dc23   2015021626

10 9 8 7 6 5 4 3 2 1

Contents

Illustrations Credits   vii

Acknowledgments   xiii

Introduction: Encountering Godard   1

1. The Politics of Violence and the End(s) of Art: Speaking (for) the Other in *La Chinoise* (1967)   19

2. The Signs in Our Midst: European Culture and Artistic Resistance in *Histoire(s) du cinéma* (1988–98)   53

3. Beyond the Cinematic Body: Digital Rhythms and In/human Breakdown   83

4. Silence, Gesture, Revelation: The Ethics and Aesthetics of Montage in Godard and Agamben   105

5. Music, Love, and the Cinematic Event   127

6. Crossing the Darkness: Metaphor, Difference, Dissymmetry in *Notre Musique* (2004)   151

7. Entering the Desert: Giving Face in *Film socialisme* (2010)   189

8. Soft and Hard/Back to Back: Erotic Encounters between Voice and Image in the Zone   207

Coda: Cinema after Language   247

Notes	255
Works Cited	291
Select Filmography/Discography	305
Index	309

Illustrations Credits

Chapter 1

Figure 1.1	*La Chinoise* (Optimum Home Releasing, 2005)	24
Figure 1.2	*La Chinoise* (Optimum Home Releasing, 2005)	24
Figure 1.3	*La Chinoise* (Optimum Home Releasing, 2005)	24
Figure 1.4	*La Chinoise* (Optimum Home Releasing, 2005)	25
Figure 1.5	*La Chinoise* (Optimum Home Releasing, 2005)	28
Figure 1.6	*La Chinoise* (Optimum Home Releasing, 2005)	35
Figure 1.7	*Masculin Féminin* (Argos Films-Arte France Développement, 2004)	39
Figure 1.8	*Sympathy for the Devil* (Fabulous Films Ltd, 2006)	40
Figure 1.9	*Éloge de l'amour* (Optimum Home Releasing, 2002)	44
Figure 1.10	Internet source: http://www.diagonalthoughts.com/?p=1930 (Accessed 1 May, 2015)	47
Figure 1.11	*Histoire(s) du cinéma* (4 DVD edition) (Gaumont Vidéo, 2007)	50
Figure 1.12	*Histoire(s) du cinéma* (4 DVD edition) (Gaumont Vidéo, 2007)	50
Figure 1.13	*Histoire(s) du cinéma* (4 DVD edition) (Gaumont Vidéo, 2007)	50

Chapter 2

Figure 2.1	*Histoire(s) du cinéma* (4 DVD edition) (Gaumont Vidéo, 2007)	59
Figure 2.2	*Histoire(s) du cinéma* (4 DVD edition) (Gaumont Vidéo, 2007)	59
Figure 2.3	*Histoire(s) du cinéma* (4 DVD edition) (Gaumont Vidéo, 2007)	63
Figure 2.4	*Histoire(s) du cinéma* (4 DVD edition) (Gaumont Vidéo, 2007)	65

Figure 2.5   *Histoire(s) du cinéma* (4 DVD edition) (Gaumont Vidéo, 2007)   65
Figure 2.6   *Histoire(s) du cinéma* (4 DVD edition) (Gaumont Vidéo, 2007)   65
Figure 2.7   *Histoire(s) du cinéma* (4 DVD edition) (Gaumont Vidéo, 2007)   70
Figure 2.8   *Histoire(s) du cinéma* (4 DVD edition) (Gaumont Vidéo, 2007)   70
Figure 2.9   *Histoire(s) du cinéma* (4 DVD edition) (Gaumont Vidéo, 2007)   70
Figure 2.10 *Histoire(s) du cinéma* (4 DVD edition) (Gaumont Vidéo, 2007)   70
Figure 2.11 *Histoire(s) du cinéma* (4 DVD edition) (Gaumont Vidéo, 2007)   76
Figure 2.12 *Histoire(s) du cinéma* (4 DVD edition) (Gaumont Vidéo, 2007)   76
Figure 2.13 *Histoire(s) du cinéma* (4 DVD edition) (Gaumont Vidéo, 2007)   78
Figure 2.14 *Histoire(s) du cinéma* (4 DVD edition) (Gaumont Vidéo, 2007)   78

Chapter 3

Figure 3.1   *Histoire(s) du cinéma* (4 DVD edition) (Gaumont Vidéo, 2007)   85
Figure 3.2   *Histoire(s) du cinéma* (4 DVD edition) (Gaumont Vidéo, 2007)   87
Figure 3.3   *Histoire(s) du cinéma* (4 DVD edition) (Gaumont Vidéo, 2007)   87
Figure 3.4   *Histoire(s) du cinéma* (4 DVD edition) (Gaumont Vidéo, 2007)   90
Figure 3.5   *Histoire(s) du cinéma* (4 DVD edition) (Gaumont Vidéo, 2007)   93
Figure 3.6   *Histoire(s) du cinéma* (4 DVD edition) (Gaumont Vidéo, 2007)   93
Figure 3.7   *Histoire(s) du cinéma* (4 DVD edition) (Gaumont Vidéo, 2007)   93
Figure 3.8   *Hélas pour moi* (Optimum Home Releasing, 2007)   96
Figure 3.9   *Hélas pour moi* (Optimum Home Releasing, 2007)   96
Figure 3.10 *Histoire(s) du cinéma* (4 DVD edition) (Gaumont Vidéo, 2007)   100

Chapter 4

Figure 4.1   *Keep Your Right Up! (Soigne Ta Droite!)* (Facets Video, 2001)   110
Figure 4.2   *Keep Your Right Up! (Soigne Ta Droite!)* (Facets Video, 2001)   111
Figure 4.3   *Keep Your Right Up! (Soigne Ta Droite!)* (Facets Video, 2001)   114
Figure 4.4   *Keep Your Right Up! (Soigne Ta Droite!)* (Facets Video, 2001)   117

Figure 4.5	*Keep Your Right Up!* (*Soigne Ta Droite!*) (Facets Video, 2001)	119
Figure 4.6	*Re Lear* (Metro-Goldwyn-Mayer Studios Inc, 2009)	121
Figure 4.7	*Keep Your Right Up!* (*Soigne Ta Droite!*) (Facets Video, 2001)	123

Chapter 5

Figure 5.1	*Prénom Carmen* in *Jean-Luc Godard vol 2* (Warner, 2005)	129
Figure 5.2	*Lettre à Freddy Buache* in *Jean-Luc Godard. Documents* (Éditions du Centre Pompidou, 2006)	132
Figure 5.3	*Je vous salue, Marie* (Gaumont Vidéo, 2010)	134
Figure 5.4	*Je vous salue, Marie* (Gaumont Vidéo, 2010)	134
Figure 5.5	*Passion/Nouvelle Vague* (2 DVD edition) (Cahiers du Cinéma, 2005)	140
Figure 5.6	*Passion/Nouvelle Vague* (2 DVD edition) (Cahiers du Cinéma, 2005)	140
Figure 5.7	*Passion/Nouvelle Vague* (2 DVD edition) (Cahiers du Cinéma, 2005)	141
Figure 5.8	*Éloge de l'amour* (Optimum Home Releasing, 2002)	150

Chapter 6

Figure 6.1	*Notre Musique* (Optimum Home Releasing, 2005)	154
Figure 6.2	*Notre Musique* (Optimum Home Releasing, 2005)	156
Figure 6.3	*Notre Musique* (Optimum Home Releasing, 2005)	162
Figure 6.4	*Notre Musique* (Optimum Home Releasing, 2005)	163
Figure 6.5	*Notre Musique* (Optimum Home Releasing, 2005)	165
Figure 6.6	*Notre Musique* (Optimum Home Releasing, 2005)	171
Figure 6.7	*Notre Musique* (Optimum Home Releasing, 2005)	176
Figure 6.8	*Notre Musique* (Optimum Home Releasing, 2005)	176
Figure 6.9	*Ici et Ailleurs* (Olive Films, 2012)	178
Figure 6.10	*Notre Musique* (Optimum Home Releasing, 2005)	181

x / Illustrations Credits

Chapter 7

Figure 7.1	Internet source: http://www.closeupfilmcentre.com/vertigo_magazine/issue-30-spring-2012-godard-is/entering-the-desert-the-book-of-film-socialisme/ (Accessed 1 May, 2015)	197
Figure 7.2	Internet source: http://www.closeupfilmcentre.com/vertigo_magazine/issue-30-spring-2012-godard-is/entering-the-desert-the-book-of-film-socialisme/ (Accessed 1 May, 2015)	197
Figure 7.3	Internet source: http://www.closeupfilmcentre.com/vertigo_magazine/issue-30-spring-2012-godard-is/entering-the-desert-the-book-of-film-socialisme/ (Accessed 1 May, 2015)	198
Figure 7.4	Internet source: http://www.closeupfilmcentre.com/vertigo_magazine/issue-30-spring-2012-godard-is/entering-the-desert-the-book-of-film-socialisme/ (Accessed 1 May, 2015)	198
Figure 7.5	Internet source: http://www.closeupfilmcentre.com/vertigo_magazine/issue-30-spring-2012-godard-is/entering-the-desert-the-book-of-film-socialisme/ (Accessed 1 May, 2015)	198
Figure 7.6	Internet source: http://www.closeupfilmcentre.com/vertigo_magazine/issue-30-spring-2012-godard-is/entering-the-desert-the-book-of-film-socialisme/ (Accessed 1 May, 2015)	198
Figure 7.7	Internet source: http://www.closeupfilmcentre.com/vertigo_magazine/issue-30-spring-2012-godard-is/entering-the-desert-the-book-of-film-socialisme/ (Accessed 1 May, 2015)	199
Figure 7.8	Internet source: http://www.closeupfilmcentre.com/vertigo_magazine/issue-30-spring-2012-godard-is/entering-the-desert-the-book-of-film-socialisme/ (Accessed 1 May, 2015)	199
Figure 7.9	Internet source: http://www.closeupfilmcentre.com/vertigo_magazine/issue-30-spring-2012-godard-is/entering-the-desert-the-book-of-film-socialisme/ (Accessed 1 May, 2015)	199
Figure 7.10	*Film socialisme* (Wild Side Vidéo, 2010)	201
Figure 7.11	*Film socialisme* (Wild Side Vidéo, 2010)	201

Chapter 8

Figure 8.1	*Histoire(s) du cinéma* (4 DVD edition) (Gaumont Vidéo, 2007)	208
Figure 8.2	*La Chinoise* (Optimum Home Releasing, 2005)	213
Figure 8.3	*Soft and Hard* in *Jean-Luc Godard Ensayos* (4 DVD edition) (Intermedio, 2011)	218

Figure 8.4	*Soft and Hard* in *Jean-Luc Godard Ensayos* (4 DVD edition) (Intermedio, 2011)	218
Figure 8.5	*Soft and Hard* in *Jean-Luc Godard Ensayos* (4 DVD edition) (Intermedio, 2011)	221
Figure 8.6	*Slow Motion* (Artificial Eye, 2006)	223
Figure 8.7	Internet source: http://www.beirutartcenter.org/parallel-events.php?exhibid=124&statusid=3 (Accessed 1 May, 2015)	225
Figure 8.8	*Armide* in *Aria* (Special Edition) (Second Sight Films, 2009)	233
Figure 8.9	*Histoire(s) du cinéma* (4 DVD edition) (Gaumont Vidéo, 2007)	240
Figure 8.10	*Re Lear* (Metro-Goldwyn-Mayer Studios Inc, 2009)	242
Figure 8.11	*Histoire(s) du cinéma* (4 DVD edition) (Gaumont Vidéo, 2007)	242
Figure 8.12	*Histoire(s) du cinéma* (4 DVD edition) (Gaumont Vidéo, 2007)	244
Figure 8.13	*Histoire(s) du cinéma* (4 DVD edition) (Gaumont Vidéo, 2007)	244

Coda

Figure C.1	*Goodbye to Language* (StudioCanal Limited, 2014)	249
Figure C.2	*Goodbye to Language* (StudioCanal Limited, 2014)	251
Figure C.3	*Goodbye to Language* (StudioCanal Limited, 2014)	251
Figure C.4	*Goodbye to Language* (StudioCanal Limited, 2014)	253

Acknowledgments

This book grew out of a chance e-mail encounter with Murray Pomerance around Cocteau. I would like to express my deepest gratitude to Murray for his immediate enthusiasm for the project and for considering it worthy of inclusion in his Horizons of Cinema series. His warm generosity, both personal and intellectual, and his unique sense of style have been an immense source of inspiration. Sincere thanks go to co-director of SUNY Press James Peltz and editorial assistant Rafael Chaiken for their exceptional support and expertise at all stages. It has been a delight to work with Eileen Nizer and Kate Suburyamo on the production and marketing of the book. Thanks also to Camille Hale for her scrupulous copyediting and Alan Rutter for his superb work on the index. I am indebted to Michael Witt for his important advice and encouragement in the early stages and his meticulous reading of parts of the book as it neared completion. The identity of the two anonymous readers of the manuscript must necessarily remain unknown, but I record my appreciation for their many insightful comments and important suggestions which proved extremely helpful in preparing the final version. The book has also benefitted enormously from conversations over the years with friends and colleagues about Godard and film in general, in particular Timothy Barnard, Leo Bersani, Nicole Brenez, Vicki Callahan, Chris Darke, Claire Denis, Thomas Elsaesser, David Faroult, Albertine Fox, Catherine Grant, Frances Guerin, Henrik Gustafsson, Eric Robertson, Jonathan Romney, Julian Ross, Libby Saxton, Michael Sheringham, Michael Temple, Alfred Thomas, Rob White, Roland-François Lack, and Phil Powrie.

Earlier versions of some chapters or parts of chapters, which I have fully updated and in most cases substantially developed and expanded, were originally published in the following edited volumes and journals: *Journal of European Studies* 40:3 (2010) (chapter 1); *The Cinema Alone: Essays on the Work of Jean-Luc Godard 1985–2000* (University of Amsterdam Press, 2000), ed. Michael Temple and James S. Williams (chapter 2); *Inhuman Reflections: Thinking the Limits of the Human* (Manchester University Press, 2000), ed. Scott Brewster, John J. Joughin, David Owen, and Richard J. Walker (chapter 3); *Cinema and Agamben: Ethics, Biopolitics and Moving Image* (New York: Bloomsbury, 2014), ed. Henrik Gustafsson and Asbjørn Grønstad (chapter 4); *For Ever Godard* (London: Black Dog Press, 2004), ed. Michael Temple, James S. Williams, and Michael Witt (chapter 5); *Vertigo* (UK) 30 (2012) (chapter 7); *Dalhousie French Studies* 45 (1998) (co-authored by Michael

Temple) (chapter 8); and *Aimez-vous le queer?* (Rodopi: Cahiers de Recherche des Instituts néerlandais, 2005), ed. Lawrence R. Schehr (chapter 8). I would like to thank the publishers for granting me permission to draw on this body of material.

Finally, I offer my special thanks and love to Jason Gittens, for always being there.

Introduction

Encountering Godard

[A]rt is getting out of yourself, like making a child. It's the only means I have to understand and change myself, to hear what others say of me, and to bring others into being.[1]

—J.-L. Godard in *Soft and Hard*

Cinema is an expansion, an extension, to the world, it's the language of the world.

—J.-L. Godard

In one of the earliest sustained accounts in English of Jean-Luc Godard's cinema, Susan Sontag sought to take critical stock of his work up to 1968 in aesthetic and ethical terms. The wide-ranging and pioneering piece called simply "Godard" (included in *Styles of Radical Will*) celebrated Godard's immense poetic will and aesthetic affirmation, arguing that his work implied a particular function for art: "sensory and conceptual dislocation. Each of Godard's films is a totality that undermines itself, a de-totalized totality" (Sontag 2009a: 163). This is because, in Sontag's view, Godard is interested "in the *convergence* of spontaneity with the emotional discipline of abstraction" (ibid.: 174; original emphasis). Just as "ideas are chiefly formal elements in Godard's films, units of sensory and emotional stimulation" (ibid.: 165), so his sensorial techniques are "something harmonious, *plastically and ethically engaging, and emotionally tonic*" (ibid.: 151; my emphasis).[2] Sontag concluded more generally: "A film is conceived of as a *living organism*: not so much an object as a *presence* or an *encounter*—a fully historical or contemporary event, whose destiny it is to be transcended by future events" (ibid.: 177; my emphasis).

One may balk a little perhaps now at Sontag's sweepingly assertive and apodictic theoretical moves. Moreover, not all her claims and insights have stood the test of time. For example, she downplays Godard's use of rhetoric, contending that Godard, unlike Robert Bresson, was "bent on destroying rhetoric by a lavish use of irony—the familiar outcome when a restless, somewhat disassociated intelligence struggles to cancel an irrepressible romanticism and tendency to moralize" (ibid.: 182). This view appears to have been proven wrong by Godard's later work, especially the mammoth *Histoire(s) du cinéma* (1988–1998) which marks a major shift in tone and mood as Godard confronts with deadly seriousness the issues of twentieth-century history and memory, clinging rhetorically to the shards of cinema and European culture even as he reworks, modifies, and transforms them. Similarly, the various points Sontag makes about melodrama and prostitution as a metaphor for the fate of human consciousness hold little currency in the light of Godard's later, more self-consciously poetic and metaphysical work. Yet the point is not really whether Sontag was ultimately right or wrong in all her critical judgments. Of far more lasting importance is the fact that she was attempting to explain what the experience of watching Godard's films drew out of her personally as a critic. The fundamental issues she raises of spectatorial response and feeling, premised on the idea that any concerted study of Godard's work requires us to bring ethics and aesthetics dynamically together, remain equally relevant today. Indeed, what makes Sontag's singular approach to Godard still so exciting and influential is her insistence that a cinema of ideas goes hand in hand with emotion and that ethics and aesthetics are intimately linked to a film's sensory, emotional, and erotic qualities. "Godard" is prefaced by an unattributed quote stating that ethics and aesthetics always converge in some form or other, that they are never separate choices, and that "the very definition of the human condition should be in the *mise-en-scène* itself" (ibid.: 147).

Sontag's attempt to establish universal truths about Godard's work and practice, and in so doing formalize a new kind of modernism, is the result of an exceptional intellectual and emotional engagement with Godard. Hers is a fully fledged and highly stylized critical response, both original and adventurous, which, by viewing Godard's early films both as philosophical (i.e., about ideas) and as the mark of a unique stylist, opens up new, fertile lines of inquiry. In fact, the reason why Sontag's remarkable literary performance remains such a powerful and inspiring model of critical reading is that it demonstrates by example that we need as critics to forge a new, imaginative, and above all personal, style of film criticism in order to grasp such an all-encompassing and shapeshifting artist as Godard. Just as a Godard film is the site of a radical encounter and material event, so the very act of writing on Godard needs to be a live, creative encounter in the critical present engaging with potentially every aspect and level of his work. This means working through, emotionally as well as intellectually, the particular challenges faced in finding an appropriate critical style equal to the task. Hence, feeling and sensation are not merely abstract theoretical concerns for the modern critic but real and concrete phenomena central to the critical enterprise. Indeed, Sontag calls in her 1964 manifesto foreword "Against Interpretation" for a complete reinvention of the critical task, declaring (and I cite at length to savor Sontag's bold, idiosyncratic language): "We must learn to *see* more, to *hear* more, to *feel* more [. . .] The aim of all commentary on art now should be to make works of art—and, by analogy, our own experience—more, rather than less, real to us. The function of criticism should be to show *how it is what it is*, even *that it is what it is*, rather than to show what it means [. . .] In place of a hermeneutics we need an erotics of art" (Sontag 2009b: 14; original emphasis). When she adds that "[s]tyle is the principle of decision in a work, the signature of the artist's will (ibid.: 32), she is talking also about a new critical style which she defines in terms of "transparence," a quality inherent in "experiencing the luminousness of the thing in itself, of things being what they are" (ibid.: 13). Both Godard's visionary "multi-cinema" and Sontag's own supremely individual critical response to it exemplify this idea of a modern erotics of art and transparence.

Sontag's dazzlingly ambitious and free approach to Godard stands out from much current critical work on Godard where, with the filmmaker now well into his eighties, there is an increasing trend to approach his cinematic project in fatalistic terms as an essentially complete oeuvre and confer on it a fixed destiny and finality. The recent co-authored volume *The Legacies of Jean-Luc Godard* (Morrey, Stojanova and Côté, 2014), for example, appears to suggest that now is already the time to provide a summative appraisal and judgment of the great director. The volume's critical animus is retrospective and evaluative, and while it contains some fine contributions, it possesses a distinctly commemorative tone not too far removed from the steady cluster of long and largely consecratory biographies of Godard (MacCabe 2003, Brody 2008, de Baecque 2011). Yet this runs the immediate risk of adopting a teleological narrative approach to the corpus and (re)periodizing it according to a set of generalizing overall perspectives often directly determined by Godard's own copious and highly seductive metacommentary on his work. Moreover, such a synthesizing, totalizing strategy overlooks the fact that each work by Godard, although an integral part of an on-going experimental process, possesses what T. S. Eliot called its own "imaginative logic" and exists on its own terms as a drama of the artistic will, some films more explicitly and self-reflexively than others, such as Godard's take on the Holy Birth in *Je vous salue, Marie* (1985). Indeed, for all the esteem (often hyperbolic) in which he is held by many, and precisely because of his progressive veneration as a "professor" and "historian" of film, he now finds himself arguably not being taken seriously enough as a still vital and innovative plastic artist urgently engaged with the contemporary world. This situation is not helped by his off-the-wall and sometimes ill-timed musings about culture and politics, for some in France the manifest signs of an irascible old devil who is fast losing the plot (for example, his deliberately provocative statement in June 2014 that he wished President Hollande would make Marine Le Pen of the Front National prime minister, "if only for things to seem to move forward").[3]

Yet Godard's live and continually evolving multimedia work remains as sharp and potent as ever in its mercurial playfulness, brooding brilliance, and moving, often haunting, beauty. It is composed of multiple tones and intensities, of intricate, interstitial folds and textures, of driving rhythms and eddies of sound, of radiant conceptual vistas and spiraling loops of ideas that incite new ways of thinking and perceiving and demand fresh forms of intellectual and creative response. It defies easy readings, insists on the mystery of cinematographic creation, and stretches the very boundaries of critical analysis and interpretation. This is especially true of Godard's work since the mid-1980s, which has become at once increasingly dense and diffuse in its referencing of historical, philosophical, theological, political, literary, and metaphysical material from the European and Anglo-American traditions, much cited at length, sometimes even in the original language, resulting in a calibrated mesh of interweaving threads and refracted networks of associations—the unique riffs and idioms of "late Godard." Yet the Godard corpus is not a smooth and seamless machine (how could it be?), and its occasional lurchings into overdrive or blockage due to oversaturation are part of the compulsive pleasures of the aesthetic encounter. As Sam Rohdie observes in the case of *Histoire(s)*, Godard's work "evokes a huge outside. And since the outside is, of necessity, always changing, subject to History, the film is never still, is always becoming, is always alive" (Rohdie 2010). Any critical expectations of conformity and stability continue to be gleefully subverted by Godard, most recently through his experimentation with digital video, resulting in rebellious, unclassifiable works like *Film socialisme* (2010). Indeed, such films, while they contribute to the daunting sense of *terribilità* often surrounding Godard, also attest to what Edward Said has called the prerogative of late style glimpsed in artists ranging from Beethoven to Thomas Mann and Jean Genet, namely its "power to render disenchantment and pleasure without resolving the contradiction between them" (Said 2007: 148). For Said, what holds these two forces in tension as they strain in opposite directions is precisely "the artist's mature subjectivity, stripped of hubris and pomposity, unashamed either of its fallibility or of the modest assurance it has gained as a result of age and exile" (ibid.), where exile is to be understood as "a kind of self-imposed exile from what is generally acceptable, coming after it, and surviving beyond it" (ibid.: 16).[4] This conception of artistic "lateness" not as harmony and resolution (of the objective world and subjective light, for instance) but rather as intransigence and dissociation applies equally well to Godard's uncompromising work of the last thirty or so years which continues to lay siege to convention and, with mounting fervor, pulverize the trappings of rational logic.

I believe, in fact, that at this pivotal stage in Godard studies we need to restore Sontag's spirit of critical commitment and adventure and her sense of the special, intersubjective status of the cinematic event by engaging intimately with his work in the live aesthetic, ethical, and emotional space of critical interpretation, and by daring to develop a new critical style and vocabulary. I am not suggesting by this, of course, that we simply imitate Sontag. Writing in the late 1960s Sontag championed an art linked to proof, which, she claimed, "is always formal (a mode of argument that is, by definition, complete)," as opposed to analysis where "there are always further *angles of understanding*, new realms of causality. Analysis is substantive" (Sontag 2009b: 198; my emphasis). Yet different times call for different measures. Rather than attempt to establish eternal cinematic and aesthetic truths about Godard based on the principle of proof, we need to pursue with greater vigor and imagination the work of textual analysis and interpretation in order to discover more what makes Godard such an incomparable and far-reaching twenty-first-century artist as opposed to merely a philosopher of film or, at worst, a didactic, po-faced recycler of ideas from the past as he is now in fast danger of appearing. Or rather we should try to combine these two approaches: on the one hand analysis with its creation of new angles of understanding, and on the other proof, the subject of which, to cite Sontag, is "the form (above and beyond the matter) of events, and the forms (above and beyond the matter) of consciousness," and whose formal means "include a conspicuous element of design (symmetry, repetition, inversion, doubling, etc.)" (ibid.). With most of the necessary groundwork of catching up with late or "lost" or otherwise "invisible" Godard now largely complete,[5] and building in particular on the recent fruits of Michael Witt's outstanding *Jean-Luc Godard, Cinema Historian* (2013), a sumptuously produced study of Godard's historical project of the 1980s and 1990s, we now have the opportunity to initiate more openly subjective readings and interpretations of his work. Indeed, it is precisely due to the rigorous objectivity and empirically substantiated claims of volumes like Witt's that other, more personal critical approaches are possible—readings that aim to convey and interpret directly the shock and surprise, the mystery and danger, even scandal, of Godard's poetic method of connecting through montage elements that wouldn't normally be brought together.

To attempt this, we will need to give ourselves the time and space to undergo *as if for the first time* the full emotional and physical experience of watching, hearing, and feeling Godard—a leap into spectatorial absorption that can often be dizzying and overwhelming or sometimes simply bewildering. Moreover, we need to trust our interpretive instincts and take the risk that we may even be off the mark in our heuristic readings. Yet the immediate intensity of the immersive critical experience is a vital first step that needs to be positively embraced. I date my own interest in Godard from the moment I first encountered *Sauve qui peut (la vie)* (1979), his return to commercial feature filmmaking after his extensive work in video and television during the 1970s with his long-term collaborator Anne-Marie Miéville, and where he sought to reinvest the possibilities and absolutes of art in an entirely new, postutopian political period defined, as the title puts it, as "every man for himself." Watching this extraordinary film dynamized by the processes of video and stop-start motion was like a *coup de foudre*—a tumultuous and indelible visceral experience of space, energy, and movement (visual, chromatic, sonic), orchestrated with such fluency and touch by Godard that the medium suddenly revealed itself in unprecedented and exhilarating ways.

Speaking only personally, Godard pushes me always to the limits as a critic and tests my critical alertness, intelligence, and sensitivity at every moment. His work encourages me to move freestyle across different fields and disciplines in order to write *on, under, with,* and *through* it stylistically. I relish this close, sustained contact. To employ the terms of Godard's favorite game of tennis, which features prominently in his work—he plays mixed doubles in *JLG/JLG: autoportrait de décembre* (*JLG/JLG: December Self-portrait*) 1995), rehearses ground strokes at home in *Soft and Hard: Soft Talk on a Hard Subject between Two Friends* (1985), ruminates on the game as the "Idiot"/"Prince" in *Soigne ta droite: Une place sur la terre* (*Keep Your Right*

Up: A Place on Earth) (1987), and even enlists former French professional tennis player Catherine Touvier for *Film socialisme*—Godard can draw me out wide as a critic, obliging me always to leave my comfort zone and abandon any prearranged game plan. Despite the occasional showstopping ace (for example, a jaw-dropping alignment of beauty and horror in montage), Godard's irresistible style of authorial play propels me invariably into long rallies where the sheer thrill and intensity of the baseline exchanges require that I create new angles in turn and move forward where possible for a face-to-face confrontation. Yet he can also suddenly cut me off at the net with a deft slice or top-spin pass (a sudden switch to slow motion, a familiar sound reconfigured, a quiver of electronic color), or else floor me with an exquisite lob from the back of the court that leaves me breathlessly counting the metaphysical space now revealed. In fact, Godard can sometimes catch me out completely with his effortless touch, from the simplest of stop-volleys to the dinkiest of drop-shots (a random close-up, an instant of hushed silence to heighten a musical motif, a spatial or transitional pause when the world appears suspended on its axis, as in the camera-as-pendulum scene of *Vivre sa vie*). I could go on.

In short, Godard's prodigious, multiform work solicits from me, indeed demands, a wide-ranging, multileveled, individual response, at once intuitive and intellectual, that crosses freely disciplinary borders and areas (art, philosophy, literature, music, aesthetics, theology, history, metaphysics) with a flexibility of method and subtlety of approach. The fluid, mutable, transformative spaces of Godard's cinema offer the excitement of negotiating new forms, new chromatics, and new harmonics in its continual (re)grafting of sounds and images with bold washes of color, searing chords, and shooting stars of ideas. This is a true cinema of the senses, with sudden rushes of multisensory, erotic, and mental energy, vibrations and stimulations, often of synaesthetic power. We "hear" images and see "sounds" in *Passion* (1981), for example, and Baudelaire's "Correspondences" is aptly recited at length in *Notre Musique* (2004). Indeed, in his groundbreaking work as a sound artist and composer of polyphonic soundtracks, Godard sculpts new, luminous sheets and textures of sonic space through an ever more complex interplay of diegetic and nondiegetic sound that oscillates between the human voice and silence, found sound and ambient noise, and live and recorded music (from the Western classical canon to popular music, jazz, and entire swathes of the ECM New Series catalog).

How can one attempt to convey such affective and intellectual intensities in Godard's work and open oneself up in the immediate present tense of writing to its multiple plastic and expressive qualities? That is, how can one engage with the full panoply of Godard's cinema without simply trying to capture and relay on the page all the intricate syncopations of Godardian montage frame by frame and also within the same frame (a process that reaches its logical conclusion in the detailed written *découpage* of sound and image), or, at the other extreme, encasing it in a grid of preordained and totalizing critical paradigms? Moreover, how can one do critical justice to the rich textual mosaic of Godard's work and its boundless aesthetic capacity to surprise without treating it merely as a repository of thoughts and ideas to be patiently itemized and cataloged, or else reducing it to a recalcitrant object to be intellectually "rationalized"? How, in short, is one to take full critical store of the visual and auditory pleasures of Godard's uniquely challenging and continually enthralling poetic works which can throb, pull, tug, elate, and ache in equal measure in the transfer of spectatorial heat and affect?

While the preferred critical model for writers on Godard remains the conventional format monograph offering a scholarly overview of the work (Roud 1967, Cerisuelo 1989, Dixon 1997, Morrey 2005, Drabinski 2008, and Morgan 2013 stand out), as well as the single- or multiauthored volume devoted to one film (notably Leutrat 1990, Locke and Warren 1995, Wills 2001) and the broader comparative study around a general theme such as self-reflexivity in cinema (Kiwan 1978, Stam 1992), other forms of approach to Godard have privileged a more personal response and sought to translate the spontaneity of his work, or what Zsuzsa Baross calls suggestively its distinctive "presentness" (Baross 2009: 137). Jean-Luc Douin's *Jean-Luc Godard: Dictionnaire des passions* (2010), for instance, an alphabetically organized series of critical snapshots and anecdotes, is a sophisticated exercise in pure cinephilia, while *Godard simple comme bonjour* (2005) by Suzanne Liandrat-Guigues and Jean-Louis Leutrat zigzags thematically across the entire corpus with serendipitous detours. The most interesting and original example of the intersubjective approach, however, is that of Kaja Silverman and Harun Farocki's *Speaking about Godard* (1998), since it brings a theorist into direct dialogue with a filmmaker. There are many enlightening passages in this extended dialogue around eight films covering the period up to *Nouvelle Vague* (1990), yet, as David Sterritt, himself the author of an important 1991 volume of close readings of selected Godard films, has rightly remarked, although "the methodology [. . .] seems eminently Godardian at first, [it] would be more persuasive if the conversations read more like lively, interactive exchanges, and less like alternating blocks of self-contained insight and opinion. Such interactivity would certainly be present if the dialogues between Silverman and Farocki had been transcribed directly from their actual conversations" (Sterritt 2000).

Another option might be to approach Godard's work through the altogether different genre of video criticism, just as Godard himself pursued his (hi)stories of cinema in *Histoire(s)* in the very medium considered its usurper and enemy, namely video (Cain to cinema's Abel, as he formulates it in *Sauve qui peut*). I recently collaborated on a short video essay around *Le Mépris* (1963) entitled *Snakes&Funerals*. The title refers to a dismissive comment made in *Le Mépris* by Fritz Lang, playing himself, that CinemaScope is "only good for snakes and funerals." Inspired by the majestic move towards abstraction and silence in the last moments of the film, when the camera tracks right to left to capture Lang's camera in the film-within-a-film moving slowly forward behind Ulysses, who faces out with arms aloft towards an indistinct blue blur of sky and sea, we sought to distil *Le Mépris* into a series of looping, denarrativized fragments and sense impressions. Our aim was to "queer" this modern-classical masterpiece about the doomed heterosexual couple by transporting it into a new kind of indeterminacy and sensory void. The orchestral theme *Camille* by Georges Delerue, which Godard never took very seriously, was rearranged on a new track and played for its underlying pathos, conjoined now with a specially recorded Finnish folk song ("The Sky Is Blue and White") featuring a single female voice. Sound and image were then brought together digitally according to the simple logic of chance. The consequences for the gendered nature of "natural" color and "straight" repetition remained inconclusive, but the close, intimate encounter with *Le Mépris* allowed us to experience directly its intoxicating poetic power and immaculate composition, yet also its peculiarly troubling and often brutal beauty.[6]

Ethics/Aesthetics/Politics

To return to the written page, and in the absence of a ready answer to these practical questions of subjective response, I wish to invoke again Sontag's central juxtaposition of ethics and aesthetics and emotion in the cinematic encounter. The very notion of encounter has, of course, important ethical connotations. For Emmanuel Levinas, who is often invoked in Godard's later work, it is an occasion for generosity and openness to the difference of the other, in contrast with the Hegelian and existentialist traditions of European thought and metaphysics, where the encounter between self and other can provoke a violent struggle for survival and preeminence (the idea, for example, that the other is knowable and can be made an object of the self). The permanent drama of Godard's work, and what makes it so endlessly compelling, is that it is always striving to encounter formally, and work through, different modes and instances of otherness and "foreign" matter, whether of race, ethnicity, culture, class, language, background, history, or gender. Indeed, Godard directly foregrounds questions of alterity in cinema both at a thematic level (the issue of how to represent the living other without denying his/her integrity— i.e., the politics of representation) and at a formal level (the challenge of how to negotiate and process the material world while also addressing the implied viewer). These two main questions, which are also issues of relationality, are often posed simultaneously in the form of a conundrum: how does one position and frame the other and viewer mutually and respectfully while at the same time filtering the recorded real, even to the point of transfiguring it poetically?

Godard's working engagement with alterity, broadly defined, is always passionate and ambivalent, conflicted and agonizing, precisely because it constitutes the daily dilemma of how to capture the real and speak on the other's behalf without subordinating him/her to purely aesthetic concerns (that is, appropriating otherness for immediate personal and artistic advantage), and in the process, reducing difference to identity and the same. Whatever format he is operating in, Godard remains admirably committed to exploring the nature and terms of spectatorship and the responsibilities of form and address, yet he keeps rubbing up against the skin of the real, that is, the historical and political ground of the Other in all its messiness and intractability. He understands instinctively, for example, that difference, to cite the filmmaker and theorist Trinh. T. Minh-ha, is a shared responsibility requiring a minimum willingness to reach out to the unknown (Minh-ha 1989: 85). At the same time, his always sensory encounter with the otherness of the real object can be a thing of simple beauty and literally "sensational," transforming the ordinary into the extraordinary and dramatically expanding our field of vision and touch. Indeed, Godard's ever-curious, often promiscuous, encounters with the physical world—those brief, unexpected, and seemingly spontaneous moments of natural beauty freed of narrative burden, when the camera, as if distracted, suddenly alights on a natural object or phenomenon—are ostensibly minor but can feel momentous, even miraculous. One such instance comes presently to mind, towards the end of *Passion*, when, during a stunning crane shot across the open landscape where a caravel lies docked in a reconstruction of a Watteau painting (*Embarquement pour Kythère* (1717)), the camera glides off gently into trees and caresses the high, snowflecked branches, accompanied by Mozart's Piano *Concerto 20 in D Minor*. As cultural theorist Sara Ahmed puts it well: "Wonder is the precondition of the exposure of the subject to the world: we wonder when we are moved by that which we face" (Ahmed 2004: 179).

Godard's remarkable aesthetic receptiveness to art in his work is but one, albeit the most tangible, expression of his fundamental investment in the always absorbing experience of beauty and the patterns of embodied signs in the world. Such an involuntary encounter is always a liminal and relational event. The cultural critic Dave Hickey, who celebrates encounters with beauty as moments when "[o]ur bodies, our minds, and the world beyond us coalesce and vibrate like a tuning fork" (Hickey 2009: 80–81), reminds us that the long history of aesthetic discourse in Western art is one of relative beauty resting upon the essential principle that, *"[i]n the moment of encounter, intricately constructed patterns of embodied reference always have the potential to completely reinvent themselves, to reinvent their own pasts and yield up the future in new, surprising, and totally unauthorized designative meanings"* (ibid.: 117) (original emphasis). What makes the experience of a Godard film so captivating is the evident delight with which he can catch himself out—and the viewer—in the very act of responding to the surprise and contingency of beauty. And it is precisely beauty's promise of radical destabilization that contributes to its striking capacity to, in the admirable words of Hickey, "locate us as physical creatures in a live, ethical relationship with other human beings in the physical world" (ibid.: 118).

Yet if Godard's cinema is directly embedded in the material world, long before any move to poetic transformation and the metaphysical is even contemplated, there is always a violence and aggression latent in this primary aesthetic drive which, as Alain Bergala describes in his account of Godard's method of shot making vis-à-vis the object and human figure, entails finding "the right angle of attack" (see Bergala 1999: 77–81). It means that any aesthetic exchange and encounter, from "the endless dialogue between imagination and work" promoted in his 1998 collaboration with Miéville for MoMA, *The Old Place: Small Notes Regarding the Arts at Fall of 20th Century*, to the intersubjective encounter between film and viewer/critic, is always of immediate ethical concern. During his press conference at Cannes for *Nouvelle Vague* in 1990, Godard instinctively employed the metaphor of tennis to explain the relational process of giving and receiving that constitutes the very lifeblood of cinema. "There's editing in tennis," he explained, adding that "[t]here's a rhythm and a cadence. It's very musical. There's silent dialogue. Cinema is silent dialogue" (Godard 1990a: 11).

In short, Godard's cinematic practice reveals not only that the aesthetic is intimately linked to the ethical, but also that these elements cannot operate in isolation from each other. Indeed, a subjective and moral approach to life (the grounds for ethics) is always linked for Godard to perception and our ways of recording the sounds and images of the immanent world (the basis of aesthetics), which is connected in turn to our lived engagement with the world of the symbolic (the politics of the biosphere). This book's simple subtitle, "Ethics, Aesthetics, Politics," reflects precisely Godard's rare ability to bring these three fields together as a rolling set of interrelated questions in generous tension. As the film scholar Fergus Daly notes in a discussion of *Éloge de l'amour* (2001), where he claims that Godard is searching by means of embodied characters ethical positions for singular modes of ethical being that would also be universally beautiful, "beauty is a matter of ethics for Godard [. . .] When Godard was asked what it might mean to be Godardian, he replied: 'to defend an ethics and an art'" (Daly and Martin 2002). I would add further that what characterizes Godard's project over the last thirty years is a constant yearning for an impossible ideal: the coming together of the ethical *and* aesthetic *and* political, such that they might finally slot together as one in perfect formation. His eternal desire is for a new and genuine relation—and ultimately fellowship—with the world in an expanding, all-encompassing politics of the aesthetic encounter.

The key to this utopian search for a redemptive unity is, of course, montage, which for Godard is cinema's unique ethical and moral code and what distinguishes it from all other forms. Indeed, montage constitutes the very basis of his thinking and lies at the core of his aesthetic, which, for all its many ideological and political twists and turns, is remarkably consistent in its deployment of formal and rhetorical figures, such as repetition and exaggeration, opposition and reversal, in particular the chiasmus. It is precisely in the processes of cinematic montage that the ethical inherent within the aesthetic is most powerfully revealed. For the primary gesture and promise of montage, already present in the silent era though in Godard's opinion never fully realized, is one of inclusion and invention of new relations across form. He talks of montage in the most basic terms as a process of "*rapprochement*" (literally, "bringing together") of unrelated objects, people, and events. To connect and (re)combine new sounds and images is to trigger new forms of thought and dialogue, and it is accompanied by a desire for judgment, expressed by Godard as a potential "scales of justice" (Brenez et al. 2006: 330). He even goes so far as to suggest that montage, or the connective act of creating relations between people, objects and ideas, is of itself a form of history. This is perhaps the closest Godard ever comes to defining the specific nature of montage which he continually reformulates in his work but which he sometimes prefers to leave in a virtual, abstract state as a magical third term, that is, as the "invisible" point, or common ground, between two pieces of film (Godard 1990b: 18).

Montage, then, is most fundamentally for Godard a poetic process of mystery and metamorphosis that embraces, recombines, and redeems even the most remote of images within the same visual and aural frame. His particular use of it as a source of creative conflict and revelation is sustained by an unquenchable desire for metaphor, fired by his ineradicable belief that cinema allows us to discover what he calls in *Histoire(s)* a "fraternity of metaphors" which intersect and connect our lives and provide social and cultural meaning. Simply put, cinema *qua* montage is for Godard a metaphor for the world, and *Histoire(s)* constitutes his most comprehensive attempt yet to harness the redemptive potential and metaphoricity of the image through the practice of montage. The ultimate challenge of Godard's concentrated acts of poetic montage is to create the right conditions for a new, transformative poetics of cinema and a crucible of emotion powerful enough to generate fraternal warmth and recharge human relations in an ideal unity of the ethical, aesthetic, and political. Naturally, nothing is guaranteed, and the fact that this mission is continually frustrated and may ultimately prove impossible imbues all Godard's work. Indeed, his perpetually renewed search accounts for his continued prolific output. The complex process of tapping directly, sometimes feverishly, into cinema's limitless reserves of metaphoricity through montage gives rise also to many paradoxes, none more acute than the fact that Godard is at his most radical not when he is explicitly political (the eventual dead end of revolutionary montage during his militant Dziga Vertov group period in the late 1960s/early 1970s offers conclusive proof), but rather when he is seeking to redefine and re-envision the very nature of the aesthetic by starting over again *à zéro*. During these moments when he renegotiates everything, he freely juxtaposes and rhetorically reverses sounds and images in order to craft through montage a new poetics of sensory energy and emotion.

Yet cinema is already a highly emotional affair for Godard precisely due to its relentless sliding back and forth between self and other, and the fact that it instantiates an ethical dilemma connecting the work, author, character, spectator, and screen through different forms and modalities of subjectivity. Godard himself raises the question of the ethical implications of this bedrock of emotion in a short text he wrote entitled "Pierrot mon ami" to promote *Pierrot le fou* (1965). Arguing for the film's "emotional unity," he states there: "This double movement, which projects us toward others at the same time as it really takes us back to ourselves, physically defines the cinema" (Bergala 1985: 259–63). Much later, in the video *Soft and Hard*, Godard adumbrates a double movement formed of internal self-development and an opening up to the Other. As the passage from the piece used as the first epigraph in this chapter reveals, art for Godard constitutes the means both to understand and change the self and "to bring others into being." Thus, if the general question of the image is always posed by Godard as a set of relations with the Other, it also comes back inexorably to matters of the self and to Godard himself as "figure." This accounts for his strong interest in self-dramatization and self-portrayal when he becomes "other" to himself. His comic turns as Oncle Jean in *Prénom Carmen* (1983) or Professor Pluggy in *King Lear* (1987) are only the most spectacular instances of his extensive experimentation in self-performance, ranging in style and tone from posed, authorial self-display and semi-improvization (the professional filmmaker at home in *Soft and Hard* and *JLG/JLG*) to studies in self-parody and ironic self-deflation (for example, the collapse of the Idiot/Prince in *Soigne ta droite*).

Raymond Bellour has eloquently captured this constant passage between self and other, interiority and exteriority, across the surface of the image in Godard's work, and I cite his conclusions at length:

> Godard is [. . .] quite close to old Nicephorous who believed in the image and thought that the evangelical message of the icon was not only equal but superior to that of the Gospel itself. The image is all the more universal and absolute in that, unlike words, it is without contradiction—there is no counter-image—and its presence is whole and immediate, without delay. It is as much the object of public worship, in the holy places it illuminates, as it is the object of an intimate relationship, in the private dwellings it transforms by its grace, and by the mystery it holds and envelops. The image thus protects those who give themselves up to it. This is what Godard dreams of, when he conceives all his films at once, and seeks to reconstruct the image [. . .] Even if only as a Christian who becomes Christ without God, Godard is destined, like the Romantic writers and so many writers after them, to be the one and the other, or to pretend to be. This is why the image, which comforts him so, frightens him also, to the point where he can't live without the "other," without an other, the person one talks to, and to whom he also addresses the image, his image, since it is also with him or her that he has made it. (Bellour 1992: 227–28)

Bellour rounds off his adroit portrait of Godard as an artist in thrall to the image as other with whom he can create his own self-image by quoting from an interview Godard gave around the time of *Passion*: "I [Godard] need an other so as not to be afraid of the image of myself" (see Bergala 1985: 511).

It is this particular aspect of otherness in Godard, the process whereby the same becomes other and the other becomes the same, that most intrigues and fascinates me about his work. I am talking here of more than a simple double movement of the kind that exists between the real and fiction, communication and noncommunication, the material and immaterial, the abstract and figurative—binaries that define all Godard's work and where his ability to shift back and forth dialectically across terms and on different planes in the blink of an eye contributes to its extreme self-consciousness. This process was already encapsulated in a short manifesto-style passage from Godard's 1957 article on Jean Renoir where he wrote: "Art at the same time as the theory of art. Beauty at the same time as the secret of beauty. Cinema at the same time as the explanation of cinema" (Bergala 1985: 118). However, I am referring to those other, preeminently formal instances of countermovement and counterformation within the progression of the work itself, notably within the operations of montage, which might appear as no more than intermittent explosions and disturbances, intervals of obscurity and distortion, yet which function as powerful forms of internal self-resistance and assume a positive status and value. For Godard's abiding trust as a committed iconophile in the "joy" of the image is derived precisely from the negativity inherent within it. A recurring Blanchotian phrase in the later work, and one of the culminating statements of *Histoire(s)*, is the following: "Yes, the image/ is joy / but beside it/ dwells nothingness/ and all the power/ of the image/ is expressed/ only by evoking nothingness [. . .] the image/capable of negating/ nothingness/ is also the gaze/ of nothingness on us/ it is light/ and it is/ immensely heavy/ it shines/and it is/ this diffuse thickness/ where nothingness/ reveals itself" (Godard 1998a, vol. 4: 299–300).[7]

I wish to prioritize these secondary, often highly graphic moments of self-resistance and internal friction, which can occur at all levels and in all registers, for this is where Godard, working imperturbably through negativity and violence, takes cinema to the point of its virtual *otherness* by turning it inside out in what seems an unstoppable process of inversion and reversibility. Indeed, Godard is often at his most genuinely moving and inspiring precisely when he is broaching new aesthetic thresholds and fully embracing the attendant risks of decomposition and breakdown. Such extreme instances, when the work suddenly appears to cut loose from itself and open up new chasms of opacity and excess, and when Godard undermines his own authority by relinquishing authorial control even to the point of apparent self-erasure, offer concrete proof of an ethical commitment to complete and unconditional self-interrogation. For this reason they constitute a moral imperative and activate a further set of double movements in his work, including creation versus decreation, the cognitive versus the intuitive, the sublime versus the countersublime, the human versus the inhuman. My aim in working the faultlines of Godard's practice and tracing such highly charged and ambivalent entanglements is not to straighten them out or synthesize them, but rather to follow them through according to their own logic, since they are the very engine and soul of his at once fundamentally humanist and profoundly materialist cinema.

A Series of Encounters: Order of Play

This book, it should now be clear, is not directly concerned with the acquisition of solid knowledge about Godard (the realm of hermeneutics) and does not pursue a form of critical exegesis culminating in the discovery of secrets and hidden truths. Nor does it seek to approach its subject as an antagonistic object of study, an opponent and adversary to be broken down, defined, and overcome in a display of critical muscle. Instead, I embark in *Encounters with Godard* on a highly personal, at times freely speculative, textual voyage into Godard's aesthetics, in a spirit of creative tension and exchange. There are no formal rules as such to this extended critical play and no exclusive *parti pris*, for what is at stake is a multileveled critical engagement with Godard's work at this particular moment in time in order to arrive at a more organically formed understanding of the nature of his audiovisual rhetorical maneuvers and multimedia practice. Moreover, I have no theoretical axe to grind or overarching thesis to prove. Proceeding on the basis that there is no one correct way or angle to approach Godard, I enter into the flesh and fiber of his work *with no strings attached*. Indeed, liberated from the need to make "sense" of the entire corpus through a systematic chronological survey, this book possesses no claim to exhaustivity, and the choice of films is wholly subjective. This means, for example, that I don't really engage with a film like *Pierrot le fou*, which, for all its modernist brilliance and bravura, has never particularly appealed to me in its all-determining heterosexuality. Indeed, I can take it or leave it (as it happens, the film will be an important point of reference). This is entirely a matter of personal taste, of course, and not meant to suggest that homosexuality is desirable for a true appreciation of Godard, one of cinema's most aggressively straight directors. I refuse any normative or essentializing notions of sexuality, whether in cinema or art and politics more generally. Further, I claim the right here to be uneven, eclectic, and polemical, and to encounter different types of Godard at my discretion. I can take his work at its most exuberant and lush, delicate and lyrical, ingenious and ravishing, but also, as and when it suits, at its most obsessive and abstruse, tendentious and mischievous, astringent and raw.

Encounters with Godard presents a series of critical match-ups with Godard on different types of surface (film, video, photography, interview, critical essay, literature). It is designed as a loose series of individual critical encounters with all areas of his later work, from his feature films and video essays since the early-1980s, when I first experienced Godard, to his later cinema, published writings, art books and installations. Informed by recent work in aesthetics and ethics of (among others) Bellour, Jacques Rancière, Leo Bersani, Giorgio Agamben, Alain Badiou, and Vilém Flusser, the book probes the subtexts, margins, and recesses of Godard's work in order to try to bring into clearer critical focus the ethics and politics underpinning his aesthetic practice, and so determine the moral economy of a style fused in a metaphorics of representation. This includes the various processes whereby Godard works through alterity aesthetically, even formulating new forms of textual otherness, precisely to offset the perceived threat of a proliferating otherness. I will attend in particular to those films that have received relatively little critical attention, such as *Soigne ta droite* and *Notre Musique*, as well as to ostensibly "minor" works such as the disturbing 1982 short *Changer d'image* (Change of Image), where Godard films himself undergoing a ritual of extreme physical self-humiliation, self-acknowledged "failures" like *Hélas pour moi* (1993), and his *film maudit*, *King Lear*. The principal method adopted is close textual analysis of chosen sequences, for I wish to stay as close as possible to the live pulse of the material in order to engage with Godard's cinematic thought in action, however hesitant, contradictory, or ambivalent this may prove. I will trace the flows and cross-currents of Godard's videographic writing and tap directly into its dynamic textual energy frame by frame, exploring at close hand Godard's passion for the shot, the surge and pounce of his cinematic framing, the dense rhetorical maneuvers and shifting rhythms of his practice of montage, his invention of new "forms that think," and his poetic and at times "sublime," intercrossings of sound and image in chiastic formation. Alert to the rebounds and deflections of Godard's game, I will address the ways he cuts across different media (from video and photography to music and literature) and brings them all together as part of his project's continuous metamorphosis of forms in the "transaesthetic" spirit of André Malraux. As Antoine de Baecque underlines, Godard shares Malraux's absolute faith in the "encounter" between man and art and also in the need to inject the image with the history of our times, since only from such a confrontation may beauty arise (see de Baecque 2013: 231). Such dual emphasis means that while I engage necessarily with the historical contexts and subtexts of Godard's work, I do not approach them in the specific terms of historiography and instead refer the reader to available critical works such as that of Witt already mentioned.

I begin with a close reading of one of Godard's key films of the 1960s, *La Chinoise* (1967), a film explicitly of montage and his first film to address head-on the complex relations between aesthetics and politics as a series of open questions relating directly to ethics. Indeed, by virtue of its context and setting (a small terrorist cell in Paris composed of men and women from different social classes and categories devoted to learning about revolutionary politics), the film adopts a self-consciously pedagogic approach to exploring the politics and phenomenology of violence, specifically the lure of revolutionary violence and its possible justification. This is intensified in one set-piece sequence by a conversation with the "real" Francis Jeanson as a model of the engaged intellectual committed to political and artistic action. Interwoven into what may at first appear a dry, technical lesson in art and politics is a passionate and fiercely self-reflexive investigation into the status of images and language as well as the nature of human love. The film's full title, *La Chinoise, ou plutôt à la chinoise* ("The Chinese woman, or rather in the Chinese way"), already indicates a move by Godard into the realm of metaphor and towards questions of style, gesture, and performance. He even remarked rather opaquely at the time of the film's release that "the movie is not a thing which is taken by the camera; the movie is the reality of the movie moving from reality to the camera. It's between them" (cited in Sterritt 1998: 29). At this crucial early stage in Godard's work and career, on the cusp of the events of May '68, which it uncannily predicts, *La Chinoise* posits the deep attraction—yet also latent dangers—of trying to collapse the aesthetic into the political and unite theory and practice once and for all. It also dramatizes the difficulty, if not impossibility, of attempting to speak for the other and asks whether cinema can ever sustain a mutual relation with the Other—indeed, whether cinema is even an ethical possibility, precisely because it trades directly in language and discourse which are intrinsically sources of aggression and manipulation. A measure of the film's strategic importance for Godard's thinking about ethics and aesthetics is that snippets from it are included in *Caméra-oeil*, his poignant contribution to the portmanteau film *Loin du Vietnam* made around the same time, where, dwarfed by a large camera, he expresses the dilemma he feels as an engaged filmmaker trying to make sense of momentous political events taking place far across the globe.

By confronting the aesthetic with the political to the point of their potential mutual destruction, *La Chinoise* establishes a rich seed-bed of ideas, creative possibilities, and open lines of inquiry that Godard will take forward, develop, and cross-fertilize in all his future work. They include the following: cinema as a form of instruction and pedagogy; the address of (and to) the other; the notion of a trans-European aesthetic tradition; montage as a material process of collage and praxis; the utopian desire for language as pure sound and matter liberated from discourse; the inescapability of human violence, including that of the word in relation to the image; the value of art as a political act and its possible transitive, social function; the relations between aesthetic form and political content (reconceived already in *La Chinoise* in chiastic fashion as political form and aesthetic content); and the duties of art and the rules of artistic engagement and responsibility. These issues will provide the key frameworks and parameters in Godard's thinking about the relations between ethics, aesthetics, and politics, just as the possibility for revolutionary change in France and elsewhere begins slowly to ebb away during the 1970s and 1980s in the wake of the failed revolution of May '68, and the very notion of history is gradually subsumed and neutralized by the dictates of state-sanctioned (postmodern) culture and the saturating uniformity of the visual sphere. Although increasingly ambivalent and skeptical about the role of art in influencing social and political change, and while refusing any simple aestheticization of politics or politicization of art (the lesson of *La Chinoise*), Godard will be consistently asking what remains of the radical potential of cinema as an art uniquely connected to the real by virtue of recording it. If cinema has lost its critical function and vocation both to communicate history and be an instrument of contestation, what, he ponders, is now left? This connects to the broader question of the redemptive power of art: does art have any real responsibility and intrinsic "value" in the debased and sterile age of the markets, as Western society drifts ever deeper into cultural amnesia and basic human rights are subjected even more to unregulated state power? If so, how might it be defined? As we shall see, ready answers to such stark questions will be lacking, and Godard is tormented daily by the historic "sins" and lost opportunities of cinema. Yet his indefatigable faith in cinematic experimentation and the possibility of his still reaching a critically aware and engaged spectator, together with his abiding commitment to interrogating the political and economic determinants of aesthetic experience, will offer a positive springboard for imagining new kinds of aesthetic and ethical resistance.

The introductory chapter on *La Chinoise* is followed by seven different types of critical encounter with Godard which together form four loose, thematic pairings or sets of play: art and politics (chapters 1 and 2); montage and ethics (chapters 3 and 4); music and metaphor (chapters 5 and 6); text and image (chapters 7 and 8). Although some chapters are more keenly focused than others on the politics of representation of the other (notably chapters 1, 6, and 8), each addresses from a different perspective the interconnected ethical, political, and aesthetic themes I have outlined. One of the book's driving principles is that all the different areas and fields encountered in Godard's ethico-aesthetic film practice overlap and interweave, even if only obliquely, setting up still further chains of thematic and formal inquiry around terms that are complementary yet may also function oppositionally, such as society and culture, art and culture, form and affect, metaphor and abstraction, portrait and figure, aesthetics and philosophy. Questions of gender and desire, for example, surface in different forms and guises in chapters 1, 5 and 8. Chapter 5 examines how Godard draws on the always original and inimitable performance of music to develop an ethics of love as revelation, while chapter 8 analyzes some of the climactic moments in his highly staged and often homoerotically infused, intertextual encounters with literature, defined specifically in terms of individual authors. Chapter 6 moves between art and philosophy as represented by Godard and Agamben respectively to throw into graphic relief the innately aesthetic structures and ambitions of Godard's cinematic approach. A number of chapters are designed specifically as case studies of one film (chapters 1, 2, 4, 6). Chapter 2, for example, examines one particular episode of *Histoire(s)*, *La Monnaie de l'absolu* (3A), viewed as a work in itself and where the relations between the historical real (the history of war in Europe), cultural memory, and the absolute demands of a sublimatory aesthetics are put under maximum strain. Some chapters are more textually dense than others (chapters 2, 4, 7, 8), and certain encounters are longer and more involved theoretically due to the particular nature of the subject matter (chapters 3, 5, 6). Yet in all cases they go the distance and demonstrate how the points of intermedial crisis and rupture in Godardian montage are mantled by his reflex use of rhetorical figures.

Although *Encounters with Godard* will not be unduly worried by issues of continuity and discontinuity in Godard's work, it will, however, establish the connecting metaphors that open up new dimensions within the cinematic medium and formalize the visual, sonic, and conceptual patterns, shapes, and contours of the corpus as they manifest themselves. The analysis of films presented synchronically, both in parallel and in counterpoint, within and across chapters, will allow the reader to appreciate more concretely the changing thematic valencies and defining formal tensions of Godard's cinema: its movements and countermovements, its intuitive and counterintuitive tendencies, its play of the sensible and figural, and its push and pull between the vertical/metaphorical and horizontal/metonymic processes at work in montage. Such a composite, wide-angle approach will highlight Godard's extraordinary investment in the plasticity and rhythms of image and sound, and the surface textures and tonalities, matt and sheen, of his multiform work. The possible limitations of such a subjective critical enterprise (partiality, provisionality, inconsistency, inconclusiveness) will, I believe, prove to be major gains since they will allow for a more supple, open-ended and creative spirit of inquiry—one where the object of discussion also sets the terms for debate and stimulates new and original forms of critical engagement and interpretive style. Indeed, the permanent challenge will be to convey and analyze as vividly as possible to both the specialist and general reader the flashes and convulsions of beauty and illumination in Godard's work without dimishing their primal power (intensity and accessibility in film criticism are, it goes without saying, not necessarily the same thing).[8]

What these moments ultimately amount to, when Godard, pushing like a painter at and against form, color and technique, suddenly changes gear and spins off in new artistic directions that appear to fly in the very face of the political, will be of paramount concern. Godard, I will suggest, lays ethical claim to the cinematic defined in the broadest terms as relationality and aesthetic and cultural resistance. Yet such a project also obliges us to ask whether there are any moral limits to his potentially infinite and endlessly refined connective poetics. Are there certain images and ideas, for example, that cannot, and should not, be brought together poetically in montage and rhetorically or erotically reversed in the name of art? This central question lies at the heart of *Encounters with Godard*, where I hope to show that while Godard is consumed by the subtle minutiae of montage, his insistence on the lived, material world and his ethical commitment to engaging with the social and the collective are never in doubt, palpable even in works such as *JLG/JLG* where he is at his most introspective. Indeed, rather than a marginal director making willfully obscure films for a chosen few, the Godard who will emerge here is a restless and radical experimenter always driven forwards by a defiant resistance to the geopolitical status quo, and with an overriding interest in open access and the sharing of the archives for the common good. Godard offers us a rare gift: the opportunity to glimpse the unparalleled potential and poetic universality of cinema, or what I shall be calling in the encounters that follow the power and mystery of the Cinematic Event.

//
1

The Politics of Violence and the End(s) of Art

Speaking (for) the Other in *La Chinoise* (1967)

—Ethics are the aesthetics of the future.

—V. I. Lenin

—*La Chinoise* is a queer film.

—J.-L. Godard

With its explosive style, frenetic action, and inflammatory talk of revolution, *La Chinoise*, a study of Maoist activists in training shot in Paris in 1967, is generally considered a uniquely prescient film forecasting "*les événements*" of May '68.[1] As Colin MacCabe has stated, no major artist was more closely linked to May '68 than Godard, and *La Chinoise* dealt directly with the anarchist/situationist and Maoist movements just as they were coming into full political being in de Gaulle's France (MacCabe 2003: 180). Yet although the film won the Special Prize at the 1967 Venice Film Festival, it was pilloried on its release as excessive and unrealistic. For those Marxist-Leninist students in particular whom Godard had consulted while preparing it, *La Chinoise* constituted both personal and political betrayals. If one of the filmmaker's intentions had been to inform his audience of the increasing impact of Maoist ideology and thinking on the student population, those same students believed he had caricatured them as "irresponsible terrorists" by making it appear that individual terrorism was their primary and absolute concern, as opposed to mass mobilization and class struggle.

Godard himself acknowledged there were fundamental problems with *La Chinoise* and much later, in January 1969, while downplaying its prophetic value, castigated himself for having produced a "reformist" film, that is to say, the work of a "solitary poet," rather than a collaboration with those that mattered. Clearly still reeling from the collective feelings of failure and disappointment at the shattering of the utopian dreams of May (the Pompidou government won the June parliamentary elections with an increased majority), he lamented that *La Chinoise* was nothing more than a film made in the lab about what people were actually doing in practice (Bergala 1985: 335). Godard was seeking here, typically, to reassess and redefine his original aims for *La Chinoise*, which included, as he had proposed in a brief "manifesto" for the 1967 Avignon Theater Festival where it was unofficially premiered, a form of aesthetic and economic counterattack ("two or three Vietnams") against the imperialistic might of the film industry (Hollywood, Cinecittà, Pinewood, Mosfilms) in order to create free, "fraternal," national cinemas. One aspect of the film he never questioned or retracted, however, was precisely its depiction of violence extending to terrorism. This was of particular personal interest and concern to Godard and formed part of his ongoing enquiry into the workings of violence at both the individual and social/political levels.

What I would like to do in what follows is to examine the various processes of violence in *La Chinoise*, at once thematic and formal, in the light not only of the events of May '68 but also of Godard's work both immediately before and after. It is a question that assumes all the more urgency in the context of the recent fortieth anniversary of the crisis and the fiftieth now just around the corner—a date that is certain to provoke yet more postmortems of its legacy (we recall that during the May 2007 presidential election campaign Nicolas Sarkozy dismissed the entire period of May '68 as nothing more than an "immoral" blip that needed to be "liquidated" from the national consciousness). I will attempt to argue that *La Chinoise* has never really been taken seriously enough as a far-reaching interrogation of the political limits of emancipatory violence and terrorism, and of cinema's very capacity to represent that process. For the film engages with something far more permanent and universal than can be accounted for by any one political crisis, however disruptive, and puts into question the very possibility of revolutionary agency promoted in the words of its jaunty, satirical theme song "Mao Mao," specially composed by Gérard Guégan and sung by Claude Channes. By examining how the militants attempt to speak on behalf of others, *La Chinoise* forces us to consider what form political action and activism should take and whether, with its latent potential for violence, language can ever help to effect change. But it also asks more generally whether one can ever hope to engage mutually with the real other at all. As we shall see, the answers to these related ethico-aesthetic questions about language, representation, and alterity require us to establish not only who is included in the radical cinematic frame and extended history of *La Chinoise* (a story that has still to be fully told), but also those others who are deliberately left out and consigned to silence.

Prehistory of *La Chinoise*

During the 1960s, the Vietnam War had begun to make itself increasingly felt in Godard's work, with odd references and allusions in films like *Pierrot le fou*, where Ferdinand (Jean-Paul Belmondo) suffers brief torture before quickly divulging the information required and eventually blowing himself up, and then *Masculin Féminin*, where Paul (Jean-Pierre Léaud) sprays a car with the words "Paix au Vietnam." Yet it is the ostensibly "minor," cartoon-style film, *Made in USA* (1966), that reveals most where Godard stood politically by the mid-to-late 1960s, for it is informed by a new understanding that politics had irrevocably changed with the infamous Ben Barka affair of October 1965, explicitly mentioned in the film. This crisis involved the bogus arrest and kidnapping in Paris in broad daylight of the exiled leader of the left-wing Moroccan opposition leader, Mehdi Ben Barka. The French secret police was eventually revealed to have conspired with both the CIA and the criminal underworld to deliver Ben Barka to Moroccan agents and then stage an elaborate cover-up (the tortured body was never found, and the file still remains open).[2] What the affair revealed for Godard was that the most important American influence was no longer simply popular culture or Coca-Cola but rather geopolitical terrorism and international conspiracy "made in USA." Indeed, Cold War France appeared now to be directly infiltrated by Richard Nixon and Robert McNamara and terrorized by a secret police force. The film, which includes the close-up of a book cover proclaiming *Gauche année zero* (Left year zero), ends with Paula Nelson (Anna Karina) responding to journalist Philippe Labro's comment that the Left and Right were now essentially the same with an open question: How then does one engage politically?

This question, and with it the issue of what new form politicized art should take, seems to have provided the intellectual starting point for *La Chinoise*. On one level it couldn't be simpler: the American-inspired capitalist democracy of de Gaulle's Fifth Republic was encouraging state terrorism, which contaminated the symbolic order itself. The film Godard made at the same time as *Made in USA*, *Deux ou trois choses que je sais d'elle*, linked, for example, the destructive regeneration of Paris by the new technocrats to the social alienation experienced by wife and mother Juliette (Marina Vlady), living in the new housing project of La Courneuve, who finances her craving for consumer goods with part-time prostitution. So intense would become Godard's disgust with French society and its contempt for its own citizens, in particular through its ossified education system and repressive forms of censorship, that when the culture minister, André Malraux, banned Jacques Rivette's film *La Religieuse* (*The Nun*) in April 1966, Godard published an open letter in *Le Nouvel Observateur* in which he described himself as "submerged in hate" and accused Malraux, a Resistance hero, of being a "collaborator." At one point in *La Chinoise* Véronique suddenly turns to the camera and takes a pot shot at Malraux with a snarling reference to his 1957 essay on the transcendence of art: "La métamorphose des dieux, M. Malraux!" ("The metamorphosis of the gods,

Mr. Malraux!"). In Godard's thinking, institutional acts of cultural and political "terrorism" demanded decisive counteracts of terrorism at every level. He quickly became alert to what he saw and heard on the Nanterre campus when he drove his new young partner and student Anne Wiazemsky there for classes. For in France, as in other Western countries, Maoist cells had been slowly forming since 1966. The Union des jeunesses communistes marxistes-léninistes (UJCML) sought to transform into Marxist rhetoric and gestures the radical philosophy of Louis Althusser, who emphasized Marxism as a science and promoted a return to the doctrinal purity of early Marx. The group published a theoretical review, the *Cahiers marxistes-léninistes*, founded by militants of the Union des étudiants communistes (UEC) based at the École Normale Supérieure, where Althusser taught philosophy. Among the ranks of the UEC were Robert Linhart, Jacques Rancière, Pierre Macherey, Alain Badiou, and Étienne Balibar, all of whom endorsed in 1966 the Great Cultural and Proletarian Revolution in China. Affecting the same idealist fervor as the young officers of the Red Guard, they fancied that they were now the political new wave in France. In fact, by the mid-to-late 1960s Mao was seen by many on the left as the sole guarantor of Marxism-Leninism. Another dissident extreme left group, the Parti communiste marxiste-léniniste de France (also mentioned in *La Chinoise*), similarly called itself Maoist although claimed allegiance to Stalin and refused Kruschev-style *détente*. Godard was put in close touch with the UJCML by a young journalist working for *Le Monde*, Jean-Pierre Gorin, who, while not a Maoist himself, began to influence the tone and direction of Godard's new film and even inspired him to visit the Chinese Embassy while on tour in Algiers.

Reprendre à zéro: Revolutionary Rhythms

La Chinoise was thus conceived as a strategic raid on prevailing reactionary aesthetics. Its "Aden-Arabie" cell (named after the communist writer Paul Nizan's violent 1931 essay, which included a famous preface by Sartre in the 1960 edition) is composed of five major characters whom Godard considered comparable to the five different levels of society established by Maxim Gorky in his play *The Lower Depths* (1902). They are: Véronique (played by Wiazemsky), a philosophy student at Nanterre and the only "bourgeois" as such; her boyfriend and actor Guillaume (Léaud); a working-class economist Henri (Michel Séméniako); a nihilist painter Kirilov (Lex de Bruijn) (his name borrowed from Dostoyevsky's *The Devils*); and finally Yvonne (Juliet Berto), originally from a peasant background and working as a maid for Véronique's parents (in an ironic comment on the rhetoric of class struggle, she will continue to polish the shoes of her fellow revolutionaries). When Yvonne warmly embraces Véronique in the first five minutes of the film, it is as if Godard were quickly referencing Louis Malle's 1965 film, *Viva Maria!* (a comedy western romp set in nineteenth-century Mexico where two feisty Marias [Jeanne Moreau and Brigitte Bardot] wage a terrorist war on a corrupt priest) in order to transport the problematics of terrorism in film into new and more difficult territory.

A transient member of the cell who arrives seventeen minutes into the film to deliver a short lecture on new perspectives of the European Left is the student Omar Diop playing himself. Introduced by Véronique as a fellow philosophy student at Nanterre and sporting a vermilion (Chinese red) jumper, Omar (Blondin) Diop was, in fact, a brilliant Senegalese student whom Godard had met at Nanterre through Wiazemsky while scouting for ideas for *La Chinoise*. A leading figure among pro-Chinese Marxist-Leninist students, he was the one authentic Maoist in the film and would later work closely with Daniel Cohn-Bendit in the *Mouvement du 22 mars*, founded at Nanterre on March 22, 1968, when students occupied the university's administration building.

In the absence of the owners (the parents of one of Véronique's friends) and thus with the rule of authority temporarily suspended for the summer, the secluded apartment functions as a crucible for revolution. It is mapped out as a series of different spaces, from the classroom to the lecture theater, and is centered visually around the display of two red books: the *Little Red Book* and the *Cahiers marxistes-léninistes*. As Rancière has put it in perhaps the most compact account yet of the film, it is as if we were witnessing here an exercise in Marxism *with* Marxism, that is, the "matter" of Chinese Marxism infused by the "principle" of Althusserian Marxism (outlined in *Reading Capital* [1965]) of learning to "see, listen, speak, read."[3] This is only half the story of *La Chinoise*, however, for it also represents Marxism in the process of becoming cinema. The cell's motto, written over the wall, is expressed in virtually cinematographic terms: "We must confront vague ideas with clear images" ("Il faut confronter les idées vagues avec des images claires"). One of the film's many formulas and refrains is the "unity" of art and politics, as well as of form and content, and Véronique even utters at one point the Sartrean mantra that aesthetics is the realm of the imaginary.[4] The film's original full title, *À la chinoise, un film en train de se faire* ("In the Chinese way, a film in the process of being made"), the second part of which is presented, as the first title in the film, against a black background in first blue ("Un film"), then yellow ("en train/ de se"), then still larger red ("**FAIRE**"), underlines that this is an instance of self-consciously performative, materialist cinema. Godard had even intended to use the newly available Philips video cameras so that the students could record their own conversations and provide their own critique, yet this proved too difficult and costly to obtain. Devoid of any initial or final credits, the film simply arrives, suddenly and dynamically, on the screen, its antirealist, "degree zero" style conveying a raw and pulsating energy and urgency. Organized around blocks of primary color (red for Maoism, blue for the workers' overalls, yellow for the Chinese race, to be contrasted with the briefly glimpsed neutral green of the countryside), it has a scattershot, pop-art feel due to its intensive collage of multiple gadgets and false revolvers, intertitles, intermittent black spacing, sudden rapid inserts, tricks of stage lighting, comic-strip images, dialogues, slogans denouncing the hypocrisy of American foreign policy and imperialism, provocations, fragments of interviews (mostly responses to Godard off-screen), assorted minihappenings, covers of magazines (notably one of Malcolm X), graffiti, a barrage of citations and dogma from journals and books by authors such as André Gorz, allusions to topical events, and *agit-prop* skits about Vietnam (the characters mime at one point Mao's assumption of power and act out those Chinese being killed by evil "revisionists"). On the soundtrack we hear newsflashes from Radio Peking, quick snippets of Stockhausen, and odd bursts of the title song "Mao Mao" based on certain formulas culled from Mao's *Little Red Book*.

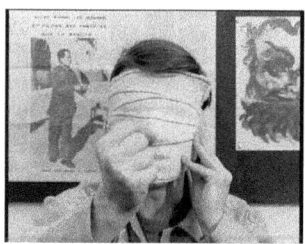  

Figures 1.1–3. Subversive rhythms: Guillaume (Jean-Pierre Léaud), a cartoon diptych, and Kirilov (Lex de Bruijn) in *La Chinoise* (1967).

The composite sonic and chromatic effect of this extraordinary work of montage (Godard claimed the film took one month to shoot and three months to edit) is of a modern symphony of sound and noise in three "movements" that, typically for early Godard, has a distinctly Brechtian ring. Indeed, Brecht is explicitly mentioned in the film and the only name to remain on the blackboard when all the other now outmoded European writers and dramatists (from Sophocles and Shakespeare to Giraudoux and Pinter) written up in chalk by Guillaume have been wiped away one by one in a silent and systematic purge. As Adrian Martin has indicated, *La Chinoise*'s formal construction was effectively dictated by one of Althusser's articles on Brecht, "Le 'Piccolo' Bertolazzi et Brecht (Notes sur un théâtre matérialiste)," the conclusion to which, a paean to a new type of spectator, Guillaume reads out at length.[5] Didactic and dialectical to the point of virtual parody, the film passes through many Brechtian levels of distancing, self-criticism, and *mise en abyme*, including shots of the cameraman, Raoul Coutard, plus camera and clapper-board. In short, *La Chinoise* destroys any pretension of a "truthful" representation of reality. Indeed, the image may be said to create its reality, since, as Kirilov expresses it chiastically: "L'art n'est pas le reflet du réel, mais le réel de ce reflet," literally: "Art is not a reflection of the real, but the real of what's reflected." Godard is thus countering with the calculated disorder of montage the proclaimed "despotism" of global capitalist imperialism rampant in the Third World (one staggered intertitle in red reads: "The imperialists are still alive / They continue to wreak despotism [*l'arbitraire*] in Asia, Africa / and Latin America"). Yet in the very same moment he is also ironizing the supercharged drills and hyperagitation of the film's militant characters whose imperative to "speak" and "do" and "act" becomes an all-consuming, almost tyrannical need (the worst insult in the cell is to be called, like Henri, a reactionary "revisionist" willing to listen to others and compromise with the Parti Communiste Français (PCF)).

The Words of Others

Towards the end of *La Chinoise*, as the narrative of terrorism eventually takes over, we finally leave the hot-house atmosphere of the cell. With Henri summarily excluded for objecting to the collective call for special combat and terrorist action, there is a drawing of lots, and Véronique is charged with the task of assassinating the revisionist soviet minister of culture Sholokov visiting Paris. As the abbreviated title *La Chinoise* had always led us to expect, our attention is now fully focused on this individual female Maoist as the vehicle of "real" violence. We follow her in her bungled mission, for she mistakes room 23 for 32 while attempting to read the reception register upside down and thus shoots the wrong man, an error which she quickly rectifies by returning to the building and accomplishing the deed. Yet if terrorist violence marks the conclusion to the cell's debates, we are not witnesses to Véronique's actions, which remain deliberately abstract (a fact underlined by the extraordinary framing of the diplomatic building behind closed gates). Instead, the film's key set-piece sequence is the slightly earlier impassioned dialogue Véronique pursues with the political philosopher Francis Jeanson on a train moving, we assume, from Nanterre to the end of the line at Saint-Germain-en-Laye (the episode is initiated by a still-frame of a station called appropriately enough La Folie-Complexe Universitaire, since renamed Nanterre-Université). Jeanson was a model of the politically engaged intellectual and a bona fide man of action. As France's leading activist for the Algerian Front de Libération National during the Algerian War, he had been put on trial in 1960 for being head of a network (the Réseau Jeanson) that supported Algerian terrorists. Found guilty of high treason, he was condemned to ten years solitary confinement though was amnestied in 1966. He now finds himself in 1967 working as, among other things, Wiazemsky's "real" philosophy teacher.

Figure 1.4. Véronique (Anne Wiazemsky) and Francis Jeanson as himself talking violence on the train from Nanterre in *La Chinoise* (1967).

Véronique explains to Jeanson that the only solution to the current blockage in the French education system and prevailing political stagnation (even renowned committed writers and thinkers like Sartre and Louis Aragon, she claims, are hopelessly out of touch) is to start again from zero by forcing students to perform manual labor (a comment greeted ironically on the soundtrack by romantic strings) and, above all, by bombing the universities. Jeanson calmly rebukes Véronique for daring to compare her fantasies of mass murder with his own defense of terrorists during the Algerian War, for he was motivated by the will of the Algerian people to emerge from colonial rule, whereas her plans represent the will of only a handful of people. "We think on their behalf," she declares brutally and fascistically, illustrating just how quickly the language games of militancy can create their own terrorism, especially if we compare it to the first dialogue between Véronique and Guillaume, which culminated in a casual invocation of alterity: "We are the words of others." Jeanson argues further that the whole populace was united in the Algerian quest for independence, or at least sympathetic to it, and thus terrorism had a particular moral force as well as realistic chance of achieving something. Since no such unity of political purpose or indeed community existed any more in France, there was instead a need, according to Jeanson, to restore in people the idea they could change the world by reinstilling a sense of creation and communication. In his own case he was seeking new forms of "cultural action" and "experiments" in the provinces, such as bringing theater to working-class audiences. His utterly reasonable if patronizing advice to Véronique is to work with friends at creating new Maisons de la Culture in the working-class *banlieues*.[6] Véronique will have nothing of this, of course. She wants action now and remains unwilling to consider the consequences. Her mission to assassinate Sholokov will not be derailed.

Throughout this entire scene Coutard's camera remains neutral, filming the two figures from the side as they sit facing each other. It is up to the viewer to assess their arguments and decide which is correct. Yet granted that Godard was whispering through an ear-piece Véronique's replies to Jeanson, who expressed his own thoughts *extempore*, which side was Godard really on here? In a long interview for *Cahiers du Cinéma* in October 1967 he declared that he was in favor of Véronique's call for mass violence and lack of compromise (Bergala 1985: 303). Although he doesn't elaborate further on this, we might add that terrorism forms a key part of the Leninist heritage, its use at any particular time to be determined by tactical, not moral, considerations. Some years later, however, Godard declared Jeanson's arguments to be more persuasive, a shift he attributed to the difference between his conscious sympathies at the time with Véronique's terrorist position and his own, more lasting, if unconscious, allegiance with peaceful kinds of political action, notably cultural.[7] Yet Jeanson's emphasis not simply on the right course of action but also on the most appropriate *form* of action takes us to the heart of the film, which began with Henri pondering socialist tactics and the feasibility of mass revolutionary force in the right "subjective and objective conditions," since the working-class no longer seemed ready to embark on a general strike or mount the barricades for higher wages (real events would, of course, soon prove such pessimism dramatically wrong). Significantly, neither Véronique nor Jeanson has the last word in La Chinoise, which goes instead to Guillaume, who finally realizes the promise of his name, a homage to the eponymous hero of Goethe's novel, *Wilhelm Meister's Apprenticeship*. He strolls through an urban wasteland, where a man paints in red the words "*théâtre année zéro*" (a link back to Made in USA, and before that, no doubt, to Roberto Rossellini's influential neorealist film, *Germany Year Zero* [1947]), in an attempt to pursue his "theatrical vocation" and goal, expressed at the beginning of the film, of achieving a socialist theater. We see him relearning the value of the essential ritual in French theater of "*frapper les trois coups*" ("striking three blows"), a sequence featuring seminaked women knocking on panes of glass, and at the end practicing door-to-door theater by consoling an emotionally distraught female neighbor with slightly altered lines from Racine's *Andromaque*. He concludes with an energetic flourish: "You need only to become Marxist-Leninist."

Is this to say that the political can solve, or simply dissolve, the problems of the personal? Such a seductively neat and simple prospect is left deliberately floating. Rancière is right, however, to regard La Chinoise as ultimately staging here a moral opposition not between Véronique and Jeanson, but between Véronique as a misguided militant and Guillaume as an enlightened actor who, with the force of his own body, articulates ("*interprète*" in the double sense in French of "interpret" and "perform") the discourse of politics and the words and gestures of revolution.[8] Earlier he had "performed" the statement "Il faut de la sincérité . . . *de la vi-o-lence*" ("We have to have sincerity . . . vi-o-lence") by shouting out the words and clenching his fist, thus engineering a self-reflexive, double performance of mind and body. Hence, La Chinoise could be said to reveal itself finally as a meditation on the theater, as it had always, in fact, promised to be (in one early mime sequence Guillaume had slowly taken off bandages around his head to illustrate that an actor, like a political militant, seeks to show what cannot be seen). Indeed, Guillaume arguably functions as Godard's ideal alter ego, representing a compromise between terrorism and the old guard as well as paving the way for a possible resolution of theory and practice. Certainly, of all the members of the cell who are confronted with their destiny at the end, it is only Guillaume who achieves a fundamental clarity and radical sense of purpose, for Yvonne is left to sell *L'Humanité Nouvelle* (the Communist newspaper), Henri announces he will return to the relative calm of Besançon or maybe East Germany to work as a chemist, Kirilov kills himself off-screen after earlier holding a gun to his head and simulating death (an apparent act of identification with the Bolshevik poet, artist, and playwright Vladimir Mayakovsky, who took his own life in 1930 and whose ideas on the unity of art and politics Kirilov freely quotes), while Véronique coolly reflects in the final frame that her murderous summer break was a detour into "fiction" that put her in touch with "reality," thereby marking her first step in a long process of personal and political transformation.

Figure 1.5. Véronique (Anne Wiazemsky) and Guillaume (Jean-Pierre Léaud) testing the discursive limits of love in *La Chinoise* (1967).

Yet more is at stake in the theoretical opposition between Guillaume and Véronique, that is to say, between the two different modalities of engaged artistic practice and militant terrorism. It comes to full light in the sequence where they speculate on the language of the future, and as Susan Sontag puts it, they submit to the impossible "arch-romantic wish to make oneself entirely simple, altogether clear" (Sontag 2009a: 187). Véronique answers Guillaume's rhetorical question "How can one do two things at once?" by suddenly declaring she is dumping him for a range of reasons, most of them petty. When he tries to reason with her she repeats virtually the same words impassively, but this time with music, playing an extract of Schubert on the record-player. Her act is merely a pretense, however, and intended as a lesson to Guillaume on how one can do two things at once, that is, with language and music, and so "combat on both fronts" (a key axiom of both the cell and the film). He claims to understand but admits to being very afraid, as does Véronique—it's not easy, after all, being a committed militant 24/7. Yet within the context of the film as a whole, this act of creating an illusion is revealed as a distinctly false strategy of subversion, staging as it does an imaginary scenario with the precise aim of achieving an effect through its affective impact. In this sense Véronique is working contra Godard, for she is composing and assembling a "reality" in order to elicit terror, while the film itself pursues an aesthetic "terrorism" through the disjunctive practice of montage—the antimimetic, deconstructionist collage that puts sound and image into constant question, and that Rivette aptly called Godard's "intertextual terrorism."

Hence, while Godard as artistic terrorist subverts aesthetically the symbolic/imaginary axis, Véronique, as an over earnest, literal terrorist, attempts to produce "real" images and the spectacle of murder. Put a little differently, militant action proves here intrinsically deficient since it leaves untouched the imaginary structure of reality (the true site of subversion), as well as the essential terror linked to the very production and holding together of the realist image. As Luca Bosetti has argued in her study of the transformative potential of terror as a subversive strategy in Godard's (and also Jacques Lacan's) work on May '68, with particular reference to *La Chinoise*, so long as militant action leaves the image intact, subversion will fail and the space of subversive agency remain elusive.[9] While Godard's film, which announces the central theme of Guy Debord's *Society of the Spectacle* (published just a few months later) of the domination of images and the replacement of social life by its representation, becomes a privileged space for symbolic displacement of the social, Véronique, as her misreading of numbers during the assassination exemplifies, lies at the mercy of the image and trapped within its fixed logic of simple inversion. Yet Véronique's blind belief in the abstract worth of terrorism is, as I have already suggested, not directly condemned by the film, and indeed, putting aside Kirilov's wild and empty declaration that he "believes" in terror ("Revolutionaries are made of terror. Give me a bomb!," he declaims), there is no agonizing moral discussion here on the validity of revolutionary violence, of the kind, for example, that propelled Albert Camus's 1949 play, *Les Justes*. Instead, with its intricate game of Chinese boxes, *La Chinoise* may be said to be firing a clear warning shot to the new generation of student agitators and imminent revolutionaries: go down the path of terrorism at your peril, for you may quickly find yourself caught in a web of illusion, error, duplication, and catastrophe.

By Any Means Necessary?

The story of Godard's own subsequent transformation into a fully fledged Maoist filmmaker, when in 1968 he renounced his unique status as film *auteur* and formed with Gorin (along with Armand Marco, Nathalie Billard, and Gérard Martin) a small film collective, the Dziga Vertov Group, is well-documented.[10] It is a story marked by his active participation in the large street protests in February and March 1968 against Malraux's attempted sacking of Henri Langlois as curator of the Cinémathèque Française which, in a curtain-raiser to the events of May, were met with an unheralded show of force and extreme violence by riot police (the CRS); his co-creation during the *événements* themselves of silent, one-reel "*ciné-tracts*" by which he attempted directly to unite theory and practice;[11] and his contribution to the "Estates General of Cinema" that took place in May and June, which united (at least temporarily) all sections of the film industry. This narrative sounds already far more smooth than it actually was, for Godard also found himself the object of much hostility from students during May '68, as evidenced by some of the slogans and street graffiti such as: "Godard le plus con des Suisses pro-chinois" ("Godard the biggest dick of the pro-Chinese Swiss," originally articulated by the Situationist Guy Debord), and: "L'art est mort. Godard n'y pourra rien" ("Art is dead. Godard can do nothing about it"). By this stage, however, Godard, like many other intellectuals and *gauchistes* of the period, including Sartre, now identified fully as a Maoist and even hit the streets to sell *La Cause du Peuple*, organ of the hard-core Gauche Prolétarienne (GP). I don't intend to rehearse here the complex and sometimes highly ambivalent story of Godard's move to political extremism and activism, nor do I wish to examine in any great detail the numerous films produced by the Dziga Vertov Group. I will, though, simply emphasize that Godard now intensified the politics of form and representation developed in *La Chinoise* by problematizing every aspect of the relationship between the political and the aesthetic in terms of voice, address, discourse, and image, and by devising multiple mechanisms (technical, semiotic, discursive) to unmask the creative process. The camera was made now to function explicitly as a weapon to subvert Western forms of representation from within and prevent any easy co-option and appropriation by the prevailing political system. The strategy worked: once films such as *Vent d'est* (1969) and *Lotte in Italia* (1970) were made, they were either rejected or banned by the television companies and media networks that had commissioned them.

One particular Dziga Vertov Group project stands out due to its repercussions for Godard's subsequent work. In 1970 he left with Gorin and Marco for Amman to shoot *Jusqu'à la victoire*, a propaganda film for Yasser Arafat's Fatah movement recording the activities of the Palestinian freedom fighters in Jordan and the Lebanon, specifically the preparations underway in 1970 in the refugee communities on the West Bank to reclaim the land occupied by Israel in 1967. Godard regarded this film as a kind of "political brochure" offering a political analysis of the Palestinians in their struggle against imperialism and providing "real," revolutionary images. The film was also intended to show didactically how the Palestinians had first to conquer a language, hence the many scenes of refugees delivering speeches, reciting poetry, pamphlets, and so on, although the project was directly hampered by the very problem of language (neither Godard nor Gorin spoke Arabic). Production was halted with only two-thirds of the film complete because many of the Palestinians filmed were suddenly killed in Amman during the Black September massacres of 1970 perpetrated by King Hussein's Jordanian troops. The recorded footage, which included Palestinian children engaged in commando exercises, was subsequently salvaged in *Ici et ailleurs* (1974), the highly confessional film essay Godard later made with Anne-Marie Miéville that worked through the collapse of the revolutionary project by addressing head-on the problems and contradictions of militant filmmaking and confronting *ici* (a white, working-class French family) with *ailleurs* (not merely the lost territory of Palestine but also the destroyed dream of collective revolutionary life). Imaging the Palestinian resistance became now a matter of restituting the speech of absent or dead Palestinians to whom, as Godard admits self-critically in the film, he had never really listened.[12] With its overlapping soundtracks and video editing techniques (multilayered superimpositions, multicolored intertitles), *Ici et ailleurs* looked very different from the original film Godard and Gorin had in mind, that is, a political analysis about history in the making, and instead appeared more an acutely personal study in self-reckoning and self-accountability (the theme of counting and figures, both of money and the dead, is omnipresent in the film). Indeed, in one sequence Godard directly implicates himself as a politically engaged filmmaker trapped in Western binary thinking and blindly splitting the world into two since he kept silent while filming fighters as they were planning a doomed maneuver ("The tragic thing is they're talking about their own death, but no-one said it"). As Miéville puts it damningly: "We wanted to make the revolution for them; in their place, we craved victory." Nevertheless, *Ici et ailleurs*, which Gorin refused to co-sign, would inspire further extensive collaboration and dialogue between Godard and Miéville across film and television during the 1970s as well as for a long time after.

Despite their serious and often noble political aims, Godard's stripped-down and deliberately rebarbative Dziga Vertov Group films never fulfilled the revolutionary function they were designed for and appear now chiefly as private period pieces, notably the violent, ideological posturings and sadomasochistic-style high jinks acted out by Godard and Gorin in their burlesque staging of the Chicago 8 trial in *Vladimir et Rosa* (1970). Indeed, some of the methods they selected as the tools for social change (images and themes of brutality, terrorism, coercion) seemed merely to replicate the very abuses of human dignity the group found so appalling in bourgeois society, like the repeated and largely gratuitous use of naked female flesh in *British Sounds* (1969) (co-directed by Jean-Henri Roger). It was a case of ever-decreasing artistic circles for Godard, who, with the fanaticism of a religious convert, seemed to be squeezing himself dry in an entirely alien political logic: the praxis of Marxist/Maoist dialectics. This creative and political dead-end was the result of an inevitable double-bind: Godard was attempting to effect change through the medium of film even though he knew profoundly that neither sound nor image had any major direct influence on the behavior of people (a fact that explains why he could never understand the need for censorship) (Bergala 1985: 308). As Bosetti puts it well, Godard's "creative nihilism," that is to say, his authentically subversive and transformative form of terror capable of liberating subjectivity from the sway of structural terror that founds the social link,[13] could never advance very far since it remained confined within the narrow limits of a creative process.

The problem remained for Godard how to take forward the creative promise embodied by Guillaume at the very end of *La Chinoise*. For the result of Godard's self-confessed "leftist trip" was an artistic impotence that one might argue was already latent in the film when Guillaume is pelted masochistically with vegetables by townspeople who pay for the privilege. Indeed, for Richard Brody, *La Chinoise* is essentially the work of a self-abasing and self-excoriating filmmaker on the verge of a political and aesthetic breakdown who applied his own attributes to Guillaume, then filmed the young man's private chastisement by Véronique and subsequent public self-humiliation in an attempt to purge himself of them. Hence, for all its daring technique, *La Chinoise* was "something of an intellectual suicide" on Godard's part.[14] This, I think, is an overly pessimistic reading of *La Chinoise*, encouraged by an overreading of the putative links between Godard and his fictional characters and by Godard's own propensity to castigate himself, sometimes even physically as we shall shortly see, whenever he appears in front of his own camera.

The theme of terrorism continued to remain very much alive for Godard, however, and he returned to it directly in *Tout va bien* (1972), one of the last films of the Dziga Vertov Group before it disbanded in early 1973. *Tout va bien* was Godard's attempt with Gorin to reach the mainstream by employing politically engaged stars such as Jane Fonda as an American radio correspondent and feminist falling out with her husband played by Yves Montand, a filmmaker now reduced to making commercials (a clear stand-in for Godard himself). Based around a wildcat strike at a factory and the sequestration of its boss by the workers (a familiar *gauchiste* tactic after '68), this work about class struggle, influenced more by Brecht than Althusser, is explicitly framed in terms of the fallout of May '68 and includes a flashback sequence reenacting the death of Gilles Tautin, a student who drowned while fleeing the riot police during the riots in June of that year near the Renault car factory at Flins. The general mood of blockage and elegy for a lost historical and revolutionary moment is eventually superseded by the spectacle of anarchic violence in the Carrefour supermarket where *gauchistes* (including Wiazemsky) first harangue the PCF salesman selling discounted copies of the latest party publication in the aisles like vegetables, then begin looting and encouraging all shoppers to do so as well—a pale version of spontaneous social revolt and solidarity within the gates of capitalism. *Tout va bien* underlines Godard's ambivalence towards violence: at once fascinated intellectually by its idea and aura, happily sharing the Maoist notion of the ideal cleansing powers of political violence in the name of the "dictatorship of the proletariat," yet also profoundly suspicious of its spectacle due to its hold on the emotions and potential for indiscriminate destruction. He claimed, even as late as 1980, that the real "inheritors" of '68 were "the terrorists" (left undefined),[15] although we note for the record that Godard himself never contemplated terrorist activity.

The Reality of Terrorism in France

To return to the particular specter of French revolutionary terrorism raised by *La Chinoise*: the powerful call for social violence and terrorism made by Véronique never translated itself into reality in France. Indeed, despite the impressive mobilization of millions of people during the events of '68 and the belief by many post-'68 revolutionaries that the shocking power of violence would force the masses to consider the prospect of revolution, no group embarked on a concerted campaign of terrorist violence in France until the emergence of Action Directe in 1979, which perpetrated over fifty attacks in the early 1980s, followed in the 1990s by the advent of Islamist terrorism (notably the 1995 bombings carried out by the Armed Islamic Group (GIA) that sought to extend the Algerian Civil War to France). The GP itself, although the most radical group post-'68, refused to kill anyone and renounced all forms of armed struggle in 1973, the same year that incontrovertible evidence reached the West of the brutal reality of Mao's China. It is also the case that separatist movements in Corsica and Brittany never committed acts on the scale of ETA or the IRA, and neither Palestinian nor other transnational terrorists struck French targets with the same ruthlessness they displayed in the Munich massacre of 1972, the OPEC ministers' kidnapping in 1975, or the more notorious skyjackings of the 1960s and 1970s. In short, France escaped the kinds of terrorism that afflicted other Western European countries such as Germany, Italy, Spain, and the UK during the 1970s. The most obvious reason for this is that de Gaulle, the focus of so much venom and hatred during '68, had already engineered his own exit from the political stage (he resigned the presidency in April 1969 and died a year later). His solidly conservative successors Georges Pompidou (who died in office in 1974) and Giscard d'Estaing (president 1974–1981) were certainly objects of scorn and caused much rancor and disarray across the Left, leading some to turn dramatically to the Right by the end of the decade like the "Nouveaux Philosophes" André Glucksmann and Bernard-Henri Lévy, yet they were far from being dictators, and France, despite various warning signs, never became a police state. Perhaps, too, the very spontaneity and vertiginous "performance" of May (what the GP derisorily referred to as a "dress rehearsal" because it seemed divorced from proper contact with French workers) had effectively preempted and "preexhausted" the need for full-scale terrorist violence. Certainly, the events had initiated a genuine social and cultural revolution (increased workers' rights, women's rights, gay rights, and so on), which many were now keen to build on.

At least some of the reason for this relatively peaceful outcome can, I think, be attributed to *La Chinoise* itself, a work by one of the most visible artists of the period and universally known. For if, in retrospect, the film appeared to get it so wrong about Maoist terrorism, and if it didn't *effect* anything as such (a fact impossible to prove, of course, although it played a clear role in inciting political action and revolts on American university campuses when screened in April 1968, notably at Columbia where rioters included future members of the Weathermen), nevertheless it made possible a much sharper awareness of the lure of political violence, as well as of the more general "hidden violence" without obvious agent that subtends, and maintains, the prevailing political and economic system. Indeed, in the way it allows us to think through—and above all see through—violence and militant activity/activism without mystifying it, *La Chinoise* may usefully be compared with Slavoj Žižek's important contemporary analysis of the subject in *Violence* (2008). Žižek argues convincingly here that subjective violence is just the most visible portion of a triumvirate that also includes two objective kinds of violence: "symbolic" violence, embodied in language and its forms, and "systemic" violence, or the often catastrophic consequences of that smooth functioning of our economic and political systems (Žižek 2008: 1). "Invisible," objective violence is precisely the violence inherent in the "normal" state of things that sustains the very zero-level standard against which we perceive something as subjectively violent. Hence, according to Žižek, we need to step back from the fascination and attraction of this directly visible "subjective" violence. Acknowledging the vital difference between the utopian events of May '68 and the apparent "irrational" senselessness of the more recent riots in the French *banlieues* during the autumn of 2005, which had no political agenda as such, Žižek speaks of an impulsive, blind "acting out," or *passage à l'acte*, that leads to (self-)destructive violence directed against one's own and which cannot be translated into speech or thought. For

Žižek, the 2005 riots need to be placed in the same context as terrorist attacks and suicide bombings, for in both cases violence is an implicit admission of impotence. The crucial difference, however, is that unlike the riots "which wanted nothing," "terrorist attacks are carried out on behalf of that *absolute* meaning provided by religion" (Žižek 2008: 69; original emphasis). If "outbursts of impotent violence are fundamentally *reactive*" (ibid.: 179; original emphasis), the clear political challenge is to produce an authentic, active gesture that both imposes and enforces a *vision*.

Whether we can ascribe finally an overarching value and status to the events and clashes of May '68 in France (for example, that of an act of pure, "divine" violence that strikes out of nowhere and instantiates what Žižek calls, employing the vocabulary of Alain Badiou, the Event) is a question requiring a longer and separate discussion. What can be said, however, is that before, during, and after *les événements*, *La Chinoise* served as an indisputable point of political reference, implicit when not explicit, by providing a compelling picture of the implications of violence and the responsibilities of revolutionary activism. Indeed, part of the film's particular force and agency is the brilliant way it problematizes the very notion and efficacy of action, from the lyrics of the title song that blur the logic of action and reaction ("Vietnam burns and I yell out Mao Mao/ Johnson laughs and I blow away Mao Mao"), to the narrative fact of the cell's abrupt dissolution. By operating, unlike the Dziga Vertov Group films, always *between* art and politics, *La Chinoise* denies any "amortization of the heart and soul" (Mayakovsky) and performs a strategic intervention in cinema, stimulating the viewer into further critical reflection and enquiry. For this reason it may be said to "impose" a vision, that of the precariousness of all political action and discourse (including cinematic), yet hardly to "enforce" it. Rather, it insists with its final title card "Fin d'un début" ("End of a beginning") on the contingent and provisional; the rest is now up to "us." That is why it is so important to stop fetishizing retroactively the film's mysterious prescience, a critical approach that has served to obscure its potent and still urgent message about both the impossibility of simple solutions and change through the practice of terrorist violence, and, just as crucially, the potential for terrorism within language and discourse itself, even that of love. (We shall come back to the specific question of political engagement and the fantasy of simply dissolving the word in "pure" action in chapter 6.) The particular history of Godard's cinema that we have traced post-'68 confirms that the notion of a revolutionary active cinema may be intellectually desirable, yet it is ultimately impossible in practice. A failed political experiment, certainly, but *La Chinoise* remains a searing and profound experience of cinema—one that will inspire Godard to take to the limit the potential of montage as an instrument of thought and direct means of engaging with the world.[16]

Missing in Action, or the Burden of the Political

Yet where does this leave ethics? Is it simply enough to say that Godard's aesthetic violence and terrorism, as we've defined it, subvert and deconstruct militant violence and terrorism? Put differently, is the ethical question posed by *La Chinoise* of how to speak for, and represent, the other while avoiding the delusion of "being the words of others" adequately resolved by the endless recombinations of montage that appear like object lessons in becoming "other" due to the fact that each individual image and sound loses itself in juxtaposition with another and is thus left unformulated and "open"?[17] Is there not perhaps something more concrete, more fundamentally "real" missing here? One crucial fact not readily acknowledged by critics is that in all the publicity images for *La Chinoise*, and even for the title song "Mao Mao," one name is curiously absent: that of Omar Diop. It could be immediately countered that since Diop is not strictly a member of the Aden-Arabie cell and is simply playing himself, there is no automatic reason for him to be presented on equal terms with the other actors. Yet Diop is not even mentioned in the detailed two-page article Godard wrote explaining his political intentions for the film, despite being so crucial to the film's elaboration of Maoism.[18] Critics follow Godard's lead and barely mention him, although his eloquent lecture is one of the film's showpiece set-sequences. In fact, his role and value will only be fully recognized by Godard much later in *Introduction à une véritable histoire du cinéma* (1980), a transcription of the improvized talks he gave in the spring and autumn of 1978 at the Conservatoire d'art cinématographique in Montreal where he pays tribute to Diop as the film's one "real character." By this time, however, Diop was dead. Expelled from France in 1969 at the age of twenty-six as a political troublemaker, he returned to Senegal where he was openly critical of the president, Léopold Sédar Senghor, and eventually detained by the authorities for planning terrorist acts. He was condemned in 1972 as a threat to state security and died in a prison cell in Dakar on May 11, 1973. The official version is that he hanged himself. However, Diop's death still remains a mystery and in all probability he was murdered.

Figure 1.6. Omar Diop as himself delivering a lecture in *La Chinoise* (1967).

I wish to stay with the idea of Diop as a real character and consider the implications of his special "realness" for Godard, since it raises some vital ethical questions about Godard's method and rhetorical engagement with the other. Godard expanded a little further in Montreal on his intentions for Diop: "I wanted him [Diop] to be the one to give the others lessons, precisely because he was black."[19] Hence, Godard positions Diop directly as the foreign (racial) other telling the indigenous white French where they are going wrong and what needs to be done politically in present-day France. Enlisted as the "real" voice and "new" image of revolutionary politics, preaching that "the road to socialism leads to revolution," Diop functions as nothing less than—yet also in Godard's ratiocinations no more than—a political philosopher, as opposed to the other members of the cell who are able to display other facets of their character, whether artistic or scientific. For this reason he is a monodimensional figure of the kind Godard will consistently expose as a limited and potentially flawed model precisely because not informed and inflected by the poetic and aesthetic. In actual fact, and highly ironically, Diop was not only a political militant but also deeply concerned with contemporary "outsider" aesthetics. He had already published a year before a probing article on Andy Warhol's *Chelsea Girls* (1966), and in addition to his work for Godard featured in a short experimental film by the late Simon Hartog, *Soul in a White Room* (1968).[20] Hence, Diop personally embodied a rare combination of radical art and politics, the very unity presented in the film as desirable but impossible and misguidedly "resolved" by the militants through their commitment to terrorism and violence.

In short, Diop is "framed" by Godard in *La Chinoise*: set up as the voice of truth and the real on the basis of his color and political creed, he is in the very same moment dispossessed of his true presence and identity and ultimately excluded from the film and its paradiscourse. That is to say, he pays the aesthetic price for being too *real* politically. This corresponds, of course, to a familiar scheme in Godard's thinking and practice of cinema, which attempts always to negotiate the extremes of Lumière (documentary) and fiction (Méliès) and craft a new and progressive compound of the two—a complicated and delicate balance. This is partly because film is a medium firmly of the present, as opposed to politics which, as Godard often states, always involves both the present and the past (Godard 1972: 225). The art of cinema requires therefore a special effort to negotiate aesthetically the irreversible present and to prevent it from becoming too real and overwhelming. To take just one brief but instructive example of this process from Godard's early work: the solid aesthetic foundations and "classic" framework of *Vivre sa Vie* (the twelve-tableaux structure and the explicit, stylized use of Edgar Allan Poe's "The Oval Portrait," C. T. Dreyer's silent classic, *The Passion of Joan of Arc* (1928), and Jean Ferrat's working-class song "Ma Môme") are created precisely to control and mediate, and ultimately off-set, the density of raw contemporary reality and real sound recorded within its frame. This basic working method and approach means that even when Godard reviews in 1959 a film like *Moi, un noir* (1958) by the ethnographic filmmaker Jean Rouch, he must first compliment Rouch on a "stunning" poetic work proving conclusively he is longer merely a purveyor of ethnographic documentaries in thrall to reality. It is notable that Godard has very little indeed to say here about the film's African setting beyond a mock-romantic comment about "Abidjan of the lagoons on the other side of the river" (Bergala 1985: 182). Indeed, Godard proposes in the article in the form of a truism that all great fiction films tend towards documentary and vice versa—a distinction he formalizes further in terms of "ethics" and "aesthetics," which, he claims, are not mutually exclusive and "necessarily find each other at the end of the path" (ibid). In other words, an ethical commitment to the real and the other must always be counterbalanced by an aesthetic filter. *Jusqu'à la victoire* is an object lesson in the mortal dangers of attempting to get too close to real historical events at the moment of their unfolding, and in the concomitant need to maintain a healthy distance from the clamor of the present. On this point Godard's project has always been nothing less than consistent, though the difficult art of finding the right formula for cinematic realism has to be learned all over again with each new film.

In his retrospective account of *Le Chinoise* in Montreal, Godard directly suggests that the film suffers from an overdose of reality and even bears the scars of ethnographic documentary. Indeed, he fully acknowledges the film's ethnographic basis and "documentary aspect," rationalizing pseudoscientifically that he "filmed it [May '68] before it really took form [. . .] cinema can be used for this, to see the creation of forms, their embryology. Embryology is something extremely mysterious" (Godard 2014: 273). So oriented towards the real, in fact, was *La Chinoise*, and so immersed in the moment with its use not only of Diop but also of Francis Jeanson, the Marxist-Leninist students he consulted, his then partner Wiazemsky and the apartment they shared together (used for all the interior scenes), that Godard even calls it here a "queer [*drôle*] film" (ibid). Yet it is Diop who bears the brunt of this *queer excess* of realness by being singled out by Godard as the film's "real" character. Which is to say, Diop is made to represent personally both the negative outcome of Godard's "detour" into political reality during the *longue durée* of May '68 (which, by the late 1970s, he was now keen to distance himself from) *and* the fundamental cinematic mistake of erring too much on the side of the real.

Hence, the story of Diop in the extended history of *La Chinoise* reveals the stark reality of Godard's strategies of exclusive otherness which can all too quickly flip over into forms of negative projection and exclusion through selective misrepresentation and occlusion. I am not suggesting for a moment, of course, that Godard's authorial "terrorism" towards the black other (the eclipsing of Diop in his very realness) can be equated with Senghor's act of state terrorism through the murderous silencing of a political undesirable. However, Godard's aesthetic violence towards the black other, whereby he inscribes Diop into *La Chinoise* as a slab of authentic otherness only then to write him out of it and, five years after his actual death, ultimately abject him as the very personification of the film's queer shortcomings, is not too dissimilar in its dizzying contradictions and *chinoiserie* from that of the naïve young terrorists who commit murder in the name of the Other. Moreover, it is symptomatic of a larger process of formal violence in

Godard's representation of the nonwhite other that cannot simply be explained as a temporary blip or blind-spot, and which, in fact, appears more like a gaping black hole in his work. For not only is there a consistent lack of genuine and sustained engagement by Godard with black characters (even when, as in *La Chinoise*, they are visible and iconic, such as Diop and Malcolm X, and when the theme of the Third World is directly sounded), but also, more troublingly, the black other is almost always rhetorically configured to perform a fixed role defined in the delimited and highly limiting terms of political realness.

I wish for the remainder of this chapter to explore the possible reasons both for the paucity of fully fledged black characters in Godard's cinema and for his acute ambivalence towards this particular instance of the real other. I begin with a brief typology of the major functions of the black African and African American figures in his work from the mid-1960s to the present.

The Face of the Black Other

The Immigrant

In the middle of *Masculin Féminin* Paul (Jean-Pierre Léaud) and his journalist friend Robert (Michel Debord) take the Paris metro where they find themselves sitting opposite two black men and one white woman engaged in a progressively more tense personal exchange that touches on issues of race and racism. We see the angry conversation unfold mainly from Paul's side of the carriage. The woman (Chantal Darget) remarks that all "Negroes" are "political assassins in the making," and one of the black men, played by the Mauritanian actor and director Med Hondo, agrees, stating: "She [Bessie Smith] is shouting kiss my big, black ass, that's what. Charlie Parker's the same [. . .] If you told Charlie, throw away your sax, and you can kill the first ten whites you see, he'd do it. He'd never play another note." In response, and to the aghast surprise of Paul, who shouts "Beware!," the woman draws a gun out from her raincoat and shoots the man dead.

The scene is, in fact, a restaging (with lines slightly altered) of the climactic scene in the 1964 play *Dutchman*, by the African American playwright LeRoi Jones (later Amiri Baraka), a political allegory depicting black/white relations in New York during the period of the black civil rights movement (the French version had just opened in Paris, and Godard used the same French cast, though neither Hondo nor Darget is credited in the film).[21] Yet Godard uses this emblematic scene less for what it actually says about race relations in the United States than for what it reveals of native French attitudes towards the immigrant other (shock, confusion, horror). Indeed, Godard is essentially co-opting the play's raw force and anger for his own personal critique of the solipsism of the new youth generation. Presented off-camera as a sound effect, the murder is passed off in the following intertitle as: "Nothing just a woman / and a man / and an ocean / of spilt blood." Indeed, apart from odd glimpses of recent immigrants eking out a shadowy existence in French society (an African man paying for daytime sex in a rundown basement in *Deux ou trois choses*; black supermarket customers becoming noticeably more animated than their white counterparts once the looting begins and the police arrive in *Tout va bien*; black faces lost in the crowd in the filler shots of the streets of northeast Paris in *Ici et ailleurs*), there is little appreciation in Godard's work of the black man or woman in contemporary France as an autonomous presence endowed with agency.

Figure 1.7. The restaging of LeRoi Jones's *Dutchman* with Med Hondo (left) and Chantal Darget in the Paris metro in *Masculin Féminin* (1966).

The Revolutionary

In *One plus One*, shot in London during the summer of 1968 and constructed around The Rolling Stones' recording "Sympathy for the Devil," a group of black militants, played among others by Diop (again uncredited), Frankie Dymon, Clifton Jones, and Danny Daniels, are filmed reciting black power and anti-imperialist slogans in a Battersea junkyard and daubing them on walls around the capital. Godard dares the viewer to be outraged by the satanic spectacle and excess of young black men receiving captive white women wearing only white shrouds stained with blood (no scenes of sex or rape are actually depicted). Yet the long, fragmented junkyard scene is also the setting for one long take of a militant reading aloud a passage about the theft of "black music" by white musicians and its popularization for white consumption.[22] The text is almost certainly extracted from the work of LeRoi Jones or Eldridge Cleaver's autobiographical collection of essays, *Soul on Ice* (1968), heavily cited in the film along with the *Black Panther Manifesto* ("PANTHERS" is scrawled along one wall of the yard facing the Thames). Cleaver's memoir, his association with the Black Panthers, and his theory of the "Omnipotent Administrator" are used by Godard here as key reference points for black militant activity, and a clear lineage of black countercultural and political figures including Malcolm X and Patrice Lamumba is quickly established. As Gary Elshaw explains, central to the scene is Godard's use of the intertitle "Outside Black Novel" which prompts the viewer both to contest what may be verbally told and to question the truth of the image (see Elshaw 1998). Indeed, Godard's overt desire to subvert and "destroy" mainstream culture draws precisely on Cleaver's mission to eradicate the dominant culture led by the Omnipotent Administrator, a symbol of repressive, white male, patriarchal power. In their joint performance of language (at one point one figure reads out a phrase, another repeats it a second later, creating the effect of a syncopated chorus), the black power activists set the aesthetic pace of the scene and inspire the continuous, interweaving camera movement back and forth across the junkyard shot in natural light. This beautiful, fluid choreographics of visual and verbal motion, liberated from the oppressive syntax both of "white" language and conventional (Western) cinema, takes further Guillaume's physical work on language and gesture in *La Chinoise* by showing black male bodies moving around each other freely and non-hierarchically. Such open receptivity to space, time and language carries a clear erotic charge. Yet the scene is also set up as an interview by two black "sisters" who have come to question one "brother" (Dymon) about the political way forward. Their conversation ends in warm thanks and mutual appreciation, as if Godard were suggesting that new kinds of political action and affinity uniting the sexes might now be possible (the film also features Wiazemsky as an urban guerrilla, "Eve Democracy").

Yet despite the evident aesthetico-political promise of *One plus One*, Godard never managed to realize his ambition to make a revolutionary film showcasing black power. The film called *One A.M. (One American Movie)* produced with the American documentary filmmakers Richard Leacock and D.A. Pennebaker was never completed, although Pennebaker and Leacock later released the shot footage as *One P.M.* It includes Rip Torn in Civil War garb talking to residents of the mainly African-American section of Ocean Hill-Brownsville in Brooklyn, LeRoi Jones reciting a text on the streets of Newark, and Godard himself personally interviewing Cleaver in Oakland. Godard was clearly out of his rhetorical depth here, a fact encapsulated by one highly awkward moment when Cleaver asserts Godard is part of the "Mafia Establishment." Again, Godard has strayed too far into "real" territory, and the strained black power elements of *One P.M.* amount to little more ultimately then voguish political wallpaper, as remote and inconsequential as the solitary poster paying lip homage to Cassius Clay on the kitchen wall in *Pierrot le fou*.

Figure 1.8. Black power militants, including Frankie Dymon with the microphone, in the junkyard in Battersea in *One plus One* (1968).

The Worker

The counterpart to the black militant in the cause for revolutionary struggle during this key period of Godard's political career is the black worker, though s/he is conspicuously absent on the production lines of the MG car factories at Abingdon filmed for *British Sounds*. Indirect reference is made in the same film to the Marxist newspaper *Black Dwarf* (edited by the prominent activist, Tariq Ali) when a front-cover photograph of black revolutionary students is suddenly flashed up with the caption "Universities under the Gun," over which is inscribed another caption (handwritten by Godard in English): "Militant sound." This sole reference to black politics and intellectuals is wholly divorced from the all-white working-class reality of the shop floor that occupies most of *British Sounds*, a film where the one black woman in a group of white feminist students at Essex University reinventing the words of a Beatles song remains all but mute in the background. A little later in Godard's work a young North African factory worker is briefly presented in the first episode of *Six fois deux* as one of the jobseekers at the local employment office, yet Godard is far more interested in black workers when they are not actually attempting to work in the current social and economic system. This is the case in *Week-end* where, in a sequence that starts with the intertitle "Monde 3" ("World 3") and ends with "Occident" ("West"), two immigrant garbage men, one West African, the other North African, pick up the two protagonists, the white bourgeois couple Corinne and Richard, and force them to do their menial work for them. The two unnamed men take it in turns to eat a symbolic loaf of bread and stare out for a minute and half directly at the camera. When Roland asks the West African for a piece, he gives him one "equal to the Congo's percentage of the annual American budget." Both workers are framed separately and talk in turn: as the Algerian speaks in monotone fashion in a voice-off, the camera films the West African in close-up, followed by the same in reverse. In what is presented explicitly as a lesson in dialectics, they tell the history of civilization from the pan-African point of view of "Nous Africains" (including both "dark" and "light" Africans) and the "*gens*" (people), which includes reference to the Maya and Aztecs. They claim the historical exploitation of blacks as the "true" genocide, a product of the "Nazism" of colonial countries, and proclaim the need for violence and "guerilla instruction." As in *La Chinoise* and *One plus One*, the nonwhite figures appear all too present and "real," delivering home truths which the fictional bourgeois couple (and the intended white viewer) are forced to hear. Silverman and Farocki rightly argue that by intercutting into the sequence other images of the film (not only flash-backs but also flash-forwards, as when the mention of Iroquois Indians provokes an image from the end of the film of cannibalistic hippies wearing Indian style head-bands), Godard is suggesting that violence and the threat of the "primitive" to Western civilization comes not from outside (that is, the Third World) but rather from within (Silverman and Farocki 1998: 103). Yet what is crucial here is not so much the dry revolutionary talk about how the Western history of mankind has resulted in a class-ridden society, nor even the justification of revolutionary violence, but rather the formal set-up itself whereby two black men stare out the implied white viewer with a fixed gaze at once silent and accusatory, indifferent and scornful. Indeed, what the scene reveals again is how Godard draws on, and requires, a certain quotient of black realness in order to generate the greater political depth he craved during this early self-radicalizing period of the mid-to-late 1960s. Hence, the function of black figures in Godard's work comes down fundamentally to the look of pure disgust which they can cast back at the more narratively developed white characters—a gaze that puts the latter, and the viewer, firmly in their place. Godard's capacity at this point in his career to capitalize on white intellectual guilt (including his own) would appear limitless.

The Prophet

In Godard's films of the 1960s and 1970s the few blacks visible, even those in the supermarket sequence of *Tout va bien*, are almost exclusively male. However, the reverse appears true in Godard's more recent work with young black and Arab women performing the role of sage or prophet foretelling the destruction of the West. *Film socialisme*, for instance, features first the actress Nadège Beausson-Diagne as Constance, although a more accurate name might be Cassandra since she serves here as a voice of doom. Even before she comes into view at the start of the film, over the image of a young white man, Mathias (Mathias Domahidy), with whom she is in conversation, she delivers the following voice-off *in media res*: "And us/ When once again we have dropped/ Africa" (Godard 2012: 7). Later, she is pictured alone in the frame and talks of "[t]his poor Europe/ Not purified but/ corrupted by suff/ering [*la souf-/ France*] Not/ exalted by humiliated/ by its reconquered freedom" (ibid.: 37). In the film's second movement entitled "Notre Europe" ("Our Europe"), the young Malian actress Eye Haïdara plays a television camerawoman for FR3 filming the Martin family. She enters into conversation with the young son whom she calls "petit blanc" ("little white boy") and shows him her Egyptian watch (the same watch glimpsed on the wrist of Constance, emphasizing the continuity between these two black female figures). She explains there are no hands on the watch to tell the time since it works according to the simple alternation of night and day (the "night of time" and the "day of time"), thus presenting herself as a conduit of superior ancient knowledge. She also talks to her FR3 colleague (Élisabeth Vitali) about Africa: "Therefore in my humble/ Opinion Africa has started off again badly" (ibid.: 59), to which the latter replies in Sartrean tones: "You mean not entered history you/ Think that What doesn't change is that that there will/ Always be bastards And all that's different today/ Is that the bastards are sincere" (ibid.). Once again, reference to black Africa reverts almost immediately to "us" Europeans and "[n]os humanités" ("our humanities"), the title of the film's third movement, leading to the central question posed here: "Quo Vadis Europa?" What this confirms is not simply that the intended viewer of Godard's films still remains essentially white and European (and implicitly male), but also that African references continue to be merely a vehicle for more pressing European matters. *Film socialisme* is precisely *not* a film about African humanities or sensibilities, even if the cruise ship visits Alexandria as part of its journey around the Mediterranean basin.[23] Moreover, the book of *Film socialisme*, although it contains most of the lines of speech uttered in the film, includes no images of Beausson-Diagne or Haïdara, or indeed of any black figures at all. The photographic portraits are exclusively of white writers, filmmakers, and philosophers, with the exception of the face of a young Palestinian fighter and a still from *Ici et ailleurs* of a young Palestinian girl singing.[24]

From this rapid overview of the key modes and strategies in Godard's treatment of black African and African American characters and themes, we see that virtually all the black figures in his work, whether performing as themselves or as invented characters, constitute essentially anonymous presences, at once visible and invisible, while adhering to a fixed set of terms and conditions of realness that have not changed since *Masculin Féminin*. Their primary function is to be on hand to provide a dispassionate, disabused, and at times brutal, gaze on the decline of the West. Cast to the textual margins and inhabiting literal and figurative "nonplaces," they are effectively obliged by Godard to carry the burden of the political, otherwise they cease to exist, certainly in aesthetic terms. Indeed, they are the ground over which Godard performs his subversive rhetorical maneuvers, for while they may articulate a vital historical, postcolonial perspective on "our" world (that is, Europe) and serve as the basis for an engaged political consciousness (and possible conscience), even generating on occasions new creative energy and revolutionary rhythms, this does not qualify them for serious inclusion in the hallowed inner sanctum of Godard's art. Moreover, as we have seen, in his specific representation of black men as always potentially on the loose, both physically and socially (they are the original "rolling stones"), Godard knowingly skirts crude and primitive racial stereotypes. *One plus One* even conjures up the colonial specter of the indigenous black male as a sexual rival stealing and raping white women. Yet for Godard it is precisely their "natural" ease with violence that makes those of African heritage so uniquely equipped and ready for revolutionary action. Such disturbing undertones to Godard's already paradoxical presentation of the black other complicate and potentially nullify those rare, exciting moments celebrating radical black expression in his work (the *prise de parole* of a historically oppressed community, the stripping down and reinvention of language, the opening up of the body to new physical and social formations).

The result of this entirely reductive and essentializing process of appropriation and projection, where Godard's conferral of exclusivity on his black characters is revealed as exclusionary and self-serving, is glimpsed in *Éloge de l'amour* in the form of the unnamed, brassy, and officious African American assistant to Steven Spielberg. Introduced in the second part of the film as an impatient figure curtly demanding road directions in her stiletto heels, she is immediately referred to by real-life French filmmaker Jean-Henri Roger (collaborator on a number of Dziga Vertov Group films) as "one of the Americans who is bothering us." In what becomes a wholly negative and thankless role, this anonymous female character has only one purpose: to *be* the face of Godard's disgust towards Spielberg and American cultural imperialism.[25] How ironic that an African American woman in another uncredited role should now become the visible symbol of the American system when blacks were once explicitly presented by Godard as noble "victims" of white capitalist society and at the vanguard of heroic revolutionary struggle. In fact, rather than herald counterresistance and radical change, African Americans appear now in Godard's imaginary to incarnate everything that is wrong with American culture and influence, precisely because they have failed to deliver on their revolutionary promise to destroy it. They have effectively sold out to (white) American values. In Godard's skewed account of political failure, blacks have therefore an even greater cross to bear than most for the political status quo and ideological bankruptcy of the West. An additional implication in *Éloge de l'amour* is that the debased American values are also specifically Jewish American, raising further troubling questions about Godard's appetitive rhetorical processes of racial appropriation, universalization, and scapegoating. We shall address these particular issues in greater detail in chapter 6, where we consider Godard's ambivalent engagement with Israel and the Jews in the context of the West Bank and Palestine.

Figure 1.9. Steven Spielberg's unnamed (and uncredited) assistant and the U.S. official (William Doherty) on the receiving end of an anti-American tirade by Berthe (Cécile Camp) off-screen in *Éloge de l'amour* (2001).

In short, during the course of Godard's career it would appear that once blacks have fulfilled and exhausted their potential as the chosen other, they are all but elided, to return only as an indiscriminate negative other devoid of either political value or aesthetic interest. They simply no longer cut it as radical others in Godard's political scheme and are forced to bear the weight of his artistic frustration and disappointment. The odd, anonymous sightings over the last thirty-five years of a black female figure naked and silent in the background of the *tableaux vivants* created in *Passion* (including Ingres's Orientalist *Interior of a Harem* [1828]), or a West African businessman wearing a *boubou* in *Soigne ta droite* physically prevented by the "Admiral" from embarking at the front of the plane and replaced on board by a boorish black teenager who runs amok in the cabin while crudely chatting up a stewardess, serve merely to reinforce the wholesale disappearance. As with Diop, it's a no-win situation: after being positively identified and projected as absolutely other and different, black Africans and African Americans are now negatively reprojected and ostracized as little more than a symptom, if not the cause, of revolutionary failure and the collapse of a certain utopian ideal of revolutionary change.

Race, Nation, Cinema: The Impossible Project

Yet how can we fully account for the extreme degree of invisibility, indeed almost total impossibility, of actual black figures and characters in Godard's later work? More is clearly at stake than the 180 degree turn in this particular area of Godard's ideological thinking, or the simple fact that since the beginning of the 1980s he has stayed largely close to home (Switzerland, France, Germany, Bosnia-Herzegovina) and focused predominantly on European culture, art, and history. A possible answer can be found, I think, if we return again to his political work of the 1970s, and specifically the fortunes of one Sonimage project with Miéville from 1978–79 planned for Mozambique. This was an immense and potentially momentous project for a newly independent Third World country that sought also to reboot and "rescue" an increasingly defunct Western cinema. Godard had signed a contract with the socialist government of President Samora Machel in December 1977 to help develop a broadcasting system untainted by Western bourgeois and capitalist influences. There was, in fact, only one movie camera in the entire country, even though independence in 1975 had also marked the creation of a new National Institute of Cinema in Mozambique spearheaded by Ruy Guerra, a key figure of the Brazilian Cinema Novo. Godard and Miéville's original idea was for a video project that could take the form of a feature-length work for distribution, to be called either *Nord contre Sud* or *Naissance (de l'image) d'une Nation*, and/or a five-hour TV series. The first two parts of the series were to be centered around a couple: a male producer and a female commentator/photographer, fictional stand-ins for Godard and Miéville to be played by actors. Godard saw Mozambique as a kind of living laboratory and a unique opportunity to identify and select the correct tools of production necessary to build from scratch an authentic national cinema and television in a completely new and virgin territory. In Mozambique, he declared, "the image is the raw material," and there were, as yet, no codes for looking. As the Malian filmmaker and theorist Manthia Diawara has written in his excellent account of the project, Godard was even ready to go like a missionary into the villages and train peasants to use the equipment (see Diawara 2003).

What emerged from Godard's preparatory visits to Mozambique was "Le dernier rêve d'un producteur" ("The Last Dream of a Producer"), a sixty-page section of the three hundredth anniversary issue of *Cahiers du Cinéma* (guest-edited by Godard himself in May 1979) that was intended as a kind of preview or teaser for the work to come. It incorporated a kind of travelogue and three collections of drawings, and notes relating to Mozambique. The "Report on Voyage no 2A of the Sonimage Company in Mozambique" was a confessional diary/photo-essay about the trip he and Miéville made together in late August/early September 1978, combining notes from Godard's own diary from their time there and photographs of the country, its inhabitants, and those assigned to the television project. It is laced with passages of critical reflection and summation in the style of *Ici et ailleurs* such as: "Power of images. Abuse of power. Always be two to watch an image, and split the difference between the two. Image as proof. Image as justice, as the result of an accord" (Godard 1979: 125). Another theme of the essay is children and their relationship with the image, making links between the youth of the country and its status as a newly born nation. The essay ends with the archly ironic, self-canceling catechism: "Who is responsible for oppression disappearing? We are. Who is responsible for oppression remaining? We are" (ibid.: 127). This passage about the fatal continuum of European attitudes to Africa is juxtaposed with the image of a young Mozambican boy, partly cast in shadow, looking up entranced towards his right. Yet despite the photographic evidence of meetings with local and international officials and reference to the views of local inhabitants, *Cahiers du Cinéma* 300 suggested little of the particular locale of the project or even its overall aims and objectives. Critical reaction was, and remains, mixed. For Daniel Fairfax the photographs display a "rare, lyrical power" (Fairfax 2010: 62), while for Brody they were neither analytical nor ethnographic, and really no more revealing than snapshots—proof that the particular significance of Mozambique for Godard, a country he was not connected to by language, history, or culture, remained blurred (Brody 2008: 414).

Godard and Miéville's experiment in Mozambique ultimately came to nothing. Deemed too costly, it was eventually shelved and Godard's contract terminated. He left the country profoundly dissatisfied with the images he had produced and with a miserable sense of having achieved almost nothing—all the more so since, as he put it rather bitterly, the authorities had totally unrealistic expectations and wanted Christmas tomorrow (as it happened, television did eventually come to Mozambique but entirely without Godard's assistance). No actual footage remains of his work there apart from the photographs used in *Cahiers* 300, although visual recollections of the project can be found in the 2003 documentary *Kuxa Kanema* by Margarida Cardoso. Diawara sums up the underlying problem in the following terms: "[A]n aesthetically radical filmmaker such as Godard simply could not function in an effective manner when tied to a government apparatus" (Diawara 2003: 119). Moreover, there was no real consideration in the project of "Africans as thinking and creative subjects who own their continent" (ibid.).[26] Godard himself acknowledged that the prospects for achieving a radical alternative to the dominant practice of television were now virtually zero: "There was a chance. A chance. It's over," he lamented (MacCabe 1980: 156). His acute feeling of total disappointment and failure as a political filmmaker remained with him for a long time, leading him to stage physically his own self-humiliation in *Changer d'image* (Change of image), a nine-minute short broadcast on French television in 1982 as part of the series "Le Changement à plus d'un titre" (Change in more than name). This could have been, as the commissioning producers clearly intended, a work about the possibilities for social and cultural change following the momentous electoral triumph of Mitterrand's socialists in 1981 after more than a decade of right-wing governments. However, Godard, sitting alone in front of a blank screen and gently interrogated by the voice of Miéville off-screen, makes it clear from the outset that he is already utterly bored by the endless debates about reform instead of direct change, preferring instead to talk about his own crisis in confidence and the impossibility of being able to respond to change by producing images of change. He expresses a wish to "show himself humiliated" since the business of making images is like giving, and above all receiving, slaps in the face. The reasons for such pessimism are unclear until a third-person male narrator (played by the Swiss dramatist and actor Jacques Probst) suddenly arrives on the soundtrack and the image is immediately replaced by another of Godard, again alone but in a different setting and this time shirtless and strapped to a chair, his spectacles on the table in front of him. He is now hit on the head and both sides of the face by an unidentified, faceless male figure in a suit. The narrator provides the context: the "idiot" (Godard) had gone a couple of years ago to a country (left vague as "somewhere" in Africa or Latin America) to work "in the realm of central television." He had been summoned on account of his "so-called sympathies for these kinds of places" and because he was "an expert in image-changing." However, the constantly changing regime, half-military and half-civilian, deported all the foreign advisors except "the idiot" whom it tasked three times with creating images of change. This excruciating simulation of torture, superimposed queasily over the first image where the screen now becomes animated with projected images, is a belated and dramatic metaphor for the manipulation Godard felt he had suffered at the hands of the authorities in Mozambique, and, more generally, within the system of cinema and television itself, now totally occupied by the state which requires art on demand.

Figure 1.10. Godard confronting his failures in front of a blank screen in *Changer d'image* (1982).

Yet in this partly fictionalized confessional short excoriating a foreign regime, Godard also puts himself literally on the rack with a self-flagellating account of his own naive "stupidity" in allowing himself to become a pawn of the system and also ultimately of his deficient cinematic method. The essential problem in Mozambique, we now understand, was again a formal confusion between the real and the imaginary and an inability by Godard to find the right configuration of documentary and narrative cinema (the narrator talks of the usual "nasty business when documentary plays with fiction"). Godard presents himself as trapped, like Véronique in *La Chinoise*, in a chiastic logic of fixed reversals: a filmmaker moving always "between the images of life and the life of images" and forced in Mozambique to provide the exact "formula" for "changing images and creating images of change," before deciding eventually to establish a new "delicate formula" that could "be seen without being told, and told without being seen." He has ended up merely a creator of "chains of images" enchained within the system (a constant visual motif in the film is a bicycle and chain in close-up). In this unsettling personal dramatization of active and passive, subject and object, where he is virtually excluded from his own narrative (once the unseen narrator arrives on the soundtrack we no longer hear what Godard is saying in front of the screen), Godard is deliberately giving himself a taste of his own medicine—the same medicine he administered in the extended story of *La Chinoise* where Diop was unceremoniously excluded as the all-too-real. How is one to move forward? How can one make a change artistically and politically? Godard states that he's not ready for any sudden change and suggests instead, rather abstractly, that he can perhaps show "*the resistance of the image* to change" (my emphasis). His thinking here is that he "can change between images" and "it's that *between* one has to show" (my emphasis). Yet the last image in *Changer d'image* of Godard lying prone on the ground outside a building and left for dead negates such modest optimism. Indeed, it reflects the fact that, three years later, and exacerbated no doubt by the recent memory of the agonizing *Jusqu'à la victoire*, a film not only unfinished but also unfinishable, he still remains mortally crushed by the overwhelming failure of his abortive Mozambique project which promised so much.

A further measure of Godard's profound and still smoldering sense of humiliation can be detected in the much later *Histoire(s)*, specifically a short, discrete section of episode 1B, *Une histoire seule*, dedicated to African themes. This reemploys some of the images and captions from *Cahiers* 300, including a photograph of Jean-Pierre Bamberger showing a young black boy how cinema is done, his camera thrusting down almost phallicly into the boy's face.[27] There is strangely no mention here of the work of contemporary African filmmakers like Ousmane Sembène, except for one reference to Souleymane Cissé's poetic "return to the source" masterpiece, *Yeelen* (1987), which, very tellingly, Godard misspells on screen as *Yeleen*. The tone is at once personal, casual, and ambiguous, punctuated by now classic, chiastic Godard formulae such as "Ce n'est pas une image juste, c'est juste une image" from *Vent d'est*, which appear rather weary and almost irrelevant in view of the urgent, postcolonial project being undertaken by black African directors to realize "authentic" images of and for themselves. In addition to Michel Leiris's 1934 book *L'Afrique fantôme*, there are assorted film references to *Moi, un noir* by Rouch (who had been in Mozambique around the same time as Godard), Robert Flaherty and W. S. Van Dyke's *White Shadows of the South Seas* (1927), and *Voyage au Congo* (1927) by Marc Allégret, presented here rather mischievously by Godard as Gide's "nephew" (he is playing on the fact that Gide's 1925 novel, *Les Faux-monnayeurs* (*The Counterfeiters*), where Édouard falls in love with his nephew, is based on Gide's relationship with Allégret, his secretary and lover). *Voyage au Congo* records the ethnographic journey undertaken by Gide and Allégret in 1925 and 1926 to document Congolese customs and, with its exotic images and ethnographical narration which Godard briefly samples here, clearly betrays a voyeuristic and ethnocentric gaze on black Africa.

One might have expected Godard at this point to mount a sustained critique of such problematic colonial material and to investigate the heritage of colonialism in cinema, yet the sequence passes by very quickly to the rhythms of John Coltrane and Otis Redding and is effectively carved in half by a return to more familiar and "comfortable" European topics such as Hitler, Mussolini and "ordinary fascism," and the history of the cinematograph within the Western tradition. Links can certainly be made here between the racialized images of black skin with 1930s/1940s fascism and the history of the camera: Allégret, we are informed, took to the Congo a Debrie Sept 35 mm cine camera, Mussolini is shown filming with a large camera, and Hitler is pictured from below with Mussolini's voice-over. Max Silverman has argued well that the phrase "ombres blanches" ("white shadows"), presented in white over a black background, should be compared with the letters "moi, un noir" printed in white over a black background, thus creating an inversion of the power relations inherent in "ombres blanches" (see Silverman 2013: 125–28). The same words are connected by Godard not only with the early cinematic device of the "fantascope" (projecting ghost-like white shadows through a magic lantern that inverts the visible world) and the 1923 silent film drama by Graham Cutts, *The White Shadow* (aka *White Shadows*) (*Ombre blanche*), but also with the explosive film *Black God, White Devil* (1964) by the radical Brazilian filmmaker and key proponent of Third Cinema, Glauber Rocha, where the legendary bandit figure Antonio das Mortes inspires the dispossessed to rise up against the forces of repression. For Silverman, the trip to the Congo by Gide and Allégret is thus recast by Godard by "its intersertion within other "journeys" through the tangled terrain of race and the cinema, which allows us to 'read' that journey historically" (ibid.: 128). Yet like the intermittent images of Errol Flynn as a former (white) slave and now pirate in the West Indies in *Captain Blood* (1935), so much of this is simply too fleeting and diffuse to make full critical sense. Godard himself gives the game away when he explains at the end of the section that he meant simply to say that cinema was never an art and still less a technology (a standard refrain in *Histoire(s)* normally rounded off with the phrase, "but a mystery"). The ultimate effect of this brief sequence, initially triggered by casual mention of Gide's 1897 prose-poem *Les Nourritures Terrestres* (*The Fruits of the Earth*) and bookended by white male artists (Rouch, Gide, Leiris, even Samuel Beckett in the form of a reference to his unpunctuated prose-work, *L'Image* [1959]), is of an intellectually uncommitted, even tokenistic, interlude framed in "counterfeit" Gidean terms as a space of eternal ambivalence.

 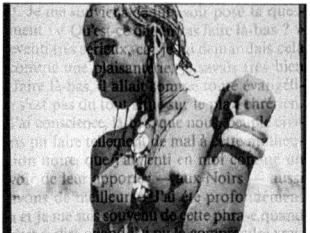 

Figures 1.11–13. Images from Mozambique in the "Africa sequence" in episode 1B of *Histoire(s) du cinéma* (1988–98).

Godard's nonengagement with African matters in *Histoire(s)* testifies to his lingering sense of artistic and political impotence induced by the failed Mozambique project and his incapacity to realize what would surely have been the most perfect encounter yet of ethics, politics, and aesthetics—one certainly far more ambitious and paradigm-shifting than the abortive American film, variously called *Bugsy*, *The Picture*, and *The Story*, which Godard was also attempting to make between 1978 and 1980 and where he would have been working entirely within the Hollywood system with Francis Ford Coppola as co-producer and major stars such as Robert de Niro and Diane Keaton. In fact, Godard's feeling of abject failure in not finding the right method, language, or codes to achieve his African dream permeates, and arguably determines, all his subsequent work, slipping metonymically into a general projection of all black Africans and African Americans as a source of failed promise and impossibility. Nothing, of course, can definitively prove or disprove this hypothesis, but that doesn't invalidate it as a theory since the degree of affect and cathexis and genuine pathos generated by the masochism of *Changer d'image*, together with his almost total disavowal in *Histoire(s)* of any real interest in Africa, carry their own highly persuasive force. Godard's immediate creative response at the time was to return decisively to something he knew intimately well, European art cinema, and it goes almost without saying that *Sauve qui peut (la vie)*, shot in Lausanne and featuring Jacques Dutronc as his alter ego Paul Godard, carries no hint at all of black skin or African presence.

The long and tortuous story we have traced of Godard's (non)encounter with African and African American influence, from *La Chinoise* and *Masculin Féminin* to *Histoire(s)* and *Film socialisme*, where the one interlinking thread is a fundamental violence to the racial other in the very name of the Other, raises major questions about the representation of difference and alterity in Godard's work and its continual balancing of the political, aesthetic, and ethical. Is there any ideal or "right" equation between these three elements that would allow for the other to exist more justly and autonomously? For if to engage with the other always involves a rhetorical process of appropriation and negative projection, can the relation ever be reversed in the other's favor? What would happen, for example, if Godard were to put aside his frustrated feelings and suspicions about black Africans and African Americans and engage with a completely different instance of the real other? In short, in a form of cinema like Godard's, which sustains itself on the rhetorical structures and metaphors it engenders, what space is ultimately possible for those who are usually configured in their very fixity and silence as the necessary condition for such aesthetic fluidity? Out of the ruins of an impossible political ideal could there eventually spring a more productive renegotiation of the relations between ethics, aesthetics, and politics—one that might also develop the potential for "resistance" within the cinematic image itself, as proposed in *Changer d'image*? And, if so, how might this resistance be formulated? These core interrelated questions constitute an abiding preoccupation of Godard's evolving ethicoaesthetic project. As we shall see in our following encounters with Godard, they will also create in his work right up to the present a permanent sense of tension and ambivalence, even profound misunderstanding and contradiction, around matters of race, culture, and the fatal attraction of the Other, real or imaginary.

2

The Signs in Our Midst

European Culture and Artistic Resistance in *Histoire(s) du cinéma* (1988–98)

History attempts to transform destiny into consciousness, and art to transform it into freedom.

—A. Malraux

Cinema is a sign, and its signs are in our midst.

—J.-L. Godard

A topos of Godard's work since the late 1980s, the opposition between art and culture, is best formulated in *JLG/JLG: autoportrait de décembre*: "[T]here is culture which is the rule/ which is part of the rule/ there is the exception/ which is art/ which is part of art/ everyone speaks the rule/ cigarettes/ computers/ t-shirts/ television."[1] This general opposition, which can be likened to many such statements made earlier in the twentieth century by Theodor Adorno about the state of the culture industry and the market, could be taken in a variety of ways. For example, as a contrast between the absolute autonomy of art and the contingencies of democratized culture, or as part of a gendered distinction Godard often draws between culture as education and production (an essentially feminine, maternal principle) and art as the adult domain of creativity (the masculine principle).[2] A little later in *JLG/JLG*, however, Godard is far more specific about the exceptional status of art, bringing together artistic heavyweights such as Flaubert, Pushkin, Dostoyevsky. Gershwin, Mozart, Cézanne, Vermeer, Antonioni, and Vigo to develop a notion of art as a fundamentally European phenomenon and experience.

In Godard's opinion the exception of art is now threatened from within Europe itself by the promotion and proliferation of European culture for all. He states: "[I]t is the nature of the rule/ to wish the death/ of the exception/ it is/ no/ it is therefore the rule/ of Europe/ of culture/ the rule of Europe/ of culture/ to organize the death/ of the art of living/ which was blossoming/ still at our feet."[3] *JLG/JLG* was released the year after the "General Agreement on Tariffs and Trade" (GATT) talks of 1993 when France successfully pursued a policy of *exception culturelle*, that is, the exception of "cultural products" such as cinema from world trade agreements. The extracts from *JLG/JLG* just cited could thus be viewed as an acerbic comment by Godard on French cultural policy advocated in the name of an integrated Europe ("a Europe of Cultures"), and its misplaced wish to legislate in matters of art wrongly conceived as culture. Certainly, if the hegemony of commodified American culture and its reactionary forces of merchandising and distribution devoid of a sense of history have always constituted a natural enemy in Godard's work (one thinks in particular of films of the mid-to-late 1960s like *Deux ou trois choses que je sais d'elle*), it is now the "new Europe" that has become his most immediate foe. As Godard declared in brutally simple terms during a conference in London in 1991 on the theme of European identity in cinema: "We have in Europe more or less lost our identity, mainly through an acceptance of American culture. For me, painting and movie-making is not culture. A novel is not culture—it's art. Mozart is not culture, but distributing Mozart on RCA compact disc is culture. This is very different. But I don't think the cure for this lost identity is to try to construct a bigger identity and call it "European."[4]

How do Godard's recent public pronouncements on art and Europe actually relate to his films? *Passion*, set in a TV studio in Switzerland (the neutral and, for Godard, often empty center of the old continent) against the distant backdrop of martial law in Poland, marked, of course, his first direct attempt to consider the status and legacy of European art, in particular their engagement with European history in the form of historical narrative. Paintings by (among others) Rembrandt, Goya, and Delacroix are presented in the film in the form of *tableaux vivants*. Ien Ang has written convincingly that *Passion* displays a specifically European nostalgic melancholy, part of a general longing for the impossible in European idealist thought which resulted historically in failed Utopias, from the Enlightenment to German unification. Moreover, it radically stages this melancholic passion for the impossible as "the impossibility of cinema itself, the impossibility of narrative, the impossibility of love, the impossibility of arriving at anything."[5] In the same doomed European vein as *Passion* are later films such as *Nouvelle Vague*, in which Europe is presented as a murky bureaucratic world of corporate capital where international industrialists and financiers circulate oblivious to the beauty and mystery of nature, and *Hélas pour moi* where Europe is treated more as a background extra, a passing object of irony (a Swiss boat named *Italy* passing in and out of the frame, a travelling salesman hauling his suitcase of goods "Made in Europe" everywhere and nowhere, a soldier always on the point of leaving for Bosnia, and so on). That said, Godard's work since the late 1980s has dealt in increasingly serious fashion with contemporary events in

Europe. *Allemagne année 90 neuf zéro*, for example, where the issue of language and culture is directly thematized (German, French, English, and occasionally Russian all overlap each other), is one of the most dense and intensive of Godard's later films and offers an aesthetic and philosophical meditation on the solitary "state" of postcommunist East Germany. *For Ever Mozart* charts the doomed progress of a young drama troupe bound for Sarajevo and exposes along the way the hypocrisy of Western countries during the Bosnian war (euphemisms such as peacekeepers). As for *Histoire(s) du cinéma*, it is literally flooded by the images of twentieth-century war in Europe, from the Spanish Civil War to the Second World War, the Holocaust, and Bosnia.

What is striking, however, is that those current events in Europe with which Godard has chosen to engage have almost no link at all with the rich heritage of European art that he draws on and cites so profusely. Godard's is an essentially classical sense of European art and culture that advances no further into the story of modern art than Francis Bacon, Picasso, and Nicolas de Staël, artists who still retain some notion of the figure. In the case of the latter, this was the last gasp of the Paris School before the center of modern art moved to New York and abstract expressionism became the order of the day. As for European cinema, it means necessarily for Godard a cinema of the past, that is to say, as Jacques Aumont has emphasized, "une Europe à trois" (Germany, Italy, France).[6] It is significant that apart from the odd fleeting reference to directors such as Coppola, Angelopoulos, Garrel, and Kiarostami, Godard makes virtually no reference to contemporary cinema in *Histoire(s)*. Similarly, many of those quintessentially European thinkers and writers to whom he refers consistently in his later work, such as Charles Péguy, Oswald Spengler, and Denis de Rougemont, were writing much earlier in the century, and all agonized in different ways over the sad predicament of contemporary Europe and European culture. Péguy's posthumously published *Clio* (1917) (subtitled a "dialogue of history and the pagan soul"), parts of which are read aloud in the last episode (4B, *Les Signes parmi nous*), is a visionary work of faith that upholds the French tradition, in particular the "genius" of Victor Hugo in whom history and poetry, matter and spirit are fully interwoven. Written under extreme personal stress and shadowed by a calm intimation of approaching war, Péguy's dialogue between Clio, the Muse of history, and the reader is a meditation on remembrance and the creative intelligence of memory.[7] Spengler's mammoth *Decline of the West* (1923), invoked in *Allemagne* in terms of the final battle between blood and money, predicts the end of Western civilization by finding analogies with the declining civilizations of the past. It is a Cassandra-like work, poised between optimism and faith on the one hand and pessimism and spleen on the other, since for Spengler cultures rise and fall in defiance of linear progress and leave nothing behind.[8] Denis de Rougemont's *Penser avec les mains* (1936) is quoted at length in episode 4A of *Histoire(s)*, *Le Contrôle de l'univers*, with Godard reading out key phrases and extracts covering the entirety of the text in chronological order. De Rougemont wrote this now little-read essay about the threatening decadence of Western culture during the rise of national socialism, and with it he sought to reinstate the powers of active, individual thought and a Western principle of community and friendship based on a new order of moral ethics (what he called the "seven virtues" such as creative imagination). This he contrasted with culture which is always "a ready-made thing and not a thing to be made or being made. It's the idea of the cultivated man rather than the creator that is associated quite naturally in our minds with culture; the idea of luxury rather than work, spiritual struggle and power in process."[9]

Underlying these very different works by Péguy, Spengler, and de Rougemont is, of course, a profound sense of what Europe and European culture should stand for. For Godard, such certainties can be viewed now only as a matter of the past, as what Europe and European art and culture once embodied or symbolized. In cinematic terms, a reconstructed notion of Europe might entail the regular programming of European-made films in every country: "The day when every television station in Europe regularly shows a Greek, Portuguese or Slovak film, whether dull or not, Europe will be created. Otherwise it will remain American" (Bergala 1998: 251). A genuinely new Europe could mean nothing more than this, yet equally nothing less than this, which is to say an impossible ideal. Thus, when Godard turns to a writer like de Rougemont, the author of other works such as *L'amour et l'Occident* (1956), it is above all to help himself diagnose the disunited, moribund state of contemporary European culture rather than to establish a clear social or political prognosis. He will never engage, for instance, with de Rougemont's numerous later essays and reports on the future of European union such as *Les Chances de l'Europe* (1962), published under the auspices of the Centre Européen de la Culture which he founded in Geneva in 1950, or *L'un et le divers, ou la Cité européenne. Deux discours* (1970), both of which argue strongly for a European federation. Yet if "Europe" and European are fast becoming only the stuff of memory for Godard, by the same token they constitute a privileged site of the imaginary, part of an open and often fantasmatic process of association, tension, transition and translation (in the literal sense, too, of moving a [dead] body). A film like *Allemagne* revels in a polyglot, pan-European artistic and historical past and imaginary, complete with frontiers, homelands, and dragons. Indeed, what Godard calls his "cinematographic unconscious," the product of his childhood reading of German literature and specifically German romanticism, his imaginary "motherland," is what can make possible an image of Don Quixote riding through the postindustrial wastelands of the former East Germany.[10]

It is by virtue of their floating status in the relentless flux of Godard's videographic montage in *Histoire(s)* that European art and culture past become, in fact, essentially open questions, or questions of form. I would like to explore these questions, and in so doing attempt to establish the specific nature of artistic "exception" and opposition to the rule in Godard's later film practice, by examining one particular episode of *Histoire(s)*, 3A, entitled *La Monnaie de l'absolu* (literally, "The change [as in exchange or barter] of the absolute"). I have chosen this episode because it exemplifies the polyphonic structure of *Histoire(s)* and is perhaps the most self-consciously European section of the work, offering an explicit and extensive enquiry into the relations between European art and history, specifically war, during the nineteenth and twentieth centuries. This aspect is highlighted in the book of *Histoire(s)* by the very first image of the third volume (Godard 1998a, vol. 3: 4): a superimposition featuring William Blake's *Europe* (an image not available in the video and even preceding the general subtitle of the book's four volumes, "Introduction à une véritable histoire du cinéma"). This illustration, where the Creator bends down with his compass, served as the frontispiece to Blake's book *Europe: A Prophecy* (1794), and it constitutes in turn a kind of foreword to Godard's own work in episode 3A by sounding a note of destiny and fatalism.

Yet I have also chosen episode 3A because it constitutes a virtual case study *à la Malraux* in artistic metamorphosis and the transformation of forms, from writing (Victor Hugo) to painting (Édouard Manet) to cinema (Roberto Rossellini and postwar Italian cinema), across the course of historical time.[11] The very title, *La Monnaie de l'absolu*, is a reference to the fourth and final part of André Malraux's *Les Voix du silence* (1951), translated into English as *The Twilight of the Absolute*. This seminal work of art history attempts to bring all artistic forms, secular and sacred, under the transhistorical umbrella of the Absolute, defined by Malraux as any authentic confrontation by human beings with a sense of their own finitude and death. Indeed, art, for Malraux, is something that ultimately surpasses the bounds of human comprehension. Malraux is a key point of reference in *Histoire(s)*. The long sequence in episode 3B, *Une Vague nouvelle*, for example, which addresses cinema as the museum of the real, harks back directly to the first part of *Les Voix du silence*, "Le musée imaginaire," and *Histoire(s)* can be read on one level as a Malrucian destruction of the institutional museum and its ideal reconstitution as a museum without walls. Indeed, as Antoine de Baecque puts it, both Godard and Malraux share a profoundly populist and prophetic belief in art and seek to dramatize our encounter and confrontation with it (de Baecque 2012: 231). This forms the basis of an "artistic theory of love at first sight" and "culture for all" whereby the overpowering emotion that a painting or other work of art can inspire opens "us" up to art and cultivates "us" (Malraux). Further, Malraux and Godard pursue a common artistic method of connecting and comparing art as the source of potential revelation, what de Baecque calls a "museum-montage" (de Baecque 2012: 234). Just as Malraux used only photographic reproductions to establish parallels within the history of art, so Godard in *Histoire(s)* employs one of the very tools said to have destroyed the aura of the work of art, namely, video, in order to reclaim meaning and another kind of aura through comparison with other works (ibid.: 228–34).

While many of the key themes of *Histoire(s)* are showcased in *La Monnaie de l'absolu* (the power—and weakness—of cinema and television, the Holocaust as a zero point in Western history and civilization, the eternal return of human suffering and death, the moral necessity of memory, however threadbare that memory may be), the episode falls into four distinct thematic parts: Europe, art, the Second World War, and cinema as a national event. I will examine each of the four parts in turn in order to show how together they present interrelated sites of crisis, struggle, and resistance. I do not propose an exhaustive close reading of episode 3A since the intricacy and depth of Godard's videographic montage here would require an entire book in itself. Moreover, although the use of music is typically rich and eclectic with extracts from Bach, Schumann, Puccini, Hindemith, Bartók, Liszt, Heinz Holliger, and Keith Jarrett (among others), I will confine myself here mainly to the visual. The detailed analysis of Godard's use of European painting and art and of the general effects of his poetic and historical formulation of montage will reveal that what he is elaborating in *Histoire(s)* is really a transnational and "transaesthetic" project sustained in part by resistance to the very idea of Europe as a unity and whole. I will then explore the general process of figuration within the rhetorical movements of Godard's montage and attempt to demonstrate that figuration functions essentially as a means of internal resistance in *Histoire(s)*. Indeed, such resistance constitutes the very ethical and aesthetic fabric of the work at the most immediate level of videographic form.

Europe

La Monnaie de l'absolu begins with Godard reciting in a choked whisper a political speech by Hugo entitled "Pour la Serbie" originally delivered on August 29, 1876 (Godard types the author and date at the end of the three-minute sequence). The speech was written by Hugo out of a sense of outrage at the actions of rival warring fictions in the buildup to the Russo-Turkish war of 1877–78 (the second major Balkan War). In it, he lambasts the reluctance of Western European nations to respond to the war in Serbia and exposes the hypocrisy of the diplomatic position adopted by Western governments when they say that to assassinate a man is a crime, while to assassinate a nation is a "question" requiring careful consideration. "What humankind knows, governments are unaware of," Hugo states, before asking: "When will the martyrdom of this small heroic nation end?."[12] The irony of Godard's choice of this speech is underscored by television footage of carnage during the Bosnian war of 1992–95 counterpointed with an image of the Mostar bridge before it was destroyed (yesterday's victim is today's aggressor), the shot of a magazine cover with the title *Bosnie: les armes high-tech*, and a photograph of François Mitterrand hidden behind sunglasses. It is extended by Godard's repetition of Hugo's mocking words "et cetera, et cetera" and the periodic tolling of a bell. At the same time, Godard presents us with a bewildering concatenation of painted images of violence, war, barbarism, and the grotesque. Goya's *Saturn*, one of his tragic *Black Paintings*, is first flashed in and out of Artemisia Gentileschi's brutal portrayal of Judith beheading Holofernes with the help of her maid. With this second image, which is suspended and repeated (and over which, in the standard restating of all the episode titles at the beginning of each episode, the title of 2B, *Fatale Beauté*, appropriately falls), Godard reminds us that the Judith and Holofernes story is linked expressly to warfare and military strategy (a Jewish widow's successful attempt to drive out the Assyrian invader and save her people). However, through sustained rapid spot editing which accentuates the violence represented in both images (the phrase "MONTAGE" is flashed up in triplicate), Godard is clearly provoking us into imagining the possible links between the represented scenes, a question we take to the next gallery of images. These are mainly details of further works by Goya (including *Great Exploits with Dead Bodies* from the *Disasters of War* series, *The Fire*, *Miracle of St. Anthony of Padua* [in the cupola of the Church of San Antonio de la Florida, Madrid], *Group on a Balcony*, and the chalk drawing *Saturn Devouring His Children*), Fuseli (*Lady Macbeth Sleepwalking*), Delacroix (*Pietà*), Grünewald (*The Temptation of Saint Anthony*, from the *Isenheim Altarpiece*), El Greco (*Christ Driving the Traders from the Temple*—the third, so-called Toledo version), and Uccello (*Deluge* and *The Battle of San Romano*, the Louvre panel). This controlled visual conflagration is also punctuated by moments of black leader, a glimpse of Velázquez's *Portrait of a Court Dwarf*, newsreel images of a Nazi death camp, and the sequence (slowed down) from Rossellini's 1948 film *Germany Year Zero* where the little boy, Edmund, walks through the rubble as he heads towards his voluntary death. The sequence comes to a rest with Monet's extraordinary portrait of his wife, Camille, on her deathbed (painted in 1879, three years after Hugo made his speech).

Figures 2.1–2. Interspotting and superimposing painting and film in the opening sequence of episode 3A of *Histoire(s) du cinéma* (1988–98).

Godard leaves us breathlessly trying to assimilate this eclectic assemblage of French, Spanish, Italian, and Swiss historical and biblical imagery. Are we meant to consider the cited paintings primarily as a demonstration of Western culture and history in crisis or as signs of a particular national culture? The penultimate image, Goya's *General Antonio Ricardos*, emphasizes the state of confusion: over the portrait of this Spanish general (killed, as it happens, during the Franco-Spanish Wars shortly after the portrait was painted in 1794), Godard types the words "Monsieur le vicomte le laquais d'Orsay," a loaded reference to the home of the French Foreign Office. He is perhaps hereby suggesting that France succeeded in blocking stronger United Nations and European Community actions against Serbia during the recent Bosnian War, a perception shared by many at the time. The exhilaration, yet also difficulty and frustration, induced by the fragmentation and defamiliarization of images, is exacerbated by other methods employed by Godard, including the filtering of images (for example, black-and-white images discolored a bloody red), the splintering of text (words cut in two, or into and sometimes over each other), and Godard's desire to use artists with and against each other (for instance, the mysterious main figure of *Deluge* is superimposed over a Renaissance image of the Ponte Vecchio). Yet in addition to the images' link with the culture that produced them and their possible new connection with each other lies the formal question of their original context. This question is articulated explicitly a few seconds later when Godard offers perhaps the most commonly recognized detail from Grünewald's *Isenheim Altarpiece*: the bent right arm and pointing finger of St. John the Baptist in the Crucifixion scene which shapes into a triangle the words: "Illum oportet crescere me autem minui" ("He must increase, but I must decrease"). In presenting just the detail of St. John, a key aspect of this supremely Catholic monument and its project of affirming a harmonious Catholic world view on the brink of spiritual crisis with the Reformation, Godard is quite deliberately gesturing towards a narrative unity and whole located forever off-screen and thus forever deferred. This fact is paralleled on the soundtrack, for Godard reproduces about two-thirds of Hugo's devastating speech almost word for word before cutting it dramatically after the statement that humanity ("*nous*") has its own "question": the little child in the mother's stomach. He thus denies Hugo's conclusion that the only possible solution to war in the Balkans is a "United States of Europe" or "Republic of Europe" (the "last port"), that is, a continental federation, with Paris, the city of light and capital of liberty, at its head. By stopping it where he does, an act as decisive as Judith's decapitation of Holofernes, Godard ends on a note of unresolved crisis and horror.

Godard's refusal even to entertain the notion of a European solution premised on the universality of French culture and civilization (a political card played by France over a century later during the GATT talks)[13] clearly reflects a belief that human war and suffering are universal concerns that are more important than any warped utopian notion of state or Republican unity. This approach can be linked perhaps to Jacques Derrida's treatment of Paul Valéry, another quintessentially European writer quoted at length by Godard at the beginning of episode 4A. In *L'Autre cap: mémoires, réponses et responsabilités* (1991), Derrida revises Valéry's "Notes sur la grandeur et décadence de l'Europe" by arguing that it is no longer possible for Europe to think of itself as the universal "brain" of a vast body, or indeed as anything more than simply a geographical "head" ("cap") to the Asiatic continent. Instead of heading towards some new form of European "capital" (in all senses of the word), it is crucial, Derrida insists, to respect "the other heading" ("l'autre cap"), or better still, "the *otherness* of the heading" ("l'Autre du cap").[14] Certainly, the (inter)textual commitment in *Histoire(s)* and all Godard's later work to movement and circulation must be read as an aesthetic move against any attempt at an imposed and fixed "European" unity, especially a vision of Europe that includes no proper account of the painful and complex experience of the Second World War. Sometimes, however, the threat of stasis is so great that it finally prevails. *Allemagne,* for example, a "border" film like so much of Godard's work since the late 1980s in that it feeds into and out of *Histoire(s)*, draws abruptly to a halt when Lemmy Caution finally reaches the capitalist neon of the new Germany, part of the new American World Order, where the "phantoms" that greeted him when he crossed the border can no longer find their "*verdigris*" home.

Art

If, then, division and fragmentation are privileged over unity both formally and thematically, should one talk primarily in terms of a "national," as opposed to European, art and culture, and if so, how? How, that is, can one create and maintain a "free" work of art which, unlike the work of an artist like Velázquez in the pay of the court, resists the rules of the state that underwrite wars. Goya, who consciously asserted the freedom of invention (or "caprice") of the artist, provides the obvious point of contrast to Velázquez and a possible model for Godard who, even more than in *Passion* where three Goya paintings were reconstituted (*The nude maja, The parasol*, and *Madrid, 3 May, 1808: Executions at the mountains of Prince Pius*), gives us here a glimpse of Goya's enormous range. Godard is, in fact, in genuine awe of painting and art, and in particular of certain works by Goya and Picasso inspired by real and traumatic historical events which, in their "thereness" and "completeness," possess "resurrectional" power at every moment. Indeed, because Western art is necessarily "high" for Godard due to its origins in the Church (he focuses almost exclusively on post-Medieval art in *Histoire(s)*), it has served as a powerful index of morality. It is Godard's view that once art entered the realm of abstraction and lost figurative contact with the historical real (a scheme very familiar in art history),[15] it was left to cinema, uniquely related to the real which it directly records, to provide a moral and ethical obligation. Yet, and this is a key opening thesis of *Histoire(s)*, cinema's moral imperative quickly disappeared as the medium became subject to commerce. Hence, while photography first assumed the colors of mourning (black and white) because it had effectively extracted life from the real, Technicolor, in all its razzle-dazzle, wished only to forget that fact. As we shall see, it is only for Godard during those rare moments when the cinematic image recovered its documentary status and allegiance to the real that cinema honored its moral function and redeemed itself.

Yet if Godard sometimes likens his work to that of painting due to the sheer physicality of montage (he has talked of the texture of *Histoire(s)* expressly in terms of "painting history" and "pure painting"), his practice of videographic montage as a form of collage operating on the boundary between word and image attempts something very different and unique, precisely because it attacks the purity and "integrity" of painting. Godard's particular insistence on montage as a form of absolute and vehicle of redemption was, of course, already present in his 1956 article for *Cahiers du Cinéma* entitled "Montage, mon beau souci" (Montage, my beautiful care), also the original subtitle of episode 3B of *Histoire(s)*, where montage is imbued with mysterious, restorative powers, even to reverse the flow of time. Now, throughout episode 3A and *Histoire(s)* as a whole, he is trying to resurrect cinema's lost potential of montage both as a transhistorical religious event and as a transaesthetic form of thought. Godard first evokes the mad and capricious lust for power of Golden Age Hollywood with its empty, "universal" wish to make the world weep in its seat (the UNIVERSAL logo is conveyed in slow-motion)—a wish, he suggests, that has now been rendered banal by CNN, American television and its "groupies" who show only death and tears for an audience that has learned *not to see* and has no more tears left to cry. We move quickly from the Technicolor explosions of Raoul Walsh's *Captain Horatio Hornblower* (1951) to a collage of Uncle Birdie rocking in his chair in Charles Laughton's *The Night of the Hunter* (1955) and terrified children running in Hitchcock's *The Birds* (1963) interflashed with a series of darkly ironic titles: "What is cinema / What does it want / Everything / What can it do / Some-thing [sic]" (the last item resting on an image of a woman singing from Abel Gance's *Napoléon* [1927]). *La Monnaie de l'absolu* then proceeds via a short bridging episode featuring a detail of Goya's own representation of *Judith* (from the *Black Paintings* series) to a more calm and reflective sequence on Manet. The link between Manet and Goya is enforced by Godard's repetition of the image of Saturn (this time a close-up detail) which is followed immediately by a detail from Manet's *Le Balcon*, an innocent group portrait featuring Berthe Morisot that reworks Goya's *Group on a Balcony*, a Hogarthian view of two women shadowed menacingly by two demonic gallants.

The story of Goya's great influence on Manet is well known in art history, and in *Les Voix du silence* Malraux provides concrete evidence of Manet's use of Goya as a model (*The Nude Maja* for *Olympia*, *Madrid, 3 May, 1808* for *Exécution de Maximilien*) (see Malraux 1951: 99–102). What is important in *La Monnaie de l'absolu*, however, is that the terms of their connection are precise for Godard. It is not really a question of an artist outstripping his precursor and model due to an anxiety of influence, in the manner, say, of Saturn desperately ingesting his offspring for fear they might become unstoppable rivals. Nor is it a question of the two artists' similar yet different representation of human violence, or of their status as representatives of a national school of painting. It is rather their link in an ongoing, universal chain and metamorphosis of artistic form. In this regard, Godard is utterly faithful to the spirit of Malraux in *Les Voix du silence*, and it is this which will ultimately enable him at the end of *La Monnaie de l'absolu* to formulate the uniqueness of cinematic form. To paraphrase Godard's voice-over: all Manet's women appear to be saying: "I know what you're thinking of" ("Je sais à quoi tu penses"), no doubt because Manet was the first painter to link the internal world to the cosmos. Even the famous pale smiles of Leonardo da Vinci, Vermeer, and Corot (examples of which Godard provides for the reader's scrutiny) proclaim, "Me first, the world after." It is for this reason, according to Godard, that Manet initiated modern painting, that is to say, the cinematograph, or form becoming speech, or more precisely "a form that thinks" ("une forme qui pense"). In Godard's version of the beginnings of modern art, which names Georges Bataille's 1955 study *Manet* as its point of departure, Manet is promoted as a "man of the cinema" not simply because his career coincided exactly with the beginnings of photography, and he looked for truth without falling into naturalism, but because his work facilitates creative thought. This is an intrinsically human moment, one of sudden mutual recognition between the viewer and subject, self and other, self and the world, and Godard repeats here a central thesis of *Histoire(s)* that cinema was initially designed for the purposes of thought but that this was forgotten immediately, the flame being definitively extinguished at Auschwitz.

Figure 2.3. A superimposition of Manet figures in episode 3A of *Histoire(s) du cinéma* (1988–98).

But there is more at stake in Godard's appreciation of Manet, and it will become clearer if I quote a key passage from Bataille's study: "[W]hat counts in Manet's canvases is not the subject, but the vibration of light [. . .] To break up the subject and re-establish it on a different basis is not to neglect the subject; so it is in a sacrifice, which takes liberties with the victim and even kills it, but cannot be said to *neglect* it. After all, the subject in Manet's pictures is not so much 'killed' as simply overshot, outdistanced; not so much obliterated in the interests of pure painting as transfigured by the stark purity of that painting [. . .] No painter more heavily invested the subject, not with meaning, but with that which goes beyond and is more significant than meaning" (original emphasis).[16] In Godard's scheme, cinematography essentially follows through the operation of modernity initiated by Manet since it sacrifices the real literally by putting it to death and then mourning it. Although "killed off," however, the real does not totally disappear; instead, the sacrifice returns the real to us and allows us to regain access to it because the projected image is effectively resurrected in light. One of Godard's primary aims in *Histoire(s)* is to privilege and celebrate film's own particular resurrecting powers and to reveal this (ironically through the medium of video) as the exact opposite of what Philippe Sollers called rather dismissively in his discussion of the work "the barter of cinema," that is, a negative, dirgelike illustration of what must be undergone, a "flood" of phantoms from the past, before a true work of painting with transcendent qualities of completeness and "thereness" can be successfully realized.[17] Indeed, one of the determining formal tensions of Histoire(s) derives precisely from the struggle played out between the destabilizing flux of cinema and cinematic history and the static pictorial image that manages effortlessly to impose itself however much Godard subjects it to the vibrations of the video machine, as at the start of La Monnaie de l'absolu. For Godard's purpose is to reverse cinema's negative status (what Sollers terms its "enormous fantasmagoria") vis-à-vis other more "refined" arts and instead reconfigure painting as the change or barter of cinema. The key here is montage which for Godard constitutes style, cinema's—and video's—unique ethical and moral code. This leads us directly to the next and third sequence concerning the Second World War, which exemplifies Godard's method of (trans)historical montage.

World War II

The bridge between the two sequences takes us from the world of Manet's Nana, via his Fifrelin accompanied by a fifing tune, to that of Zola pictured with his photographic camera and the last words of his 1880 novel, Nana, "à Berlin! à Berlin!," pictured in close-up (this is the influence of technology on the evolution of literary form, here naturalism). This in turn leads to Jean Renoir's silent 1926 film Nana starring Catherine Hessling (claimed by Godard incorrectly as the first co-production with UFA),[18] to Goebbels and the shot of Jean Gabin being gunned down in Marcel Carné's 1938 Quai des Brumes, a film originally meant to be filmed in Berlin as the last UFA co-production but which was banned by Goebbels. This quick-fire chain of connections is merely a preparation, however, for the core element of the six-and-a-half-minute sequence: the compressed crossing in time of two trains and the elaborate train of associations it produces. To summarize in brief: in March 1942, Danièle Darrieux, along with other French stars such as Suzy Delair, Albert Préjean, and Junie Astor, traveled from the Gare de l'Est in Paris to Berlin as guests of UFA. In the same year, Irène Némirovsky, a young French Jewish writer, returned to Paris from the South in order to retrieve a bracelet and was promptly arrested before then being deported from the same station to Auschwitz. Godard refers to Némirovsky as "that fool Irène in the next train," a reference to Louis Aragon's erotic novel Le Con d'Irène (Irene's Cunt), published clandestinely in 1928. These two facts become a site for further criss-crossings of associations. Némirovsky had scored a blockbuster hit in 1930 with her book Le Bal which was immediately adapted for the screen by Wilhelm Thiele in the 1931 film of the same name starring Darrieux in her first major role (pictured in close-up is a page of her Journal describing the success of Le Bal). Notable by their absence on the train, however, were Alain Cuny and Marie Déa who starred together in Marcel

Carné's *Les Visiteurs du soir* of 1942, a still from which is shown featuring Cuny as Gilles (one of the two envoys of the Devil with Arletty) and Déa as Lady Anne, both chained up and turned to stone. Godard intones, "Their hearts were beating, beating, beating" ("Leur coeur battait, battait, battait"), in honor of a love that cannot be suppressed but which serves to express the momentous urgency of the decision taken by Cuny and Déa not to take the train and effectively collaborate.

Figures 2.4–6. Three key moments in the extended train sequence in episode 3A of *Histoire(s) du cinéma* (1988–98).

Such tense unloading of historical freight continues with the representation of a train moving right to left, a detail from Kandinsky's *Murnau, View with Railway and Castle* (1909), in which are embedded moving images of a train traveling *in the opposite direction* though dramatically slowed down. It concludes with contemporary footage of Cuny repeating the question he posed to Déa in 1942 concerning the train, this time to Juliette Binoche as she reads aloud a poem by Emily Brontë on impending death (juxtaposed on the soundtrack by General de Gaulle celebrating the liberation of Paris in August 1944).[19] The last image, superimposed over the contours of Binoche's body, is of a reclining nude by Nicolas de Staël.[20] This dizzying procession of wartime references is already dense enough, but the resonances proliferate even further if we consider that Catherine Hessling was first noticed by Renoir's father, Auguste Renoir; that the typed words "la romance" produce an image from *La Vénus aveugle* (a 1941 melodrama by Abel Gance dedicated to Marshal Pétain) of Viviane Romance, an actress who also took the train with Darrieux and her group; that the phrase "Gilles, no, not that of Drieu" refers also to the title of an autobiographically inspired novel by the writer and collaborator Drieu la Rochelle;[21] and that finally, inscribed in segments across the middle of the sequence as we hear Pétain instructing his followers in the need for long-term suffering and atonement (his speech of 17 June 1941), is the French translation of the famous phrase from William Faulkner's *Requiem for a Nun* (1950): "The past is never dead, it's not even past" (Faulkner's first novel, we recall, was *Soldier's Pay* (1926) about the uneasy return of a war hero, translated into French as *Monnaie de Singe*).

Taken as a whole, the sequence is structured as a site of intersection between various journeys positive and negative, all of which feeds into a double movement of repetition and reversal. The term *battement* itself functions as a double movement since it indicates not only the beating and palpitation of the heart but also an interval of time (as in the phrase "un battement de vingt minutes," a wait of twenty minutes between trains). All the elements are, as it were, crossed through and in some cases crossed out, for Godard also pursues a process of self-correction initiated earlier in episode 3A where the caption "erreur" flashed up shortly after his erroneous statement that Erich Pommer was the founder of Universal (it should have been Carl Laemmle). This process continued with the written correction seconds later of Dolores del Rio misidentified by association as the actress in the extract shown from *Captain Horatio Hornblower* ("Erreur Virginia Mayo") (the soundtrack talked of King Vidor's 1932 *Bird of Paradise* starring Del Rio), and, in the Manet episode, with the almost spontaneous correction of the pianist he evokes, "my Miss Clara Haskil" (a Jewish performer hounded by the Nazis), by the caption "erreur Martha Argerich" stamped over the image of one of the latter's CD recordings. In this third sequence Godard recognizes his confusion over the dates in the war, 1942 and 1944, and signals this with the caption "Error two years before." I would like to suggest that this series of double movements corresponds to the rhetorical figure of the chiasmus, or the placing crosswise of elements, which can take the form of practically any strategy of reversal or specular reflection that crosses the attributes of inside and outside.[22] As such, it does no more than formalize the many key features of Godard's videographic style evident from the beginning of *La Monnaie de l'absolu*, including the interflashing of images, their fading in and out, superimposition and absorption, whereby each image opens up to another in a continuous process of traversal. The very first images of Goya and Gentileschi, specifically their representations of human arms engaged in unbearable violence— from man as perpetrator of violence (Saturn holding up his child [son or daughter?] to eat)[23] to man as the victim of violence (Judith beheading Holofernes)—indicate that the central drive and direction of this episode are inversion and reversal. Images bridge anonymously over each other, as in the first bridging part of episode 3A itself where the phrase "Don't tell stories, my child" ("Ne raconte pas d'histoires, mon petit"), typewritten over a shot of Godard, is immediately reversed as: "Tell stories, my man" ("Raconte des histoires, mon grand").

Hence, if each image decontextualized and deallegorized, is effectively transformed metaphysically into a kind of epiphany, a manifestation of the mystery of cinematographic creation (one thinks ahead to Godard's appreciation in episode 4A of Hitchcock as the greatest creator of forms this century on account of the fact that what one remembers of his films are not the narratives but the visual details, that is, objects at their most concrete because suddenly thrown into light), nevertheless it is the case that each image has the potential to be motivated rhetorically in recurring patterns and structures.[24] Moreover, it is precisely because Godard's poetics of montage embraces all forms of image and can subject them to similar processes of reversibility and superimposition that it manages to reverse the overwhelming autonomy and self-sufficiency of painting—all images become equally "present." In short, Godard's fundamentally democratic method of videographic montage displaces and disperses the potential power of painting and prevents it, if only temporarily, from overwhelming and blocking the video flow. What counts above all is the performability and transformability of the image within a larger signifying system rather than any innate expressivity it may possess. Furthermore, this process, which, as the episode of the trains highlights, traces the relations between life and art, possesses a specifically historical dimension. Robert Bresson's 1945 film *Les Dames du Bois de Boulogne*, for example, produced during the last months of the Occupation and the beginning of the Libération, is presented by Godard as a film of French resistance for lack of any other. Its penultimate scene of Élina Labourdette whispering, "I will fight" ("Je lutte"), is linked poetically to the moment in 1944 when the "Maquis des Glières" Resistance group was about to fall. Such editorial maneuvers allow Godard elsewhere to suggest that montage as "*rapprochement*" (that is, the act of creating relations between people, objects, and ideas) is, of itself, a form of history; indeed, that montage and history are one and the same process.[25]

Cinema as National Event

What value, though, ought we to ascribe to Godard's rhetorical crossings? Do they carry Christian connotations of the cross as symbol of the crucified Christ, the Savior and Word, an idea potentially at odds with the Jewish significance of the episode (Némirovsky, Haskil, the Holocaust, and so on)? This question is elaborated in the fourth and last sequence of episode 3A where Godard develops the notion of cinema as a means of national renewal at a precise historical juncture. We move from a highly symbolic instance of aesthetic resistance (the lovers of *Les Visiteurs du soir*) to the notion of cinematic form itself as resistance. There is once again a short bridging episode where Godard considers institutionalized remembrance (the public celebrations for the fiftieth anniversary of the Liberation of Paris) and laments the present state of cinema and television, reminding us that the "citadel" of the CNC (now the Centre National du Cinéma et de l'Image Animée) was originally set up under Vichy. Such a media spectacle, Godard claims rather wildly as he slows down images of the former *résistants*, ostracizes free spirits like Guy Debord (who actively opposed the French war in Algeria) and the "gentle and valiant" poet Claude Roy (who took part in the Resistance) because French cinema never liberated itself from the Germans and Americans (cue an image of Rangers on horseback in hot pursuit from John Ford's *The Searchers* [1950]). His statement that such blind commemoration, courtesy of Japanese digital cameras, will allow yet again the dead to remain unburied (a role once performed by poets) is matched by images of the scene from *Pierrot le fou* where Marianne (Anna Karina) talks of the many *maquisards* who died anonymously and about whose lives one knows nothing. Godard then extends the idea of resistance by first proposing poetry as a form of resistance—a fact well known by Osip Mandelstam, but Russians these days, Godard sighs, are no longer well known. The black-and-white photograph conveyed here in the form of an iris shot is not that of Mandelstam, in fact, but of the French resistance poet Louis Aragon, who, as a lifetime communist, fell directly under the Soviet influence (his image is superimposed over a printed page of his collection of mordant and wholly disabused poems, *Le nouveau Crève-coeur* [1948], written in the immediate aftermath of the Liberation and very different in mood from *Le Crève-coeur* [1941], which included the love poem "Elsa, je t'aime" cited earlier during the train sequence). Godard then moves to his central focus, a case of resistance in cinema: Rossellini's *Rome, Open City* (1945), the only film to resist the occupation of cinema by America and Hollywood uniformity. It was natural that this event occurred in Italy because, according to Godard, the country had twice betrayed and thus needed to reverse its total lack of identity. With *Rome, Open City*, the only time a (commercial) film was not made by people in uniform, Italy refound itself as a nation ("Italy simply regained the right of a nation to look itself in the face"). Godard's further controversial claim here is that no other European country produced resistance films as such, not even Poland. Indeed, he summarily dismisses Andrzej Munk's uncompleted and posthumous *Pasazerka* (*Passenger*) (1963) (briefly glimpsed) and Wanda Jakubowska's *The Last Stage* (1948) as films of expiation. After all, Poland, he states, ended up welcoming Spielberg, where "never again" ("plus jamais ça") became "it's better than nothing" ("mais c'est toujours ça," literally "but it's still that"). France during this period, meanwhile, was producing films like Claude Autant-Lara's *Sylvie et les fantômes* (1946), a romantic comedy.

What is so remarkable about the nostalgic roll-call of Italian postwar films that follows, which seems more like an extended advert for an already well-covered period of Italian cinema (brief sequences juxtaposed from *Senso, The Leopard, Bicycle Thieves, The Swindlers, Paisà, Germany Year Zero, Stromboli, Bitter Rice, La Strada, Umberto D., La Terra Trema, Amarcord*, and *Teorema*), is that Godard presents it in the form of silent cinema. A song by the popular French-Italian singer/songwriter Riccardo Cocciante celebrating the glories of Italian as an all-embracing, inclusive, and universal language is simply dubbed over the parade of images and allowed to play unhindered to its natural end. Godard also superimposes snatches of extracts (in their original) from Dante's *The Divine Comedy* and Ovid's *Art of Love*, assorted phrases of Latin interwoven with Italian around the themes of vision, imagery, light, change, and divine power, ending with a statement on the immanence of love: "Qui nimium multis non amo dicit, amat" (literally, "He who says much and to many that he does not love, loves"). By allowing the images essentially to speak for themselves (some sequences, like that of de Sica's *Umberto D.*, even retain their original editing, rare in *Histoire(s)*), Godard is actually respecting the common production method of Italian cinema during that period. His argument is that what made *Rome, Open City* so unique and served to create a tide of Italian neorealist films by Fellini, Visconti, Pasolini, de Santis, and others, was that the Italian and Latin poets of the past effectively "passed over" the visual track since sound was never recorded on location at the same time as the images. Godard would seem thereby to be utterly faithful to Rossellini's adage (famously endorsed by the primary theorist of cinematic presence, André Bazin) which he types in at the end over an image of the director: "Reality is there, why manipulate it?" ("Les choses sont là, pourquoi les manipuler?"). If important aspects about the production and technique of *Rome, Open City* are omitted here (the fact, for example, that despite its frequent newsreel appearance the film comprised simulations and reconstructions of recent events shot in the same location), it is because Godard proposes the film primarily as an act of resistance against American cinema (a scene from a Western in color is briefly viewed). *Rome, Open City* was a totally unexpected and spontaneous free artistic act, shot in adverse conditions beyond the limits of the studio system, and it realized cinema's full potential, unique among the visual arts, to operate at a popular and national scale, literally projecting an entire people's new, future self-identity. The sudden moment when Italy beheld its own image was a rare, cinematic gesture of historical incarnation, one that, as Marie-José Mondzain has shown, also originally occurred in America where cinema provided the new country with an account of its history, the story of its birth.[26] For this reason, *Rome, Open City* allowed cinema in some way to redeem itself after its abject failure to record the Holocaust. Yet Godard actually goes further when he argues elsewhere that only a Christian country like Italy could retrieve its identity so successfully in the image, since only the Christian religion is directly concerned with images.[27] It is as though the history of a new cinematic movement must necessarily enact a major transformation according to the narrative of the Passion, the miraculous process whereby God incarnates himself through Christ, who, through His Passion (the Crucifixion and then Resurrection) restores the visible and the fallen image of Man. This idea may help to explain the attention given here and elsewhere in *Histoire(s)* to the agony of the Communist Manfredi's torture by the Nazis in Rossellini's film. The idea is pursued in the following episode 3B, *Une Vague nouvelle*, where Godard claims that the image is of the order of redemption ("careful, that of the real"), thus giving further significance to the quote attributed by Godard to St. Paul and which he cites throughout *Histoire(s)*: "The image will come only at the time of the resurrection" ("L'image ne viendra qu'au temps de la résurrection").

Rome, Open City exemplifies Godard's idea of art as freedom and as exception (the sudden advent of Rossellini), and of identity through difference (the Italian nation within Europe). Yet it is not on this social and historical high note that episode 3A actually ends, since Godard also needs himself to perform the specificity of film and video as a medium over and beyond its capacity to record visual reality. What is at issue is precisely cinema as a process and art of manipulation. There is thus a sudden return to French in the last series of captions, "une pensée qui forme / une forme qui pense," a chiastic formation that harks back to the Manet episode (where we note in passing that the idea of silent cinema was already evoked in Godard's phrase: "It was silent cinema in the company of my Miss Haskil"). This chiasmus effectively repeats the chiastic play of repetitions, double movements, and corrections that we have traced throughout episode 3A as one single moment of reversal. Indeed, one might say that the previous compulsive play of error and association, encapsulated by the phrase flashed earlier on the screen, "the mechanical sentence starts up again," and where, for example, a reference to a wartime tune about a girl called Marguerite (Julien Carette's "Si tu veux, Marguerite," originally from Renoir's 1937 film, *La Grande Illusion*, which implores "Marguerite" to make him happy by surrendering her heart) was enough to justify the image of a young Marguerite Duras counterpointed by a key phrase from her 1985 work *La Douleur* about the torture of a suspected collaborator ("Must just hit, how real it is, how right") ("Faut frapper, que c'est vrai, que c'est juste"), has now been reversed into a single message. The perpetual movement of displacement, of error and *errance*, has been finally controlled by a folding together of the Italian Renaissance and Italian modernism at the turning point of a chiastic inversion. The first part of the sentence is written over a black-and-white photograph of Pasolini head down and eyes hidden under sunglasses—this is intellectual thought in the agonizing process of being formed. It is then reversed over the small detail, almost impossible to recognize out of context, of a figure from Piero della Francesca's cycle of frescoes, *The Legend of the True Cross*. The detail, a face staring serenely out of frame into the distance, is taken from the scene entitled "The Exaltation or Restitution of the Cross" in reference to Heraclius's return of the cross to Jerusalem according to the Golden Legend. Once again, therefore, we are dealing with a Christian image in terms of resurrection, and it is worth noting historically that this fresco was commissioned as part of an attempt to renew the Catholic Church by bringing together its different parts and engineering a *rapprochement* with the Eastern Church.

Figures 2.7–10. Pasolini and Piero della Francesca folded together chiastically in the climax to episode 3A of *Histoire(s) du cinéma* (1988–98).

The linking of Pasolini with Renaissance art is, of course, a pure act of montage on Godard's part, a simple yet willfully ironic manipulation which directly contradicts the spirit of Rossellini and his idea, typed by Godard onto the screen, that "[t]he camera is the screen." Moreover, in conversation with Alain Bergala, Godard connects directly the idea of "a thought that forms" not only with bad cinema (Pasolini is not specifically mentioned) but also with the state, that is, the controlling of thought, rather than its spontaneous revelation through montage. Godard declares: "'The State is the thought that forms.' I believe more in a form that thinks [. . .] In cinema it's the form that thinks. In bad cinema, it's the thought that forms."[28] The unexpected link made between Pasolini and Piero at the end of *La Monnaie de l'absolu*, one that ties together the two principal art forms explored during the episode, is exemplary of the type of transfer and poetic (as opposed to intellectual) thought proposed earlier in the Manet sequence. As such, it may be said to herald a new relationship between self and other and self and world defined in general historical terms, since Godard insists here on historical incarnation as part of a larger process of continuity and evolution, including that of Latin into Italian. Montage, not available to the other "finer" arts, is what enables cinema to become something more than cinema and so qualify as art as defined by Malraux. It therefore has the value of an absolute with an extra-aesthetic, or rather transaesthetic, dimension. (To recall Adorno: where art is experienced purely aesthetically, it fails to be fully experienced even aesthetically.)

Of course, this is only a temporary point of resolution. *Histoire(s)* comprises a serial structure and the proceeding *à suivre* already reverts back self-reflexively to Pasolini: a shot of the intellectual talking bird from his 1966 film, *Hawks and Sparrows*. Yet what the sequence brilliantly reveals is that the figure of the chiasmus not only constitutes one of the defining features of Godardian montage, but also possesses in his work a specifically Christian dimension as the visual epitome of the Savior's Passion and Redemption. It can be linked in this respect to another formal process in *Histoire(s)*: Godard's identification by means of a small cross of the saints and martyrs of French cinema such as Vigo, Cocteau, and Renoir. Moreover, if we consider *La Monnaie de l'absolu* in its entirety, it could justifiably be argued that the four sequences constitute themselves a (loosely defined) chiastic structure, the turning point of reversal being the crossing of trains: war / art / war / art (cinema as an art born after Auschwitz). Finally, Godard's joint emphasis on the physical aspect of montage and the spiritual act of incarnation accounts perhaps for his resurrection of de Rougemont's essay *Penser avec les mains*, which, at a key historical juncture, preached the decisive and liberating violence of creative thought as an integral part of a universal "dialectics of incarnation" to which even divine thought yielded with the agony of God's son on the cross.[29] For this reason, in addition to the phrases extracted by Godard in *Le Contrôle de l'univers*, which conclude with the statement that an act is the judge of time and justifies Man's hopes for salvation, we might just as appropriately select others from *Penser avec les mains* such as the following: "*incarnation* is an act reducible neither to conformity nor escape, and what is more— and this is crucial—will arise out of a surge of thought towards an end it invents or has seen. It's the thought that acts, which knows where it's going" (de Rougemont 1936: 223–24; original emphasis); "the act reincarnates us. The primacy of the spiritual is the primacy of the person creating, of the 'thought that thinks' over 'the thought that is thought'" (ibid.: 247); and "man in his capacity as man is truly a creator, but a creator created [. . .] and his limits are those of personal incarnation. That is his order and reality, and the place of his redemption" (ibid.: 248). The transformative power of individual creative thought is what, both for Godard and de Rougemont, allows for and demands a personal moral judgment. In his own account during one interview of the complex train episode in episode 3A, Godard remarks: "That is where the connection is. You can show the past and the present. A thought is there. A wish also to judge. There is a story."[30] (Compare de Rougemont in a passage cited almost word for word in episode 4A: "I believe in the appeal of facts. Let us consider the times and the places in which we live, our given particular situation, and the concrete appeal that thus emerges, and after that LET US JUDGE" (ibid.: 125).)

La Monnaie de l'absolu, then, offers a continually evolving analysis of the national and universal status of art. At the beginning, European art is presented as a reflection of European history and the constant struggle for power and conflict between city- and nation-states. This is to be contrasted with the direct encounter with the cosmos in Manet. By the end, however, a kind of clearing and resolution is reached: art must be seen above all in national terms since this is what ensures continuity, in the case of Italy from the painting of the Renaissance to the renaissance of Italian cinema and Italy as a country with Rossellini. Indeed, the historical need for state and national identity is what gives art and cinema its primary motivation and meaning. Exceptionally, Italian neorealism, being a genuine movement of the people (this is Godard at his most residually Marxist), had nothing directly to do with the state, which seeks above all to reproduce an image of itself. In fact, as a "free act" *Rome, Open City* contradicted the many kinds of state-sponsored and sanctioned art that Godard is fond of listing in *Histoire(s)* and elsewhere. In *Allemagne*, for example, in addition to Velázquez and Giotto, he offers the example of Dürer, who "destroyed nature on his canvases" and is even proposed as the precursor and predecessor of Nazism. In *For Ever Mozart*, the message could not be clearer: the nation opposes the State. The rather conservative implication of this form of national aesthetics is that there can never be a total break with the past: even the most radical avant-garde expression or statement (Manet, Picasso), when placed and viewed in its national context, represents only a temporary and minor discontinuity within a larger, more fundamental continuity, that of artistic tradition. Yet in episode 3A Godard suggests, paradoxically, that it is as a direct result of being formed in regional and national terms that cinema as an art can accede to something transnational and therefore universal, eternal, and transcendent. A film by Rossellini is of the order and sublimity of a Piero fresco.

The problem today, of course, is that in a unifying, post–Cold War Europe based on the free flow of capital, where the traditional model of the nation-state has become outmoded and with it the notion of national boundaries, a narrative of nation is no longer available to bridge the necessary recontextualizing of meaning. It thus makes an event on the national scale of Italian neorealism impossible to duplicate. Indeed, with the narrative of nationhood so deformed (Serbia being an obvious case in point),[31] and with all distinctions between East and West, past and present, at risk of being lost, the solemnity of art is increasingly irrelevant to the construction of a national identity. As Jeffrey Skoller has argued in his Deleuzian reading of *Allemagne*, rather than ideas becoming universalized knowledge, they are simply ill-remembered signifiers of a vague memory. Germany has become a deterritorialized world of signifiers of past events, he suggests, and the film in turn constitutes a flea market of allusions and references to a past of German culture and ideologies (Freud's Dora turns into Goethe's Charlotte Kestner, which leads to Thomas Mann's *Lotte in Weimar*, then Schiller, and so on).[32] Yet it could be argued, perhaps, that Godard's stubborn belief in some profound and always complex notion of national culture and identity within his massive elaboration of a pan-European imaginary is of salutary value at the present political juncture, since it serves to avoid what Jürgen Habermas has called in his discussion of the formal and functional transformations of the nation-state in post-Wall Europe "the arrogance of post-nationalism."[33] It is perhaps in this light, too, that we can best appreciate Godard's affinity with the French writer and media theoretician Régis Debray, with whom he has been the most forthright in his views on art as a specifically Western (read: Christian) phenomenon now at its end.[34] Part of Debray's general project is a defense of the image and a reawakening of our obligations and duties to it. He is the author of *Vie et mort de l'image: une histoire du regard en Occident* (1992), which bemoans the current tyranny of the visual (the realm of the videosphere) and emphasizes the need for otherness, incompleteness, and the transcendental (as opposed to mere transparency). What is interesting, however, is how this approach dovetails in Debray with a kind of national republicanism expressed most forcefully in *Le Code et le glaive: Après l'Europe, la nation?* (1999), an essay that proposes to examine "a Republican conscience" and delivers a hatchet job on "Euroland." For Debray, the supranational or federal model leads to the worst possible outcome: nations without a state (that is, inorganic bodies), and, at the top, a state without people (that is, an organ without a body), leading in the case of France back to the feudalism of the Ancien Régime.[35] While I do not wish to claim Godard as a political theorist in the same mold as Debray (Godard is, after all, an artist, not a politician, and Debray needs to be viewed within a particular French political context that stretches from de Gaulle to the emergence of the far right), nevertheless it is striking to note the similarity in tone and emphasis between Godard's strong sense of nationhood in cinema and Debray's desire to restore the discourse of passion and war (if not *la patrie*) as part of a tradition of nation-states that recognizes the "values" of a nation accreted over time, that is, the barter (*monnaie*) of history which, Debray asserts, is currently being buried under the vocabulary of international banking and legalese. Debray argues vigorously that the concept of a new European megastate based in Brussels denies the essential role of *lieux de mémoire* and of what he calls "le tragique de l'histoire," which includes myth, the people, a shared heritage and a common will, factors equally foregrounded and valorized in *Histoire(s)*.

I would like now to return to *La Monnaie de l'absolu* since the new Europe may, in fact, be only the most obvious figure of impossible unity and of the ongoing crisis of fragmentation and decontextualization in Godard's endlessly self-reflexive work which is sustained by other forms of missed totality. I am thinking, for example, of the extracts and cited ideas linked poetically and chiastically across different forms and media in each main episode of episode 3A, in particular the details of paintings that refer to an outside whole and which alone justify Godard's repeated use in *Histoire(s)* of the Beethoven axiom: "The perfect union of several voices prevents, all in all, the progress of one towards another" ("L'union parfaite de plusieurs voix empêche, somme toute, le progrès de l'une vers l'autre"), as well as of the statement (one of many by Robert Bresson cited in the work): "If an image looked at separately expresses something clearly, and if it presents an interpretation, it will not transform itself on contact with other images. Other images will have no power over it, and it will have no power over images. Neither action nor reaction."[36] I would argue, in fact, that Europe is really only a privileged metaphor in Godard's work for the more immediate problem of the process of cinematic and videographic form, specifically montage, because it operates as an eminently reversible concept. After all, his definition of an ideal Europe in cinematic terms is similar to his dream scenario for the state funding of films in France, which imagines that if the state were really serious about funding cinema, it would out of obligation pay repertory cinemas to show a certain number of films a guaranteed number of times, even those lacking an audience.[37] Such reversibility of ideas raises the question whether, in fact, there are any aesthetic limits to Godardian montage, for so omnipresent is the theme of Europe and European art and history, a veritable memory bank of images, that at times it seems merely to act as the spur for yet further chiastic formations—a bankable quotient of recorded reality available for videographic creativity and its endless self-reflection. The more forms to be crossed through, the greater the possibility for reversibility, transfiguration, and resurrection. From the painting of history to the history of painting, the trace of history becomes essentially just another "sublime" element, in the Kantian sense, too, of history being beyond our immediate comprehension?[38]

What value ought we to attach precisely to the many chiastic moments crafted by Godardian montage? Do they represent simply a compromise solution, a temporary stop-gap of sense in lieu of a total meaning, whether of Europe or art or nation or history? I would like to suggest that Godard's rhetorical play of montage itself forms part of the only theme that can be said to unify episode 3A, that is, war and its resistance, a theme which, as we have seen, is kept on the move in different forms as a political, military, and artistic concept. To say that montage is itself the subject of interrogation and displacement for Godard is not simply to say that it constitutes a form of resistance to encroaching uniformity—that of the unified global superpresent supplied by today's televisual and digital communications where the different processes of history and memory, as well as of art and culture, risk being flattened if not canceled out. Certainly, Godard's practice of desynchronization, translation, ambivalence, tension, mystery in the complex folds and texture of videographic form, which results in a continued openness to the Other (whether defined as image, form, or idea), amounts to a form of aesthetic and ethical resistance. In the concluding episode of *Histoire(s)*, *Les Signes parmi nous*, where he positions himself almost overrhetorically as a filmmaker/artist engaged in combat with France as a morally bankrupt nation, Godard berates (in terms not too far removed, ironically, from Gaullist fears of globalization) "the systematic/ organization/ of unified time/ the instant/ that global tyranny" (Godard 1998a, vol. 4: 279–86). Yet the question of montage in *Histoire(s)* is at once more involved and original than that. Let us revisit Godard's intercrossings of form.

As we have seen, these are intense and dynamic moments of combination and crossing through artistic form, history, idea, even gender. Whether Godard is moving into or away from details, color-filtering images, splintering and reversing texts (words cut in two, or into and sometimes over each other, the same with music and the sounds of war), counterpointing art and cinematic image, or playing off an artist with and against himself or another (e.g. the different shades of Goya at the start of 3A, the pictorial image of a bridge superimposed over the detail of another), the emphasis is always on movement and process, or *trans*, rather than on "the between" (Deleuze)[39] or the *"entre-images"* (Bellour).[40] Indeed, *Histoire(s)* pushes to new limits what Kaja Silverman and Harun Farocki have correctly identified in *Passion*, namely, a process (or trope) of transferral, transition, transposition, and transformation. In *Passion*, they argue, where cross-cutting is a privileged vehicle for establishing the derivations of a term from its ostensible opposite, "the transfer between the senses of sight and hearing represents a critical component of the Godardian sublime [. . .] a potentiality operating specific to cinema."[41] A full measure of the Godardian sublime operating in *Histoire(s)* can be gained by referring to one of the most remarkable aesthetic moves in *Histoire(s)* that occurs towards the end of episode 1A, *Toutes les histoires*. Godard has just evoked the power of wartime newsreels to redeem cinema's primary documentary status by presenting brief clips of George Stevens's 16 mm color footage of the Auschwitz and Ravensbrück concentration camps ("39–44 martyrdom and resurrection of the documentary"). Suddenly we are confronted with an extraordinary composite image that superimposes over gruesome pictures of piled-up corpses in the ovens a scene from Stevens's own later black and white film, *A Place in the Sun* (1951), where the rich heiress Angela (Elizabeth Taylor), cradles her lover, George (Montgomery Clift), in close-up by the side of a secluded lake. This is followed by the moment when, after bending down to kiss her lover (staggered by Godard in slow-motion), she leaps back to her feet and, with her right arm outstretched, declares her intention to marry him. The action is stop-started and the original soundtrack replaced by a short extract from Paul Hindemith's *Viola Sonata (Opus 11, no. 4)*, a key composer for Godard since the late 1980s.[42] In addition, the entire image is enframed by the operative detail from Giotto's *Noli me tangere* (the "Easter Morning" scene in the Arena cycle of frescoes at Padua), which is tilted 90 degrees so that it appears as if Mary Magdalene is actually descending from the clouds like an angel (the hands of the risen Christ are just visible bottom right of frame). This is a *détournement*, so to speak, of the sacred kind. Mary's outstretched hands seem to encircle Taylor, drawing her up into the heavens as if in the form of an iris shot. Christ's prohibition against touching (the risen Christ is just visible bottom right of screen) has been stunningly reversed by Godard in a new and unheralded form of touching across form, encompassing art, cinema, and video—a kind of hypertripping and troping by Godard such that all the various elements banal and divine are stretched to their limit and reversed. It is accentuated by Godard's voice-over which states: "O what wonder to look at what one cannot see/ O sweet wonder of our blind eyes"—words which rework those of the priest in Georges Bernanos's 1936 novel, *Journal d'un curé de campagne* ("O what wonder to be able thus to give what one does not own oneself, O sweet miracle of our empty hands").[43]

This highly unsettling juxtaposition of beauty (natural and aesthetic) and

Figures 2.11–12. Sublime misappropriations: footage of the camps superimposed with *A Place in the Sun*, over which is then superimposed a torqued detail of Giotto's *Noli me tangere*, in episode 1A of *Histoire(s) du cinéma* (1988–98).

personal happiness with the unspeakable horror of genocide, which relies on our knowledge that Loon Lake in Stevens's film (his version of Theodore Dreyer's 1925 novel, *An American Tragedy*) is also a place of death (George's former pregnant lover Alice [Shelley Winters] whom he plans to kill, will accidentally drown here), exemplifies Godard's idea of cinematic vision (as opposed to the mere act of looking) as a form of historical recognition through inversion. If, as Godard suggests, Liz Taylor radiates such a "deep" and "secular" yet "somber" feeling of happiness (Bergala 1998: 172), it is precisely because, via the logic of reverse extremes, Stevens had filmed the camps. Yet the scene has become a major bone of contention for readers of Godard who question precisely the religious implications of the sequence. Most notably, the philosopher Jacques Rancière worries that the figure of Mary Magdalene in Giotto's *Noli me tangere* has been transformed by Godard into an angel of resurrection.[44] Godard, Rancière argues, effectively divorces the figures from their plastic and dramatic context (whose meaning, after all, was absence, separation, and the empty tomb) in order to impose an absolute image, that of cinema's redemption.[45] Certainly, *Histoire(s)* appears to offer here the temporary illusion that the fateful and ignominious story of cinema's inexorable decline might actually be reversed and sublimated. Sublime crossings and transfigurations of this kind, whereby a wake for the dead (the recorded trace of history as a graveyard of the dead) is transformed into rapture ("martyrdom and resurrection"), are the result of Godard's manipulation of montage as a metapoetic form of thought, that is to say, "thinking with one's hands" (de Rougemont). They constitute what Youssef Ishaghpour has aptly called *"images-pensées,"*[46] and display Godard's conceptualizing power and consummate skill in inventing and grooming "forms that think." For this reason, they may be said to exemplify the authority of Renaissance painting that he is so fond of citing and its force as an instrument of scientific knowledge and innovation. But these "maximal" instances of metaphorical mastery, proof of Godard's enormous creative and poetic will, risk becoming in themselves totalizing interpretations. Sollers has talked of Godard's incessant cogitation and meditation,[47] and Godard himself virtually admits that the process is compulsive, irresistible, and potentially unstoppable when he types on the screen at one moment in *La Monnaie de l'absolu* that "the mechanical sentence starts up again." Chiastic formations even extend between episodes (1B, *Une histoire seule*/2A, *Seul le cinéma*). In fact, Godard is always so far ahead of the viewer in making the intellectual connections and processing links across form and time that the result can sometimes feel like the opposite of a free, creative act. Moreover, it is hard not to question or even simply reject Godard's leanings towards the transcendent with his clutching of the details and shards of religious ideas and iconography as a nostalgia for the plenitude of meaning in cinema and art—another manifestation, perhaps, of that European nostalgic melancholy for the impossible.

This is not the whole story, however. There is another way of looking at mystery in *Histoire(s)*, one that is not necessarily religious, since there exists in Godard's videographic montage always a secondary countermovement, or what we might call a "minimal" moment of metonymy. For despite their many obvious and different formats, physiques, and frames, some images are linked and molded together by gesture, profile, and outline. At the very start of *La Monnaie de l'absolu*, for example, the image of one of the children's bodies being devoured by Saturn appears to marry the form of a *Disasters of War* image by Goya over which it is superimposed. Similarly, the shape and contours of some of the deathly forms from the *Disasters of War* series are taken up in the spread-out arms of Fuseli's *Lady Macbeth*, while superimposed approximatively over the figure of Binoche is de Staël's *Nu Couché Bleu* (or Godard's own pastiche of it). To take the sublime sequence of *Toutes les histoire(s)* that we have just encountered: a few seconds before, and as if in preparation for it, a Rembrandt etching, *Self-Portrait: Wide-Eyed*, an eternally youthful expression of Western subjectivity peering as if in disbelief at the horror down the line at Auschwitz, arises out of an image from Munk's film *Pasazerka* of prisoners performing Bach, such that the black lines of Rembrandt trace and link up with the black-and-white lines of the prisoners' uniforms (on the soundtrack Godard cites Malraux: "art, that is, what is reborn in what has been burnt" ["l'art, c'est-à-dire, ce qui renaît dans ce qui a été brûlé"]). Shortly afterwards, and following further instances of metaphorical crossing through Impressionism and different periods of religious painting (the black-and-white images of Rembrandt and Munk merging into Monet's [blue] *Impression: Sunrise*, which leads to the central sacred detail of Mary with the infant Christ from the *Isenheim Altarpiece* [in red], reversed immediately into the main detail of a St. John the Baptist's beheading), we see a still from Murnau's *Nosferatu* of Count Dracula, his outstretched, cloaked arms interlocked with a detail multiply flashed of Picasso's *Guernica* (a major point of reference in *Histoire(s)* because inspired by a contemporary event and possessing eternal, resurrecting power). Finally, pictorial images of human faces looking up in agony and terror (again from Goya's *Disasters of War*) complement Stevens's color images of the gaping, open-mouthed, disembodied victims of the camps.

What we are witnessing here are really "horizontal" moments of confluence,

Figures 2.13–14. Second-degree montage: tracing relations between the human form across Rembrandt and Munk, Murnau, and Picasso, in episode 1A of *Histoire(s) du cinéma* (1988–98).

contiguity, conjunction, and coincidence within the "vertical" pull of Godard's rhetorical and imaginary maneuvers. They trace the interrelations of human form at the level of silhouette, shape, and figure, and, in the more casual and supple patterns thus produced, reveal real objects eager to take abstract form. The raw immersion in Italian neorealism in *La Monnaie de l'absolu*, a series of emotional movements and gestures running from pain to sensual joy, is only the most overt example of this type of basic and spontaneous association and connection which is always material, proximate, local, and specific. Moreover, such play of surface detail operates in complete silence since it is never directly commented on or integrated and rationalized as part of an argument or thesis. It is a pure, affective moment of seeing and feeling rather than of interpretation, and may even appear sentimental and naive in comparison with some of the dense, aggressive intellectual processes and formations that we have unpacked and described. This mode of montage characterizes Godard's collaborative work with Miéville with its slower, more deliberate pace, for example, the video essays *Soft and Hard*, *Deux fois cinquante ans de cinéma français* (1995), *The Old Place* (1998), and *Liberté et Patrie* (2002) (a study of the life and work of the Vaudois artist Aimé Pache) which share the same, more measured techniques of slow dissolves and superimpositions, and which, in the case of *The Old Place*, extend the sense of continuity and interconnection evoked by a key phrase (a quote from Benjamin about messianic time): "What already has been will be, and what will be has already been." A more general progression in Godard's later work might also be established if, like Aumont, we acknowledge that since *France tour détour deux enfants*, which explores the human body as the very paradigm of representation and expression, Godard has shared the former desire of Western art to paint and show human feelings directly beyond language.[48]

To put it another way, the nonlinguistic resists any totalizing conceptualization or theorization in *Histoire(s)* and preserves its mystery. In the terms proposed by Jean-François Lyotard in *Discours, figure,* the sensible or figural is privileged over discourse. Lyotard's book was, of course, an attack on the structuralist project which, in his opinion, was too quick to translate things (historical material reality) into signs, thereby erasing the force or desire intrinsic in seeing. For Lyotard, on the contrary, the work of art offers desire not images in which it will be fulfilled and lost, but forms whereby it will be reflected as play and as unbound energy. Although he did not refer specifically to film, the views Lyotard presents are perhaps just as pertinent, if not more so, in the cinematic context. "The transcendence of the symbol," he writes, "is the figure, that is, a spatial manifestation which linguistic space cannot incorporate without getting disturbed, an externality which it cannot internalize into signification. Art is posited in alterity in its quality of plasticity and desire, curved extension, opposite to invariability and reason, diacritical space. Art wishes for figure; "beauty" is figural, unbound, rhythmic [. . .] All discourse has its *vis-à-vis*, that to which it is opposite [. . .] The cognitive function carries within itself that death which sets up the *vis-à-vis*, that death which makes the density of reference."[49] In *Histoire(s)*, the figural is above all the human figure at its most concrete and literal, and the work's meaning ultimately lies somewhere between the figural and the awesome reach of Godard's Sublime. That is why, finally, the concluding chiastic sequence of *La Monnaie de l'absolu*, which marries the tortured face of Pasolini with a calm, enigmatic Piero detail, is so important, since it also marks a temporary break and resolution in the work's inherent struggle between sense and the sensible.[50]

The problem of resistance has thus become even more fundamental than our analysis of episode 3A had prepared us for, since the very form of *Histoire(s)* seems consistently to be resisting the logic of Godard's own rhetorical maneuvers. The greater, more radical question of artistic "exception to the rule" is therefore actually the work's resistance to its own constructions and primary processes through, paradoxically, a direct and immediate "collaboration" of forms. Not only do these two competing aesthetic drives provide for a fascinating encounter between the intuitive and the counterintuitive that generates much of the internal drama and rhythm of

Histoire(s). More crucially, the work essentially cuts itself loose at regular moments from Godard's guiding drive towards aesthetic sense and knowledge. Whether one sees this as a necessary masochistic move on Godard's part (and by that I mean as a healthy expression of creative impotence that preempts the pitfalls of total mastery and potential inaccessibility) is a matter for debate. What can certainly be said is that *Histoire(s)*'s own internal self-resistance through the tracing of boundaries between figures and objects is what, in fact, makes possible the general (metacritical) thematization of resistance in *La Monnaie de l'absolu*. One might say further that Godard's singular oppositional stance in *Histoire(s)*, by which he self-consciously resists totalization (his own), is arguably the only artistic position possible when, in the face of the continuing massive horror of European history that he relays so powerfully to the viewer in his later work, he would surely prefer to court impotence, deadlock, and failure indefinitely rather than risk the dogmatics of affirmation. The highly paradoxical nature of this last-ditch act of aesthetic affirmation, forced *in extremis* like the highly charged statement made in *For Ever Mozart*: "To resist means not to be had (from behind) by History" ("Résister, c'est ne pas se faire avoir par [derrière] l'Histoire"), might usefully be compared with that of the philosopher whom we mentioned at the very beginning of our discussion, Theodor Adorno. Like Godard, Adorno viewed the Holocaust as an end point of human civilization and as a result had a sense of permanent catastrophe. Out of a defeatist politics of political pessimism, however, Adorno generated a compensatorily rich negative dialectics that constantly undermined and defeated any idealizing synthesis, even though he never fully abandoned the concept of totality, or totalizing idealism.[51] *Histoire(s)* seems at times to move in the particular direction indicated by Adorno of contemplating "all things as they would present themselves from the standpoint of redemption." Perspectives, Adorno explained, "must be fashioned that displace and estrange the world and reveal it to be, with its rifts and crevices, as indigent and distorted as it will one day appear in the Messianic light."[52] Godard's similar aesthetic strategy in *Histoire(s)* perhaps explains his hesitant and oneiric final resort, but resort nonetheless, to one of the ultimate totalizing and idealist concepts, that of creator, in the closing moments of the work.

Can the pioneering and uniquely challenging work of *Histoire(s)* provide in any way a political blueprint for stemming what Godard posits throughout as the encroaching uniformity of the global superpresent supplied by today's televisual and digital communications, where the different processes of history and memory, as well as of art and culture, risk being flattened out? Probably not. In the end, *Histoire(s)* defines itself as a site of ongoing struggle and resistance not simply against culture, Europe, the state (to some degree all synonymous now for Godard), nor even, as was the case with Adorno, against easy readability (for Adorno, we recall, only difficult art and philosophy such as his own escaped reappropriation by the market system). More profoundly, the work is engaged in a permanent process of internal self-resistance whereby it forms a connection, however uncertain, contingent and minimal, with the immediately human and social. Godard offers here irrefutable proof that the forms of art—the forms that think—can help lay the basis for new forms of ethical being. If, in the last analysis, this unique creative resource is also to be described as a "European art film" (and I think it should), it is precisely because it interrogates and reverses relentlessly the meaning of each of those terms and demands that we, in turn, reconsider and redefine received notions such as national and European art and cinema as part of our duty of discovering what Godard calls, in the form of an open, eternal mystery, "the signs in our midst."

3

Beyond the Cinematic Body

Digital Rhythms and In/human Breakdown

> What have I got to do with all of this?
>
> —J.-L. Godard in *Histoire(s) du cinéma*

> Godard is a catastrophe and he's proud of it.
>
> —A. de Baecque

Body, Machine, Affect

What kind of subjectivity is possible in the era of digital technology? Or, put a little differently, what kind of self can emerge when the basic human concept of analogy appears destroyed, and when, for the first time, bodies and objects are becoming virtually disfigurable and refigurable in real time? In a provocative discussion of the artificially constructed digital image, Vilém Flusser has proclaimed that the self should now be regarded as a "digital distribution," a realization of possibilities arising from the dense distribution of what he calls "point elements."[1] According to Flusser, in the new field of criss-crossing human relations we are but "'digital computations' of swirling point-potentialities" and therefore "projects" of alternative worlds.[2] In his view, there is ultimately little difference between truth and apparition, science and art. Such an extreme leveling of technology and human endeavor is becoming increasingly common, notably in French postmodern theory and philosophy, where, in the words of Arthur Kroker, subjectivity is more a "possessed individualism," pushed at this terminal phase of technological society "to a point of aesthetic excess [such] that the self no longer has any real existence, only a perspective appearance as a site where all the referents converge and implode."[3] Such a view has not gone by unchallenged, of course. Eve Kosofsky Sedgwick and Adam Frank, for example, dispute what they see as the habitual privileging of digital models wrongly equated with the machine over analog models wrongly equated with the biological. They warn of important dangers for theory if it relies on a rigorous adherence to an antiessentialist model of digital on/off representation. A "hygienic" form of theory, they argue, can find itself theorizing different affects as affect, itself an essentializing gesture since essence is simply "displaced from the analogic possibility of finitely multiple qualitative differences to some prior place where an undifferentiated stream of originary matter or energy is being turned (infinitely) on or off.[4] Inspired by the work of the American psychologist Silvan Tomkins, Sedgwick and Frank propose instead a "repertoire of different risks, a periodic table of the infinitely recombinable elements of the affect system, a complex multilayered phyllo dough of the analog and the digital."[5]

The tension underlying any opposition between the human as analogical and the digital as inhuman is showcased in remarkable fashion by *Histoire(s) du cinéma*, where the two sets of terms are configured respectively as the cinematic and the video/electronic. Cinema, a recorder of reality, is fundamentally an art of the index and, as such, has long represented for Godard the only proper basis of invention and creation.[6] In *Histoire(s)*, however, he cuts into the substance of a hundred years of screened agony, pain, happiness, and joy to stage a confrontation between human emotion and the potentially dehumanizing effects of electronic technology. Apart from the specific electronic techniques provided by on-line video such as "keying" (the collaging of multiple visual images), inserting, compositing, captioning, and rapid "spotting" and flashing, the effects obtained here are largely derived from early cinema such as juxtaposition, dissolves, cross-cutting, iris shots, slow-motion, fading in and fading out, fast-forwarding and rewinding, and above all superimposition in its slow and gentle mode whereby the original filmic image is retained in a composite frame. Indeed, in a highly concentrated visual process already initiated in *Numéro deux* (1975), Godard fully exploits the capacity of on-line video to hold images, add to them, erase them (partially or entirely), recall them, and layer them *ad infinitum*, often with equivalent processes on the soundtrack. The video screen of *Histoire(s)* thus becomes a palimpsestic space of inscription, with the spoken and written texts, classical and modern music, stills, documentary newsreels, paintings, drawings, cartoons, and computer graphics all acquiring the equal, fleeting, material status of a trace and phantom. Yet it is not simply that new connections, interferences, and resonances spring up every time a new image or sound is presented. As Cyril Beghin argues, Godard's on-line video editing is a poetics of transformation and animation that embraces both the synthesis and the analysis of movement.[7] Figures from different images undergo similar motions, rhythms, and vibrations, such that each image is opened up to others and loses its referential and mimetic force. The effect is enhanced by Godard's complete disregard for the original intertitles of the silent films he cites (the only titles used are his own), as well as by the overlay of his rhetorical structures. His typewritten titles have the additional effect of being ideograms, a fact that serves to highlight the act of enunciation rather than the statement itself and encourages slippage from the semantic level to the phonetic. Sam Rohdie puts it well when he states that Godard's "massive deframing of the cinema" in *Histoire(s)* "de-writes" by breaking logical connectives, creating dissonances, and activating explosions of montage that break down, distort, pulverize, and disintegrate sounds and images (Rohdie 2012: 86). The resulting kinetic energy turns motion back into yet further emotion.

Figure 3.1. Controlled electronic overload in episode 1A of *Histoire(s) du cinéma* (1988–98).

In pursuing new forms of cogitation through the senses ("Cogito ergo video" Godard types on the screen at one point), *Histoire(s)* offers perhaps as close a glimpse of Henri Bergson's theoretical realm of pure perception as has yet been captured, since each visual and sonic element interacts directly with another and so allows for the totality of the past to appear present at every moment. By wresting sounds and images from their original plastic and dramatic context and effectively "decreating" them (the operations of suture and identification in the extracted film sequences such as shot/reverse shot are not maintained), Godard arrives here at a virtually presyntactical realm of pure sound and image. He thus achieves what he had been attempting for a long time: to dissolve the solidified word into particles and so arrive (to use the terms of *Prénom Carmen*) at a stage *avant le nom* (before the name), before the order of linguistic and cinematic syntax has taken over and sounds (and with them the "virgin image" ["l'image vierge"]) have lost their immediacy, freedom, and innocence. Each sound and image appears as if transformed into a pure epiphany, a manifestation of the mystery of cinematographic creation and the sensible experience of matter. This is particularly true if we bear in mind that Godard's appreciation of Hitchcock as the greatest creator of forms of the twentieth century rests on the fact that what one remembers of his films are not the narratives but the visual details—objects at their most concrete and material because suddenly thrown into the light. Such a formal process of decreation might usefully be compared with that of *Passion* and *Scénario du film* Passion where, as Libby Saxton has carefully shown, the energies celebrated by the philosopher and Christian mystic Simone Weil in *La Pesanteur et la grâce* (1947) are visualized in kinetic form. Weil proposed the term "decreation" as a way of describing the energy of grace liberated through the ethical act of renouncing or "decreating" the self—an act of "moral gravity" that energizes the soul. Saxton shows convincingly how both *Passion* and *Scénario du film* Passion move between the real material body and immaterial/spiritual presence, between human stasis and supernatural kinesis, to the point that human forms are dematerialized and the distinction between the physical and spiritual is all but abolished (see Saxton 2014: 62–67).

We have already witnessed in the previous chapter how the pure, affective moments of seeing in *Histoire(s)*, a secondary level of montage, work with and against Godard's major rhetorical maneuvers. If we now focus explicitly on the spectatorial overload and "chaos" produced by the work's multiple rhythms, pulsations, vibrations, and intensities, we can, of course, talk loosely of the experience in terms of trauma. After all, cinema is so connected to the real by virtue of recording it that it comes directly under the influence of death. It is death at work (Cocteau), and since the story of the twentieth century is one of war and the camps, there is literally an overkill of death. The faces caught in early newsreels are like disembodied ghosts in Godard's machine, and they set up through repetition, overlap and replay endless cycles of mourning, a pathos only heightened by the fact that the very material of film, nitrate, is steadily decomposing. Allen Meek has explored well the issues of affect and trauma in *Histoire(s)* in specific relation to Godard's engagement with the Holocaust.[8] Yet there are other, more immediate critical ways of engaging with the material and emotional impact of the work's sensorium of the past and its proliferation of affect within the general context of Godard's evolving poetics. One such is provided potentially by Steven Shaviro in *The Cinematic Body* (1993), a study of "embodied" cinematic vision in the work of David Cronenberg, Rainer Werner Fassbinder, and Andy Warhol which proposes a new dynamics of filmviewing at once mimetic, tactile, and corporeal.[9] Exploring the affective responses of his own intoxicated viewing body as well as the multiple interactions, affects, and transformations of the bodies on screen, Shaviro reveals that cinema can offer a shattering, masochistic pleasure of obsessive passivity and abjection due to the spectator's abandonment to free-flowing sensation and visual fascination. Indeed, by instantiating an ambivalent, viscerally real, and at times terrifying, nonsignifying "body" (defined here not as an object of representation but as a zone of affective intensity), cinema brings the viewer convulsively face to face with the signs and stimuli of an ecstatic otherness that can be neither incorporated nor expelled.[10]

The cinematic body theorized by Shaviro, which goes beyond current Lacanian film theory grounded in lack and castration anxiety and privileges physiological excitation over fantasy (fantasies of sadistic control and fetishistic voyeurism), allows us to conceive of *Histoire(s)* in terms of a video body of affect, or, better still, "videographic" body of affect, in view of the fact that the digital image subordinates the photographic and cinematic to the painterly and graphic (for example, the computerized hand-painting of digitized film frames). The "hypertrophic surplus of immediate sensation," which Shaviro describes in detail, matches exactly the experience of Godard's Heraclitean flux of material. Indeed, Godard is fully conscious of the epic nature of his direct encounter with rereleased raw emotion. The extended sequence at the start of episode 1A, for example, where a microphone swings slowly into frame as he gears up like a performer to take hold of the beast of cinema, is a moment of pure theatrical suspense and visual fascination. Yet the notion of a purely mechanical videographic body of affect in *Histoire(s)* is, of course, complicated by the physical presence of Godard's own body, which functions as the principal site of encounter between the human and the inhuman. Godard is everywhere within the work, as image, voice, and editor, whether in the persona of bespectacled intellectual puffing on his cigar in his study while cutting into own films to confect a new edit (in one extraordinary moment in episode 1B he replays over his face the final scene of *Le Mépris* where the film crew, featuring Godard, recreate the return of Ulysses to his native land), or as a shaman-like figure getting down and dirty in the heat and sweat of his night-time laboratory (he even goes topless in episode 2B).

 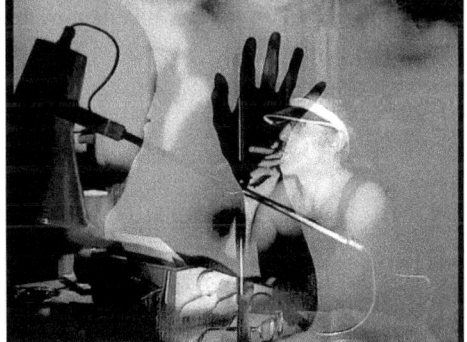

Figures 3.2–3. Godard editing over himself in episodes IB and 2B of *Histoire(s) du cinéma* (1988–98).

If such ubiquity suggests supreme narcissism on Godard's part, this is pushed to breaking point since his body itself participates in the digital effect. He is quite literally immersed in the frenzy of his material, offering himself humbly to the viewer as a kind of functional tool on a par with Amplex, Agfa, Video and Audio, among which he lists himself in the closing credits to each episode. Indeed, if Godard figures personally in *Histoire(s)* as cinema's memory with montage serving as his individual signature, he is also visibly consumed and even shattered by the sheer exorbitance of the sounds and images he calls up, in particular of the newsreels of war-time executions and the devastating scenes of torture in films like *Rome, Open City*. In the crowded blare and spume of the screen, his figure and skin are often obscured, spotted, and superimposed to the point of invisibility and his voice technically mangled, thus rendering him even more radically discomfited than the masochistically inclined male heroes of his feature films of the 1980s and 1990s.[11] There are occasions, too, when the computerized editing appears to operate beyond his cognitive control. We experience with Godard the elation and anxiety caused by the layout and font of words fragmenting, splintering, and bifurcating (e.g. "his toi toi toi re"), of key phrases and sentences stammering forth, dilating and decomposing. The constant play on the title word *Histoire(s)* ("with an s and sometimes SS") is emblematic of this general contagion. Such paroxysms of the machine match and exacerbate the many instances in *Histoire(s)* of objects spiraling out of control into chaos, from the tumult and convulsions of newsreels recording war and human slaughter to the more individual and intimate images of disarray, for instance, the shot in episode 1A from Boris Barnet's *By the Bluest of Seas* (1936) of a woman losing the pearls of her earrings as they cascade down both sides of her face.

Godard has always understood very clearly that the imaginary disturbance of "emotion" is an intrinsically physical process, as he demonstrated in his enlightening presentation of *Pierrot le fou* (see "Pierrot mon ami" in Bergala 1985: 259–63). The potential ethical issue this raises has been highlighted by Richard Dienst, who writes of *Pierrot le fou* that the emotion generated whenever images are redrawn together "always brings both the prospect of unification as well as the threat of disorientation and uncertainty. Emotion makes you feel alive only by opening your borders to the energies of other lives [. . .] in the moment of emotional transport, there sparks an image" (Dienst 2000: 31–32). This raises, in turn, important questions about the function of emotion and the senses in contemporary postmodern aesthetics. How much further does Godard's new videographic body of compressions and elasticities go beyond the cinematic body as defined by Shaviro? Does the programmed audiovisual ferment of *Histoire(s)*, which directly implicates its manipulator-composer, simply magnify the ecstatic affect already available in film, or does it constitute something else even more radical and unique to the electronic medium? Further, to return to our opening question, to what extent can one talk of a digitalized self? I propose to examine these related issues by entering into the electronic flesh of *Histoire(s)* and analyzing two set-piece sequences, one from the beginning and one from the end of episode 1B entitled *Une histoire seule*, which together bring to a head, quite literally, the crisis between the analogical human and the digital inhuman. While it is clearly impossible to convey the total emotional experience of viewing these sequences, where sounds and images are in constant evolution and can transmute within the space of a second, we will nonetheless be able through close textual reading to define the nature and limits of what is human and inhuman in *Histoire(s)*. As we shall see, Godard's encounter with the video/digital machine is at once rhetorical and poetic, and the sparks and flashes of energy created through montage in *Histoire(s)* always carry the promise of a new poetics of illumination.

The Fall: Performance and Poetic Will

The first minutes of episode 1B immediately plunge the viewer into a masculine context of outsider artists such as Paul Gauguin and Jean Cocteau. Godard refers to Jean Delannoy's *L'Éternel Retour* (1943), a modernization of the love story of Tristan and Isolde scripted by Cocteau, although typically we are offered instead a clip from Cocteau's own film *Orphée* (1949), starring his former lover, now friend and collaborator, Jean Marais. Godard repeatedly implores on the soundtrack: "What is my (hi)story? What is my relationship to the (hi)story of cinema? What have I got to do with all of this?"[12] This becomes a refrain taken up as if in an echo-chamber by another unidentified male voice who relays the additional fear of being haunted by a "*chuchotement continu*" ("continuous whispering") audible even after his television has been turned off. This statement of powerlessness in the face of the machine contrasts with the consummate authority of Cocteau's own voice-machine. After a brief discussion of his own 1987 film *Soigne ta droite: Une place sur la terre* (linked, via Heurtebise, the driver of Death, to *The Eternal Return*), and following the arresting superimposition of a cubist portrait by Picasso in post-Guernica green and yellow ochre over shots from a Western, Godard introduces the final gory moments of the shoot-out on the cliff in *Duel in the Sun* (1946) (dir. King Vidor), where the weak heroine Pearl (Jennifer Jones) finally exacts her revenge on her lover, the lecherous outlaw Lewt (Gregory Peck). This Technicolor climax to a typical, if extreme, Hollywood tale of sex and death gives Godard the opportunity on the soundtrack to deliver one of his key themes: that cinema once possessed, due to its inherent powers of ambiguity, the capacity to engender new ideas and sensations, yet limited itself to being an agent of spectacle and archetypal (nineteenth-century) narrative.

What Godard does with this sequence is to stagger and decompose it, intercutting in stages the phrase: "The image will come at the time of the resurrection" (a classic religious thesis attributed elsewhere by Godard to Saint Paul), while at the same time redubbing the soundtrack with the chilling theme music from Alfred Hitchcock's *Psycho*. This is taken over in turn by the lugubrious tone of a Leonard Cohen song, *Night Comes On*, about male loss and separation ("And there's nothing to follow, there's nowhere to go/ She's gone like the summer, gone like the snow/ And the crickets are breaking his heart with their song/ As the day caves in and the night's all wrong"). The tragic climax of the original film sequence, which closes on Peck's blood-strewn face, is ironically suspended and deflated by Godard's intertitle "oh! Temps" ("Oh! Time"), a pun in French on "au temps" ("at the time") in the phrase: "The image will come at the time of the resurrection." This pun is clearly a metacritical comment on the nature of the filmic image and filmic time, and indeed, the sequence is introduced symbolically at the beginning as a battle between Sound (codified here as masculine) and Image (feminine). This split amplifies the criss-crossing of text and image that occurred moments earlier when Godard's statement, "All that has passed through cinema has been marked by it" was immediately reversed and contradicted by his typing on the screen of the phrase: "but about other mourning I'll keep quiet and so begins . . ."

Figure 3.4. Deconstructing the shoot-out sequence from King Vidor's *Duel in the Sun* with Jennifer Jones in episode 1B of *Histoire(s) du cinéma* (1988–98).

Hence, in a *tour de force* deconstruction of classical cinema, Godard reconfigures sound and image in order to generate critical ideas and sensations that have nothing to do with the emotions of the prerecorded cinematic material he is citing. The mood created is a mixture of loss, confusion, doubt, frustration, expectancy, and apprehension. In addition, we see that the passage of film into the video/digital machine provokes repetition and inversion. Indeed, the overriding rhetorical feature of *Histoire(s)* is the proliferation of chiastic processes of inversion, understood in Paul de Man's sense of the term as any strategy of reversal or specular reflexion that crosses the attributes of inside and outside.[13] A constant play of oppositions, divisions, and inversions is already in evidence at the start of the first episode. The typewritten statement from Virgil, "hoc opus/hic labor est," is followed by the intercutting of different pairs of eyes, by shots of Godard filmed first in pink light then in blue, and eventually by an orchestrated criss-crossing of short excerpts from classic French and Japanese cinema. An internal machine of patterns and refrains is quickly established with Godard inverting key ideas and mantra-like phrases such as: "Redites-le/le redites" ("repeat it/the repeated"), "histoire de la solitude/ solitude de l'histoire" ("(hi)story of solitude/solitude of (hi)story"), and "actualité de l'histoire/histoire des actualités" ("actuality of history/(hi)story of the newsreels"). The continual flux of chiastic formations in *Histoire(s)*, starred by minicrosses of approval placed theatrically next to names like that of filmmaker Jean Vigo, pushes *Histoire(s)* even further into the realm of the mechanical, and indeed may be read on one level as a threatening sign of the inhuman.

Let us now fast-forward to the closing stages of episode 1B, which repeat and transpose some of its key elements (Cohen, *Soigne ta droite*, Hitchcock), and where male self-destruction is again a powerful theme. The build-up to the episode's conclusion is an extended series of cinematic and pictorial heterosexual embraces running *pêle-mêle* into each other, while on the soundtrack, to the ascending organ of Bach's *Have Pity on Me, God*, we hear Charles Ferdinand Ramuz reciting an extract from his short 1921 text "L'amour de la fille et du garçon" (The love of the boy and the girl) (1921), about a young man seducing a girl and entering places "one normally doesn't dare to go or see." The graphic, perverse nature of this voice-off is complemented by male fetishistic moments from Dalí and Buñuel's *Un Chien andalou* (1929). The sporadic intercutting of titles like "Lost in the Fog" and "Au paradis perdu" (Lost in paradise) increases the emotional impact of the sequence, as does the visual reference to Gauguin's painting *Words of the Devil* (1892), depicting the sexual shame of a Polynesian woman. The theme of the sexually licit and illicit is further developed visually by an excerpt from the Italian neorealist film *Two Pennyworth of Hope* (1951) by Renato Castellani, where a young woman, inviting a man towards her, quickly crosses herself (Godard stop-forwards the action) and turns towards the statue of the Madonna in the foreground, pushing it, and the camera, away. This dramatization of religious *pudeur* casts the viewer in the unexpected role of a voyeur whose enjoyment is deliberately blocked. A single female voice, that of Maria Casarès who played the Princess (Death) in *Orphée*, then starts up on the soundtrack, reading with quiet intensity what is, in fact, a small extract from the French translation of Martin Heidegger's "What are poets for?" (published in 1950 although written in 1946).[14] Heidegger's essay is a disquisition on the question posed by Hölderlin in his elegy "Bread and Wine" of the value of poets in a "destitute time," and it leads Heidegger to a consideration of Rilke as the modern poet. The recited passage (which omits from the original the elements relating to the wine god and ether) reads as follows: "Poets are the mortals who sense the trace of the fugitive gods, stay on the gods' tracks, and so trace for their kindred mortals the way toward the turning . . . But who has the power to sense, to trace such a track? Traces are often inconspicuous, and are always the legacy of a directive that is barely divined. To be a poet in a destitute time means: to attend, singing, to the trace of the fugitive gods."[15]

During the reading of this passage, which hinges on humankind's possible "turning" ("*le chemin du revirement*"), a remarkable physical and highly concrete turning is also recorded. The word "hélas!" ("alas!") has just been uttered in a low, deep, and prophetic male voice (an excerpt from the soundtrack of *Soigne ta droite* that retains the wailing voice of Catherine Ringer in her recording studio in the background, as if in counterpoint,), and Casarès is preparing to utter the word "chantant" ("singing"). Meanwhile, on the image-track, a still image from Bergman's 1949 film, *Prison* (aka *The Devil's Wanton*), of the alcoholic journalist Thomas (Birger Malmsten) and the prostitute Birgitta (Doris Svedlund) huddled together beside a cinematograph and gazing off-screen towards the viewer, is now interspotted with the facial detail of a generic-looking Byzantine icon of an archangel in a red robe and with a bright yellow halo. It seems as if the icon were the very image being projected in *Prison*, and it quickly expands in an iris-out to cover the entire frame. Now, suddenly, we are exposed to the dramatic moment in *Soigne ta droite* when, in his burlesque role as the Idiot/Prince, Godard, with a copy of Dostoyevsky's *The Idiot* in his hands, is knocked into by another figure disembarking from the plane just as he is being presented with a pile of large cans of cine film (the footage of the completed film-within-a-film). The cans crash in a loud cacophony, and Godard appears to fall head-first down the aircraft ramp. We hear the words "ça suffit!" ("that's enough!"), and the image is promptly cut. The soundtrack picks up again the thread of Heidegger's sentence with "attentif/ à la trace/ des dieux enfouis" ("attentive/ to the trace/ of the fugitive gods"), and the image, now restored to silence, offers a full-frame of the archangel which had subtended the crash (its face was superimposed over the center of the image of Godard's fall, specifically the cans of film). The screen also becomes now the site of writing of a phrase that had begun over the frame of the archangel seconds before Godard's explosion into the image, but which appeared blocked and suspended at the words "ne te fais ("don't do") due to the missing final part of the French negative ("ne . . . pas"). The phrase restarts and, though staggered, is now motivated into a complete Pauline sentence about human love and hope through collective unity: "ne te fais/ pas de mal/ ne te fais / pas de mal /car nous sommes tous/ tous encore ici" ("don't cause yourself/ harm/ don't cause yourself/ harm/ for we are all, all still here").[16]

Another series of movements and connections is also brought to fruition. The slow voice of Cohen returns to the soundtrack, but not the earlier discordant, mournful rasp of *Night Comes On*, rather a gentler and more contemplative, even lyrical, Cohen accompanied by a soothing female voice. They sing together softly as if in unison: "If it be your will/ that I speak no more/ and my voice be still/ as it was before." After the sexual disarray and cacophony of the Ramuz text and the antiphony of "hélas!" and Ringer's voice used in the build-up to the crash, this has the euphonic force of a reconciliation between male and female, even, in the light of the sacred icon, of spiritual calm and recovery. In the case of the still from *Prison* of the couple at once separated and united by the projector, it is now briefly spotted in turn by the archangel, over which is inscribed in red "L'ANGE" ("ANGEL"), forming a startling triple superimposition. It is as if Bergman's image, which has haunted this entire episode in a range of styles, sizes, and formats (close-up detail, negative, positive, tinted), has now finally been activated. Another element that is reintroduced is Hitchcock, but a very different sort of Hitchcock from *Psycho*. The last part of the Pauline sentence ("for we are all/ all still here") is inscribed over a short extract (stop-started) from *Vertigo* (1958) where Scottie (James Stewart) saves "Madeleine" (Kim Novak) from drowning in San Francisco Bay. This segues into a scene early in Albert Lewin's *Pandora and the Flying Dutchman* (1951) when Pandora (Ava Gardner) swims out one night to meet the Dutch captain Hendrick (James Mason) on his yacht. On the sound-track, meanwhile, we hear recorded phrases from the bowels of history of Hollywood production: an anonymous shout of "This is a picture!" over *Vertigo*; "Cameras!" over *Pandora*. Over this last sputtering image appears the caption "à suivre" ("to be continued"), the linking device in early French silent film serials. Episode 1B is now finally over.

Figure 3.5–7. *Prison*, an archangel icon, *Soigne ta droite* and *Vertigo* brought together chiastically in the climax to episode 1B of *Histoire(s) du cinéma* (1988–98).

The affirmative force of the penultimate image from *Vertigo*, which stands in sharp opposition to the destructive climax of the *Duel in the Sun* sequence earlier in the episode, depends on our filmic knowledge that Scottie successfully rescues the woman he thinks is the suicidal "Madeleine." Yet, of course, from the moment Scottie saves "Madeleine" (a woman who does not exist), he is drawn ever deeper into a spiral of deceit, illusion, and obsession that entails the death both of the real Madeleine (pushed off a tower) and of her impersonator, Judy (who falls off the same tower), a fact that makes the final message of serial continuity highly ironic. Similarly in *Pandora*, when Pandora reaches the yacht, she discovers Hendrick painting a picture of her posed as her mythical namesake. Pandora will attempt to save Hendrick, even after discovering that he is the Flying Dutchman, and will swim out once again to meet him on his boat towards the end of the film. However, the two are doomed and will die together at sea in a storm. Hence, rather than restore a sense of harmonious calm and closure to 1B, these final ambivalent snatches of fatal narrative release a jar of human confusion and catastrophe. Everything has now effectively been reopened and put into question: not just the foundations of heterosexual love, but also the image as a vehicle of the truth. In case we were in any doubt about the fundamental nature and import of this instability, over the images from *Vertigo* and *Pandora* an unidentified (and just audible) male voice reflects in academic tones on the status of the image and its relationship with reality, both spiritual and material. He ponders whether Christ is a man or the image of a man, or whether in the Eucharist Christ is present in reality or only symbolically, and finally whether the filmed image of a man is a real man or already the fiction of a man. Needless to say, no answers are forthcoming, and the only certainty here remains yet more reversibility ("à suivre").

Viewed as a whole, the closing polytych of episode 1B constitutes a spectacular multichiastic event of inversions and ironic counterpoints triggered by Godard's crash. The criss-crossing of elements in formation extends from the interspotting of *Prison* with the archangel (the icon is first spotted into the still, then vice versa), to the contrasting of the crystalline voice of Casarès invoking male poets with the softer, "feminized" Cohen, the repetition and negative inversion of the phrase "ne te fais/ pas de mal" culminating in a self-folding, four-part structure ("car nous sommes *tous,/ tous* encore ici" [my emphasis]), and finally the inversion performed across gender (male "saves" female in *Vertigo*, female "saves" male in *Pandora*). In addition, the typed letters of the Pauline sentence are initially blue but are then recolored white against first black, then sea-blue. The fact that *Pandora* was only added into the mix by Godard in the 2007 DVD version of *Histoire(s)* reveals once again his seemingly unstoppable chiastic compulsion. Indeed, the chains of inversion that define this work will resume immediately in the following episode (2A), the title of which, *Seul le cinéma* (The cinema alone, or Only the cinema), already performs chiastically with *Une histoire seule*.

With this degree of formal intricacy, Godard's restaging here of his own hyperstylized act of falling physically *into* the image is clearly more than just a dynamic, literal illustration of one of the key tenets of *Histoire(s)*, namely, that the invention of cinema originally afforded people the unique chance to "project" themselves directly into the world. Equally, it represents far more than a simple comic figuration of Ramuz's young man falling abjectly to his knees in voyeuristic fascination. By falling down with his cans of film, Godard would appear to be enacting hyperbolically the fall of cinema and taking on the burden of cinema's suffering. It might even be argued that he is also staging proleptically his own death as a founder of modernist cinema—one who now finds himself reduced to relative obscurity in the contemporary era where his films, even when they are distributed, usually attract only a limited audience (*Soigne ta droite* ranks as one of the rarest of his later works). Certainly, the idea of the fall and catastrophe is a recurring trope in his later work and directly linked to feelings of personal failure, notably in *Changer d'image*, where, as we noted in chapter 1, he films himself being beaten for his cinematic shortcomings during the abortive Sonimage project in Mozambique in the late 1970s. The theme runs right through the later corpus up to and including his exhibit in 2006 at the Centre Pompidou in Paris, *Voyages(s) en Utopie, Jean-Luc Godard, 1946–2006*, which arose out of the ashes of his ill-fated multimedia project *Collage(s) de France, archéologie du cinéma d'après JLG*, almost as an emaciated, inverted version of its original projected self. Godard's practice has, of course, always flirted with danger and potential failure, a process often ritualized as an aesthetics of breakdown. Indeed, according to André Habib, who rightly suggests that the "beauty and paradox" of Godardian failure is evident even in a short like *Lettre à Freddy Buache* which anticipates its own refusal by those who commissioned it (even before it was actually refused), Godard's "performances of failure" "perform something of cinema's possible impossibility,"[17] such that failure may be read as the very condition of a film's possibility. Such an experimental strategy arguably corresponds to the radical Durassian model of progress in cinema through controlled destruction, for example, *Son nom de Venise dans Calcutta désert* (1976), which literally hollows out and dissolves, clinically and systematically with the same soundtrack, the visual beauty and human figuration of *India Song* (1975).

The most obvious instance of this process in Godard's work is surely the seldom seen *King Lear*, which presents itself from the outset as an abandoned object. Yet perhaps the most intriguing and instructive case, and one that merits a short diversion in our discussion of *Histoire(s)*, is *Hélas pour moi*, written off by many critics as an unmitigated mess and failure and virtually disowned by Godard himself at the time, who described it as "inside out" because an inversion of his original intentions (it recorded the presence, rather than absence, of God). The scale of the "disaster" is even greater when one considers Godard's lengthy preparations and the care he took to ensure the film's success. He wrote perhaps for the first time a meticulous, full-length screenplay (inspired by Jean Giraudoux's adaptation of the legend of Alcmena and Amphitryon, *Amphitryon 38* [1929]) and secured the services of global star Gérard Depardieu, then the incontestable god of French cinema, to incarnate the double figure of Simon and God—an exceptional meeting between Go*dard* and Depar*dieu*, as the promotional material put it. Yet Depardieu, who at one point becomes "soluble" in water, abandoned the set early on in frustration with Godard's work habits, leaving the film, which offered itself early on as a "proposition de cinéma," still "à la trace de Dieu" ("following God's footprints").[18] The signs of confusion are not hard to see for the film's ruin is registered on a formal level as disturbance and breakdown. As Douglas Morrey has well observed, when the sexual act takes place, just visible beneath a near-abstract shot of the rising sun reflected on the lake is the image of a hand stroking a penis, followed by a very rapid series of shots in which the sun is intercut with images that are too dark and pass by too rapidly to make out (including copulating genitalia). Hence, the film's central event, "the supposed sexual congress between a god and a mortal woman, occurs before we have had a chance to register it on anything other than a subliminal level."[19] Unable to establish anything concrete about what exactly happened, Abraham Klimt (Bernard Verley), an investigator introduced by Godard as part of a last-ditch effort to salvage the film, promptly exits the film. The relentless concern in *Hélas pour moi* with the events of the past (including even a double flash-back) appears blurred and confused, like the repeated, almost mechanical use of out-of-focus. In short, the image is continually blocked in its own tenebrous slurry (it is made explicit at one point that cinematographic grammar is "deficient" and "renders demeaning any attempt to show things naked"). As such, *Hélas pour moi* performs only negatively: something like *Je vous salue, Marie* (the varied use of Bach, the talk of body, love, and the soul), and something like *Nouvelle Vague* (the theme of return, the shores of Lake Geneva), yet neither. The film, as one of the intertitles puts it, is as if "aimé pour rien" ("loved for nothing"), in the very image of Simon/God/Depardieu.

Some critics have attempted to recuperate *Hélas pour moi* in the express terms of the sacred,[20] but what is most crucial here is the particular value of negation in Godard's artistic practice, conveyed formally by the narrative dead-ends and the sudden, unheralded explosions of sound and image and other effects of distortion that punctuate the work. For what may seem complete breakdown could also be read, within the context of an evolving multimedia process, as a radical form of aesthetic breakthrough. Moreover, the film does attempt to redeem itself when all seems lost and over, and the possible means are once again rhetorical. As the final list of credits (minus the director's name) play out over a black screen, *Hélas pour moi* suddenly takes off in a new direction with an unidentified young female voice (almost certainly Rachel) talking of something unknown and clandestine, while also insisting on the impossibility of resolving the mystery. Over a deep-focus shot of a cornfield with a horizon line of trees where Rachel can be discerned riding her bike from left to right, the voice-off begins: "At night, when I wake up, I know it has nothing to do with what is near or far, or with something that has happened to me [*un événement m'appartenant*], or with a truth capable of speech. It's neither a scene, nor the beginning of something." At this point, an older male voice (no doubt Klimt) interjects: "An image." She replies: "Yes, an instant, but sterile. Someone to whom I am nothing, and who is nothing to me. a point, and beyond that point, nothing in the world is strange to me." The man cuts into the last words with the just audible phrase: "A figure?," to which she replies: "Yes, but without a name, without a biography, which refuses to remember, which doesn't wish to be recorded. It's present but not there. Absent and yet nowhere else." "Completely beyond the real, then?," the male voice suggests, to which she responds: "If they say it is connected to the night, I reply no. Night doesn't know it." The man expresses frustration at this lack of clarity ("But what are you talking about, Miss?"), prompting her to deliver the ultimate noncommittal statement of the film: "If I'm asked, I reply: 'Then there's no-one around to ask me about it.'" The true end of the film has now finally been reached.

What is remarkable about this absolute refusal of personal revelation, which underlines the impossibility of language and knowledge to comprehend and name liminal events, is that, following a partial repeat of the long-shot of Rachel on her bike and then a glimpse of her on a separate occasion from an open apartment window, and just as the voice declares, "If they say it is connected to the night . . . ," a moon suddenly becomes visible in the night sky, moving at great speed in the frame from right to left. Although far away in extreme long-shot, it appears reasonably clear and in focus. Then, unpredictably, it changes course and turns left towards the camera which appears to zoom forward as if approaching it head-on. In the very process of increasing in size, however, the moon loses its sharp outline and focus, its yellowish white color transforming into a pale blue hue. Denied entry into the clarity of close-up, it remains as if suspended in the limbo of midshot towards the left of the frame. After a few seconds, and once the voice-off has reached its conclusion, the elusive, blurry, blue sphere disappears, and the image is definitively cut.

Figures 3.8–9. The opening and final images of the short sequence following the end-credits of *Hélas pour moi* (1993).

This would seem on one level a rather hackneyed cinematic *trucage* with which to conclude the film, employing as it does a traditional female symbol of the waxing moon to convey the expanding mystery of one woman's individual but oddly impersonal experience. Yet taken as a whole the sequence is a subtle, poetic construction across sound and image that reinvents the film's themes of distance and unknowability, with the form and shape of the moon serving as an aesthetic figure inaccessible to the basic processes of cognition. Indeed, it constitutes a pure cinematic event of opposing movements and lines of flight: left to right/right to left; distance in focus/proximity out of focus. This affective, chiastic mix of intimacy (threatening) and withdrawal (reassuring) encapsulates some of the key aspects of Godardian montage as we have been defining it. It also returns us to an earlier moment in the film when a young girl by the lake talked of a peculiar "blue deeper than blue" that strangely "persists." If the moon seems cold, distant, and sterile, this stunning movement of color and abstraction constitutes a gesture towards the *au-delà* that arrives from the *en-deçà* of the image. As if the divine subtended the aesthetic project and could declare itself even during apparently minor moments? Or as if the image had miraculously elevated itself into an icon and the redemption claimed by the past had finally materialized? We can only speculate. Certainly, this entirely unexpected aesthetic opening up of a new dimension of mystery and unreadability, an insistence on a space beyond analysis, helps to reclaim *Hélas pour moi* which erred too much on the side of visibility (the presencing of God). For this reason, formal disaster could be said to operate as cinema's internal means for redeeming the disarray and confusion of production.[21] Or, put another way, the disaster of *Hélas pour moi* arguably engenders its own resurrection, and that of cinema itself, by disclosing new thresholds of cinematic practice. *Hélas pour moi* might usefully be compared in this respect to the more recent *Film socialisme* where Godard appears deliberately to lay digital waste to his current method and style in order to recharge and redefine his cinema.

We can now return to episode 1B of *Histoire(s)* with a keener sense of the potential aesthetic gains of driven negativity in Godard's graphic, metaphysical fall. Godard's body effectively acts itself as the chiastic point of reversal, the self-deflating, absent center of the typewritten sentence: "ne te fais/ pas de mal/ car nous sommes tous,/ tous encore ici." The ironic effect of such a chiastic fall is of a positive turning point, like the "turning" traced by poets for their fellow mortals in Casarès's voice-off, for, as we have seen, it reverses (albeit only temporarily) sexual chaos into poetic and spiritual calm, and it carries the (short-lived) promise of a Pauline return to a spirit of human kinship and community glimpsed in the image of recovery in *Vertigo*. It is precisely by provoking a brief escape from the internal chiastic machine that Godard's falling/failing body creates the possibility for the episode's closure (we are reminded here of John Guillory's figural legend of the chiasmus: origin [a], divergence [b], repetition [b], return [a]).[22] Which is to say, by personally embodying the chiasmus, Godard tropes on it and renders it human. Or, put a little differently, he incarnates the inhuman in order to actualize the human. This rhetorical movement is at once affective and aesthetic, for the image from *Vertigo*, received in its original context as a perfunctory image of suspense, is now charged with a genuine pathos ("This is a picture!"). Hence, Godard's violent eruption into the image testifies directly to the generative force of the cinematic image within the new video and digital context. We might even say that the cinematic image, which was previously reduced to absurdly short flashes of sensation and intensity, has been momentarily resurrected in the video/digital machine as a properly "virtual" image, that is, one in which, to return again to Bergson, past and present are superimposed.

That we might view the closing moments of episode 1B aesthetically in this way is encouraged, of course, by the presence of the archangel, which raises a different set of questions from the minimalist drawing by Paul Klee of a child angel (*Forgetful Angel* [1939–40]) used at this point by Godard in the initial version, where the angel's sad eyes were bowed down as if in empathy with the forces of human history, memory, and forgetting.[23] It is not just a matter of angels *qua* angels, of which there are many in episode 1B and throughout *Histoire(s)*,[24] but rather of the particular iconic nature and status of the archangel. The holy image is presented here as an object of perdurability: it remains visually solid and serene through the crash and chaos of Godard's fall when everything else appears fleeting and intermittent, and despite itself also being subjected to multiple bombardments. Moreover, by placing the icon in the very epicenter of the falling reels of film, Godard is consciously alluding to, and drawing on, the original power of the icon which united art and belief and was invested with a level of meaning denied to contemporary image-makers. By employing the icon chiastically with Bergman's *Prison*, a film that foregrounds cinematic innocence and promise (the silent, slapstick farce entitled "Death and the Devil" projected by the couple temporarily reverses Birgitta's depression and allows her to articulate the truth of her terrible past, so bringing her closer to Thomas), and, further, by spotting the icon such that the archangel's wings now appear to radiate out over the talismanic image of the projector like an illuminated halo, Godard is arguably clinging to what he calls in the work and elsewhere "the childhood of art"—his sacred notion of the unprecedented potential of the new medium of film for human discovery and revelation. Yet Godard knows only too well that such moments of "real" meaning are precisely "fugitive" and transient, even illusory, and that there is, alas, no real escape from the Fall of the contemporary, supersaturated visual sphere where not only God but also History and (increasingly) Art are becoming invisible. The possibility for the type of plenitude inherent within the iconic image cannot be entertained here for more than a few seconds, and, as we have seen, we are returned almost immediately at the end of 1B to the primary vertigo of confusion and reversibility, making any notion of where "*ici*" ("here") might be an object of ironic and tragic speculation, especially in view of the narrative outcomes of *Vertigo* and *Pandora*. The cinematic image would thus appear to be doomed simply to perform its own lack of meaning—nothing ultimately can be redeemed. Yet, as we've also seen in chapter 2 with his remarkable montage of Giotto, Elizabeth Taylor, and Auschwitz in *Histoire(s)* 1A, Godard is irresistibly drawn into iconic temptation and will sometimes proceed to resurrect history and approximate the sacred *as if it were still possible*.

But we can go even further here, I think, and read the final moments of episode 1B in the particular context of the sublime, an overt theme in Godard's recent work, notably *Prénom Carmen*, which ends with a reference to Rilke's first *Duino Elegy*: "For Beauty's nothing/ but beginning of Terror we're still just able to bear."[25] The videographic body of *Histoire(s)* functions exactly like the elusive, unbound, sublime object which, in its received Kantian sense, exceeds any finite frame and can only be represented (if at all) as a failure of representation. Certainly, by making the video/digital frame incorporate, fragment, and dismember every kind of visual image, Godard renders even more monstrous film's originally heterogeneous nature, that is to say, its hybrid form of image and narrative. What we witness, in fact, in *Histoire(s)* is almost a parody of the three-stage process of the romantic sublime as defined by Thomas Weiskel, with its normative stage before alterity has been apprehended, the traumatic phase that challenges the subject's dignity by means of the drastic contrast opened up between the apparently insurmountable powers of a tremendous object and his/her own disorientation, and, finally, the reactive phase, or moment of poetic sublimation, when the subject experiences elevation and empowerment through the restoration of blocked or occluded power?[26] For we see that, following a period of electronically induced formal and sexual breakdown, Godard regains a measure of authorial dignity by "penetrating" cinematically the electronic frame in a state of virtual collapse. However bracketed and self-ironic this quintessentially postmodern moment may appear, the structure of transcendence nevertheless prevails, and Godard as creator imposes himself romantically as master of the video/digital machine, even appropriating Hitchcockian imagery as his own. Not the least of the ironies of this sublime formation is that Godard executes it while his cinematic body is at its most literally exposed and vulnerable.

New Vibrations, New Feelings

What is the ultimate force of Godard's display of poetic will, his personal self-troping, which seems to take absolutely literally Merleau-Ponty's statement that the ability to conceive space (here cinematic and videographic) depends upon our being "thrust into it by our body"?[27] Does this moment of sublimation really signify, as the final written and spoken messages of episode 1B intend, a movement away from daemonic self-abjection? Moreover, what are the implications for the new digitalized image if an intensified, "real," cinematic body provides the ultimate emotional and aesthetic recourse? The penetration of Godard's videographic machine by his own cinematic flesh marks, as we have said, the moment when the inhuman is transformed and reinvested as human. Almost against the odds Godard retains the notion of a self that can, if only intermittently, regain authority over the pervasive power of electronic technology by casting it in the sacred terms of the unnatural and inhuman. We think ahead also to the last, highly personal stages of *Histoire(s)* where the tone changes as Godard pursues an ethical and philosophical discussion on the nature of humanity and human relations, delivering statements such as

"Love of those who are closest is an art" and "Amor omnia vincit." In the moving and supremely romantic climax which superimposes a yellow rose over an image of Godard's face, itself superimposed over a reproduction of Francis Bacon's second *Study for a Portrait of Van Gogh* (1957) (a painted landscape featuring a solitary male walker), Godard's voiceover recites Jorge Luis Borges's transcription (in his short 1952 essay "The Flower of Coleridge") of a line by Samuel Coleridge about waking from a paradisiac dream with a flower in his hands: "if a man/ if/ a man/ crossed/ paradise/ in a dream/ [and] received a flower/ as proof/ of his passage/ and on waking up/ found/ this flower/ in his hands/ what's to say/ then." The following four short, simple words, the last heard in *Histoire(s)*, are by Godard himself: "I was that man."[28] This final resort to the culturally consecrated act of the author signing off his individual work completes the clearest argument yet made by Godard for the fundamental relevance of fiction and fantasy.

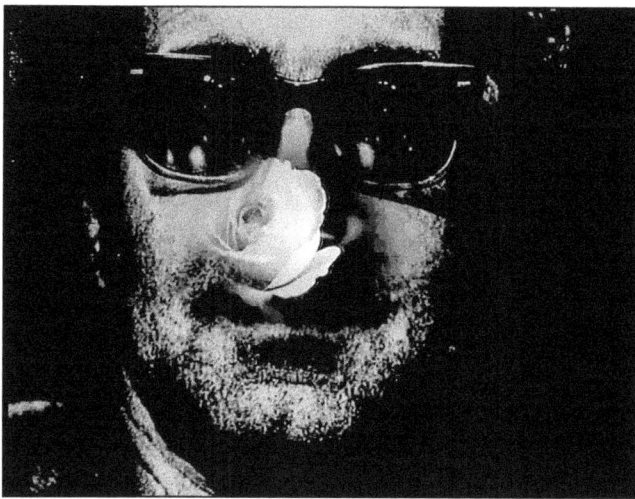

Figure 3.10. Godard's self-portrait in the closing moments of episode 4B of *Histoire(s) du cinéma* (1988–98).

Godard seems to be indicating at such moments that the romantic sublime still has potent relevance in the digital era, although clearly, if the videographic body is transcended, it is not so much to a space "beyond" as to somewhere yet deeper (the vague "ici") within the machine. In Godard's sublime reversion to his own cinematic self, his autobiographical body plays out the romantic narrative of the poet as a "tracer of traces," the unique status of which was already emphasized in the visual arrangement of the key phrase of the *Duel in the Sun* sequence where Godard divided the word "L'image" into "L'i" / "mage" ("magus"). "Trace," too, is a key term for Godard. Elsewhere he has stated that the history of cinema is the only one that possesses its own traces,[29] while in the video piece *Scénario du film* Passion he looks to the Old Masters for traces of an "image to be made." In short, a self-styled journey of discovery into new ideas and sensations has been redirected here into a nostalgic contemplation of traditional myths and dualisms (self/other, mind/matter, and so on). One is tempted to call this merely sentimental, with its negative connotation of uncritical, except that whereas in *Vertigo*, for instance, sentimentality brings about Judy's downfall (she became overattached to Madeleine's necklace, her reward for the murder), in *Histoire(s)* Godard's romantic self-reinstatement also demonstrates a form of self-critique that bears on the very nature of his position as a film- and video-maker. It throws into clear light, rather than resolves, the central problem of finding a resolution between the digital and the cinematic/analogical.

We can perhaps best appreciate the kind of "aesthetic" sentimentality at issue here by referring to Jean-François Lyotard's discussion of art and communication in *The Inhuman: Reflections on Time* (1988). Starting with Kant's notion of a "community of feeling," or *sensus communis*, Lyotard argues that new technology (the realm of the concept and communication) entails the loss of an immediately communicable sentimentality. That is to say, its reception precludes the here-and-now of aesthetic presentation.[30] He poses the following questions: "If we accept that assumed communicability is included in the singular aesthetic feeling, and if we accept that this singular aesthetic feeling is the immediate mode, which is no doubt to say the poorest and the purest of a passibility to space and time, necessary forms of *aesthesis*, then can this communicability persist when the forms which should be its occasion are conceptually determined, whether in their generation or in their transmission? What happens to aesthetic feeling when *calculated* situations are put forward as aesthetic?"[31] Godard's physical encounter with the electronic machine plays out these questions, and the response obtained seems to indicate that there is still a space and time for the kind of "sentimentality" that one finds in the slightest sketch by a Cézanne or a Degas (to cite Lyotard's example). Godard makes of techno-science a place and moment for immediate passion and contemplation. Such an act serves to restore faith in the possibility and freedom of art which, in Godardian thought, has been all but eroded by institutionalized "culture." What again, however, makes Godard's modality of presence and reception so ironic in *Histoire(s)* is that it is achieved in the sublime mode, precisely where, according to Kant, passibility to anything except lack cannot occur because the free-floating forms which arouse the feeling of the beautiful are absent.

This point can be further developed by returning again to the figure of the chiasmus in the specifically poetic context of Rilke. Véronique Fóti has shown how Rilke's poetry often anticipates Merleau-Ponty's theory of embodied perception, in particular his concept of noncoincident bodily reflections, a *perpetuum mobile* of nontotalizable referrals and reversals that subvert the apparent self-identity of polarized opposites.[32] According to Fóti, Rilke's absolute poetic language, the language of angels and even of the gods which results from a process of cosmic sedimentation and alchemical transsubstantiation accomplishes the quasivisible presencing of what Merleau-Ponty calls the invisible of the visible, or the given in the visible. This is inner without ceasing to be the world. Figuration, as the chiastic, noncoincident interconnection of seemingly disseuvered polarities, is achieved through the "inward-turning" of the tropology of a poetic language that articulates itself at the limits of the sayable as "ingathered throw" (*gesammelter Wurf*). This type of figuration is, I would claim, exemplified by Godard's gesture of throwing himself cinematically into the videographic image. The act is followed by an image, that of "Madeleine"'s rescue in *Vertigo*, which is also pure metaphor (Greek *meta-pherein*, "carrying across"). In the process, Godard proves that a reconciliation of form and flux can, after all, be contrived in recreated "plastic" form. If poetic language situates itself ideally at the precarious intersection of two silences, one of which is prelinguistic and the other in excess of language, the visual image, Godard implies, can only properly operate intermedially, at the cross-section of the cinematic and the videographic/digital, in other words, between two modes of the inhuman, one aesthetic or sacred and the other technological. This apparent contradiction, which, as we have seen is also that of two kinds of chiasmus, is held in continual suspense in *Histoire(s)* where the digitized electronic command is permanently haunted and disturbed by cinematic stories of the self, and where some form of living body always remains "to be continued" and sublimated.

Such a powerful insistence on the proximate body, evident, too, in other works by Godard such as *Scénario du film* Passion where he places his hands flat against the *page blanche* of a white projector-screen, clearly goes against the general drift of postmodern theory which privileges depthlessness. We referred at the beginning to Flusser's idea of digital computations, which leads Flusser to conclude somewhat fancifully that the more beautiful the digital apparition in computer art becomes in today's "whirring nothingness," the more "real" and "truthful" are its projected alternative worlds (he plays on the German noun *Schein* ["apparition"]. which has the same root as the adjective *schön* ["beautiful"]).[33] Yet even Scott Bukatman's more comprehensive theory of cybersubjectivity, which skillfully uses Merleau-Ponty's model of subject construction to show that the invisible processes of electronic technology construct a body that is at once material and immaterial, is dramatically different from the outcome reached in *Histoire(s)*. Bukatman posits that if the master enters the machine, the machine, in turn, becomes a part of the human, a new body, thus freeing the mind from bodily limitations and providing "a place for the return of *the omnipotence of thoughts*" (original italics).[34] Godard, by contrast, in continuously laying bare what Keats called in "Ode to Psyche" the "wreath'd trellis of a working brain," never disentangles his chiastic intertwining of the human body and inhuman machine, just as he never ties down the digital to an aesthetic term like beauty which, in its more sublime moments, exceeds definition. Equally, he never retreats to the all-encompassing notion of a digital unconscious, however distributed or collectively constructed. Nor does he fantasize a posthuman *au-delà*.[35] Instead, Godard seeks to expand the affective, transformative potential of the technological image which is able to draw on what he terms in *Histoire(s)* cinema's "formidable power of transfiguration," that is, those moments when it accedes to the transcendent level of painting and when art is "reborn in what has been burnt." Towards the end of episode 1A, for example, we behold a Rembrandt self-portrait rising out of a newsreel image of the death camps. Bergala has convincingly argued that Godard is searching at such moments for a new kind of image that would provide a form not only of resurrection but also of redemption. Each present moment of *Histoire(s)*, Bergala asserts, constitutes a lightly corrected version of a past event: cinema's abysmal, and for Godard criminal, failure to film the camps?[36]

So far our discussion of aesthetic emotion in *Histoire(s)* has centered mainly on the visual image. Yet by exposing the viewer to a vertigo of stimuli and affect, Godard's face-to-face with technology opens up the more general question of the function of the senses in postmodernism. How can we take full account of the intense orchestration of sound in *Histoire(s)*, which sometimes has four soundtracks operating simultaneously, without falling into the essentialist trap of positing the aural-auditory mode as pure feeling and, in the process, of merely reproducing the absolute split between cognition and feeling (the idea that feeling belongs to the body and that the body is really inaccessible and resistant to language and thought)? It is a trap that Lyotard himself does not escape when he offers two modes of the inhuman, the negentropic and the aesthetic, and evokes the aural-auditory as a special mode of the sublime inhuman. In specific relation to music, he describes a "sound-feeling" prior to any objectification or "audition."[37] Steven Connor, in a recent article entitled "Feel the Noise: Excess, Affect and the Acoustic," which examines the twentieth-century opposition between feeling as an auditory and acoustic experience and the cognitive operations of reflection and judgment experienced in terms of the eye, is rightly suspicious of this type of "'othering'" of affect,[38] quite distinct from that achieved in Romantic thought where feeling becomes a sacred and inhuman (if always fragile) gift. Connor expresses the guarded hope that new communicative and representational technologies will reconfigure the relations between the senses and so allow for a transformation of the links between feeling, thinking and understanding.

The crucial need to reevaluate the mutual implications of affectivity and cognition is, I believe, what is ultimately at stake in *Histoire(s)*, where Godard is showing precisely how human thought and emotion have been formed and transformed during the course of the twentieth century and into the twenty-first. By engineering a relentless chiastic switching or referral of the senses to the point of visual cacophony and white noise, and by revealing how the human self can only be conceived now fractally as a reversible and deflationary figure distorted by vibration and contradiction, the videographic body of *Histoire(s)* signals a possible way forward. We have witnessed only a small section of *Histoire(s)*, and there is much important research to be done in this area. Yet in a work which, in its very scientific ambition, deliberately cultivates mystery (Godard repeatedly invokes Robert Bresson's cinematic axiom: "Retain for yourself a margin of vagueness"), there will surely be no final conclusion to this process. Just as the technological inhuman operates necessarily in tension with the sublime inhuman, so (digital) thought and (human) emotion become impossible to separate. It may well be, Godard suggests, that it is only by consistently pushing human emotion to new thresholds—to the point, that is, where the human becomes so inhuman that new forms of human sensibility will need to reveal themselves—that we will have any real chance of staying afloat in an increasingly virtual, yet still intractably real, cybernetic age.

4

Silence, Gesture, Revelation
The Ethics and Aesthetics of Montage in Godard and Agamben

> Ethics is aesthetics from within.
>
> —P. Reverdy

The short, schematic article by Giorgio Agamben on Godard's *Histoire(s) du cinéma* published in *Le Monde* in October 1995, the only essay he has devoted thus far exclusively to Godard, distills the central ideas of a lecture he delivered on Guy Debord around the same time entitled "Difference and Repetition: On Guy Debord's films" (1995).[1] At stake is the nature of history in the cinema. For Agamben, it is necessarily messianic because nonchronological and linked to salvation. Montage constitutes the means and condition for this salvation, specifically the processes of "stoppage" and "repetition" whereby images (and sounds) are freed from their meaning and exhibit themselves as such, and we as spectators must undertake the task of (re)construction. *Histoire(s)* thus comes down to an act of "decreation" and an "apocalypse" of cinema in the different senses of the term, including that of revelation. Similarly, Debord's cinematic practice dismantles the image to *reveal the gesture*, exemplifying cinema's aim not simply to create but also to decreate what exists in order to produce something new. By rendering visible the means and the medium of cinema through repetition and stoppage, both Godard and Debord actively harness cinema's potential for resistance against the spectacularization of politics and the control of information and public opinion by corporate media.[2]

I do not wish here to compare and contrast at length Godard's approach to repetition and stoppage as it has developed since his extensive video work of the mid-to-late 1970s with Debord's dismantling of the "disembodied spectacle" through techniques such as *détournement* that subvert capitalist signs and culture. Important links can certainly be made between Debord's "anticinema" and works like *France tour détour deux enfants*, which slowed down human movement and "decreated" the lines of linear, rational thinking through the use of stop-start motion to reveal, in the words of Gilles Deleuze, the constitutive spaces and interstitial "silences" between images, or the "between-two of images."[3] Yet the possibility of establishing a critical relationship between Godard and Agamben will not come down simply to a connection or otherwise to Debord,[4] still less to Deleuze.[5] Instead, I want to return specifically to Agamben's article on *Histoire(s)*, which concludes with the wonderfully suggestive phrase about the work's messianic drive. Agamben states: "The true messianic power is this power to return the image to this 'imagelessness' ['*sans image*'] which, as Benjamin said, is the refuge of all images." Agamben is clearly talking here about the way that, just as in Debord's fractured cinema where the images of the mediatized world are ripped from their narrative context and placed in a montage, each image in *Histoire(s)*—defamiliarized, decontextualized, de-allegorized—is effectively transformed metaphysically into a kind of epiphany and manifestation of the mystery of cinematographic creation. Indeed, each new pure concrete object and detail, when thrown into the light, enacts this same miracle. (Agamben writes in the Debord essay, paraphrasing Benjamin, that in the messianic situation of cinema "[e]ach moment, each image, is charged with history because it is the door through which the Messiah enters.")[6] Attempting to redeem cinema as a site of the messianic promise contained in the image, Agamben is clearly drawn to Godard for whom montage carries the potential to "redeem" the real. There is, however, something implicit in Agamben's article that needs to be fully acknowledged: Godard's messianic practice of montage is operating in a wholly different realm from that of Debord. The Debord essay ends on a very particular note. Following his clear distinction between the two different ways of showing "imagelessness" (the "*sans image*") and making visible the fact that there is nothing more to be seen (Debord's project contrasts with pornography/advertising which acts as though there are always more images behind the images), Agamben concludes: "It is here, in the difference, that the ethics and the politics of cinema come into play."[7] These words are flagrantly missing in the Godard article. Why should this be?

The emphasis on the ethical and political is part of the general thrust of Agamben's small but urgent body of writing on film, which insists that any notion of gesture in the cinema remains a preeminently ethical rather than aesthetic concern. In "Notes on Gesture" (1992), his key study of how bourgeois "gestures" based on the illusion of subjective identity and unity were definitively destroyed at the dawn of modernity (along with the aura of the image and the idea of a natural language as complete and inherently linked to meaning), and where he also makes the case for a purely gestural cinema that exhibits the conditions of cinematic montage and the medium as pure means, he states the following: "Because cinema has its center in the gesture and not in the image, it belongs essentially to the realm of ethics and politics (and not simply to that of aesthetics) [. . .] The gesture, in other words, opens the sphere of *ethos* as the more proper sphere of that which is human."[8] The assumption here is that the image now revealed as gesture leads surely to ethics as a more "proper" and privileged domain than the aesthetic for discussing the human, and, by extension, that the ethical is distinct from, and perhaps superior to, the aesthetic. Hence, *Histoire(s)*, which is a profound exercise in aesthetics as well as film historiography, does not quite cut it in Agamben's ethical scheme, despite the fact that, in his own words, it is directly prefigured by Debord's *Society of the Spectacle* (1967), and, more crucially, that stoppage links cinema specifically to poetry, where the form (rhythm, poetic technique) can be placed at odds with the meaning, making cinema therefore "a sustained 'hesitation between image and meaning.'"[9] In fact, Agamben's work seems perpetually suspended on a question, namely what, in practical concrete terms, should the next stage of the critical project of cinema be after one has exhibited the medium and duly exposed the illusion of the image and the spectatorial set-up? Can there/should there be any kind of aesthetic surplus? Indeed, does the aesthetic have any real role or function now? Or is the only "safe" option to ensure that the aesthetic realm is always pulled back towards ethics?

I want to consider these particular questions, and in so doing assess the validity of Agamben's views on the messianic, that is, "non-aesthetic," status of Godard's work, by reading Agamben's theory of ethics and gesture in the cinema against a rather obscure and marginal work in Godard's oeuvre—one, however, that directly extends his exploration of the (meta)physical gesture in his work of the early 1980s and which is driven by the messianic idea of an ending (the end) as salvation and redemption. *Soigne ta droite: Une place sur la terre* has been critically overlooked and woefully underrated, despite its generally favorable reception in France upon release.[10] This is the reverse of *King Lear*, a *film maudit* made around the same time which suffered from a lack of proper distribution (it was released in France only in 2002), but which has steadily been recuperated as a vital forerunner of *Histoire(s)* due to its explicit references to film history and set-piece sequences on projection and montage.[11] On the surface *Soigne ta droite* is disarmingly light, even whimsical, being in part a personal homage to Jacques Tati (the title conjures up the boxing term of Tati's 1936 short, *Soigne ton gauche* [*Keep Your Left Up*], directed by René Clément) as well as to other exponents of slapstick film comedy such as Harry Langdon, Buster Keaton, and Jerry Lewis (*The Family Jewels* [1965] and *Smorgasbord* [1983] are directly evoked). Yet the film is similarly premised on the end of cinema and imbued with the mood of loss and death, although it explores in very different ways the ethico-aesthetic question of how to retrieve the image and resurrect cinema in a post-Chernobyl, digital world of global capitalism, neotelevision and political apathy.[12] With its satirical portrait of the service industries and the cold, cynical ethos of money, quick-grab gratification, and noncommunication, the film reflects not simply the growing sense of social and political confusion and disenchantment in France at the time (notably the beginning of "cohabitation" between the Socialists under Mitterrand and the right under Chirac), but also the malaise of contemporary state-sanctioned cinema and culture which has "imprisoned" the image and with it human relationality. In interviews to promote the film, Godard bemoaned the loss of the documentary gaze and of the idea of art as a means of showing and sharing things, part of the vanishing signs and gestures of mutual dialogue.[13]

In fact, although *Soigne ta droite* may appear structurally as one of his most loose, aimless, dispersed, and flagrantly meandering films (a series of sketches tied together without the hook of an obvious pretext as in *King Lear*), it is actually one of his tightest and most complete conceptually. Its narrative premise is announced at the very outset in a voice-over explaining that the Idiot/Prince, a filmmaker in exile, has been given one last chance by those "at the top" (unspecified) to "save" himself by completing a film from scratch in one day and delivering it in the capital for projection that evening. "Then, and only then, will his 'numerous sins' [also left unspecified] be forgiven." The voice-over by the unnamed "Man" (François Périer) presents the film and leads it along, giving us the illusion of taking part in the act of its creation. What we watch as we follow Godard as the Idiot/Prince take a trip first by car, then a plane commandeered by a suicidal pilot (there will be a near-death experience for all on board), is what may, or may not, feed into the film that has been commissioned. We are thus dealing with a film gleefully exhibiting its own means of production and exposing itself both as film and fiction, while also recording a possible return and passage to cinematic recuperation: delivery as potential deliverance and the lifting of a "curse." Indeed, *Soigne ta droite* is concerned directly with the status and fate of the cinematic image in terms of sin and redemption: can cinematic lack or error be righted, and if so, how? Specifically, can the final stage of a film, its projection, provide a means of salvation? Such underlying existential themes make *Soigne ta droite* a supremely philosophical film, and not simply on account of its many gags, which, if taken literally, define it in Agambenian terms as an exemplary philosophical exercise in gesturality. Agamben writes in his important conclusion to "Notes on Gesture":

> The gesture is [. . .] communication of a communicability. It has precisely nothing to say because what it shows is the being-in-language of human beings as pure mediality [. . .] it is always a *gag* in the proper meaning of the term, indicating first of all something that could be put in your mouth to hinder speech, as well as in the sense of the actor's improvization meant to compensate a loss of memory or an inability to speak. Cinema's essential "silence" (which has nothing to do with the presence or absence of a sound track) is, just like the silence of philosophy, exposure of the being-in-language of human beings: pure gesturality. (original emphasis)[14]

We shall return shortly to the particular implications of linking gesture, silence, and mediality.

But *Soigne ta droite* is also unparalleled in Godard's work for its sustained and systematic engagement with one particular literary source: Hermann Broch's extraordinary novel *The Death of Virgil* (1945). This *magnum opus* is a key point of reference in Godard's later work: already in *Soft and Hard* he had read out some passages with Anne-Marie Miéville concerning art's "despair" and "cruel beauty," and in episode 2B of *Histoire(s)* the actress Sabine Azéma will read out selected extracts on the same theme. In *Soigne ta droite*, while many authors circulate around the themes of death and deliverance, including Dostoyevsky (who provides the name of Godard's character permanently reading *The Idiot*), Racine, Lautréamont, and André Malraux (reworked passages from *Lazare* (*Lazarus*) (1974), a reflection on death occasioned by Malraux's miraculous recovery from a near-death experience of sleeping sickness and which explores themes of sacrifice, suicide, choice, fraternity and redemption),[15] entire sections of Albert Kohn's 1955 French translation of *The Death of Virgil* are recited at length by Périer on the soundtrack, providing the film with a center of gravity. Godard cites exclusively from "Fire—the Descent," the second stage in the Latin poet's final nineteen hours of life during which he agonizes over whether to burn the manuscript of the *Aeneid*, which he now regards as a failure because the society he eulogizes doesn't correspond to reality. Just as Virgil stands out from his miserable fellow men he passes in the slums, so the Idiot/Prince stands out in his quiet, self-possessed dignity from the cynical world he passes through. Broch, an Austrian Jewish writer who began the novel while briefly interned in a Nazi camp before being rescued, represents for Godard the artist at war with his chosen form but who, in the very act of creating, produces a unique statement of rare beauty about the triumph of art and the imagination. *The Death of Virgil* is an unstoppable, breathless, sumptuous flow of language in long, lyrical sentences rich in sensual imagery, and it generates many of the terms that appear in the film (emptiness, sacrifice, solitude, the soul, laughter, the universe, salvation, twilight, grace, the law). *Soigne ta droite* rehearses, too, some of the text's stylistic qualities: its perpetually expanding and endlessly self-correcting ruminations, its reversible chiastic formulations, and its fondness for interjections. Assorted fragments of the intertext are stitched together by Godard and then repeated (sometimes almost immediately) in ever new and surprising ways over different visuals in a continuous process of recombining, retouching, and recomposing. *King Lear* had included a reworking of Pierre Reverdy's prose poem "L'Image" (1918), a powerful manifesto for the complex images of Godard's later work and a model of montage as the distant and just association of ideas generating so-called true emotion "because born outside of all imitation, all evocation and all resemblance."[16] *Soigne ta droite* takes the poetics of emotion to an entirely new level, however, since Broch provides a model of decreation conceived not as a philosophical concept in Agambenian terms but rather as a process of poetic experimentation (the word is used explicitly in the novel). Metaphor becomes metamorphosis and transmutation, and repetition is experienced as difference and variation in an endless, ever more intricate and subtle movement of modification, reversal, permutation, reformulation, and amplification.

Figure 4.1. Godard as the Idiot/Prince in flight in *Soigne ta droite* (1987).

Soigne ta droite thus offers a fascinating case of two different forms and means of revelation, one messianic, the other poetic, and it does so through set sequences of audiovisual decreation. Although it doesn't actually employ stop-start motion, its pushing of the cinematic image out of and beyond itself to the point of abstraction (the "*sans image*") and to something more poetic, even musical, marks the culmination of an intensive period of cinematic experimentation by Godard inspired by the "derealizing" techniques of videographic montage, from *Sauve qui peut (la vie)*, which was also a reinvigorated return to the body and the "homeland of gesture" (Agamben), to the distortion and transformation of the art image in *Passion* and *Scénario du film* Passion.[17] By examining in detail Godard's immersive encounter with Broch and poetics through the prism of Agamben, and thus submitting a philosophy of cinema to a concrete instance of aesthetic practice, I want to put to the test Agamben's assumptions about the "neutrality" of the aesthetic sphere in film, and specifically about cinema as simply the setting for "gesture" understood as both the demonstration of mediality, which subtracts from "the false wholeness of identity or the falseness of the image as unity," and, more critically, "the harnessing of the collapse of subjectivity and aesthetics."[18] I will argue that by aesthetically investing the primary cinematic gestures of projection and montage, Godard draws out some of the key, underlying principles of Agamben's theory of gestural cinema while also exposing some of its limitations as a philosophy of film. To illuminate Godard and Agamben mutually in this way will allow us to appreciate the particular significance of Agamben's writing on cinema for thinking not only about Godard, but also about the very relations between the ethical and the aesthetic.

The Law of the Crystal: Revealing the Image from Within

Soigne ta droite plays out as a kind of virtual film where everything is being piloted: the allegorical-style sketches that are being performed for the eventual possible film by the Idiot/Prince; Fred Chichin and Catherine Ringer (the French pop rock group, Les Rita Mitsouko) searching for the right sound and harmony as they lay down tracks for a new album (Godard mixes final versions of the songs with their nascent forms, producing a strange interfragmentation of finished and unfinished music); the Individual (Jacques Villeret) assuming multiple roles as he tries to find "a place on earth" (as gardener, as bored golfer's caddy, as suicidal actor, as lothario waltzing with a mysterious silent woman who strips for him); and above all the same shots and passages being tried out and rehearsed in different sequences and then repeated. The recurring, teasing image of the half-open French window facing out towards the sea and sky at Trouville (the beach is always framed by doors and a balcony which mediate our access to the water) is linked directly to a passage from *Lazare* about Westerners "dramatizing" death as the door that one passes through to go from one room (life) into another (the beyond). This crystalizes the theme of light and its relationship to the other side as the film's dominant metaphor for its confrontation with death (Godard, in fact, shoots deliberately in the direction of the light source here). This is a film forever about to pass new limits, borders, and thresholds in a gesture of opening up to the world and to the light, like the casual, flickering reflection of a window frame captured on an apartment wall in the form of star.

Figure 4.2. Fred Chichin and Catherine Ringer (Les Rita Mitsouko) laying down tracks in *Soigne ta droite* (1987).

A strong earthbound sense of linear narrative direction is retained, however, as we count down in anticipation of the delivery and projection of the Idiot/Prince's film, *Une place sur la terre*, and a potential event of cinematic salvation through a resolution of form. The process is set in motion by the one "spectacular" moment of cinematic gesture in the film when Godard, on being presented with a pile of large cans of cinema film (the footage of the completed film-within-a-film), is knocked into by another figure disembarking and falls down an aircraft ramp in loud cacophony. We have here a by-now-familiar Godard theme of the (self-)sacrifice required of cinema linked to its concrete "fall," and, as we saw in chapter 3, the sequence will be directly incorporated into the final part of episode IB of *Histoire(s)* where it is juxtaposed with Maria Casarès reciting on the soundtrack a French translation of Heidegger's "What Are Poets For?." As the Idiot/Price lies on the tarmac the pilot's wife negotiates with him to purchase the film simply because the cans gleam like diamonds. The film has now looped the loop: the pilot has bought the film in which all the characters we have seen are playing, and it can therefore now be projected. Yet *Soigne ta droite* is also moving in other directions guided by other manifestations of cinematic gesture, starting with a long, six-minute sequence in the train (intercut by shots of Les Rita Mitsouko in the studio) with a police inspector (Rufus) deporting the Individual, now a Belgian prisoner, over the French border. The Individual's right arm is handcuffed to the curtain rod of the window (a reference to Jean-Pierre Melville's *Le Cercle rouge* (1970), which also featured Périer), and we see the handcuffs in close-up focus, then out of focus, against the passing landscape as the two figures indulge in an old game of insults, trade memories of happier times of political comradeship (evocations of Sartre's dirty political hands in *Les Mains sales* [1948] abound), and consider the "errors" and "suffering" that history does not allow.[19] There is an unexpected move towards fraternity and solidarity when the inspector extends his hand towards the cuffed wrist and makes physical contact, the two arms thus meeting at the apex of a triangle. Yet the gesture is revealed as empty and goes nowhere. What follows is a formal counterresponse to the failure of communication and gesture through a series of set pieces focused on the very grammar of cinema, and which develop the notion of gesture in a continuously evolving process of metaphorization and poetic transformation of the cinematic image: first focus pull, then projection, finally montage.

As the voice-over by Périer explains over a close-up shot of Ringer deep in thought that he forgot to say that the policeman on the train towards the border forgot to utter the words "what would one do without the dead?" (circularity and commentary appear boundless in this film), Godard cuts on the word "policeman" to a blurred, out-of-focus image rendered abstract. The dark shape that runs vertically down the frame is gradually brought into focus and revealed as a wooden pole with lines of barbed wire in dark silhouette against a pale sky. On the word "sentence" the shot is cut to an extreme close-up of barbed wire, this time in focus. The wire soon recedes out of focus and dematerializes in the light to the point of its virtual disappearance. Simultaneously, the camera moves slightly upwards to disclose a jumble of human figures strewn on the ground. Finally, several shots later, over a close-up of a young woman lying face down, and as Périer begins another compressed remolding of a passage from Broch, Godard cuts abruptly to a shot of barbed wire running diagonally in focus across the frame. On the soundtrack we hear: "The Individual shuddered, and in a final piercing through of the dream's border, with a final shattering of every sort of image, in a last shattering of memory, the dream grew [. . .] he growing with it: his thinking had become greater than any form of thinking [. . .] it became a second immensity [. . .] it became the law that caused the crystal to grow [. . .] stated in the crystal, stated through music, but over and above that, expressing the music of the crystal." At the mention of "a last shattering of memory" the barbed wire withdraws out of focus, before being once again restored to full focus with the phrase "a second immensity." This arresting *plan-séquence*, a play of shifting movement, countermovement, and redefinition within the image, comes to an end with a return to Ringer and Chichin in the studio peering up into the artificial light.

Daniel Morgan rightly states that Godard's nonnarrative use of focus pulls explores "the resources of aesthetics in and through cinema" and takes mythic (i.e., nonlinear) time out of profane time (i.e., time as history and duration).[20] In these moments of uncertainty, he argues, it's the look of images, not what they represent, that becomes the attraction—one that is extended by a further instance of focus pull almost immediately after. This time two seated figures staring blankly in a café are held in a background flux of gently pulsating colors and amorphous forms for almost fifteen seconds before being gradually pulled into focus. While Morgan is certainly right about Godard's foregrounding here of the processes of perception, making this a supremely (meta)cinematic moment, more needs to be said about this extended formal scene and its iconography. To the roars of a large sports crowd accompanied on the soundtrack by heavy metal clanking, the Individual is pictured lying in a section of a stadium with other people barely alive and breathing (an obvious reference to the Heysel Stadium disaster in May 1985). Yet this also, of course, evokes the internment camps for deportation during the Holocaust such as the Vélodrome d'Hiver in Paris in 1942, and when one figure on the stadium floor says he lives in the Hôtel Terminus (the title of Marcel Ophuls's 1988 documentary on Klaus Barbie), the allusion to concentration camp victims in a mass grave is unmistakable. This is developed further when we consider what is being related by Périer simultaneously on the soundtrack: "[A] second immensity, it became the law that presides over the development of crystal." The association with Kristallnacht is complete. Moreover, the Individual's remark about suffering is matched with a shot of Ringer, the daughter of a Holocaust survivor, looking straight at the camera (the whole sequence is effectively bookended by shots of Ringer). The voice-over continues in a separate phrase extracted directly from Malraux: "Death is the path towards the light."

Figure 4.3. Another extended focus-pull in *Soigne ta droite* (1987).

Yet the focus pulls are not only an ethical matter but also an object of properly cinematic strangeness and beauty that seems to come from within the image itself. They are a pure effect of the camera yet somehow appear in excess of it, in a constant movement of repetition, expansion, and extension. Godard, I would argue, is tapping here into the kinetic potential of the (silent) image to release its latent energy and capacity for movement *through* form and *out of* form. The pulls also constitute, in conjunction with the soundtrack, a familiar Godardian chiastic reversal between image and word. In the first instance, as we hear "his thinking had become greater than any form of thinking," the wire diminishes in size and dematerializes into a formless blur, thus joining the "immensity" articulated on the voice-over. In the second case, however, as the image comes back into focus, we hear synthesizers in free-flow, as if the sound and image were now working together in mutual dilation and distension: the image comes into being through the surge of sound. Music can help restore objects into focus and bring them back to life. The passage from Broch itself brings the theme of music directly to the fore with its utterly mysterious chiastic-sounding and self-extending phrase about the dissolution of thought and its transformation into a second "immensity": "it [his thinking] became the law that caused the crystal to grow [. . .] stated in crystal, stated through music, but over and above that, expressing the music of the crystal." Hence, the idea of *decreating* the image ("a final shattering of every sort of image") is matched precisely by the advent of the music of the crystal on the soundtrack. (It is a crucial fact that although the visual image may sometimes appear blocked by repetition in *Soigne ta droite*, the soundtrack of voice and music always seems to be moving forwards and continuously evolving in a live process of creativity and annunciation.)

I want to suggest that, in a manner which has much to do with Agamben's subtraction of gesture from within the image, something latent within the image is imposing itself here. It is greater than all thought and for the moment has no name, except for the oxymoronic, ethereal beauty of the phrase "the music of the crystal," which has the poetic force of a montage of opposing terms (solid/diffuse). It is indeed something miraculous, as made clear by the continuation of Malraux's phrase on death that immediately follows: "One knows this when one has returned from something like it." Crucially, Godard qualifies this quote by adding: "From music, perhaps. But which is going to rise up from ancient times." In *Soigne ta droite*, as in Broch, the potential for accelerating intensity and amplification—a voyage into ever-deepening, resounding, enveloping, penetrating, radiating, vibrating profundity and emotion, or "*rayonnement*"—appears inexhaustible, like the flow of music itself. A different manifestation of the same poetic movement and play with form occurs in the scene on the golf course, when the camera suddenly lifts up into the trees and drifts through the branches to the music of Ringer's distorted voice as it gently swells into being. This unheralded harmony of music and image is only brief, and it happens as Périer intones another full passage from Broch about a still deeper silence transmuting into waiting like a further irradiation of light, and the need to achieve a creative act in order to move beyond the law of destiny, random chance, and dreams and so overcome the evil spell. He invokes

> a still stronger irradiation, perhaps even a second and more pervading immensity, in order that from this one *the divine might stream out freshly again, abolishing evil forever*. It was an undirected waiting, as undirected as the radiation, but for all that directed to the waiter, the dreamer; it was a sort of invitation to him to make a final attempt, a last creative effort to get *outside of the dream, outside of fate, outside of chance, outside of form, outside of himself*. (My emphasis)

Music for Godard always stands for something prior and original and reversible, both passive and active, since it both inheres within, and *gestures* beyond, the image, in positive, salutary extension.[21] In the case of Les Rita Mitsouko, the continual ebb and flow of extended synths, swirling reverb and other digitally enhanced vocal and musical effects forming and deforming provide the film with its sensuous, sensurround wrap and sonic extension.

Just as there is a running opposition in Agamben between "gesture" in the singular and "gestures" in the plural with their false unity, so in Godard, who also roams freely between the concrete and abstract, there are two kinds of valency of the image. The train episode was framed by an "obvious" and highly loaded image of hand gesture as sign of (failed) political solidarity—a physical gesture within the image that demands to be decoded. But there's also another image *as* gesture: a more abstract and self-reflexive, yet also more properly cinematic, kind of image that exhibits itself as such and entails a loss of clarity and meaning. This is a decreation of the image pushed now to the level of mystery, silence, and unreadability, and ultimately beyond the normal bounds of legibility and vision to the realm of the "*sans image.*" For Agamben, gesture "is the other side of the commodity that lets the "crystals of this common social substance" sink into the situation."[22] In the hands of Godard, however, the commodified image gives way to an idea of crystal that escapes social definition and takes the situation of cinema to an altogether different, abstract, and poetic realm. This process of transformation reveals itself as a moment of extreme beauty that resists simple definition and is best left in the raw, mineral state of "the music of the crystal." It is not just that Ringer herself embodies this, for the reasons given: music is a liminal movement at the frontier of the senses where the image becomes light and silence becomes sound. The law of music subsumes all others: language, repetition, fate, dreams.

Stabbing Darkness in the Back: The Silence of the Gesture

Godard immediately takes these ideas further within the framework of projection which plays out in different forms in the final stages of the film and is formally initiated by a blunt gesture of repetition through the reinsertion of the film's opening credits. The first instance is a pure gag conducted in silence. The screening of the Idiot/Prince's completed film *Une place sur la terre* sees the airline pilot and his wife take up their places along the Seine and simply gaze out upon Paris after their brush with death. This is cinema reenvisioned as Bazin's "window on the world." The gag not only undermines knowledge by underlining the constitutive gap of *Soigne ta droite* (we will never "know" if the film by Godard's character is the one by Godard we've been watching), but also it presents cinema in ideal Godardian terms as a shared and ritualized public site of subjective projection whereby we project creatively onto the "real."[23] Yet this moment of (self-)projection is also framed in the express terms of human gesture: the pilot salutes what he gazes at off-screen, while his wife appears to be praying in front of it, her converging arms replicating the triangular shape limned by the policeman and the prisoner's hands on the train. Projection is thus being presented as a metacinematic gesture that stands in counterpoint to abortive political gesture and carries the open promise of renewed collective relations.

The second scene of projection takes place shortly after in the more traditional setting of a projection booth with Périer now assuming the role of projectionist and donning blue overalls for the occasion. It is prefaced with a cut to yet another shot of the sun setting over the water taken from within the room in Trouville with its half-open French window, as if waiting for some new type of poetic turning or troping and transformation. A clock ticking on the soundtrack furthers the mood of suspense and expectation of what the "real" projection will reveal. We again hear the passage from Broch used for the second sequence of focus pull about whether evil still existed and the need to wait for the day-star to obtain a reply from the voice of the Universe. This passage is now extended, however, by a separate passage about silence (also derived from Broch) that includes another chiastic construction centered on silence and muteness: "This time the awareness of their fault leaves them speechless, their lack of words renders them this time aware of their fault."[24] Silence morphs effortlessly into vision in the words that follow, yet this is reversed almost immediately into nonvision: "[B]eholding this silence, the man also yearned to open his mouth in a last mute cry of horror. Yet still while seeing it, almost before he had really seen it, he no longer saw anything." This silent, double movement of vision and nonvision is matched in the image in a totally unforeseen way. After checking the equipment and setting up the reels, and as we hear a delayed repetition of the portentous phrase "But it's in the back that the light will stab the darkness," Périer finally presses the button. Ignition. Except that Godard refuses us entry into the auditorium to see the image projected onto the cinema screen, still less the beam of light striking it. Instead, we remain firmly within the borders of the booth like a cave or grotto—but for what kind of new image exactly?

Figure 4.4. François Périer preparing for the final event of cinematic projection in *Soigne ta droite* (1987).

We glimpse two brief shots, separated by another image of the French window, of the celluloid passing though the projector and reflected in a plate of glass in the center of the dragon-like apparatus. Two initially indecipherable images can just be made out, yet at an angle, a little like the blurred images of the focus pull, though here with the extra complication that they seem to be extreme close-ups of something human enlarged and inverted by the reflection, as well as in suspended motion. The first image contains a small smearing of red, like human lips coated in lipstick; the second appears more upright and is devoid of color. These are composite images of the human and the mechanical, of reflection and shadow, created by the projector's silhouette against a white wall and the frames of celluloid passing through the projector and reflected and magnified in a mirror.

In this prismatic and chromatic play with motion, size, perspective, and color, the cinematic image is exposing and exhibiting itself as pure process. Mute like the suffocated human cry in the Broch passage, these strange, silent images recall the extreme close-ups of silent cinema contained in *Histoire(s)* (the open-mouthed female figure from Eisenstein's *Battleship Potemkin* [1925], for instance), or, better still, the hybrid images of faces of cinema in the book of *Histoire(s)* where each miraculous image resurrected from the video machine appears to be screaming in the eerie silence of the page. In both cases we are being asked to consider the relations between knowledge, beauty, aesthetic form, and the real. We know that these evanescent, abstractifying images are not an "error" because they constitute a deliberate repetition in a tightly edited sequence of montage. Indeed, the repetition of the pivotal phrase about the light and darkness generates a self-reflexive drama of repetition and interruption revolving around the dividing image of the half-open window frame. On the soundtrack we hear Ringer's voice, more a hushed reverb whisper than a fully vocalized phrase, celebrating two girls dancing at a bar, a song heard earlier during the scene of the excluded young girl but delivered now in a strange, ethereal, sonic burst that complements the seemingly intractable images. Yet it is enough to establish a relation between the silent gesture of suspended lips and the female voice and for us to read the two disembodied images evoking silent cinema as radiations of Ringer herself.

We have been through the ringer here! We have moved across different forms of reality in the blink of an eye—so fast, in fact, that we barely see the image for what it is exactly, except *as* image, thereby escaping the claws of cognition and interpretation. Godard is typically forging a path out of his own signifying chains: the film's inherent structure of repetition of shots is ruptured by the act of repetition itself which results in a totally new kind of shot in the film. In the intensive *mise-en-abyme* of repetition, mediation, and framing (the repetition of film frames within the frame of the projector enframed within the image), cinema is taken self-reflexively to the borders of silence. In the process, projection is revealed ultimately as an *effect* of montage. Further, the disturbance (*fracassement*) and vibration within the logic of repetition that reverberates with the violence of the action related ("stab the darkness") result in an explosion of the image that opens it up to the ever-deepening, obscure, unfathomable mystery of cinematic creation beyond control and containment. This act of self-exhibition and revelation in the moment of projection as montage, a material moment of pure energy and light, is also an act of release: the figure of Ringer, as uncontrollable and "unframable" now as her earlier involuntary gesture of tapping her fingers on the table to the rhythms in her head during a break in recording, escapes the symbolic frame it was briefly held in during the focus pull moment (the confluence of crystal and Kristallnacht) to become simply film *rolling through*.

Figure 4.5. The Individual (Jacques Villeret) looking at the young girl behind the French window peering in, in *Soigne ta droite* (1987).

We can loop this moment back, as the lyrics of the music invite us to, to the film's other female image-within-the-image: that of the young girl outside on the balcony at Trouville looking at the Individual through the glass and reflected in miniature in the facing mirror at the back of the apartment (she was effectively imprisoned within the frame while remaining outside it). It was a brutal image of exclusion: the window slams back repeatedly on her face. A figment possibly of his own imagination (she disappears when he barks "Come in"), the excluded girl was associated with the noise and life of the world outside opposed to the narcissistic self-seclusion of the Individual reliant on his prerecorded phrases from Beckett on the tape-recorder for any contact with visual reality ("An image had appeared . . ."). He stands, in fact, as a metaphor for the individual, self-sufficient image which, for Godard, endorsing Robert Bresson, thwarts the cinematographic system because it risks not transforming itself through contact with other images.[25] For what is at stake for Godard is always the performability of the image within a larger signifying system rather than any innate expressivity it may possess. The gesture of montage is thus now fully revealed as one of inclusion and new relations or communication across form: a poetic process of mystery and metamorphosis that embraces, recombines, and redeems even the most vulnerable and remote of images within the same visual and aural frame. The final image, the last in a three-stage edited sequence of the recurring still-frame images of the half-open window, is of the sunset, but in an intense form that casts the much closer window frame in shadow against the dense, white cirrus clouds to create the effect of a black-and-white image. It gleams with possibility. All is still to play for in this ultimate return to something approximating photography or silent cinema since all is still to be heard. The final words of the voice-over invoke Broch again, but in a passage not heard before: "And then, very gently, as if not to alarm him, the whispering that the man had already heard a long time before, before even his very existence, started again." We can link this final affirmative note of nonresolution and mystery—the continuous advent of sound as ungraspable and uncontainable as the light—to *The Death of Virgil* itself which ends with a continuous "rumbling" and "flooding sound" of the elusive, ineffable Word beyond all understanding, language, and speech.[26] We can never know for sure if the originary "error" and curse of *Soigne ta droite* have been lifted and redeemed by the music and light of the crystal. Instead, we're left with the continuum of *light as sound*—the unquenchable hope of the recovery and redemption of love and innocence.[27] (The film's repeated passage about Dostoyevsky's obsessive interest in the torture of an innocent child (a reworking of Malraux) always carried, of course, its own counterresponse: "the smallest act of heroism or love is no less fascinating than torture.")

A similar type of recursion to the gesturality of silent cinema occurred in the last stages of *King Lear* where it took a nonhuman form. Wearing a loose, white, shroud-like dress Cordelia had led a white horse (the pale horse of Death?) into and out of a woodland clearing, her father Learo lamenting: "She's gone forever. She's dead as earth. Lend me a looking glass." The sequence was sealed by a *tableau vivant* of Cordelia dead, stretched out on a rock by the side of the lake as Learo stands with his back to us holding a shotgun and facing the lake and sky like a Rückenfigur in a Casper David Friedrich painting. This highly ambiguous image of death and incest appeared to correspond to the "new image" of cinema reborn that William and Edgar were looking for following the sacrifice exacted by cinema (Pluggy's death). It is accompanied by a female voice-over quoting the rapturous ending to Virginia Woolf's *The Waves* (1931) about a proud horse ridden by the narrator against the enemy, "Death." Suddenly, after the intertitle: "King Lear / A Study," the white horse that Cordelia had led away now returns, and in a dynamic, wild form. Photographed in long-shot by the water's edge, the horse races into the left foreground as if towards the camera and past the viewer in stop-start motion. The shot, lasting only a matter of seconds, had the electroshock force of a sequence in early primitive cinema projected and seen as if for the first time, like Muybridge's horses captured in pristine motion. Indeed, the horse seemed to silence language in its tracks with its rare and fleeting beauty (the loud recital of a Shakespeare sonnet by Mr. Alien [Woody Allen] in the editing suite ceased and only a light background hum or drone was audible). As Marc Robinson has elegantly put it, this is an image whose beauty is "its own justification."[28] Moreover, the horse carries no one on its back and is thus free of the burden of death or of any other type of symbol. It veers off-frame, destination unknown, as mysteriously and autonomously as it sprang into motion. In fact, like the immediate sensation of vision as nonvision in the Broch passage, it all happens so quickly that we cannot grasp its meaning: the horse runs free, as it were, beyond cognition and easy interpretation, and can't be contained or reduced to an object of scientific knowledge. Dislocated in the film, without authorship or direction, it can be experienced only as motion and beauty and release.

Figure 4.6. The revelation of motion: Cordelia's white horse released into stop-start motion in *King Lear* (1987).

This stunning shot thus stands in direct contrast to the symbolically encased, static *tableau vivant*. The fact that it is stop-started means that we receive it directly as a pure effect of acceleration and deceleration. Indeed, it is a supremely metacinematic moment of exhibition and projection, of pure means as Agamben would term it, like dance. For it is not an expression of anything specific but rather an event of pure gesture and affect happening *now* in the filmic present. This sudden bolt of energy and sensation presents the image as a uniquely cinematic sequence of edited motion in time, and there is something precisely musical about it, in the sense that, as I will attempt to show in chapter 5, music enjoys a concrete and plastic status in Godard and can operate autonomously and spring eternally afresh in time.

In a film such as *King Lear*, which hangs heavy like so much of late Godard with the betrayed promise of silent film that was never allowed to find true montage before spectacle and the master narratives of sex and war took over (one of the film's many instances of betrayal and "violent silence"), it is precisely by tapping into the rich kinetic deposits of silent cinema that Godard finds a way forward *against death*. This is nothing less than a liberation of the image as gesture which thus becomes the name for all that is *not* image. Yet if the horse in free motion evokes a Muybridge study, it also harks back to another Muybridge image of a soldier carrying a gun, presented by Agamben as an example of the breakdown of bourgeois gesture (we don't know what the solider is doing or where he is going). What occurs in Agamben's work under the sign of lost bourgeois gestures and meaning in the mechanical age of reproduction returns in Godard as pure gesture and mystery in the postmodern age. Which is to say, what Agamben would adduce in the case of the bolting horse as a historical sign of the dissolution of gesture, that is, the moment when, as he describes it in "Notes on Gesture," cinema helped destroy the meaning of human gestures at the dawn of modernity and then proceeded to commemorate their loss obsessively, often in glaring close-up, is replayed positively here as pure cinematic energy—released into the light as the pure joy and ineluctable beauty of the image. In other words, the ethically negative in Agamben returns in Godard as ethically and aesthetically positive. What I am suggesting here is that the event of beauty in Godard's cinema, released via stop-start motion in an uncontrolled rush of energy, means that gesture is always ethico-aesthetic in its nature and mystery. It is not simply that cinema must expose and display its own means of production (a mere question of formal method and style), but also that it must enter a new realm of mystery and undecidability that lies within and beyond the literal image and is formed of opposites. This is the territory of montage which, if properly executed, can generate the flash and energy of the unexpected and unimagined, a sign of cinema's eternal self-renewal.

Hence, Agamben's philosophical proposition of gesture as "a moment of art subtracted from the neutrality of aesthetics" and "pure praxis"[29] runs counter to Godard's artistic method. *Soigne ta droite*, like *King Lear*, takes us at privileged moments to the far shores of the poetic and aesthetic where the image, reconceived and remade in montage, is restored to its original silence and lost aura (the last words of *King Lear*, taken from the play, are a reaffirmation of both touch and silence: "If that her [Cordelia's] breath will mist or stain the stone, why, then she lives"). Silence has, in fact, a fundamental role in Godardian montage, in particular the double movement of montage in *Histoire(s)* where, as we saw in chapter 2, "horizontal" moments of confluence, contiguity, conjunction, and coincidence, which resist the vertical pull of his characteristically dense, rhetorical, and aggressively intellectual maneuvers, constitute a kind of countermovement in the videographic montage: a "minimal" moment of metonymy whereby images are linked and molded together by contour, outline, gesture, silhouette, and profile. Such nondiscursive moments of association, contiguity, and conjunction trace as if spontaneously the interrelations of human form at the level of shape and figure. This play of detail operates as if in silence since it is never directly commented on or integrated or rationalized as part of an argument or thesis. Indeed, throughout *Histoire(s)* the nonlinguistic resists any totalizing conceptualization or theorization and thus remains a pure affective and inclusive moment of seeing and feeling rather than one of interpretation. More generally, the ethico-aesthetic in Godard is poetic adventure, surprise, flash, affect, combustion, and he can make it happen *now*. The force and challenge of his later work is precisely to jump-start and recharge cinema and human relations by delivering on the promise of silent cinema through the alchemy of poetic montage, a crucible of emotion capable of generating fraternal warmth. This is the beauty and the passion of Godard's cinematic gesture.

Figure 4.7. A final iteration of the half-open window onto the sea and sky in the closing sequence of *Soigne ta droite* (1987).

Cinema: The Sphere of Pure Means

Agamben the philosopher has thrown into powerful relief Godard the artist. In *Soigne ta droite* Godard starts out from a position of imagelessness (the end of cinema) and sets about retrieving and recuperating it by returning it to silence and the *sans image*. For Godard, the power of cinema and cinematic montage is to release the image from its frozen state by revealing its transformative potential and poetic extensibility. Cinematic gesture, or the mystery and aura of the image in cinema, is taken always beyond a strictly physical level to something increasingly abstract, on the borders of music and operating as pure affect. Godard's cinematic gesture—the gesture of refinding and resurrecting cinema today through montage—always involves an emotional return from the dead. This is the moment when Godard's work suddenly appears to revert to the forms of silent cinema, and it invariably functions in the chiastic mode of repetition as reversal and return. Such mediality is congruent with the shared aims of Agamben and Debord, who reveal how the essential silence of cinema can expose our being-in-language or "pure gesturality" by making us reflect at privileged moments of stoppage and repetition on the image *qua* image. Yet while he may consistently promote the idea in *Histoire(s)* that the cinematograph was an instrument designed for thinking and for creating "forms that think" (and certainly the complex processes of montage at work, its sublime crossings and transfigurations, testify to Godard's powerful manipulation of montage as a form of thought), Godard is fully aware that there must also always be a margin for beauty, error, and mystery, or the unexplainable and unknowable.

Something beyond explicit discourse; something like the crystal of the music which transforms from light into sound before it can be intellectually grasped. Devoted to creating the conditions of a new transformative ethico-aesthetics, Godard recovers gesture *aesthetically* as the realm of the poetic *and* the ethical (relationality/communicability). Indeed, for Godard, the ethical is inherent within the aesthetic and will be revealed in the unique poetic processes of cinematic montage ("at the time of the resurrection").

Godard's natural commitment to the poetic and the aesthetic as a means of revealing the ethical thus complicates any simple notion of his work as messianic in nature. As André Habib remarks of the images of nature flooding Godard's work of the 1980s, "[t]he time of the resurrection is not a messianic return, but rather a *parousie*, a 'second event' that redeems the real through images, the resurrection of a *presence*, lyrical and transformative, of cinema's aura" (original emphasis).[30] Of course, such undimmed faith in the ethics of the aesthetic, in an "infancy" of the image, may seem naïve and nostalgic, perhaps even regressive, but, as with the more intuitive, material counterdrives of *Histoire(s)*, Godard positively embraces sentimentality and child-like wonder in *Soigne ta droite* and in the concrete terms of poetic reversibility. As the Idiot/Prince he talks with his fellow female passenger of the "smiling regret" he sometimes feels—an apparent contradiction in terms but which doesn't spoil either of the two terms or feelings: "Time is therefore vertical here: sentiment is irreversible, or rather, the reversibility of being is sentimentalized here. The smile regrets, and regret smiles." This is inspired by Baudelaire's idea of "le regret souriant" as analyzed by that most aesthetically attuned of modern philosophers, Gaston Bachelard, who saw the image as representing the "vertical instant" of poetry: a time in which ambivalent sentiments can co-exist without being reduced to antithesis, simultaneity, or succession.[31]

To conclude, the possibility of redemption provided by the image, now revealed in its full potential as "gesture," is *real* in Godard—an eternal and self-renewing hope and optimism, the residue perhaps of his lingering socialist belief in an alternative future. Putting aside for a moment the obvious paradox and pathos of an artist passionately seeking to engage with his audience in the heat of the cinematic encounter and transmit the sparks of poetic illumination and revelation even though his films are no longer guaranteed a theatrical release (*Soigne ta droite* is a prime example), the portals of love and transformation always remain open for Godard, at least poetically speaking. For Agamben, however, all is always already over: the gestures of the nineteenth-century bourgeoisie are no more and can only be mourned, interminably and irremediably. For a philosopher like Agamben, any temptation to soar to aesthetic transcendence is simply not an option. "Notes on Gesture" ends with the statement: "*Politics is the sphere of pure means, that is, of the absolute and complete gesturality of human beings*" (original emphasis).[32] Godard's work proves otherwise by replacing "politics" with "cinema." Yet in both cases gesturality entails the resurrection of the human in all its materiality, physicality, and fraternity, or what we might call in shorthand form "the body of cinema" shorn of all preestablished meanings and values (however Christian the themes of resurrection and recuperation may sometimes loom in Godard). It is this shared, absolute commitment to the human that encourages the idea that Godard and Agamben may eventually engage with each other directly, and that artist and philosopher will cross over to each other in their very differences through the incandescence of cinematic traffic.

5

Music, Love, and the Cinematic Event

> If I speak in the tongues of mortals and of angels, but do not have love, I am a noisy gong or a clanging cymbal.
>
> —1 Corinthians 13

> Music is beyond, whereas literature and cinema are on earth.
>
> —J.-L. Godard

The Infinity of Music

For a filmmaker so knowing and eloquent about his own method, Godard is singularly unenlightening about his use of music. When not simply silent on the matter, he often adopts a cavalier public attitude to what is without doubt a major creative resource. During a radio interview in 2002 with the film critic Thierry Jousse devoted to his practice of music and creation of "sound screens," Godard flaunts the fact that he is not a musician and repeats his by now standard line that it was the music producer and head of ECM Records Manfred Eicher who suggested, and voluntarily supplied, much of the music in his films since the mid-1980s.[1] In addition, serial music such as Boulez is peremptorily dismissed, and even the contemporary composer David Darling, whose work is omnipresent in Godard's later work, is downgraded and miscategorized as "minor" film music. This type of impatient reaction reaches a comic level with Godard's screen persona, notably in Anne-Marie Miéville's *Nous sommes tous encore ici* (1997), where the irascible "Lui" complains that classical works are now played much faster than when originally performed and thus offer no comfort. In fact, whenever he can, Godard chooses to divert the discussion of music to questions of art and painting on which he has a well-honed discourse and possesses even practical experience, including his unique collaboration (already noted in chapter 1) entitled *Film-tract No. 1968* (aka *Le Rouge*) with the artist Gérard Fromanger with whom he attended drawing lessons during the late 1960s. It is as if Godard were absolving himself of any knowledge of music, as though his wide-ranging use of the Western musical canon were simply instinctive and beyond analysis. Composers he uses are credited in his films, but this is often a half-hearted gesture, the lists of names remaining distinctly vague and incomplete. Ironically, the only real moment in his work where there is any serious attempt at a discourse on musical history occurs in *Week-end* where, as the camera tracks 360 degrees around the piano in the farmyard, the traveling musician Paul Gégauff explains that all modern music springs from Mozart. And Mozart will remain uncontroversially the standard icon of Western music for Godard right up to *For Ever Mozart* and beyond.

Why should Godard wish to draw such a marked veil over his musical practice, especially when the sound design of his films over the last thirty-five years or so has become ever more musically dense and complex, often comprising whole swathes of the ECM "New Series" catalog, and when his collaboration with the sound editor and engineer François Musy since the early 1980s has proved to be one of the most consistent and fertile?[2] This is a basic question that has been evaded by most critics who consider Godard a remarkable exponent of film sound yet prefer to follow his lead and approach him more as a "painter of images" or even sculptor carving audible space, as in the case of *Prénom Carmen* which explicitly evokes certain Rodin statues during the love scenes set in Trouville (see Godard's illustrated presentation of the film in Bergala 1985: 557–73).[3] This state of critical affairs is all the more unfortunate for the fact that the soundtracks of later works like *Nouvelle Vague* and *Histoire(s) du cinéma* are commercially available and ripe for analysis. Godard even remarks of *Nouvelle Vague*: "[M]y film, if you listen to the soundtrack without the images, will turn out even better."[4] It is essential from the outset to emphasize the steady and frankly astonishing evolution in Godard's use of music. Bach, Beethoven, and Mozart were all in play in the early shorts, of course, leading to their ironic dissection and counterpointing with contemporary images in the feature films of the 1960s (Bach, Vivaldi, and Schubert mixed with Stockhausen in *La Chinoise*, for instance).[5] This was extended by Godard's calculated and parodic overuse of specially commissioned theme music in films like *Le Mépris* (by Georges Delerue), *Pierrot le fou*, and *Week-end* (both by Antoine Duhamel). After his complete refusal to engage with music during the Dziga Vertov Group period on the grounds that it was bourgeois and elitist, Godard's return to commercial filmmaking in 1979 with *Sauve qui peut (la vie)* marked not simply a return to theme music (the commissioned electronic music by French-Lebanese composer Gabriel Yared), which determines here the stop-start rhythm of the image, but also the explicit formulation of a question that will haunt his subsequent work: "c'est quoi cette musique?" ("what's that music?") (the film's final section is expressly titled "Musique"). The works that follow are flush with music. In the timeless chords of the classics and church music in *Passion* (Ravel, Mozart, Beethoven, Dvořák, Fauré), it has a comforting function, helping to smooth over and render equal the opposed worlds of love and work, bosses and workers. *Prénom Carmen* presents in close-up the rehearsal of a series of Beethoven late string quartets (9, 10, 14, 15, 16) by the Prat Quartet, while *Je vous salue, Marie* unfolds as a kind of antiphony between its two featured composers, Bach and Dvořák.

Figure 5.1. The Prat Quartet rehearsing Beethoven in *Prénom Carmen* (1983).

Coinciding with the first episodes of *Histoire(s)* in the late 1980s, however, a whole new set of composers emerged, from early modernists such as Paul Hindemith, Anton Webern, Béla Bartók, Arthur Honegger, Arnold Schoenberg, and Dmitri Shostakovich, to contemporary composers and musicians such as Darling and Ketil Bjørnstad, Arvo Pärt, Heinz Holliger, and Giya Kancheli. The same sets of chords, harmonic phrases, and melodic tracks of these composers, by turns plaintive, strident, elegiac, and menacing, are heard across the different works of the 1990s, giving a powerful sense of identity and coherence to the period. Hindemith, in particular, who is first heard in *Le Rapport Darty* (1989), and who provides much of the initial steam power for *Histoire(s)*, constitutes a vital connecting link. In the case of Bartók, he is used in episode 1B, according to Godard, precisely as a substitute for the films that should have been made in Hungary during the first half of the twentieth century but were not. Significantly, the chosen extracts of these composers are played usually from the beginning of a section or movement and are allowed to continue, even if they are temporarily silenced or halted in their progress. Which is to say, Godard's new respect for the integrity of the musical sample means that it now has time to install itself on the ear and register its own direction. This is particularly noticeable in *Histoire(s)*, where, although Hindemith may be fragmented or Bach's *Prelude and Fugue in C Major* interrupted three times in succession (to take just two examples), still the music manages to impose itself, and often all the more clearly, resulting in sustained passages of music.⁶ In *Allemagne année 90 neuf zéro*, which is structured as a series of variations, composers like Bach and Webern not only prevail over a rapidly changing image-track but are also thematized in different ways. Gavin Bryars's doleful *After the Requiem* establishes early on the tone of the film, which is both an elegy for the vanished ghosts of German culture and a celebration of German music that has been tainted by the war and the legacy of guilt created by Hitler.⁷ To make a further small but crucial point: with the exception of the rehearsals by the contemporary French pop rock group Les Rita Mitsouko in *Soigne ta droite*, this varied music is almost exclusively prerecorded and thus operates on a highly different level from that of *Sauve qui peut* and *Prénom Carmen*, say, where live music takes center-stage in the image and as such can prove fatal.⁸ In the former, an orchestra plays Yared's theme music live on the side of the street following Paul Godard's car accident; in the latter, the string quartet arrives in time to accompany the death of Carmen at the hands of the police.⁹ In short, music becomes in Godard's later work an index of continuity and perdurability.

Again, in view of such major shifts in experimentation whereby music assumes an increasingly concrete and plastic role in his work, why should Godard fall so silent on his use of music, making it almost an untouchable object? He is clearly not just being coy or strategic. Music *is* a mystery for him, and part of its unique power is that he feels unable to define or decipher it. It is ineffable; it simply *is*.¹⁰ Even in a film like *Numéro deux*, dealing with blocked channels of communication and desire linked to violence, consumerism, and politics, music enjoys a special status: that of the unbelievable, or, more specifically, that of "seeing the unbelievable" ("*voir l'incroyable*"). This means seeing what is normally hidden from view, that is, the sexual realities of the nuclear family (see Fox 2015). The expression derives directly from the lyrics of Léo Ferré's song *Tu ne dis jamais rien* which Vanessa and her grandfather listen to at one point on headphones in a brief, shared moment of relative calm from the oppressive "factory" of family life. The same expression is used by Godard to describe the profound personal effect music often has on him:

> Music expresses the spiritual, and it provides inspiration. When I'm blind music is my little Antigone; it helps to see the unbelievable. And what has always interested me is the fact that musicians have no need for the image although people involved with images need music. I've always wanted to be able to pan or track during a war scene or love scene, in order to see the orchestra at the same time. And for music to take over at the moment when there is no more need to see the image. For music to express something else. What interests me is to see music—to try to see what one is hearing and to hear what one is seeing.¹¹

The final chiastic twist of this passage is a familiar rhetorical move by Godard, of course, and it lies behind the aesthetic conceit elaborated in *Passion* of "seeing" Fauré (*Piano Concerto for the Left Hand*) and "hearing" Rembrandt (*The Night Watch*).

The specifically romantic implications of Godard's approach, which promotes music as primarily a state of feeling, have already been well noted by Jacques Aumont, who runs with the idea of Antigone and accounts for Godard's obsessiveness with regard to music in terms of the maternal, since this involves immersion in an infinitely retold melody. According to Aumont, Godard is interested principally in the "idea" of music, or rather in the idea that he can make of the musical idea, and specifically in the "surging forth" ("*surgissement*") of that idea. With each instance of music, Aumont writes, Godard is looking for an idea or feeling in its raw state and power.[12]

It would be tempting to pursue further the psychoanalytic implications of Godard's relationship with music, especially since he acknowledges that he came to music via his mother's interest in Schumann. It could certainly be argued, for example, that music represents another aspect of Godard's "heterosexual fix," since whatever period of classical music he chooses to engage with, it is most usually with instrumental and symphonic forms, occasionally choral, but very rarely the operatic which, in its hybrid excess, can harbor gender instability, even perversion. One thinks of the grotesque sequence at the very start of *Sauve qui peut* where the unlocatable female soprano voice-off segues into a scene of gay male paranoia, with Godard's alter ego Paul (Jacques Dutronc) physically rebuffing the mature Italian bellboy who pursues him into the hotel car-park with confused memories of the night before and begs: "Ream me! Ream me the way half the navy did! There's nothing like a little good clean 'round eye'!." Paul's violent counterreaction recalls his namesake's (Jean-Pierre Léaud) utter confusion and shock in *Masculin Féminin* at glimpsing two men kiss in a cinema toilet. It may be compared, too, with the spectacle of male narcissism and self-absorption presented in the 1987 short *Armide*, the soundtrack of which is composed of different extracts from Jean-Baptiste Lully's opera, notably act II, scene 5, "Enfin, il est en ma puissance" ("At last, he is in my power"), although on first hearing it sounds largely the same piece. The struggle between opposing forces on the part of the two young cleaning women who vacillate between wishing to attract the bodybuilders' attention and entertaining fantasies of murderous revenge for feeling sexually ignored (they draw a knife on the back of one man then withdraw it, and shout out separately at the end "Oui!" and "Non!") is reflected and amplified on a formal level precisely by the tension created on the soundtrack by Godard's rearrangement of scenes and the fact that the flow of the music is consistently interrupted by silence.[13] The twin features here of male indifference and (dis)continuous musical sound were also explored in the earlier video short *Changer d'image*, where Godard films himself being physically beaten by another man. On the soundtrack he is denigrated as "the idiot" by a third-person narrator while concussive orchestral music (possibly Beethoven though it remains deliberately generic and indiscriminate in the brutal din) plays on heartlessly in the background. The contemporaneous video short, *Lettre à Freddy Buache*, offers a counterexample: Godard films himself close to the turntable while listening attentively to the whole euphonious sweep of Ravel's *Boléro*, as if unwilling to relinquish any authorial control and thereby expose himself to unforeseen emotional disturbance or sexual danger.

Figure 5.2. Godard listening to Ravel in *Lettre à Freddy Buache* (1981).

Such a fixed thematic approach would, however, reduce Godard's rich and multiple sonic perspectives to a single fantasy complex and suggest merely an ongoing Oedipus-like struggle with the classical Grand Masters. Indeed, according to this reading, Godard would still be stuck in the groove of Éric Rohmer's *Le Signe du lion* (1958), where in a cameo role he played a partygoer listening again and again to the same opening bars of the slow movement of Beethoven's *Ninth String Quartet*. To return to the passage cited above, it would also entirely overlook how Godard positions music as something both already "there" and "other," at the limits of his artistic practice. Music inspires him to create and beckons even when the visual image proves redundant. A concerted wish by Godard to negotiate and channel this apparently inexhaustible source of artistic desire might perhaps help to explain his increasingly involved investment in music over recent decades. Yet this is still to remain on the level of authorial motivation. Can one talk of a particular musical "idea" or theory in Godard?

Rather than attempt to answer this question by offering an exhaustive account of all the various kinds of music employed by Godard (including *chanson*, American popular song, and free-form jazz),[14] I shall limit myself to studying the evolution of Godard's engagement with the classical tradition. I will take two emblematic works of the mid-to-late 1980s, *Je vous salue, Marie* and *Nouvelle Vague*, and examine in detail a key musical turning point in each film, which I shall then also relate to other films of the same period. I will argue that far from being a reassuring hook in his work (a way, for example, for the viewer to endure heavy subject matter and intensive montage), still less a supplementary tool of innate expression, Godard's use of predominantly tonal and melodic music goes to the very heart of his artistic and intellectual project, precisely because it allows him to move beyond the usual chiastic boundaries of his thinking.[15] Further, music (and Hindemith will be an exemplary case) comes to constitute what I shall be calling "the cinematic event," for it functions directly as the very index of cinema in its ideal Godardian form, marking the space where the cinematic as conceived by Godard in its specific relation both to human love and history (the two progressively central themes of the later corpus) is most able to reveal itself. I will conclude my discussion with a formal analysis of *Éloge de l'amour*, which marks the logical culmination of Godard's experimentation with music and its integral link to the primary processes of love and memory operating in his work.

Hail Mary, Music of Love

The first fifteen minutes of *Je vous salue, Marie* offers a virtual medley of Bach's greatest hits, with extracts taken from a variety of forms both sacred and secular, including church music, piano, and organ (Godard has talked of the film being a kind of documentary on Bach's music).[16] In particular, the *Toccata in D Minor* and *Prelude and Fugue in C Major* burst forth repeatedly, even if temporarily thwarted by silence, and *Jesu, Joy of Man's Desiring* greets the birth of Jesus. Bach will eventually be joined by Dvořák, specifically the first and second movements ("Allegro" and "Adagio, ma non troppo") of Dvořák's highly romantic and stormy *Cello Concerto in B minor (op. 104)* (1895). The solo cello of this concerto first arrives in the film when Gabriel and the child angel discover the face of Mary (played by Myriem Roussel) and perform the Annunciation, and it will also figure extensively in the film's middle section. Like the Bach segments, Dvořák is taken *in medias res*, and together these two composers form a kind of cosmic pull in the film that matches the extraordinary sky-/solar-/moon-scapes without ever simply illustrating them (as was arguably the case with the self-consciously sublime set-piece sequences in *Passion* featuring, for instance, the "Agnus Dei" of Fauré's *Requiem*). Godard exploits the full dramatics of sound by fading the music in and out and by increasing or decreasing the volume of both the minor and major keys in an array of mounting crescendos and delicate diminuendos. The music is persistently barred from developing until the end of the film when the clear shape of a melodic phrase, the final "reconciliation" chorus of Bach's *Saint Matthew Passion*, provides the climax. It is thus maintained in a state of perpetual annunciation and surprise, impelling Eva to declare: "It's a wonder that any phrase arrives. There could be nothing." As Godard himself puts it, the film is not about climaxes but rather "signs in the beginning. Signs in the sense of signals, the beginning of signs, when signs are beginning to grow. Before they have signification or meaning. Immaculate signs in a way."[17]

Through music a timeless zone of possibility and transition is produced in the film, and the action remains always "*en ce temps-là*." Marie herself will make contact with this external continuum, if only fleetingly, during her agonizing spiritual confrontation with God and when her body encounters her soul. As for Godard, he, too, is in search of a cinematic *kairos*, or what we might call more mechanically in view of Mary's job at the petrol station its necessary "biting point." This occurs in Marie's room just after she has instructed Joseph (Thierry Rode) in the true meaning of love. Instead of wishing to possess Marie as before, Joseph, filmed from the side, removes his left hand from her abdomen, asking "Is that it, I love you?" ("c'est ça, je t'aime?"), to which she replies "yes." His discovery is greeted by the arrival on the soundtrack of the second movement of Dvořák's concerto. By twice repeating the gesture of holding his hand to her naked body then slowly withdrawing it, he comes to understand that love is also a question of letting go and welcoming the otherness of the other. The strings of the concerto continue with greater volume and intensity into the next shot, a frontal close-up of Marie's naked body, where Joseph practices again the same gesture. The film then records a new and unheralded type of musical event: the dramatic intercutting of Dvořák with Bach. We cut from a shot of Marie suddenly turning round and exposing her behind (Dvořák), to a panoramic shot of a sky shrouded in dark, wispy clouds into which we are immediately transported forwards and horizontally through a short zoom (Bach). The Dvořák concerto then quickly resumes and a single cello takes flight as the camera pans briefly across the sky, reaching a small clearing in the clouds where it is held for ten seconds. The cello carries over into the next sequence back on land (a succession of bushes, fields, flowers). The supernal frisson generated by this dazzling interelemental and intermusical sequence, a formal embrace (Dvořák/Bach/Dvořák) where the aural edit is always just slightly ahead of the visual, is registered directly by the forward thrust of the aerial zoom.

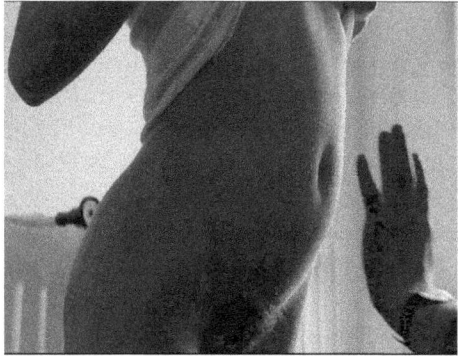 

Figures 5.3–4. Joseph (Thierry Rode) learning to love Marie (Myriem Roussel) followed by a cut to the sky in *Je vous salue, Marie* (1985).

How should we read this horizontal, musical movement forwards, which is evidently more than a simple counterpointing of the baroque and romantic? Godard talks in an interview with Katherine Dieckmann of privileging the horizontal when it comes to sound:

> I try to work not with an idea of vertical sound, where there are many tracks distinct from one another, but horizontally, where there are many, many sounds but still it's as though every sound is becoming one general speech, whether it's music, dialog or nature sound. *Je vous salue, Marie* had more of a documentary use of sound than other films I've done. It's simple in a way: there's dialogue, direct sounds, and music.[18]

This account of the horizontal leaves out, however, the play of the image. Another point Godard makes in the same interview, specifically about Bach, is more pertinent. After asserting that Bach was the music of Martin Luther who attacked the way the Catholic Church makes images, he states the following:

> Bach's music can be matched to any situation. It's perfect. When you play it *in reverse*, it sounds almost the same. It's very mathematical. You could play it in the elevator, like Muzak. It blends itself. Bach is the perfect musician for the elevator.[19] (my emphasis)

This ever so slightly scandalous notion of background classical music is confirmation that Bach constitutes the musical ground of *Je vous salue, Marie*. It also reveals that at this stage of his practice Godard is conceiving of Bach in predominantly reversible terms. By inserting Bach as it were horizontally within Dvořák to record a cinematic event and so reach the vital biting point (which, as we have said, is also the moment of human love and its recognition), the film moves, however, beyond the purely abstract or conceptual (the logic of reversibility) and arrives at something far more direct and immediately affective (leading Marie in a voiceover shortly after the zoom to talk of experiencing the light like a glowing fire).

This type of formal countermaneuver along the horizontal axis is not new in Godard's work, of course, and operates at a range of levels. It occurred already very graphically in *Vivre sa vie*, a film composed of long takes placed together side by side such that each, according to Godard, could be self-sufficient (see Sterritt 1998: 6), and which showcases the purity of sound since both dialogue and background noise were recorded as direct sound. During the famous pendulum sequence, the camera metronomically crossing back and forth the dead space between Nana and her potential new pimp, Raoul, suddenly stopped midway between them, and the anxious silence of their locked stares in the static frame was broken only by a nervous laugh from Nana that immediately drove the camera horizontally back towards her, as if drawn magnetically by the love of Godard for his model and then wife, Anna Karina. In *Sauve qui peut* Godard deliberately adopted a nonhierarchical leveling of sound by approaching sound "lengthwise" ("en longueur") and working with only two tracks, thus avoiding the usual vertical stacking of different tracks to be organized in the postproduction phase (see Bergala 1985: 469). This helps to explain in part why the final sequence features a live orchestra. But the maneuver is perhaps most visible in *Histoire(s)*, where it can be read more specifically as a matching of the vertical and metaphorical by the horizontal and metonymical. As

I argued in chapter 2, dense, rhetorically motivated formations of montage (for instance, the superimposition within a single frame of shots of the concentration camps, a stop-started sequence from George Stevens's *A Place in the Sun* (1951), and a *Noli me tangere* representation by Giotto), are off-set by nondiscursive moments of association, confluence, contiguity, conjunction, and coincidence, moments that trace the interrelations of human form at the level of silhouette, shape, and figure. These far more basic and spontaneous associations by Godard are material, proximate, local, and specific, and as such they offer a purer, more inclusive moment of seeing and feeling than the more mental act of cognition and interpretation.

In short, by means of its horizontal cinematic event, music in *Je vous salue, Marie* is shown to partake of the same mystery as human (as opposed to divine) love, and as we have seen, and as Marie (previously a violinist in *Prénom Carmen*) herself acknowledges here, it is "always in advance of us." Furthermore, it retains its virginal and annunciatory force in the film even after the images have begun to fade following the birth of Jesus and have acquired a flat, *National Geographic*-style aspect. One could read the film more generally as a personal statement by Godard that music remains a locus of creativity and experimentation even after the visual shock of cinema (the period of the New Wave, for instance) has lost its aura and images have become simply clichés. By comparison, *Détective*, made quickly to finance the completion of *Je vous salue, Marie*, might appear minor, almost throwaway Godard. Yet *Détective*, as free and generous in its use of Schubert and Honegger as it is restricted within the walls and mirrors of the Hôtel Concorde, lays the essential groundwork for *Je vous salue, Marie*. The film announces itself with Schubert's *Unfinished* even before the first image arrives, and the dense soundtrack of familiar classical bars and passages creates real dramatic tension above the corny B-movie plot that continues even after the final credits have fallen away. The concluding musical high underscores Ariel's parting words, a repetition of those she uttered at the very beginning: "because love is eternal." As in *Je vous salue, Marie*, the music is already here, already there, unfolding of its own accord in a Sontagian moment of "transparency," a continuous act of stereophonic love (*Détective* was, in fact, Godard's first experiment with Dolby stereo).[20] The use of Honegger's *Liturgical Symphony* (No. 3) (1945–46), in particular the pounding, portentous military march of its third part "Dona nobis pacem," may seem completely unjustified and even inappropriate here, yet precisely for this reason it soars forwards and ever higher above the visual frame.

Détective and *Je vous salue, Marie* complement each other perfectly in their common project of "trying out" music, and they set the tone for much of Godard's production of the mid-to-late 1980s: works like *On s'est tous défilé* (1988), a light, almost incidental parade of assorted music (Mozart, Honegger, Leonard Cohen, Barbara Streisand) that matches the interflashing of fashion images and art, and *Puissance de la parole*, a meditation on the vibrations of the cosmos where any musical connection is potentially possible between Ravel, Bach, Beethoven, Cohen, and John Cage. In each case, what prevails is the inimitable capacity of music to spring to the fore and operate in the filmic present, rather than merely to be a vehicle for prior meaning. The effect produced is of a creative *act* in the present tense. Compare such works with *King Lear*, a film "shot in the back" riddled with captions such as "fear and loathing," "no thing," and "everything over," and where a "violent silence" haunts the world. Even if William Shakespeare the Fifth is able to gather and even recreate for himself visual signs of the recent dead past (he flashes up images of cinematic icons as well as works by the Great Masters, projects spectral images within a *camera obscura*, lights sparklers, replays filmed sequences of resurrection from Cocteau's 1951 short, *La Villa Santo-Sospir*, etc.), all the musical sounds employed in the film (Darling/Bach/Honegger/Ravel) are as if frozen and skewed in an indecipherable bassline slur. "Edgar, it's a pity there is not music," Julie Delpy complains to Leos Carax near the end. Yet if, as Godard states, music is the most powerful of all the arts because it "supports everything,"[21] it is also the hardest to retrieve and restore to life once it has all but disappeared.

The Tracks of Love

Music returns in force three years later in *Nouvelle Vague*, which begins with the caption "Incipit Lamentatio," proceeds to "Acta est Fabula," and concludes with "Consummatum est." Something has happened during the course of the film, but what exactly? Music no longer seems to be simply annunciatory in the manner of *Passion*, where the opening tracking of a plane's vapor trail through the clouds was accompanied by the romantic rush and yearning of Ravel (*Piano Concerto for the Left Hand*). Still less is it explicitly thematized as in *Je vous salue, Marie*, which told of the Annunciation of the Divine and the Cosmic. In the more fractured historical world of Godard's later work, the emphasis will now be on keeping the fragment of music intact and clear, but to what effect? *Nouvelle Vague* clearly bears the weight of the past, and not simply due to its title referring to the New Wave and Godard's own cinematic history. In its choice of location, the shores of Lake Geneva (Godard's childhood home), we also detect the traces of Godard's slightly earlier video short, *Le Dernier mot* (1988), his first and highly somber attempt at historical reconstruction. There, Bach was used exclusively to record the last moments of the young French Marxist philosopher Valentin Feldman, executed by the Nazis in 1942. In *Nouvelle Vague*, on the other hand, which is set in the contemporary world of international business, the soundtrack encompasses Werner Pirchner, Hindemith, Heinz Holliger, Schoenberg, Dino Saluzzi, Meredith Monk, Paul Giger, and David Darling. Hindemith predominates, however, with extracts of varying length taken repeatedly from his 1933–34 symphony *Mathis der Maler*, *Trauermusik* (for viola and string orchestra, 1936), and three different viola sonatas. Typically, while almost everything in the film is articulated verbally in the unremitting barrage of quotes, texts, and captions, no mention is made intradiegetically or otherwise of the specific music employed. The caption "Solo cello and voice," for instance, is not attributed to any one composer or composition and simply floats by. It is precisely for this reason that the music seems protected from the choking nets of discourse and knowledge and remains always an enigmatic and potent force. Moreover, however long they are played, the extracts are usually taken from their beginning and quickly repeated. The opening of the second movement of *Mathis der Maler*, entitled "Entombment," for instance, is repeated six times in succession (not always swift) in the first half of the film. The effect of permanency which this creates is well attested by the blind writer and storyteller Claire Bartoli in her intuitive, poetic appreciation of the soundtrack of *Nouvelle Vague*. She writes: "Beyond the realm of words, the music expressed as the inexpressible fluid enchantment returns like a memory, never to abandon us. It is also fragmented, inserting itself into the score of sound. And yet I feel its permanence, in slow waves [. . .] [the music] lunges forward with the spoken words, charging them with intensity."[22]

Nouvelle Vague begins with Saluzzi's "Winter" from *Andina* (1988), followed by Darling's "Far Away Lights" (from *Journal October: Solo Cello* [1980]), and closes with exactly the same works, though in reverse order. This complements the many other chiastic features of the film, which hinges on the possible resurrection/reincarnation of a middle-aged man ("Lennox") wearing a crucifix. It is divided into two parts: the first, where the headstrong Italian countess Elena (Domiziana Giordano), heiress to a business empire, dominates the drifter Roger Lennox (Alain Delon), whom she encounters by chance and installs in her life; the second where she is controlled by his apparent brother and metaphysical double, Richard Lennox (Alain Delon), who suddenly turns up after his death and takes active control of her company's affairs. Each part culminates in a boating scene during the crossing of Lake Geneva with radically different outcomes. In the first, Elena accidently pushes Roger overboard and, knowing he can't swim, coolly and impassively allows him to drown in front of her. In the second, which takes place on more choppy waters, she herself is saved from drowning by Richard. The film's chiastic framing structure is further emphasized in the booklet of the 2-CD set produced by ECM Records in 1997 (an audio version of the entire film remixed digitally by Musy), which offers a musical breakdown of each CD on facing pages.

In fact, the chiastic status of *Nouvelle Vague* is at once compounded and undermined by an error in the simple yet imprecise breakdown copyrighted to Godard, an error effectively endorsed by the even vaguer detailing of the music in the special issue of *L'Avant-Scène Cinéma* on *Nouvelle Vague* (nos. 396–97). The booklet would have us believe, wrongly, that three different pieces of Hindemith are used in the last quarter of each CD. The problem is essentially this: on the second disc, after the use of the dramatic start of the fourth movement of Hindemith's *Sonata for Solo Viola* (*Opus 25, no. 1*), we are supposed to hear an extract from "Entombment" from *Mathis der Maler*, followed by an extract from *Trauermusik*. This would match the three-part Hindemith series that occurred near the end of the first disc and that comprised the following: i. the opening from "Entombment"; ii. an extract from the equally slow and not dissimilar first movement ("Langsam") of *Trauermusik* (specifically the bars of the brooding second section that begins after fifty-five seconds), played twice to confirm the ominous atmosphere as Elena and Roger head out to water; iii. the start of the third and final movement of *Mathis der Maler,* "The Temptation of Saint Anthony," with its nervous uncoiling into a full and explosive crescendo during the build-up to the moment of drowning. Such symmetry would appear to exemplify Godard's chiastic compulsion which we have encountered throughout his work. However, what is actually heard on the second disc and on the soundtrack of the film are the first and second stages of the first movement of *Trauermusik,* played now in order from the beginning for the first time and separated by a gap of around twenty-five seconds, thus producing a musical sequence that lasts altogether around two minutes. In other words, we witness a continuous development (albeit temporarily paused) of the same music, rather than its repetition or effective reversal. Hence, the lure of the chiasmus is registered only by the "reader" of *Nouvelle Vague,* not by the viewer or listener of the film who is able to appreciate the music more fully as a celebration of repetition as difference. The final words of *Nouvelle Vague,* where water is an agent of both death and rebirth and "Lennox" is both Roger and Richard in a continual ebb and flow, take the form of a shared male voice-off: "It's not the same" / "it's another." What the error reveals is therefore highly instructive: while music may seem to conform to Godard's chiastic thinking, it always outstrips and supersedes the chiasmus during the moment of its performance. Indeed, Godard's nonchiastic use of Hindemith highlights that music is always free and fluid and cannot be easily controlled or contained on the page in neat formulae and structures. That is why, of course, Godard draws on it so much: it is never the same but always "other" and always original.

Yet more is at stake in Godard's engagement of Hindemith in *Nouvelle Vague,* for, as in *Je vous salue, Marie,* a process of formal reversal can be seen operating elsewhere at the junction of sound and image in montage. *Trauermusik* initially occurred in the first half of the film, where it was almost immediately repeated three times, set in motion by the lawyer Raoul's advice to Elena: "Think about it!" ("Pensez-y!"). When the piece appears again in its more extended form in the second half, it is to accompany the most extraordinary shot in the film, luminously photographed by William Lubtchansky and surely one of the most remarkable Godard has ever created: the soaring lateral tracking shot across and above land triggered instantaneously by the edit that arrives as soon as Richard reaches forward and clasps tight Elena's arm waving frantically above the surface of the water. The shot begins with the camera tracking slowly backwards at a slight angle to the ground and passing a tree in the right foreground. It then proceeds to skirt the high ridge horizontally with the lake visible below in extreme long-shot, before capturing Lennox as he runs up the steep slope to join Elena and accompany her back through the country estate towards the mansion. The red of their bathrobes is offset by the lush green woodland (echoes here of the primary colors of the couple in the grounds of Cinecittà in *Le Mépris*), and he shouts to her, as if Eurydice to Orpheus, "Don't turn round!," a command that produces a ripple effect in the suspended silence of the landscape. The camera then cranes gently high above them, ascending first laterally then frontally, before letting them disappear naturally behind the trunk of a large tree that comes to occupy the center of the frame. This long, majestic, continuous tracking shot from the trunk of one tree to the canopy of another, borne aloft by *Trauermusik* and enhanced by the shimmer of long shadows and silhouettes formed by the low angle of the sun, literally scales new heights in the film. Sweeping effortlessly, transcendently, through space and time, it both recapitulates and transumes the continuum of the film's earlier tracking shots, even one as striking as the lateral tracking first left to right, then right to left, through the mansion at night. As for the music, it continues for another ten or so seconds after the visual image has been replaced by the printed caption, "Omnia Vincit Amor," and a new scene has begun the other side of the mansion.

Figures 5.5–6. Elena's (Domiziana Giordano) rescue by Richard Lennox (Alain Delon) immediately followed by the long, lateral tracking shot in *Nouvelle Vague* (1990).

The first horizontal, then vertical, traversal of the landscape accompanied by the continuously unfolding sound of *Trauermusik* may also be read, of course, as a formal unraveling and gradual defusing of the intensively chiastic event that has just taken place: not simply the criss-crossing of arm and hand above the water, but also the intercutting of sound and image it precipitated. For as the camera moved forward to greet Lennox's hand in the act of pulling Elena out of the water, the cut to the tracking shot immediately propelled us backwards over land through a hydraulic effect of motion: forward push in water, backward pull on land. Like the elemental encounter of Bach and Dvořák in *Je vous salue Marie*, this formation of movement and countermovement is made possible by the sheer energy generated: the physical gripping of human skin, the material friction of montage. In fact, the aquatic intercrossing of arm and hand is already a replay of a terrestrial meeting of hands that occurred in the first minutes of the film when Elena, after discovering Roger Lennox lying by the side of the road, moved her hand slowly from the right of an open, abstract frame of the landscape to embrace his own rising up painfully from below. This highly pictorial touching of hands in close-up, evoking most obviously Michelangelo's God reaching out to Adam in the Sistine Chapel, celebrated a "free" gesture, the gift of human love (Elena: "O what miracle to be able to give what we don't possess"; Roger: "Miracle of our empty hands" [a reworking of Bernanos]). Crucially, it takes place in the bosom of the natural landscape which continues to remain in focus within the frame and is not canceled out by the movement of the hands. Indeed, what is most prominent in this originary scene is the presence of a large tree with a wide trunk to which Roger clings for dear life after running into frame from a speeding lorry. The entire sequence appears to revolve around it (just moments before, in his opening voice-over about the narrative he wished to relate, Delon stated he would be "content with the shade of a tall polar tree in its mourning"). Moreover, the event is stretched out in time by a pan left from the tree to the road (i.e., from the opposite direction) which records the movement of the lorry followed by Elena's car as it screeches to a halt. Her eye is immediately caught by the tree's branches and the sun glinting through the leaves; transfixed, she stays in the car to admire the natural spectacle conveyed now as a subjective point-of-view shot. It is as if her sudden realization of the eternal beauty and quiet presence of the centuries-old landscape inspires her to offer her hand in a simple expression of human love and care for a stranger. Trees are now implanted as a central motif, and other stunning arborescent moments will later follow when the camera simply pans upwards through branches and foliage, often to the tune of Hindemith ("Entombment").

Figure 5.7. The gift of human touch: hands embracing in *Nouvelle Vague* (1990).

Yet in the extended, "postchiastic" tracking shot through the landscape, Hindemith is not the only auditory element. There are two separate voice-overs which accompany in succession the two different parts of *Trauermusik* and allow us to appreciate further the particular function and value of music in *Nouvelle Vague*. Speaking first in Italian, Elena, who had earlier cited lines from Dante's *Purgatory*, recites an extract from the first canto of *Inferno*, a passage that, in its second part, would appear to work against the image:

> Then was the fear a little smoothed which had endured in the lake of my heart all that long dolorous night. And as he who with labored breath, having come from the open sea to the shore, turns back to gaze at the perilous waters, so my spirit, still fleeing, turned once more to look at the ravine [*Trauermusik* stops] which never before let any go alive. (subtitles of DVD)

The baton is then passed on to Lennox, who, speaking in French in the third person, focuses our attention further on this stunning visual event and its composite of internal differences across nature, time, language, and gender:

> It was as if they had already lived all this. Their words seemed frozen in the traces [*Trauermusik* resumes] of other words from other times. They paid no heed to what they did but to the division which set today's actions in the past and parallel actions in the past . . . They felt tall, immobile, above them past and present: identical waves in the same ocean. (subtitles of DVD)

This second poetic passage, which, in a heady coincidence of opposites, invokes the movement of water as the camera passes over land, suggests that the now reconciled characters are themselves like trees, tall and motionless in their new calm, and thus at one with nature (Delon is both *in* the landscape visually and *over* it audially). Further, it helps us to understand better the play of elongated shadows on the ground as a physical representation and dispersal of the lines and movements of memory—a process of recognition whereby the events of the present are experienced as different from, yet also uncannily similar to, those which took place in the past ("identical waves in the same ocean"). This process of similarity through mutual difference is presented as fundamentally musical in nature, for the second part of *Trauermusik*, a piece already familiar to our ears but not heard from the beginning until this point, appears both the same, yet different. In this brilliantly self-reflexive sequence of cinema, magnified by the fact that Delon's scenes on the boat directly evoke his earlier self in René Clément's *Plein Soleil* (1960), Hindemith arrives afresh, *as if for the first time*, exactly as the play of similarity and difference between past and present is being formally recognized on the soundtrack and the tracking shot that echoes all others is pursuing its unique path. It is not just that music allows the workings of memory to resound in the present moment of its performance. Even more significantly, music here performs its very own act of montage: the moment when the same is suddenly revealed as different, an event of transformation as thrilling as the act of human love and rescue.

Nothing, of course, indicated that *Trauermusik*, a restrained lament gently disclosing deep emotions and undercurrents (it was originally written for the sudden death of George V on January 20, 1936), could inspire or sustain a tracking shot of such magisterial force and elevation, one that swells time and space simultaneously and brings Elena and Lennox (Richard and Roger) together with nature. Yet within the cascading series of forms and inversions created here by Godard, the stately, measured sweep of viola and strings proves exactly right for the slowly ascending and always evolving tracking shot of love. Pitching it a little higher, it is as though, in this supremely musical moment, *Nouvelle Vague* had transcended time and being itself. Herein lies the crucial difference between Godard's use of music in *Nouvelle Vague* and *Je vous salue, Marie*. If, in the earlier film, classical music (Bach and Dvořák) still operated romantically as a mode of the celestial sublime and lasted only for as long as it took to achieve the film's biting point, in *Nouvelle Vague* the sublime musical moment projects itself ever forward in time to the modernist beat of Hindemith who eventually surpasses the visual image. When *Trauermusik* runs over into the next scene it immediately heralds a new and positive equilibrium of male and female, life and work, with the couple's decision to leave together by car for further adventures, she still in charge of the company, he with a controlling hand in its affairs. The irresistible flow of music is thus what both drives forward the cinematic moment and manifests it as an ethics of love.

Such a proactive, salutary combination of music and cinematographic shot is found also in other works by Godard of the 1990s. In *Allemagne année 90 neuf zero*, specifically its fifth "variation," the first part of the second movement ("Allegretto") of Beethoven's *Seventh Symphony in A major* (1813), takes us into the film's first major tracking shot, a brisk and brief lateral tracking from right to left past Lake Wansee as Lemmy Caution exclaims: "O beloved land, where are you?." The music is immediately replayed twice, the second instance transporting us over the boundary into the film's sixth variation ("The decline of the West"). This solemn, processional music is Beethoven at his (comparatively) more muted, taken at the very start of the movement before it reaches its inevitable crescendo. It is kept therefore at the stage of desire, eschewing completely the original resolution of the movement which imagined two lovers who must separate for a few moments in order to enjoy a greater bond (this could be read on one level as a highly ambivalent comment by Godard on German reunification). In *JLG/JLG* the first camera movement of the film is instigated by the first movement of Hindemith's *Trauermusik*: a slow, meditative, forward tracking through the house, then laterally past the video monitor showing a black-and-white film, before finally resting in front of the table where another video camera lies. A little later, we ride a repeat of this tracking shot, now a lateral tracking inside past the bookshelves accompanied by the same Beethoven used in *Allemagne* (the tracking shot is then immediately reversed and matched with Darling in a contrapuntal musical form).

The key problem with *Hélas pour moi*, of course, a film we discussed in chapter 3 in the context of Godard's performance of breakdown and failure, is that it never really achieves ignition, still less an adequate biting point, by means of a musical tracking. Indeed, as the film's key themes become ever more explicit and prosaic (Simon #2/God/Depardieu: "events are what happens and has a meaning"; Klimt: "the music is raising us all to this spot of light"), so the music finds itself consigned to the background to join the phantom matter preached by Klimt. Hence, the first tracking shot right to left that takes in a boat on the lake is accompanied by a short piece by Darling which began in the previous shot. The musical effect is dispersed and even mute, like the film's odd mixings of indeterminate music that achieve no real dramatic effect. Indeed, the smashing Kancheli chords become almost redundant, like the film's division into "books" that simply loses steam around the half-way mark after the intertitle "Book Five." No definitive or enduring sense of futurity through music is ultimately possible in *Hélas pour moi*.

The Cinematic Event

What "happens" in *Nouvelle Vague* and the other achieved films of Godard's later period like *Allemagne* and *JLG/JLG* is, of course, essentially an act of montage, which, as these works keep reminding us, brings together for the first time elements not predisposed to being linked. If this involves normally opposed composers (Bach and Dvořák), it can also be as simple and as profound as matching the music of mourning (Hindemith) with the lightest of lateral tracking shots. To invoke the repeated message of *Histoire(s)* (a citing of Pierre Reverdy's "L'Image" [1918]): "What is great is not the image but the emotion which it provokes . . . The emotion thus provoked is true because it is born outside all imitation, all evocation, and all resemblance." This process of cinematic juxtaposition and substitution has always carried a distinctly musical charge for Godard, and it is already there in the Bazinian sentence cited with such graphic gusto in *Le Mépris*: "The cinema substitutes for our gaze a world in harmony [*qui s'accorde*] with our desires."[23] But what *Nouvelle Vague* further demonstrates is that music can also generate formally of itself the originality and emotion of montage. As we have seen, the same piece of music may sound the same, yet each instance of its playing is different and unique. Moreover, unlike a textual quote, it cannot be replaced by, or substituted for, anything else. It is, as it were, irreducible, untranslatable and nondeconstructible, acquiring with each repeated play an even greater self-sufficiency and permanency. The fact that Godard chooses largely to avoid opera and Lieder means that the musical phrase retains its "natural" *élan* and is not diverted or derailed by the tricks of discourse. That again would be to risk conventional textual citation and with it Godard's standard reflex of rhetorical reversibility. Just one musical note can be compellingly present, even momentous. As Mark Swed writes movingly of *Histoire(s)*: "Listening, we linger, hang on to, fall in love with (whether for the first time or anew) every note [. . .] music that is so familiar and that we thought we "knew," he [Godard] makes us feel for the first time."[24]

By taking a movement of music not at its climax but at its very beginning, and sometimes just the opening snippets or the prelude before the theme or leitmotif succumbs to variation, Godard maintains music invariably in its proleptic and revelatory mode, in a continual state of becoming. For, in what Edward Said calls its very "reticence" and "allusive silence" (Said 1991: 16), music will never run the risk of staleness or complication because it remains forever "open," like an eternal hope or promise. It thus incarnates the spirit of Mozart, and this even in the film *For Ever Mozart* where Mozart actually features very little. A classic Mozart flourish at the start of the film is cut up and rendered staccato before transmuting into the music of Darling and Bjørnstad, as if Godard were denying Mozart primary status within the film precisely to capture its Mozartian essence. This is the case even when Godard is referring to twentieth-century composers who were inextricably linked to the periods in which they were working (the rising tide of European fascism, the Second World War, the Cold War, etc.), and whose music was clearly affected by their own personal fates (one thinks in particular of Hindemith,

Bartók, Webern and Shostakovich).[25] Indeed, however historically laden, sad, and melancholic, music in late Godard always records a free and positive act of creation. By contrast, the image, as *Je vous salue, Marie* demonstrated so clearly, is ultimately no longer recuperable, and Godard knows this, however hard he tries in *Histoire(s)* and elsewhere to reinscribe its original documentary capacity.

The notion of music as a creative "event" has always been present in Godard, of course. To return to *Week-end*, Gégauff's piano recital is presented explicitly as a "happening," an "ACTION MUSICALE." Yet in Godard's later work, the primacy, permanency, and projection of music may actually be said to constitute *the* cinematic event, since it offers perhaps the only means now to register a cinematic absolute of the kind claimed in *Histoire(s)*, that is, cinema's unique potential to "look at the world looking at it," and its uncanny ability to forecast and anticipate historical events (Renoir's *La Règle du jeu* [1939] and Chaplin's *The Great Dictator* [1940] are the favored examples). Certainly, it has the status now of an ideal, like the Image continually promised during the silent era but never realized, namely the event of "montage." Moreover, it never operates less than as a mystery, which for Godard was cinema's essential function ("neither an art, nor a science, but a mystery"). In addition, emotion and lyricism, which once existed in silent cinema and then disappeared as if people were ashamed of them, are possible now only in the performance of the musical extract or, more rarely, when editing can itself rise to the level of a clear musical passage.[26] That so much of Godard's music of the later period is either sad or angry emphasizes that in the very gesture of recovering the essence of cinema through another form (i.e., music), Godard is also mourning cinema's current impossibility. The extreme pathos of this situation finds its natural obverse in the high pitch of the squawking birds that punctuate bathetically so much of the later work.

Yet if the unstoppable promise and direct summons of music inspire Godard's still-burning passion for the cinema, evident in such disarming public statements as "cinema remains for me a cause for hope,"[27] it is precisely because music is intimately linked to the primal call of love which reverberates through time. We have already seen how both *Je vous salue, Marie* and *Nouvelle Vague* showcase the process of love as a gradual recognition of the other and the free giving of the gift of life.[28] Elena remarks at one point that what is not resolved by love remains forever in suspense, and I would argue that the climactic musical tracking shot of *Nouvelle Vague* does achieve this desired resolution. Indeed, music acquires such determining value in Godard precisely because it both conveys *and* instantiates the annunciatory and revelatory power of love. Again, it does so beyond all resemblance and imitation. Godard may be equally in awe of painting, but this can generate both creative excitement and nervous rivalry, leading him in *Passion*, for example, to stage the Grand Masters as *tableaux vivants* and then dismantle them in an ongoing process of deconstruction/reconstruction. For as long as he is unable to compose or play music, it will never become something to try to copy or imitate. Not unexpectedly, his project from 1988 through 1990 to make a film entitled *La Neuvième Symphonie* (The Ninth Symphony) was eventually aborted.

I have been employing the term "event" deliberately for its echoes of the "Truth-Event" in the work of Alain Badiou, who uses it to account for that unpredictable moment when something is suddenly imposed on us from the outside by a traumatic encounter that shakes us to the very foundations of our being. This is an event of revelation occurring in a totally different dimension from that of Knowledge and the ontological order. Love as a singular encounter and process is a prime instance of the Truth-Event delineated by Badiou and further expounded by Slavoj Žižek in his recent work.[29] It reinscribes a properly metaphysical dimension, where the infinite Truth is eternal and *meta-* with regard to the temporal process of Being. For Badiou, *the* example of a "Truth-Event" is Christianity: the Event is Christ's incarnation and death, its ultimate God is the Final Redemption, and its subjects are the believers who search for signs of God. Here is how Žižek describes the event of Christian Truth:

> The Christian Truth [. . .] is the one of Revelation [. . .] Truth is not inherent, it is not the (re)discovery of what is already in myself [the Socratic philosophical principle] but an Event, something violently imposed on me from the Outside through a traumatic encounter that shatters the very foundation of my being.[30]

Mindful that for the later Lacan love is no longer merely the narcissistic screen obfuscating the truth of desire but "the very way to come to terms with the traumatic drive," Žižek also equates the Christian Truth-Event with the psychoanalytic moment of "traversing the fantasy":[31]

> [P]sychoanalytic treatment is, at its most fundamental, not the path of remembrance, of the return to the inner repressed truth, its bringing to light; its crucial moment, that of "traversing the future," rather designates the subject's (symbolic) rebirth, his (re)creation *ex nihilo*, a jump through the "zero-point" of death-drive to the thoroughly new symbolic configuration of his being.[32]

Love, the greatest of the three Pauline principles of faith, hope, and love since it marks a New Beginning and offers a way out of the deadlock of Law, its prohibition and its transgression (through desire), is defined by both Badiou and Žižek as fidelity to the Truth-Event.

Taken together, Badiou and Žižek allow us to understand how far Godard has reached in his practice since he expressed his consuming desire for music in the passage cited at the beginning of our discussion. By allowing music to enter freely into his work on its own terms and acquire the status of an original and unstoppable Event, he has traversed the "blind" fantasy whereby he was Theseus to music's Antigone. The desire for music has now become the love of music which, as we have seen, operates as the very essence of cinema in its ideal form. *Histoire(s)*, we know, presents a Godard who, having been so indelibly marked by the event of cinema that he claims to have no other home, remains utterly faithful to the unlimited mystery and potential of "the cinematic." Two of the recurring aesthetic formulae of *Histoire(s)*–"The story, not the person who tells it" and "Believe, whatever happens" (the assonance of the original French "Crois, quoi qu'il arrive" is emphatic)—refer also to Godard's early days in the New Wave when cinema stood for the films that could not be seen and thus required faith in an invisible image. By personally "embodying" cinema in *Histoire(s)*, Godard performs an act of passionate devotion to the cinematic form. To take only one of the subjective stances towards the Truth-Event proposed by Badiou, that of the Master, we might say that Godard, as inventor of new forms of critical and historical montage, orchestrates formally the Event of Cinema in order to guarantee its continuity. As he explains during one particularly effusive moment: "The cinema is the love, the meeting, the love of ourselves and of life, the love of ourselves on earth, it's a very evangelical matter, and it's not by chance that the white screen is like a canvas [. . .] the screen as the linen of Veronica, the shroud that keeps the trace, the love, of the lived, of the world."[33]

The obvious question raised by such statements from Godard is whether his current use of music should be considered to some extent specifically Christian, especially when he can also refer with such ease to an "honest and secular Christianity" while explaining the influence of Wittgenstein on the phrase just cited ("Believe, whatever happens").[34] After all, Hindemith and Pärt may be classed as modern Christian composers in the long line established by Mozart and Fauré, and in Pärt's case *Passio* is a defiant expression of the Catholic faith. Similarly, Honegger's *Symphony No.3* draws directly upon the liturgy of the Catholic mass for the dead. As Jullier as noted, the long and gentle "reverberations" of music in Godard's work can relate symbolically for the enlightened listener to sacred music, even when nonovertly religious composers like Darling and Bjørnstad are being used. (Keith Jarrett is unusual in this respect in that the titles of the two hushed and eerie piano compositions from *Dark Intervals* [1988], which Godard reprises throughout *Histoire(s)* and other recent works, are actually religious in nature ["Hymn" and "Ritual Prayer"] although, significantly, they refer to form rather than content.) Yet what we have witnessed is that Godard's artistic conscience is ultimately post-chiastic, and when he turns to Christian narratives and iconography he is operating more in the fluid realm of available aesthetic and cultural metaphor. The Christian legacy for Godard is primarily that of Western art guided by the notion of love as the defining event of human existence, and this absolute general principle accounts for his deep fascination with Catholic writers and thinkers, notably Françoise Dolto, who sought to unite her faith with her practice of psychoanalysis which she regarded as both scientific and spiritual.[35] Ultimately it is not the religious or sacred content of the music that matters most to Godard, but rather its fundamental status as tonal music and its natural extension and projective qualities. The force of his repeated Pauline message in *Histoire(s)* and elsewhere, that "the image will come at the time of the resurrection," lies above all in its *mode* of articulation in the musical tense of Godardian montage rather than in any strictly literal sense, Christian or otherwise, the term "image" may denote.

In the particular case of Hindemith, it is highly significant that Godard employs the original symphony *Mathis der Maler* rather than the subsequent opera. Which is to say, he uses the third movement of the symphony rather than the sixth scene of the opera, "The temptation of Saint Anthony," of which it forms the basis. There, following the vision in which Mathis sees himself as a latter-day St. Anthony holding out against the temptations of wealth and power and of the heroism of war and sensual delight, St. Paul the Apostle utters to the lost artist the redeeming and admonitory words: "Go forth and create." Certainly, Godard cannot escape the influence of the later opera, which determines how one reads the symphony, but the urgent summons of its artistic message is conveyed formally in Godard's work through the performance and advance of the music, in the insistent, driving repetition of the opening passage of the symphony's third movement. For this experience alone Hindemith comes to function for Godard as a kind of perpetual Reveille, a call to artistic arms.

In the case of another contemporary composer, Kancheli, a Georgian in exile from his native Tiflis and composer of major works such as *Trauerfarbenes Land* ("Land That Wears Mourning"), Godard refers throughout *Histoire(s)* (especially episodes 2A and 3B) and *JLG/JLG* to the dramatic opening of *Vom Winde beweint* (1992), a "liturgy" for solo viola and orchestra. This one shockingly loud and raw minor chord from the piano is held for a long minute, releasing into the air soundwaves that are allowed to die away in their own time. Writing of another very similar piece by Kancheli entitled *Lament,* a work composed in 1994 for violin, soprano, and orchestra where fragments disappear even before they fully appear and pass immediately into a *fortissimo* explosion, a violent cataclysmic *tutti,* Žižek remarks on the eruption of the Real in all its brutality and evil: "The subject takes the risk of putting himself forward; the Other strikes back with all ferocity."[36] In the particular way that *Vom Winde beweint* springs forth seemingly of its own accord in Godard's work, sometimes in silence, sometimes over other music, at times in quick succession, and always powerful enough to provoke a cut in the image, it is the pure and indefinable emotion created by the musical event that matters, and the fact that this nameless, almost unholy sound without apparent object continues to expand and consolidate itself through space and time.

In Praise of Music

If all Godard's successful films are thus really to be conceived of formally as love melodies—for the cinema, art, the viewing public—only one, of course, explicitly bears that message in its title, *Éloge de l'amour*. Again, while there is endless discussion in the film of cinema (documentary film/Spielberg), art and painting, writing and philosophy (Georges Bataille, Simone Weil, etc.), music passes by virtually unnoticed. What is new in Godard's work, however, is the degree to which the musical element has become distilled, for while there is some variation (the odd extract from Pärt and another ECM composer of largely string music,

Karl Amadeus Hartmann, as well as occasional references to French film composers such as Georges Van Parys and Maurice Jaubert), one gentle, sparse, and elegiac twenty-five-second segment by Darling and Bjørnstad predominates. The tune is heard in truncated form at the very beginning of the film and then reproduced close to twenty times in different forms, tones, and volumes, sometimes interrupted or suspended, but always there and always reappearing as if new.

Darling and Bjørnstad are able to "carry" Éloge, indeed to provide its very rhythm and backbone, because by this stage within the Godard corpus they have acquired their own history and significance. They seem to anticipate the flow of images and by themselves operate the cinematic event as we have defined it—as a sustained chord of promise and futurity. If Éloge appears to some critics even to be composed formally like music (for Marie Anne Guerin it is a "hymn to the image,"[37] while for Amy Taubin it has the beating of a late Beethoven string quartet since the shards of images and black spacing, along with speech and music, are treated almost as individual notes and can coalesce into something akin to melodic phrases or harmonic textures), this is surely because of the continuous flow of the apparently slight but unstoppable globs of Darling and Bjørnstad.[38] The sudden spectacular switch one hour into the film from black-and-white 35 mm to color digital video is actually of secondary aesthetic importance, as is the obvious fact of the film's reversible structure whereby it comes around full circle, the ending meeting the beginning in the middle.[39] Likewise, the repeated chiastic use of the captions "de l'amour" ("of/about love") and "de quelque chose" ("of/about something") advance the film no further than other repeated captions such as "Deux ans avant" ("Two years before") and "Archives" in the film's second part. Indeed, the film's structure functions far more humbly as a tool of character contrast between the young misguided filmmaker Edgar (Bruno Putzulu), attempting in vain to compose a cantata-cum-opera about Weil, and his more focused creator (Godard) who trusts, as always, only to instrumental or symphonic music in order to perform his cinematic act.

This is not at all to downplay the historical element of Éloge, which features the story of two former Resistance fighters and is visually drenched in moody night shots of Paris that radiate echoes of the Second World War (including even close-up shots of commemorative plaques), the New Wave, and the French cinematic tradition in general (Vigo, Renoir, etc.). On the contrary, the use of music enacts history at both a concrete and metaphorical level, for the playing and replaying of the same few critical bars creates duration (the horizontal axis) and generates of itself the processes of memory (the vertical axis). Always moving forwards in linear fashion, music is the past recasting itself poetically into the future. As such, it manages to escape the fatal nexus of money, cinema (Hollywood), and history for sale that results in the film in the very betrayal of memory. In short, music in Godard is history, its mourning, *and* its transcendence.[40] The very title of Schoenberg's 1917 string sextet, *Transfigured Night*, much used in both *Nouvelle Vague* and *Histoire(s)*, signals this effect. Far more even than painting, music continually exemplifies the resurrectional status of art as defined by André Malraux and endorsed by Godard throughout *Histoire(s)*: (literally) "art is what is reborn in what has been burnt." It thus offers an aesthetic model for Godard, not only because it enables him to step down from the cross of his chiastic thinking, but also because it imprints itself within a larger, more intersubjective and inclusive process, that of memory. Like universal "sovereign" love, as *Éloge* now defines it following Georges Bataille, this relies on the recognition and respect of difference within the totality of the whole—of the kind of relations that exists, for example, between the past and the present and between the loved one as object and the lover as subject, however much these instances overlap and can sometimes fuse.[41]

Figure 5.8. Edgar (Bruno Putzulu) moving through altered states of landscape while on the train back to Paris in *Éloge de l'amour* (2001).

Éloge thus marks the most advanced sublimation yet of Godard's artistic desire *for* music. Moreover, it suggests that the love of/for music may not only offer a highly valuable means of creative thinking, but also constitute a potentially powerful ethical foundation. We shall explore this possibility further in our discussion of *Notre Musique* in chapter 6 where we consider music as a metaphor for human relations due to its relational nature and its capacity to bring people together. Certainly, when articulated verbally by Godard himself in works like *JLG/JLG*, the idea of love can become self-absorbed and inflated ("I said that I loved/ there's the promise/ right now/ I must sacrifice myself/ in order that through me/the word of love/ has a meaning/in order that there is love/ on earth"). In *Éloge*, too, it can become caught up chiastically as soon as Godard attempts to translate it into discourse (for example, with the phrase "La mesure de l'amour, c'est aimer sans mesure" ["The measure of love is to love beyond measure"]). However, in the inimitable performance of music, which always arouses us as if for the first time, Godardian love and cinema find their most original, consistent and open expression.

6

Crossing the Darkness
Metaphor, Difference, Dissymmetry in *Notre Musique* (2004)

Cinema is made with what is called negatives in every language. And you draw a positive from this. And this specific element of photography is a metaphor which is more than a metaphor, it's a kind of reality.

—J.-L. Godard

The principle of cinema: go towards the light and shine it back on our night, our music.

—J.-L. Godard in *Notre Musique*

When is a bridge not a bridge? Or rather, when does a bridge no longer function metaphorically as a bridging of opposites? That is to say, are there any limits to metaphoricity in the cinema which Godard defines, as we have seen, as the privileged realm of "a fraternity of metaphors" made manifest in the very process of montage? These questions come urgently to the fore in *Notre Musique* (2004), which takes place in a quintessential space of metaphor, Sarajevo, capital of Bosnia-Herzegovina, metaphor now for a new Europe following the lifting of the city's four-year siege in December 1996 and the end of the Bosnian War. As Godard puts it: "Sarajevo [is] a metaphor for Europe, with people who feel that they're separated from others and at the same time are with us, with something to be reconstructed together" (Godard 2004a). The symbolic locus of the ongoing reconstruction of this historic city is the sixteenth-century Ottoman Old Bridge over the Neretva River in Mostar, a small medieval town nearby ("Mostar" means "bridge-keeper"). An emblem of Bosnia's multiethnic society and shared cultural heritage, the bridge (commonly referred to as the "Old Man") linked the separate Christian and Muslim communities but was destroyed in November 1993 by Croatian shells. At the time of the making of *Notre Musique* it was in the process of being reconstructed stone by stone as part of a UNESCO project under the supervision of French engineer Gilles Péqueux, who also features in the film.

Godard is asking in *Notre Musique* both what it really means to say that cinema provides a fraternity of metaphors, and, more generally, what the underlying connections and bridging links are that bind us together socially and culturally. And he does so in this unique geographical site of metaphor by effectively putting metaphor to the test through the processes of montage and its capacity to create *rapprochements* between different elements. Already, the titular term "notre musique" is to be understood as a metaphor for human existence itself, with "musique" and the collective pronoun "notre" standing for "our" European way of living and being (*savoir-vivre*) (the film critic Jean-Michel Frodon calls Sarajevo a "shareable, inhabitable mental place" [Frodon 2004a: 18]). This metaphorical shift was already evident in Godard's original short preparatory text for *Notre Musique*, "Projet de film," which includes a chiastically arranged parenthesis about music: "notre musique, qui nous parle et parle de nous" ("our music which speaks to us and of us speaks").[1] In fact, the film was originally intended as a personal tribute to the music producer Manfred Eicher, founder of the Munich-based record company ECM. The project never materialized, although typically the film's soundtrack offers a rich and enterprising range of ECM composers, many already familiar in Godard's later work such as Arvo Pärt, David Darling, Ketil Bjørnstad, Meredith Monk, Keith Jarrett, Heinz Holliger, György Kurtág, and Hans Otte, but some also new to the Godard listener such as Tomasz Stanko, Anoaur Brahem, Alexander Knaifel, and Trygve Seim, complemented by the lush, symphonic swells of Sibelius and Tchaikovksy.

Yet while *Notre Musique* contains no visible traces of Eicher or other musicians, it showcases an array of writers, poets, and artists who suggest in different ways the possibility for new connections and correspondences between the arts, science, cinema, and politics. Among the writers and artists featured in person is Juan Goytisolo, author of a searing eye-witness account *Cuadernos de Sarajevo* (1993) much admired by Godard, and who offers reflections on vision and revelation, darkness and memory from his 1997 book, *La Forêt de l'écriture*, a plea for a return to the values of conviviality and a creative revolution to counter modern barbarism. Also included are the French author/sculptor Pierre Bergounioux, the writer/philosopher and video-maker Jean-Paul Curnier, and the actor Jean-Christophe Bouvet playing the fictional "C. Maillard." (The French philosopher Antonia Birnbaum and the German sociologist of violence and terror Wolfgang Sofsky are similarly acknowledged in the closing credits though not present on screen.) The most important figure to feature in the film, however, along with Godard himself, is the late Palestinian poet Mahmoud Darwish, who takes part in a set-piece interview with a fictional freelance reporter from the Israeli newspaper *Haaretz*, Judith Lerner (Sarah Adler). Darwish, of course, goes back a long way in Godard's work and was a companion-in-arms politically during the late 1960s/early 1970s. The unfinished

Jusqu'à la victoire, a propaganda film by the Dziga Vertov Group commissioned in 1969 by the militant Palestinian group Fatah, includes a poem by Darwish entitled "Je résisterai" ("I will resist"), read aloud by a young Fatah girl in the bombed out ruins of the Jordanian village of Karameh where the Fatah headquarters were located.[2]

Godard's direct engagement with the aesthetic in terms of metaphor is made fully explicit in *Notre Musique* through reference to Baudelaire's poem "Correspondances," recited in part off-screen in the burned out National Library. We hear the opening quatrain of the poem read by a woman who picks up by chance a copy of *Les Fleurs du Mal* lying in a pile of books: "Nature is a temple in which living pillars/ Sometimes give voice to confused words;/ Man passes there through *forests of symbols*/ Which look at him with understanding eyes" (my emphasis). On a purely structural level, too, *Notre Musique* is metaphorically and symbolically loaded. It is divided into three sections or "kingdoms" that recall a medieval, Dantesque triptych organized polyphonically by refrain and counterpoint with chorale-like sequences. The first is "Hell," a ten-minute collage of documentary and fictional scenes of war and calamity (including 9/11) in the style of the early episodes of *Histoire(s)*, though the effect created here is very different, for an aesthetic polarity is formed between the complex visual excess of highly processed and mangled images generating a palpitating display of lustrous primary colors and the continuous, uninterrupted sounds of Hans Otte's piano music that punctuate it with clanging, biting chords. With this opening the film announces it will not be directly concerned with history and the politics of historiography like *Histoire(s)*, but rather with the ethics and politics of aesthetic difference. The second kingdom, "Purgatory," which takes up most of the film, is based around a lightly fictionalized restaging of Godard's own visit to the 2002 Sarajevo conference, European Literary Encounters, at the Centre Culturel André Malraux. It records various kinds of human interaction and encounter which take place in a limbo of transitional "nonplaces": airport lounge, hotel lobbies, bars, moving taxis and trams, and so on. The third and final kingdom, "Paradise," is a short section entirely different in mood and style and presented as a film-within-a-film.

Notre Musique quickly establishes itself as a dense, liminal space, at once real and imaginary, where different people and worlds meet and which draws from some of the founding myths of Judeo-Christian Europe. The languages spoken by the Egyptian Jewish interpreter and translator for the conference, Ramos García (Rony Kramer) (Russian, Spanish, French, Hebrew, Arabic, English) bespeak the geopolitical cartography of Europe's (post)colonial relationship to the Middle East. Yet the film also experiments with different ways of approaching otherness, both thematic and formal, such that aesthetic questions of cinematic form, difference, and metaphor are directly linked to ethical considerations of identity, race and ethnicity. The film features for the first time in Godard's work three Native Americans who are portrayed in different forms and styles, at one point in full traditional regalia. Striking and mysterious, speaking only English, they are played by the actors George Aguilar and Léticia Gutiérrez, and by Ferlyn Brass as himself. They appear completely "other" in the film: their skin color and costumes ensure they exist outside the binaries of black and white, and they engage with no one else, despite their occasional (unsuccessful) efforts to enter into dialogue with the locals. Indeed, they remain all but invisible to those around them, wandering through the film like ghosts, at once part of the diegesis yet also at a remove from it, as if haunting the European consciousness (and conscience) by provoking questions of identity, belonging, and place. Free-floating, unpredictable, and seemingly autonomous in a film dealing directly with modes of discourse (poetic, personal, official, political, aesthetic, social, philosophical, pedagogical) as well as of communication (dialogue, interview, translation, conversation, interpretation), they would appear to herald in Godard's work a totally new and affirmative kind of encounter with absolute difference and the alterity of the irreducibly other.

Figure 6.1. Godard and the interpreter Ramos García (Rony Kramer) in *Notre Musique* (2004).

But how, *Notre Musique* asks, can one bridge the gap and cross to the Other without crossing it out? Will the radical otherness of the Native Americans, heightened, like Godard's former chosen others, Africans and African Americans, by their graphic difference in language and skin color, be fully heard? Or will Godard's new outer rim of alterity be revealed as merely a mercenary requirement for yet more figures of otherness in his imaginary scheme? In short, is a realistic, mutual encounter with the other possible here? We can rephrase these questions in more directly formal terms which lead back to my opening enquiry: can the bridging mechanisms of metaphor in *Notre Musique* be rewired to allow for a more ethical presentation of the other? For the film sets itself up explicitly as an artistic challenge, even dare: in a fixed space spanned symbolically by the Mostar bridge which literally haunts the background of the image, is it possible to keep the live, intersecting currents and circuits of metaphor on the move and from congealing into symbol? Put simply: how can one both sustain the adventure of metaphor and bridge the divide with the Other?

What makes *Notre Musique* so powerful is that these interrelated questions of ethics and aesthetics play out in a clearly delimited political context (the new postwar era of official forgiveness and reconciliation in Bosnia-Herzegovina) and are posed explicitly as theoretical issues in the set-piece sequence of Godard's master class to film students half-way through the film about how to read images, where his role and responsibility as an artist come under direct scrutiny. It is by working carefully through the multiple, overlapping layers of metaphor and otherness in *Notre Musique*, and by comparing Godard's articulated theory of montage as a *rapprochement* of different elements with his actual practice of cinema here, that we shall attempt to address these various questions. For *Notre Musique*, a film expressly about human relations and positionality (already the title proclaims "our" music as opposed to "yours" or "theirs"), constitutes perhaps the most far-reaching investigation in Godard's work of the combined ethical, aesthetic, and political value of metaphor in cinema in its relationship to the real. Yet if, as always, Godard explores the possibilities of the medium in order to obtain poetic traction and generate forms of internal self-resistance, here it will not be by resorting to his now standard, default practices of chiastic reversal and poetic formulae (the rhetorical processes we have been tracing in detail in this book), but rather by attempting to take metaphor to its bursting point—to the point where it is potentially more than metaphor, and a means not simply of transfiguring reality but also a form of reality in itself. As we shall see, the real other, like metaphor, is never simply the other in Godard, but part of a proliferating chain of otherness that winds back inexorably to the realm of the political, in this case the hyperpolitical. We begin with Godard's master class demonstration of his theory of montage as *champ/contre-champ*.

The Theory of Montage: The Poetics of *Champ/contre-champ*

Godard works in his master class through the long history of image-making approached from a variety of perspectives (from genre to film grammar and ideology) in order to pinpoint the specifics of cinematic form, that is, the play of difference between images and sounds in montage. He posits at the start the impossibility of correctly identifying a particular documentary image of battle ruins (the example given is Richmond, Virginia, during the American Civil War) since it appears to resemble all other images of war, whether World War II or Bosnia. He immediately counterpoints this with the magical power of the aesthetic image by means of a short staged reconstruction of the young Bernadette of Lourdes recognizing her vision as Marian only upon beholding the Byzantine icon of Our Lady of Cambrai ("no illusion, no depth, the sacred"). What then follows is a series of ten or so examples of *champ/contre-champ* of varying significance and value. A combination of two separate stills of Cary Grant and Rosalind Russell from Howard Hawks's *His*

Girl Friday (1940), for example, where both are on the phone smiling and making the same gesture (Grant is facing right off-screen, Russell looks across towards the left), is presented as a failed instance of *champ/contre-champ*. A-4 size copies of the stills are held aloft by two film students who place them in turn one over the other. According to Godard who is pictured at this moment from the point of view of the audience, one would need the original sound to realize the difference of the images, so identical are they in style and production, for Hawks has failed to appreciate the function of *champ/contre-champ* as an instrument of differentiation. In Godard's poetics, the substance of the image lies in its alternation, which produces the shock of recognition of a double perspective. Yet his underlying point here that Hawks can't tell the difference between men and women is not developed, despite the obvious androgynous tendency in some of Hawks's films where men can act "feminine" (as in *I Was a Male War Bride* [1949]) and women can perform the dominant role. Thus the claim, while clearly influenced by Godard's knowing choice of Cary Grant, a closeted gay actor in Hollywood, remains rather forced and unsubstantiated.

Figure 6.2. Juxtaposing Cary Grant and Rosalind Russell in Godard's master class in *Notre Musique* (2004).

Another instance of *champ/contre-champ*, this time presented as successful and executed by Godard himself, juxtaposes a contemporary black-and-white photograph of refugees fleeing on donkeys behind barbed wire, and over which is printed the word "Kosovo," with a color painting of the Israelites' exodus from Egypt by donkey accompanied by the title "Egypt." The same images (minus the captions) were already used, in fact, in a sequence from *The Old Place* with a voice-over commentary by Godard and Anne-Marie Miéville (artistic director on

Notre Musique) about the process of montage as *rapprochement* influenced by the Benjaminian idea of the fleeting resurrection of the past in the image ("like stars move with and against each other to form a constellation, so certain things appear to move away from each other to form certain images"). Here, the two images are followed by a third that has no title and would seem to be that of a dead child covered in a shroud, possibly a news image from the Rwanda genocide. "You see in truth that truth has two faces," Godard declares emphatically.

One of the last examples of *champ/contre-champ* offered by Godard revolves around the image of a castle taken from a book by the German physicist Werner Heisenberg who visited Elsinore Castle before the war. A countershot is provided: the same book describing the castle as that of Hamlet. First the "real" ("uncertainty"), then the "imaginary" ("certainty").[3] As Godard later put it in one interview, again in Benjaminian terms, the image at this particular moment is created by the text in the manner of poetry, "like two stars whose *rapprochement* produces a constellation."[4] Clearly, this reimagining of shot/countershot as the objective critical comparison of different images has little to do with its standard function in commercial narrative cinema as a means of identification with character through subjective point-of-view formal procedures that aim to channel and contain, and ultimately cancel out, otherness. Indeed, *Notre Musique* resolutely eschews subjective point-of-view and classic shot/countershot. What is being proposed here instead is a theory of seeing and reading the image *asymmetrically* and *metaphorically* by means of the exchangeablity of terms afforded by montage. As always in Godard, cinema is about learning the right way of seeing (*voir*) and receiving (*recevoir*) the sounds and images of the world. He commands: "Try to see something. Try to represent something. In the first instance, look at that. In the second, close your eyes."

Having begun his lesson with the image of a human skull and the Blanchotian idea, discussed earlier in the introduction, that the image is joy precisely because it is surrounded by the void ("Image is happiness. But beside it dwells nothingness. The power of the image is expressed only by evoking nothingness"), Godard concludes in exuberant, almost evangelical terms that cinema is metaphor and a path to human enlightenment: "The principle of cinema: go towards the light and shine it back on our night, our music." The accompanying image of a swinging light-bulb lighting up the darkness and creating new shadows in its path is an obvious reference to a sequence in Henri-Georges Clouzot's 1943 study of moral ambiguity during the Occupation, *Le Corbeau* (*The Raven*), where a lighted bulb swinging back and forth across a globe points allegorically to the murky shadows of the *années noires*. Cinema may wish to be both master of the visible and master of the chasm in which the visible crosses the invisible, yet the cinematic apparatus advanced here by Godard is always, uniquely, a matter both of poetic transfer (Greek *meta-pherein*, "carrying across") and moral relativity.

So endeth the lesson. Yet one not taken very seriously by the students themselves who appear unengaged and unconvinced by Godard's dogmatic and often peremptory, absolute statements like, "You'll see it's the same thing!" and "It's worse when the two things are similar," and who end up talking over him. This is not simply the result of a clash of different generations, however. The problem is clearly linked to Godard's haughty approach and style whereby he defamiliarizes himself as "Jean-Luc Godard" and offers himself in a deliberately unflattering, even self-lacerating, light as the "Master." Indeed, he appears here to be exposing his own narcissism as the great Auteur and, in the process, debunking—even potentially discrediting—his own authority. For he invites no discussion at any moment in his lecture, and even the translator, Ramos García, who is seen arriving at the start, and with whom Godard was filmed earlier at the airport in deep conversation about the nature of "exodus" (specifically the difference between "exodus" [*l'exode*] as the conclusion of a Greek tragedy and "the Exodus [*l'Exodus*]" as the permanent condition of exile and expulsion in the biblical account of Moses leading the Israelites out from Egypt into the Promised Land), utters no word of dissent. The one student who does venture a question, one that has nothing directly to do with what Godard has just presented and concerns the potential of digital cameras to "save" cinema, receives no response. For in a sequence that insists on the standard set-up of projection whereby all in the audience are directed to look forward together in unison at one image (in this case Godard), the premise of such a question goes against all Godard stands for in his poetics and metaphysics. He is pictured at this moment in close-up and isolated in the frame—a ghostly, silent, solitary figure in silhouette staring into the camera as if into the void. This encapsulates the unsatisfactory nature of the lecture: a nonencounter with the other with whom no real dialogue seems possible.

Why Godard should portray himself in such highly ambivalent fashion remains for the moment unclear. What can be said at this stage, however, is that the portrayal of Godard as recalcitrant professor is matched visually by the way he is constantly repositioned by the camera and never occupies a fixed position within the frame. In fact, in its very weakness and lack as a traditional lecture and encounter, the master class presents a powerful staging of difference not simply through the numerous types of images covered by Godard but in the very way the sequence is shot and presented. Just as he is simultaneously translated by a female interpreter, so the camera tracks restlessly back and forth across the young audience, from front and behind, at different distances and angles. Moreover, in the moment of their exposition in *champ/contre-champ*, each image is placed concretely on top of another, thus creating a temporary reverse field. Which is to say, difference is never a smooth and pure process based on a simple parity of terms and equality of representation: only one image is brought to the light and prioritized at any one time. The result is a continual tension and process of evaluation according to different criteria, notably the poetic impact and persuasive force of the bridging together of particular terms in montage. For this reason, the form of the master class may be said to offer a lesson in itself of the poetics of montage as difference—one that emphasizes the very *contrariness* and resistance within the structure of *champ/contre-champ*. Every sequence in the film, in fact, instantiates difference and relativity, relationality and translation (from the Latin *translatio*, "to bring across"), by refusing simply to fuse opposites and by outlawing the apparent, fixed certainties of the overliteral and symbolic. It also means that, taken as a whole, *Notre Musique* is not simply a blanket illustration of *champ/contre-champ*. There are other types of montage at work which, like the secondary, more instinctive, metonymical level of editing in *Histoire(s)* explored in chapter 2, revolve around shape, color, figure, and form and produce entire clusters of links and free associations, in particular around the motif of flowers. The focus of the present chapter, however, will remain exclusively the operations of *champ/contre-champ*.

In short, *Notre Musique* puts an absolute premium on difference, including the basic (meta)physical binaries of the various stages of the cinematic process: negative/positive (analog film processing), fields/reverse fields (montage), light/darkness (celluloid projection). As such, the film goes well beyond any simple idea of cultural dialogue or transnational exchange. Indeed, Godard totally refuses the model of the polite diplomatic encounter or institutional hospitality towards the invited other and insists instead on a spirit of radical refusal. He has come to an official place of encounter overseen by a multinational peacekeeping force (the SPOR) precisely to stage a series of missed or nonencounters, replacing a publicly agreed upon set of political terms and conditions of engagement with his own formal and aesthetic ones. The formal art of asymmetry, while giving flesh to Godard's redefinition of cinema as "our night" and "our music" and the surpassing of strict binary sense, seems entirely appropriate in view of the historical context of Sarajevo, since the ethnic conflict in Bosnia involved three main parties (Muslim Bosniaks, Orthodox Serbs, Catholic Croats) who were continually developing new ties and alliances. There is a frank acknowledgment here by Godard that while the students may seek easy solutions to the questions of cinema, there are no quick-fix answers, no opposites to be neatly united, and no simple bridges to mend or cross—only more difficulty and ambiguity and difference to work through and negotiate via montage. For this reason, the whole of *Notre Musique*, and not just the master class sequence, is, despite its general surface calm, a fractious, refractory, and often highly uncomfortable film in its (non)engagement with a variety of forms of otherness—an engagement that continually rubs up against the fact of incomprehension and often lack of mutual understanding.

Godard's master class raises the basic question whether the use of cinematic form, buttressed as here by a set of lubricating metaphors and "prolonged echoes" (Baudelaire), can serve directly to produce a more ethical presentation of ethnic and racial difference and so allow for the safe passage of the other—what Goytisolo describes at one point in the film, where he calls for a creative "revolution" reinforcing memory and giving substance to images, "a safer, more serene crossing of the darkness" for those living. To establish whether, and for how long, the real, living other can continue to remain "other" while functioning as a living entity in Godard's desired *champ/contre-champ*, formulated as here in terms of difference and asymmetry, also entails addressing the core theme of responsibility towards both self and other. This theme is announced at the very beginning of the film by a female voice-off, which, over terrible images of mankind's inhumanity, asserts the need for mutual forgiveness in the religious terms of the Lord's Prayer: "Forgive us our trespasses as we forgive those who trespass against us. Yes, as we forgive them, and no differently." The second sentence is repeated on its own a little later, thus acquiring greater weight and importance. The same voice then adds, chiastically: "We can consider death in two ways: one, as the impossible of the possible; the other, as the possible of the impossible." The sequence closes with Rimbaud's radical statement: "Now, 'I' is another." During the master class the theme of forgiveness is approached from the perspective of presumed guilt, but in a spirit of pure artistic disavowal. Godard remarks: "It is said that our language [i.e., the visual language of filmmakers] arbitrarily cuts objects out in reality; it is said as if we were guilty." He even recites the famous line from Racine's play *Phèdre* about the additional tragedy of rendering morally culpable those who are essentially innocent of any crime (Phèdre imputes the malady of her tragic love for her step-son Hippolyte to a vengeful diety): "When you [Oenone] know my crime, and the fate that afflicts me/ I won't die any less, but will die more guilty" ("Quand tu sauras mon crime, et le sort qui m'accable,/ Je n'en mourrai pas moins, mais j'en mourrai plus coupable"). This eclectic and enigmatic set of statements about personal responsibility and public accountability, which retreats from the possibility of absolute guilt (and with it unconditional exoneration) and moves instead into the more complex and diffuse realm of poetics, subtends the entire film. Yet it also obliges us to ponder what, if anything, there might be to forgive about Godard's self-performance here and his practice of the relativity of cinematic truth in relation to the other.

Theory into Practice: Occupying the Reverse Field

If, as Godard has suggested in interviews, the one genocide to rival the Shoah is that of the slaughter and virtual extinction of the Native Americans, could it be that the only "good" Americans now in Godard's ever-decreasing circles of radical otherness are the Native Americans intermittently glimpsed in *Notre Musique*, precisely because they still remain outsiders in North American society? After all, as a people of the "Fourth World" they are without political autonomy or self-determination, forced to exist within a system that has been imposed on them and to which they have been forced to adapt (most usually not), and where their tribal languages are now fast disappearing, if not already extinct. Dissidence, resistance, and a refusal to be co-opted by the System are part of their daily life. Indeed, the Native American tribes continue to figure in the European and Anglo-American imaginary as perhaps the least known, least represented and least understood of all North American communities. Godard ensures we remember their historical fate by citing in the opening section, "Hell," fragments of John Ford's *Fort Apache* (1948), and Cy Endfield's *Zulu* (1964) (the sequence is accompanied by a quote from Montesquieu: "And so, in the time of fables, after the floods, there appeared on earth men armed for extermination"). Yet if it is indeed the case that Native Americans have now replaced Africans and African Americans in Godard's cinema as a primary index of political resistance, what might be the terms and conditions attached to such an identity and status? Already in *Passion* the link between Native Americans and language had been raised by the director, Jerzy Radziwilowicz, in conversation with Hanna Schygulla: "Do you know why the white men killed all the Indians? Because the Indians didn't say, 'I don't understand.' They said, 'Me no understand' [. . .] So the white men killed them, not because they didn't understand, but because they didn't say it right. That's all." And Godard will later pursue the idea of a radically "other," nonnormative form of language with his use of "Navajo English" subtitles in *Film socialisme* that recall the old Hollywood Westerns where the wild Red Indians speak in choppy phrases, or "Injun English." These arresting compound subtitles (a single line, no punctuation or conjugation of verbs, nouns stitched together, sentences lumped together as one word) are not in pidgin English or Tonto speech but constitute rather a new and unique hybrid. Godard's simple appropriation of the tribal name "Navajo" to describe his invented language (expressly intended with evident sting for his Anglophone audience, though they are also available as an optional extra on the French DVD of *Film socialisme*) is, of course, on one level deeply insensitive, even offensive. Yet, on a purely formal level, might not such distortion and undermining of language and syntax *from within* also achieve finally what the shortlived project to create a new, black, revolutionary language and vocabulary discussed in chapter 1 could not, namely the explosion of Western syntax? In the particular case of *Notre Musique*, might, in fact, the free, undoctored speech of the Native Americans recapture, albeit in a different, nondeclarative mode, some of the utopian promise of black counterdiscourse glimpsed in *One plus One*? More generally, could these wholly new characters in Godard's cinema be accorded full agency and autonomy as real, flesh-and-blood characters, rather than be made simply to function as reductive types or fixed symbols, whether of oppression and revolt or their obverse, American hegemony?

The three Native Americans are observed in various combinations on seven separate occasions and in different kinds of shot: a series of long-shots of Aguilar and Gutiérrez in the ruined National Library; Brass and Gutiérrez cavorting together outside the Holiday Inn as Judith passes on her way to interview Darwish; a medium close-up of Aguilar listening in on Judith's interview with Darwish like a silent witness; a close-up of Aguilar and Brass waiting together in the hotel for Gutiérrez to descend the marble staircase in open sandals (another close-up that evokes Zoya's [Galina Vodyanitskaya] bare feet moving down a set of steps in the snow in Lev Arnshtam's *Zoya* [1944]); a rapid, inserted close-up of Aguilar and Gutiérrez huddled together on the street like migrant gypsies, he playing a flute, she singing along; an extreme long-shot of Aguilar, Gutiérrez, and Brass loading up a car near the Mostar bridge and heading off out of frame; and finally an image of all three in traditional costume in front of the Mostar bridge with Brass mounted on a horse, first in long-shot, then in much brighter medium long-shot. In the case of the National Library sequence, the most extended and composed of deliberately rough dry edits (there is nothing "smooth" or "natural" about the presence here of these "alien" beings), Aguilar and Gutiérrez declaim in turn a series of lines on the nature of mutual otherness, collective identity, and human *rapprochement* that take the form of open, rhetorical questions: "Isn't it about time, stranger, for us to meet face to face in the same age? Both of us strangers in the same land, meeting at the tip of an abyss?" These powerful words, the origin of which is left unidentified, are not acknowledged at all by the older male librarian to whom they are directed, and indeed, at one point, another female librarian even attempts (unsuccessfully) to wrest a book away from Gutiérrez. The scene is peremptorily cut, and the Native Americans are gone.

Figure 6.3. George Aguilar and Léticia Gutiérrez in the National Library in *Notre Musique* (2004).

We shall come back shortly to the full implications of this recited passage. What is important for the moment to recognize is that, as Burlin Barr puts it well, Godard presents the Native Americans as "remainders" outside the realm of (or possibility of) discourse.[5] Which is to say, these spectres or *"revenants"* demanding to be heard are always potentially present in the frame. Yet the final apparition of all three in tribal outfits in front of the Mostar bridge is clearly a fabricated image by Judith who in the previous shot is seen taking photographs of the Native Americans. The spectacular change in their clothing and physical bearing is a reflection of what she chooses to see. As Barr rightly suggests, Judith is seeking through her viewfinder a verification of preconceived ideas and attempting to reconstruct what she already knows: Native Americans as exotic, nonwhite others and instantly recognizable as a symbol or type. Barr states: "The Native Americans in warrior 'ethnic' garb 'appear as a phantasm' rather than as flesh-and-blood, contemporary subjects" (Barr 2010: 79). The other has thus become simply the object of a photo-op. Judith's professional efforts at documentation, however well-intentioned, result therefore in yet another instance of erasure: the Native Americans are cast according to her own cultural and political preconceptions and not by their own continuing attempts at self-definition, which include creating in the very site of another episode of recent genocide (Sarajevo) the possibility of establishing a new political voice. Hence, in suddenly becoming ultra-visible as "other," they are immediately reconsigned to obscurity and enjoy no agency or autonomy over their own mute image. In short, as with the conspicuous and noisome African American woman in *Éloge de l'amour* mentioned in chapter 1, Judith's confected image of the Native Americans in their flagrant display of difference represents the very *screening out* of difference rather than its celebration.

Figure 6.4. George Aguilar, Léticia Gutiérrez and Ferlyn Brass pictured by Judith in front of the Mostar bridge in *Notre Musique* (2004).

Judith, we recall, has come to Sarajevo to discover a fresh way of thinking about the relationship between Palestinians and Israelis as well as to attempt to arrange "a simple conversation" ("juste une conversation") on the topic of atonement between her absent grandfather and the French ambassador, Olivier Naville (Simon Eine), a member of the Resistance in World War II who had hidden Judith's grandparents in his garret in 1943. Lauded by Judith as a "free man," Naville hesitates to accept her invitation only because, he says, he would need to relinquish his job for the French Diplomatic Service, implicitly suggesting that such a conversation would raise uncomfortable questions about French responsibility for persecuting the Jews during Vichy and aiding the Germans in the deportation process. Striving for reconciliation and a true dialogue, Judith embodies hope and intellectual passion (Naville compares her to Hannah Arendt, an image of whom hangs on the Embassy walls), yet she also proves blinkered in her idealistic and overdetermined approach towards reconciliation, for she aims to converse only about psychology and morality. Moreover, in her (non)engagement with the Native Americans, Judith reveals herself here to be an artless digital photographer/journalist with no real aesthetic sensitivity or understanding of the poetics of *champ/contre-champ*. Oblivious to the creative and ethical possibilities of a "free" aesthetic, she would seek instead to freeze audiovisual and conceptual mobility and flux, surprise and transformation, into a "false" aesthetic image and fixed symbol of unity and reconciliation.

Judith's false image staged in front of the Mostar bridge brings to the fore the always latent question of the status of the bridge, still in the process of full reconstruction and over which human figures can periodically be seen walking. At its most positive, the bridge may be said to exist as a site of pure potential: the (re)bridging of opposed banks as a possible new and meaningful dialogue and reconciliation between Muslims and Croatians. Judith certainly sees the bridge in these terms, projecting onto it, and Sarajevo in general, her own hopes for peace and reconciliation between Israel and Palestine. Yet until that reconstruction is complete, the bridge remains arguably a static symbol of a destroyed idea of Europe as the coming together of different cultures and communities. Certainly, the artificial image produced by Judith suggests that for the moment the bridge risks being no more than a convenient yet ultimately empty symbol of intercultural exchange in the temporary and circumscribed cosmopolitan space of encounters and linguistic difference that is the international literary conference. Yet Godard characteristically invests supplementary aesthetic and philosophical meaning into the Mostar bridge. Immediately prior to Judith's photographic ruminations is an entire seven-minute sequence about the bridge, including amateur archival footage of its destruction in 1993 by Croats, slowed down and color-enhanced, thus making it an object of aesthetic contemplation. The scene details the bridge's physical recovery and forensic reconstruction and includes a pedagogical sequence set in a primary school where children attempt to talk about the future (Judith watches the history of the bridge being taught to children who then rehearse a song on the subject). The engineer Péqueux is also heard off-screen explaining to Judith that it's not simply a question of restoring tourism. He states: "We must restore the past and render the future possible. Combine the pain with the guilt," adding with a supremely Levinasian turn of phrase: "The relation between me and the other isn't *symmetrical*. At the start the other matters little in my regard [*à mon égard*]. It's his business. . . . For me, he's the one I'm responsible for. Here, a Muslim and a Croatian" (my emphasis). Judith, who just happens to be reading Levinas's *Entre nous* (1991) by the bridge, responds in kind: "We are guilty for everything and everyone. Myself as much as the other." This celebrated phrase is, of course, a key founding principle of Levinas's work derived from a passage in Dostoyevsky's *The Brothers Karamazov*: "We are all responsible for everything and guilty in front of everyone, but I am that more than all others." The dialogue continues. Péqueux: "The bridge has two faces and one truth." Judith: "That's difficult: if the face says 'Thou shalt not kill,' how can we make a face with stones?."

Figure 6.5. Judith (Sarah Adler) on the numbered stones of the Mostar bridge in *Notre Musique* (2004).

This discussion about two faces, truth, and the self/other relation is intensified by the fact that as it unfolds we both see and hear Judith speaking, while we only hear Péqueux (though his legs are intermittently visible). This is just one of the film's consistently odd and "unnatural" physical groupings and formations of people positioned together off-center in the frame and usually at an angle. In fact, Godard's formal strategy of insisting on otherness here and elsewhere in the film, part of his desire to keep sound and image, and image and image, always on the move and in asymmetrical relation so as not to force a false symmetry of form, clearly matches, and draws out, Péqueux's Levinasian statement about the asymmetry of self and other. In fact, Levinas's philosophical delineation of asymmetry informs directly the film's general ethical concerns regarding the face of the other. Levinas's theory of the ethical subject, we recall, is centered on a person's radical responsibility for a human other (what he calls "*le pour-l'autre*") which precedes any notion of individual freedom and even truth itself. Indeed, personal identity is defined solely in terms of infinite responsibility for the other. This absolute need of alterity makes us exist; only the other gives meaning to the self ("je est un autre" just as "l'Autre est un Je"). The other's face thus has the status of an epiphany. The conventional framework of the law enters only by way of the presence of the Third, for when I am face to face with the other to whom I am infinitely responsible, there is always a Third involved. From that moment (discussed at length in *Entre Nous*) new questions arise: how does my neighbor whom I face relate to this Third? Is he the Third's friend or his foe or even his victim? Who, of the two, is my true neighbor in the first place? (see Levinas 1991: 30–38). Such insistence on the necessary presence of the Third may help also to explain another recurring feature of *Notre Musique*:

that of a persistent third (sometimes even fourth) presence or "eye," which, as Barr rightly claims, is always on hand to witness the social exchanges. An obvious example is the young unnamed female conference worker who never speaks but is consistently glimpsed in the frame of the image. Such moments, according to Barr, "make visible the subaltern [. . .] marginal subjectivities" (Barr 2010: 84), as if Godard were positing alterity as a position of witnessing and perception rather than merely trying to account for otherness or assimilate it (ibid).[6] Certainly, this formal strategy of the Third eye serves as a natural counterpart to the theory of *champ/contre-champ* and is of a piece with the asymmetry of sound and image in *Notre Musique*, its decentered framing of the figure, and, of course, its ternary structure.

However, for Levinas the legal relationship with the Third, necessary as it is, remains always grounded in the subject's primordial ethical relationship to the other. The responsibility for the other, that is, the subject as the response to the infinite call embodied in the other's face which is simultaneously helpless, vulnerable, and issuing an unconditional command, is, for Levinas, fundamentally *asymmetrical* and *nonreciprocal*: I am responsible for the other without having any right to claim that the other should display the same responsibility for me. The ethical asymmetry between me and the other addressing me with the infinite call means that I should be ready to take responsibility for the other even to the point of taking the other's place and becoming a hostage for the other. For these reasons the ethical in Levinas is incompatible with the political: ethics involves an asymmetrical relationship in which I am always already responsible for the other, while politics is more the domain of symmetrical equality and distributive justice.[7]

As Irmgard Emmelhainz emphasizes, by postulating via Levinas that we are all guilty for everyone and everything, *Notre Musique* is suggesting that the wish to establish relationships of restitutionary debt is really beside the point. An attempt at a new beginning based on restitution and cultural rehabilitation as a way towards forgiveness was, of course, made in Sarajevo. Yet, as Emmelhainz suggests, rehabilitation is not able to rearrange the past since it reestablishes the past as it previously existed, and as "novelty," rather than readjusting and accounting for it. It neither promises nor guarantees forgiveness, which provides at least a potential means of breaking away from infinite debt and, along with making a promise, offers the possibility of new beginnings (Emmelhainz 2009: 854). With this in mind we can perhaps place in clearer perspective the film's opening voice-over statement of qualified forgiveness that tropes on the Lord's Prayer. The film would be appearing to advocate, *contra* Levinas, that unconditional relations with the other (here in the form of absolute forgiveness) are not possible in practice, and that one should aim instead for some kind of equivalence and parity. The fact that this voice belongs, as we later realize, to Judith obliges us to relate the idea of forgiveness to her particular wish for "just a conversation" on the topic of atonement, as opposed to the pretension of "a just [i.e., rightful] conversation" that was, as Emmelhainz notes, the dubious premise of the discourse of reconciliation and forgiveness in the Balkans inspired by the recent Oslo Accords of 1993 and 1995 between Israel and the Palestine Liberation Organization (PLO) (see Emmelhainz 2014). Yet *Notre*

Musique is also making it very clear, precisely in Sarajevo as a preeminent space of cultural reconciliation and dialogue, that the possibilities of personal atonement are extremely limited. Not only does that "simple conversation" not actually happen in the film, but also forgiveness and the appeal to reason cannot easily form the basis of an ethical encounter, especially when the stakes of collective destruction are so high.

The question of a possible ethics and alterity of war becomes, of course, even more pressing when the war in question is with one's immediate neighbor, as was the case in Bosnia. Emmelhainz summarizes well the complexities of this dilemma: "Is it a matter of acknowledging guilt and suffering, or asking for forgiveness? Is it a matter of judgment and trial, establishing a relationship of infinite debt? Can it be reestablished with a promise, with forgiveness, or redress? How can the bond between men and the world, destroyed when the neighbour turns against the self, be restituted?" (Emmelhainz 2009). Once war is over, the vanquished enemy becomes the survivor, "an other," as opposed to "the Other." Emmehainz again: "Thus, the survivor is not the Other, it is someone else ("un autre") after having undergone not only the destruction—which is to make something created pass into nothingness—of her life-world, but also the destruction of the bond that is "in-between" men, which is the link to the world" (ibid.).⁹ This is the message, too, of the film's references to the *indélibile* in the work of the Holocaust survivor and writer Jean Améry, whose essay "Torture" from *At the Mind's Limits*, an account of "his Auschwitz," is cited in its French translation. The essay's final paragraph (slightly reworked by Godard) is recited by "C. Maillard" who remarks in the taxi as it passes through the ruins of Sarajevo: "When it's all over, nothing is the same/ Violence leaves a deep scar/ A trace of the oblivion always remains./ The trust in the world that terror destroys is irretrievable./ Violence severs the safe line." As Alan Wright emphasizes, resentment is ultimately for Améry the only possible precondition for an ethical encounter between the victims of the Holocaust and the German people, since the difference between victim and perpetrator must not be dialectically neutralized but accepted and integrated absolutely (Wright 2012: 10). Wright concludes correctly that for late Godard also, "[t]he ravages of Time and the wreckage of History cannot be repaired through any act of forgiveness or appeal to reason" (ibid.).⁸

Are we to infer from these various arguments that the ethical and political as presented in *Notre Musique* must always remain, as in Levinas, incommensurate and incompatible? Further, if we are always to read the other *asymmetrically*, does that preclude the possibility of negotiating ethical responsibility in the messy day-to-day world of politics and social history? Put differently, is the elegantly simple, abstract equation of absolute ethical responsibility, like the high theory of *champ/contre-champ*, impossible to put adequately into practice, especially in a film like *Notre Musique*, which adopts in large part a documentary mode and takes place within the complex historical and social-political boundaries of Sarajevo?

In the absence of an immediate answer, let us return to the Mostar bridge, which, despite repeated views of its reconstruction from different angles and in different formats, we never really get close to, still less stand on top of or walk across. Indeed, it is clear from Godard's master class that any "real" crossing or transfer in this film will need to function at a metaphorical rather than strictly literal or symbolic level. No one image or metaphor, however potentially dynamic, is allowed to literalize the film's poetics of bridging and *rapprochement* of ideas and realities through montage which alone for Godard is capable of reformulating human relations and generating understanding. This essential fact informs every key encounter in the film, for national forgiveness and ethnic reconciliation is always more than simply fixing a bridge connecting two societies and cultures pitted against each other. Indeed, if the bridge represents anything at all in Godard's stripping away of the all-too-easy symbolic memorialization of a historic monument in the name of unity and reconciliation, it is that it, and metaphor more generally, connects only virtually and through difference, generating in turn yet more difference in an endless flow of metaphoricity. To cross the Mostar bridge literally in the film is an impossibility; it can only "bridge" opposites figuratively. Yet precisely out of such literal impossibility comes a potentially limitless possibility of figuration. All of Godard's thinking and work on metaphor in *Notre Musique* is founded on this simple yet crucial fact. Indeed, the film's figurative density is the very sign of Godard's success in dismantling symbol and ensuring the flow of metaphor. Hence, the real, concrete literal bridge of stones, and Péqueux's misconceived if noble attempt to renumber them all in order to reconstruct the bridge in the name of historical accuracy, become effectively irrelevant to Godard's poetics of cinematic bridging and *rapprochement*. Indeed, it may only constitute the ground over which such a poetics is ever possible.[10] By crossing through so many strata of difference in a vast, dynamic network of cultural associations, *Notre Musique* prioritizes the poetic and imaginary over the drive to obligatory reconciliation and commemoration partly endorsed by Péqueux. If there is any bridging to be done in *Notre Musique* it will take us beyond the purely visible and concrete—to the point, in fact, that what we see in front of us is not actually the point at all. For to "see" properly in cinema we need to work and read through the explicit image (the recorded real and its many aporia) in order to grasp aesthetically and ethically the implicit, operative metaphor, that is to say, the very act of producing meaning.

The Color of Metaphor: Native Americans/Jews/Palestinians

It is at this point that we need to return to the passage jointly recited by the Native Americans in the empty shell of the National Library, a building, we recall, which, with its Muslim-inspired architecture, served as the central repository of Bosnian written culture and was deliberately targeted by Orthodox Christian Serbian ultranationalists in August 1992 as part of a strategy of cultural erasure. The lines about being mutually other in a pending encounter of two peoples who are both strangers to the same land derive, in fact, from Darwish, specifically his long prose-poem entitled "The Last Speech of the Red Indian," cited here in selective and modified parts.[11] The poem is based on a speech by Chief Seattle, one of the last chiefs to surrender formally to the American government. Prefaced by a direct quote from Chief Seattle on death as a transitional state, it refers directly to Christopher Columbus and establishes an implicit link between America in 1492 and Palestine in 1948. Darwish addresses the destructive legacy of Columbus and the fate of the Native Americans "in the ash of legends."[12] As Emmelhainz indicates, and in line with what we have just established regarding the processes of reconciliation and reconstruction in Bosnia-Herzegovina, the postcolonial *plainte* heard here is beyond claiming restitution and recognition or singing a nostalgic elegy to what was lost (Emmelhainz 2009: 881). Instead, the words confer on Columbus a list of "rights" that pertain to his particular way of mapping the world according to the dictates of colonial cartography. However, what the Native Americans will never grant him is the right to believe that all men are equal. The recited poem continues:

> Let Columbus scour the seas to find India,
> It is his right!
> He can call our ghosts the names of spices,
> He can call us Red Indians,
> He can fiddle with his compass to correct his course,
> Twist all the errors of the North wind,
> But outside the narrow world to his map,
> He cannot believe that all men are born equal
> The same as air and water,
> The same as people in Barcelona,
> Except that they happen to worship Nature's God in
> Everything,
> And not gold.

Thus do the "Red Indians" convey their past-present status as the inevitable outcome of a historical event that has perpetuated inequality and further humiliation in spite of the universal proclamation of the equality of all humans. Darwish's inferred juxtaposition here of the Native American ordeal with that of the Palestinians hinges on the form of colonization both peoples have undergone. In each case the experience of disaster has been, as Chief Seattle put it, that of "the end of life and the beginning of survival" (ibid.: 883). Differently from Latin American, Asian, and African colonial and postcolonial processes, Native North Americans and Palestinians have not just been exploited but rather expelled from their land, their histories systematically erased, and their cultures suppressed. In the words of Chief Seattle, the "colonialists' appetite [. . .] devoured the earth and left behind only a desert." For the Native Americans suffered not only mass extermination but also the further horror of having their names and languages all but extinguished in the process. In the case of the Palestinians, while they have retained their language, they do not officially "exist" as a people because Palestine has never really existed as a land. Both peoples thus share the predicament of how now to assert their historical presence in the face of historical and geographical effacement, dispossession of their land, and collective punishment.

What is the exact force of Godard's effective endorsement of this equivalence between the Palestinian discourse of absence and that of the "Red Indians"? The Native Americans are, in fact, located at the center of a recurring tension in his work between Jew/Israeli and Arab/Palestinian, which takes the form here of an opposition between two different types of aesthetic strategy. On the one hand, Judith appropriates their visual image and identity for her own political purposes; on the other, their only major speech is prewritten by Darwish. This opposition comes to a head when Judith interviews Darwish. As we might expect by now, this is a heavily formalized and asymmetrically staged interview between the fictional Judith as a young Israeli journalist asking questions in Hebrew, and the real Darwish as a much older and celebrated Palestinian poet/intellectual responding in Arabic (Darwish is actually reciting lines provided by Godard based on an interview printed in Hebrew between Darwish and the Israeli writer Helit Yeshurun in 1996). In an oblique approximation of *champ/contre-champ* that once again does not conform to the standard cinematic set-up of shot/countershot and avoids subjective POV shots, Darwish is filmed at the start in silhouette with his back to us while facing the window and looking out towards the Sarajevo cityscape in the background. The axis is changed when Darwish is pictured from the front top left of the frame, with Judith now viewed from behind in the bottom right. Darwish's assertion that "the truth always has two faces"—a statement preempting Godard's lecture on the image and directly contradicting Péqueux's idea of the bridge as having two faces and only one truth—triggers a frontal shot of him facing Judith. The interlocutors are now formally engaged in a meeting of gazes, or points of view, under the watchful eyes of Aguilar as the ever-present Third. Indeed, to acknowledge the simultaneous existence of each of the two faces is precisely to infer the presence of a third position or term. To reinvoke Godard's theory during the master class: the reverse-shot is not the "other" of the shot, but "the same" in a different situation. Hence, two sides of a common story are brought together visually face to face and, as in an ideal *champ/contre-champ*, they present *difference in kind*.

Darwish and Judith are both in search of a new dialogue across race, culture, generation, and gender, based on their shared love for the same land. Fueled by a spirit of reconciliation and forgiveness, Judith dreams of setting aside entrenched differences. As for Darwish, he explains that literature since Homer has been on the side of the winners, and it's now his job as a Palestinian poet to speak for Troy, that is, history's losers. Darwish: "I wanted to speak in the name of the absentee, in the name of the Trojan poet. There is more poetic inspiration and humanity in defeat than in victory. Even in defeat there is deep poetry, and probably deeper poetry. If I belonged to the victor's camp, I would participate in demonstrations in support for the victims." The interview becomes almost a combat of words among the vanquished. Darwish to Judith: "A people with no poetry are a defeated people." Judith: "You say there's no more room for Homer and you are the Trojan's bard and you love the vanquished. You're talking like a Jew!" Darwish explains further the paradox of the

Palestinians: they have the misfortune of having as their enemy Israel, a state that enjoys unlimited international support, yet they also enjoy the great fortune of having the world's media focused on their plight precisely because the Jews are the center of attention: "You [the Jews] have brought us defeat and renown [. . .] they [the world's media] only take an interest in me [Arab] because of you [Jew]."

Figure 6.6. Judith (Sarah Adler) interviewing Mahmoud Darwish in *Notre Musique* (2004).

The encounter between Judith and Darwish foregrounds some of the film's key issues: the cyclical exchangeability and transhistorical relationship between the defeated and the conquerors; alterity, ethical responsibility, and atonement; and the central significance of metaphor to all questions concerning race and culture. In fact, Darwish's crucial collection of interviews with Arab and Israeli journalists and writers during the 1990s entitled *La Palestine comme métaphore* (2002) is directly referred to here when Judith reads out a line from it—one that immediately becomes a bone of contention between the two. Darwish claims that the cited phrase "If they defeat us in poetry, then it's the end" has been mistranslated from the Arabic, insisting: "One can read it differently." The title, *La Palestine comme métaphore*, already clearly suggests that Palestine (which is, after all, a Hebrew word: "Falestine") remains deeply embedded within the Western (colonial) imaginary. A quick snap-shot of the major themes from the volume reveals, moreover, how closely Darwish's approach resonates with Godard's metaphorical method and thinking in *Notre Musique* and his later work in general: the ironic unfolding of history and its confrontation of self with other; the imperative of poetry and the imagination; the overlapping and interdependence of cultures; the false concept and promise of the state; and a commitment to the oppressed and defeated. In fact, both Godard and Darwish deal in universal terms with the human condition and dare to speak in the name of *"nous"* by examining the landscape of history, collective memory, and the intrinsic links between self and other, identity and its otherness. Similarly they favor "nonexistence," both aesthetically and existentially. Like the moving image for Godard, so poetry for Darwish represents the continual tracing of absence. Moreover, if Godard feels exiled in contemporary cinema, Darwish remained physically removed from his native village of Birwa in Palestine (he resided in his later years in Ramallah). In both cases, much is predicated on loss and a permanent sense of suffering, death, and war. As the title of one of Darwish's collections in English puts it, "unfortunately, it was paradise."[13]

The translator of the interviews in Arabic included in *La Palestine comme métaphore* is the historian Elias Sanbar, Darwish's official French translator who was responsible for introducing Darwish and Goytisolo to the project of *Notre Musique* at Godard's request (he was also present at the 2002 Sarajevo conference attended by Godard).[14] Godard had first met Sanbar during the shooting of *Jusqu'à la victoire* on which he acted as translator and intermediary, and the three hundredth anniversary issue of *Cahiers du Cinéma* featured (p. 17) a letter by Godard to Sanbar dated July 19, 1977, where he discusses the terms "Jew" and "Muslim." Sanbar, whose works include *Palestine 1948: L'expulsion* (1984); *Palestine, le pays à venir* (1996); and *Les Palestiniens dans le siècle* (1994), as well as a documentary entitled *Mahmoud Darwish: The Land as Language* (1998), which he co-directed, is credited in *Notre Musique* simply as "Mémoire" (Memory), a clear reference to his book, *Les Palestiniens. La photographie d'une terre et de son peuple de 1839 à nos jours* (2004).[15] In this remarkable compendium of visual images and documents detailing the *mise en image* of the Palestinians through history (every available known style and format of image of the Palestinians produced either by themselves or by others—historical, staged, propagandistic, touristic, photographic, studio confected, cinematographic— is examined), Sanbar recounts how the invention of the *daguerrotype* propelled a wave of photographic campaigns by the Western empires into the Holy Land in the mid-to-late nineteenth century, with the result that Palestine was effectively obliterated by the colonial gaze. The book provided vital background information for Godard, who had wished initially for *Notre Musique* to be a direct statement about Palestine but felt unable to return to film in the Middle East. Hence in part his reason for choosing Sarajevo and restaging the 2002 conference, a natural site of confluence for artists and intellectuals in real and existential exile.[16] Like Godard, Sanbar shares an absolute belief in the image as a means of proof and testimony. At one point in the book, under the title "Rendre Visible" ("Making Visible"), Sanbar even analyzes an iconic photographic image taken of the filming of the *Jusqu'à la victoire*, concluding: "Gazes that link together to try to say what a Palestinian refugee camp is in 1969."[17]

The shared aesthetic, historical, and political interests of Sanbar, Godard, and Darwish converge directly around their common understanding that the tragic fate of the Native Americans is equivalent to that of the Palestinians. Indeed, *Les Palestiniens. La Photographie d'une terre et de son peuple de 1839 à nos jours* contains a devastating reference to the genocide of American Indians. In the section "Trois Portraits, Deux Regards" ("Three Portraits, Two Gazes"), Sanbar reproduces a photograph from the 1880s of a "Peau-Rouge" ("Red-Skin") called Daisy, which he juxtaposes with the portrait of a Palestinian woman, "La mariée de Bethléem" ("The Married woman of Bethlehem"), produced by the French photographic studio Maison Bonfils. Sanbar writes that the two images effectively show the same woman with identical decors and interchangeable characters—a woman who is destined to disappear.[18] In his other important study of the same year, *Figures du Palestinien. Identité des origines, identité de devenir*, Sanbar discusses at some length the parallels between the expulsion of the Palestinians from their native land and the persecution of the Native Americans during the American conquest of the Midwest and far west (the subchapter "Peaux-Rouges" explicitly references Godard's views on American imperialism).[19] The parallels will be spelled out directly, and not merely metaphorically, in Godard's later *Film socialisme* where Sanbar appears as himself and where footage of the Nazi death camps in slow motion is followed by two clips, the first from John Ford's *Cheyenne Autumn* (1964), showing women and children of the forced Cheyenne exodus, the second from Claude Lanzmann's 1994 documentary *Tsahal* (an aerial shot of an Israeli fighter jet patrolling the coastline as a voice-over intones "Palestine"). As Henrik Gustafsson has shown, the linking of two colonial enterprises in North America and the Middle East, not only through their shared myth of a promised land but also on account of a similar rationale legitimizing the eviction of its former inhabitants, underlines their common ignorance of territorial sovereignty and citizenship (Gustafsson 2014: 222–23). The sequence recalls, too, a set-piece of montage in the first episode of *Histoire(s)* where, after a meditation on the Nazi camps and a quote from Lanzmann (the train pulling into Treblinka in *Shoah*), there follows a color photograph of a Palestinian boy marching with a burning U.S. flag. Superimposed in the flames are images from D. W. Griffith's *The Birth of a Nation* (1915), followed by a tracking shot of John Wayne racing through a Native American camp in Ford's *The Searchers* (1965). Allusions to the Navajo reservation in Ford's Monument Valley pervade *Histoire(s)*.

We can thus better appreciate now that the entire Mostar bridge sequence in *Notre Musique* featuring Native Americans is essentially about the Palestinians and their demands for visibility and recognition. While it may seem that Godard is letting the Native Americans speak in their own voice and irreducible difference as the other (in this film of perpetually missed encounters they do not engage in dialogue with anyone other than themselves), they are not actually able to speak their own words but simply relay a poem that co-opts their history and discourse as a metaphor for speaking about Palestine. In this playing off of one other with another, the viewer is obliged to read metaphorically *through* the three Native Americans in order to grasp the "real" picture, namely, the fate of the Palestinians. This is a highly instructive example of the way Godard can move through otherness by generating still further otherness, yet not in the express interests of the other but ultimately to reduce the other to the same. Hence, although both clearly heard and seen in *Notre Musique*, the Native Americans, conscripted in an escalating, self-reflexive chain of metaphoricity, function as merely a figure and vehicle (and arguably decoy) for a more contemporary and immediately pressing instance of otherness that is not their own.

In short, the Native Americans striving to be recognized through language and images are no less—yet also no more—than potent figures for the Palestinians who have always been for Godard the true revolutionaries because they are an exemplary oppressed and disinherited people. In 1970 he declared to Andrew Sarris: "The Palestinians are the real Marxist revolutionaries, the disinherited of the earth, but they never speak of socialism and radicalism [. . .] Al Fatah and the Palestinians will eventually overthrow all the corrupt regimes in the Middle East, be they bourgeois Arab or American Zionist" (Sterritt 1998: 56). A far from convinced Sarris acknowledged that Godard believed blindly in Al Fatah as the instrument of a benign transformation of the Arab vision from the holy warfare of Mohammed to the class warfare of Marx. It goes almost without saying that the vital role and value accorded to the Palestinians and Arabs in Godard's thinking are diametrically different from that of Africans and African Americans who have morphed dramatically over time from revolutionary other to reactionary same. By contrast, the special status of the Palestinians in Godard's work has changed extremely little since the days of his collaboration with Darwish and the Feddayin in Amman. It is significant, too, that although *Jusqu'à la victoire* was aborted largely due to the advent of war (conceptual and financial issues were also a factor), it was, unlike Godard's impossible project for Mozambique, at least salvageable and recuperable as a new and entirely different film, *Ici et ailleurs*.

We are entitled to ask if the aesthetic processes at work in *Notre Musique* are any more ethically desirable and "just" than Judith's intrinsically false photographic treatment of the Native Americans. For Godard's impressive commitment to keeping metaphor on the move and not reducing the Native Americans to mere symbol is assured only by appropriating the otherness of the other and making it work instead as figure. The metaphorical reading of one people through another (here the Palestinians through the Native Americans) in a real space (Sarajevo) that itself serves as a metaphor for Palestine, exile, and cinema more generally,[20] matches exactly the formal asymmetry (pushed gleefully at times by Godard to the level of dissymmetry) of *champ/contre-champ*. Hence, both forms of figuration, though very different in approach and design, end up effectively erasing the visible, present other. Such, one might argue, are the ethical perils of a cinematic method founded on the standard cinematic principles of field and reverse field, positive and negative, doubling and inversion, and sustained by metaphor which is always greedy for more raw material. Yet it raises again the question we asked earlier regarding the Native Americans: how does the Palestinian other ultimately fit within the inner workings of Godard's film poetics, and what are the particular terms and conditions of this other's presence? We have already seen how Darwish is foregrounded in his interview with Judith. We need now to return once again to Godard's master class where the most politically charged instance of *champ/contre-champ* revolves around the common history of the Jews and the Palestinians.

Jew ≠ Muslim: Poetic Transfer

Following the controversial sequence in *JLG/JLG: autoportrait de décembre* where he drew a "stereophonic" Star of David (a kind of mystical hexagram) out of two triangles, one overlaid in reverse on the first, in order to demonstrate the ironic unfolding of history ("there was Germany/ which projected Israel/ Israel which reflected/ this projection/ and Israel found its cross/ and the law of the stereo/ continues/ Israel projected the Palestinian/ people/ and the Palestinian people/ in turn/ carried its cross" [Godard 1996a: 28]), Godard promotes in the master class of *Notre Musique* the provocative idea, virtually *de rigueur* in his later work, that Jewish prisoners on the verge of death in Nazi concentration camps during the Second World War were sometimes described as "Muselmänner" ("Muslims").[21] "Muselmann" was, in fact, the term used by the Nazis to describe those so severely ill, exhausted, malnourished, and faceless and deprived of speech and experience, that, as Giorgio Agamben puts it, they were the living dead on the point of "bare life" (Agamben 2002b: 55). For Agamben, as for Primo Levi, the Muselmann, this threshold figure between the human and the inhuman, was, in fact, "the exemplary, privileged "complete witness; to the Holocaust" (Agamben 2002b: 165). In the specific context of Godard's film historiography, the Jew reduced to a Muselmann was also, as Michael Witt suggests, "the ultimate witness to the atrocities of the Holocaust that cinema failed to be" (Witt 2013: 186). Godard had first aired this idea in *Ici et ailleurs* through the linking of two key images both located inside camps: a young Fedayeen woman patrolling a border fence in a refugee camp in Jordan, and archival footage (originally employed in Alain Resnais's *Nuit et Brouillard* [1955]) of bodies being dragged and dumped into mass graves in a Nazi camp in Poland after the liberation. It was accompanied by the words: "Here's a Jew in such a state the SS call him a Muslim [*musulman*]," the term "Muslim" designating the final act to seal the destruction of the last remnant of the Jewish people.[22]

Yet in the master class of *Notre Musique* Godard's *rapprochement* of terms goes even further. He first juxtaposes the image of a face captioned by the word "Juif" ("Jew") with another image of a Jew in a concentration camp on the threshold of death accompanied by the word "Musulman." He also cites orally a reflection on the precariousness and political contingency of visuality by Louis-Ferdinand Céline, who wrote in 1936 (in *Mort à crédit* [*Death on the Instalment Plan*]) that the facts no longer speak for themselves, for already "the field of the text has integrated [*recouvert*, literally 'covered up'] that of vision." Godard then attempts to bring the Jews and Palestinians together as two communities of survivors and exiled peoples by juxtaposing what seem to be two quite similar photographs, one in color, the other black and white, of a crowd of people gathered around a small boat in shallow water. In a new and entirely unexpected contortion of the real versus fiction binary that underpins all his work, he states: "In 1948 the Israelites walk on water into the Promised Land; the Palestinians walk into the water to drown: Shot and reverse-shot: the Jewish people joined fiction, the Palestinian people documentary." Godard's use of the French word *"noyade"* ("drowning") invokes the *"Nakba"* ("catastrophe"), the term often used by Palestinians, like "transfer," to refer to their exodus and displacement at the time of the Israeli Declaration of Independence during the 1948 Palestine War. For Godard, the Jews entered the world of legend (the Promised Land was an "eternal fiction" for the Jews since biblical times, he will later declare in Alain Fleischer's documentary, *Morceaux de conversations avec Jean-Luc Godard* [2007]), whilst the Palestinians were consigned to reality. The message of this highly contentious concatenation of terms is clear: the cost of Jewish identity is the physical expulsion of others and their ongoing cultural erasure.

Figure 6.7–8. The provocation of shot/reverse-shot: Godard juxtaposing the "Israelites" and the Palestinians in his master class in *Notre Musique* (2004).

For Emmelhainz, Godard's seemingly abstract assertion that Palestinians fell into documentary refers concretely to the fact that Palestinians have increasingly presented themselves through documentary and other forms of documentation as a people with a history and as victims of Israeli expulsion and occupation—part of their political project to highlight their cause and promote the liberation of the land where their history was written. Indeed, documentary functions for the Palestinians precisely as a type of politicized memory detailing their collective lives before the Nakba, as well as a form of collective identity which state sovereignty and territory would normally provide. In fact, according to oral historian Sonia Nimr, the task of remembering in order to transmit and preserve "what was" has replaced the centenary tradition of storytelling in Palestine.[23] It is one of the reasons why, in the case of Palestinian self-representation, the struggle is also one for the "right to narrate." For Hamid Dabashi, meanwhile, there is currently a mimetic crisis in Palestinian self-representation because everything has become too fictive to be fictionalized and too unreal to accommodate any metaphor. The result is a "traumatic realism" through visual and literary documentaries in a frenzy to create records of silenced crimes and victimization (Emmelhainz 2009: 653). It has triggered an attempt by Palestinians to recover the human emotions generated by their ongoing displacement and exile, whether in the form of personal confessions, writing-reportage, or literary responses to the events. An explicit plea is made, in fact, in *Notre musique* for individual belief as the right to fiction. "C. Maillard" states: "I only believe myself in stories where the witnesses have their throats cut."[24]

Yet Godard's particular *rapprochement* of the terms "documentary" and "fiction," "Palestinians" and "Israelites" (the latter often used by Godard in preference to "Jews" or "Israelis," no doubt due to his growing up in a right-wing family where such words were terms of insult and abuse), forms part of a larger *champ/contre-champ* as dissymmetry involving the Jews and Palestinians—one that Godard fleshed out in interviews around *Notre Musique* where he stated (following Sanbar) that the Israelis found the "other" in the Palestinians, but the Israelis are not the chosen other of Palestinians. In fact, Palestinians had to construct their own "image as other" ("[u]ne image d'autres'"), that is, as what Europeans since the colonial period have called simply "the Arabs," because up until then they had existed only textually (Godard 2004c: 21). Godard is adamant that by inventing a bridging of this kind he is not suggesting that the Shoah and the Nakba are the same thing, merely establishing a *"mise en relation,"* that is to say, a way to interrogate facts which arise but which cannot otherwise be related. He declares: "The shot and the reverse-shot do not mean equivalence, they rather pose a question [. . .] When the Israelis found 'the other' in the Palestinians [. . .] they had to encounter them face to face. Whereas for the Palestinians it is not the same thing, Israel is not the 'other' of Palestinians. This dissymmetry constitutes a true shot/reverse-shot, a forming of relations between terms that poses questions rather than equates them" (Godard 2004c: 20). Godard is treading a fine line: on the one hand he wishes to make complex authorial parallels and correspondences by bridging together different terms and ideas, yet on the other he claims these are not strict or binding equivalences and function merely as open questions to be made sense of by the viewer. Of course, on one level Godard is simply pointing out that the West's response to events in the Middle East and the West Bank is almost invariably asymmetrical, and also exposing the nature and history of common asymmetrical oppositions such as "Palestinians and Jews," "Israelis and Muslims," the "West and Islam," which have naturalized nationalistic, ethnic, and religious distinctions. The problematic equation of nation, religion, and ethnic identity has not only transformed the Palestinians into the "others" of the Israelis, but also has encouraged any critique of both Israel's exclusive origins and its continuing policies regarding land resettlement to be characterized as anti-Semitism.

Witt effectively endorses Godard's attempt at intellectual self-justification here when he suggests that Godard's "technique of *rapprochement* in no way implies a direct equivalence between the various elements that he brings together, but rather a process of dynamic inter-activity and the production of critical thought resulting from the effects of what Vertov termed the *interval* between them" (Witt 2013: 181). But does this view perhaps let Godard off the hook too easily and allow him *carte blanche* to make any political linkages and bridgings he so chooses, whatever their effect and provocation? (Strangely, in the same interview referred to, Godard dilutes the poetic and political force of this stated strategy by suggesting that the camera serves as the *contre-champ* of the projector.) The film critic and curator Dominique

Païni, who collaborated unsuccessfully with Godard during the mid-2000s on the abortive project for the Centre Pompidou in Paris, *Collage(s) de France*, is surely right when he wrote in a letter to Godard that the filmmaker has inadvertently "frozen" the relations between the real world and the world of images by letting personal "ideological resentment" get in the way of the aesthetic. For if anything, according to Païni, Israel has now become documentary (the Zionist project has after all been achieved), while Palestine has become fiction (cited in de Baecque 2010: 796). Païni is accusing Godard of not reversing his political propositions with the same freedom and alacrity he naturally applies to his aesthetic formulations. In order not to be led up the garden path by Godard into ethical and political error, we shall need, Païni implies, to do this vital critical work for ourselves. Meanwhile, for the film critic and historian Jean Narboni who, in *Morceaux de conversations avec Jean-Luc Godard*, takes Godard to task for his *rapprochement* of Jews and fiction versus Palestinians and documentary in *Notre Musique*, Godard appears to be qualifying the Jewish notion of the Promised Land as a wild, "immemorial dream" or "fantasy" ("*chimère*"), that is, as an unrealistic, utopian, and illegitimate biblical fiction (cited in Fleischer 2011: 119). In the process, the Bible, which for Jews constitutes the supreme point of reference, is disqualified as pure fiction and a "mere detour" (ibid). What Godard is really saying with his act of montage, according to Narboni, is that Palestinians are legitimately part of the incontestable real, while the Israelis are part of the unreality and "lie" of fiction.[25]

Notre Musique requires, in fact, that we place it in the expressly anti-Zionist context of *Ici et ailleurs* which addressed in often agonizing terms the problem of how to relay politically the voice and image of the Palestinian other, especially when that other has been drowned out by ideology and mainstream Western media. It also included in one notorious *rapprochement* an image of Golda Meir juxtaposed with that of Hitler. On the soundtrack we also hear Hitler using the word "Palestinian," commonly employed during the 1930s to describe those Zionists who were eking out a life in ancient Judea and Canaan, the territory then under British mandate (the term was not really used to describe Arabs living in Israel

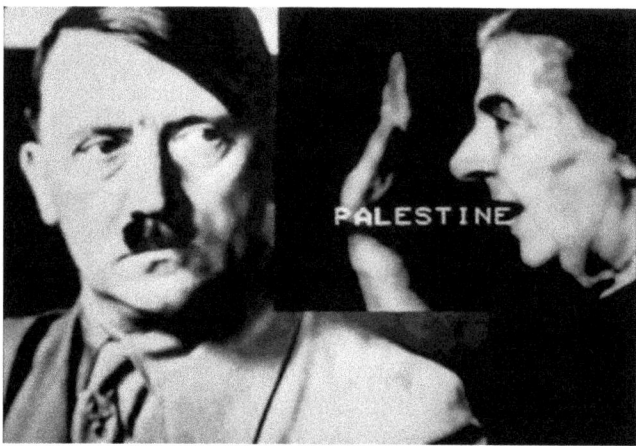

Figure 6.9. Hitler juxtaposed with Golda Meir in *Ici et ailleurs* (1974).

until the 1960s). In another key conversation from *Morceaux de conversations avec Jean-Luc Godard*, Narboni argues that the juxtaposition of Hitler and Meir was clearly intended by Godard as an equivalence between what the Nazis did to the Jews and what the Jews are currently doing to the Palestinians. He adds that even Godard's pro-Palestinian friend and admirer, Gilles Deleuze (who, we note, not only championed Godard's interstitial method of montage in *Six fois deux* [see Deleuze 1992] but also published an article with Sanbar referring expressly to the Palestinians as the "Indians [i.e., American Indians] of Palestine" [see Deleuze and Sanbar 1982]), found it difficult to defend him on this insulting parallel. Godard responds to this accusation by immediately disqualifying Deleuze as a Parisian celebrity with his own local agenda. Yet the crucial question of "who" exactly are the Palestinians in terms of a political community, and "who" may speak for them, remains a serious and fundamental concern for Godard, and he will return to it in *Film socialisme* where he confers on both Palestine and the Palestinian state the same territorial status at the level of language, in the process underscoring the asymmetry between the status of the land and the unacknowledged people in their obliterated state (see Emmelhainz 2014).

Godard is not done yet in his ratiocinations of *Notre Musique*, however. For while it may appear that the Jews and Palestinians are twin elements in the particular conjunction of race and alterity during the master class, the film's pivotal *champ/contre-champ* remains that aligning the Palestinians with the Native Americans. Godard puts it in the clearest of terms in the cited interview: "The true shot/counter-shot of the Palestinians is doubtlessly less Israel than the Indians" (Godard 2004c: 20). In other words, in yet another turning of the metaphorical screw, what might appear in *Notre Musique* to be exclusively about the historical relations between the Jews and Palestinians must be read in more metaphorical terms (the very terms Godard has been instructing us to adopt throughout the film) as actually about the Palestinians and Native Americans. Therein lies the truest equivalence, and in Godard's merry-go-round of others the Jews are represented as no more than the means to achieve it. This simple fact belies the apparent obsession with the Jews attributed to Godard by many critics like Antoine de Baecque who see the Jewish question as Godard's persistent blind-spot since the 1970s due to what they represent for him, namely, the victim become executioner (de Baecque 2010: 796).

The Eternal Double Bind

Our analysis of the stark implications of Godard's sophisticated aesthetic maneuvers in *Notre Musique* corresponds in large part to that proposed by Jacques Rancière. For Rancière, Godard's dissymmetrical presentation of the Native Americans in *Notre Musique* in order to denounce oppression (the injustice suffered by the Palestinians likened first to the fate, both military and poetic, of Troy, then to that of the Jews assassinated in the camps, and finally to the silence of a former French resistance fighter [Judith's grandfather]), is, in both aesthetic and political and ethical terms, profoundly muddled and unsatisfactory. On the one hand, the speech of the Native

Americans resounds in the empty library so that the European dialogue of injustices may never be forgotten. On the other, togged up in parodic Red-Skin feathers with their horse in front of the Mostar bridge, they denounce the clichés of the European imaginary. Yet these two distinct kinds of denunciation, which, according to Rancière, should really be conjoined, cancel each other out, since the bodies present on the screen do not have the autonomy that would allow them to form a synthesis of sound and image. Indeed, the Native Americans are presented as mute and have no effective agency or autonomy as real living bodies because they are irrevocably split between sound and image (Rancière 2011: 123–24). In fact, Rancière rightly argues, the film's denunciation of the stereotypes of the image serves only to take away the Native Americans' power of speech and give it back to the "sovereign voice" (i.e., Godard), who organizes the endless attrition between the *lieux communs* of discourse and the brutality of the images which interrupt them, as well as between the visual stereotypes and the poetic speech that throws into relief such proof. Rancière concludes convincingly that Godard's ironic dialectical politics, whereby the words turn inconclusively around the *champ/contre-champ* and the Israelis enter into the color of fiction while the Palestinians exit towards the black and white of documentary, appears to be going around in circles.

Yet, of course, on a purely artistic level *Notre Musique* could not be more straightforward. It's not simply that for Godard the only racial and cultural difference that really counts is ultimately Palestinian. Let us turn to the one black face visible in *Notre Musique*, that of the African American marine in the third and final "Paradise" section which plays out as the short film-within-a-film, also called *Notre Musique*, made by the film student Olga Brodsky (Nade Dieu), a French Jew of Russian descent. Olga is in Sarajevo with her uncle Ramos en route to Tel Aviv to protest against the subjugation of Palestinians by the State of Israel by performing a "gesture for peace"——an act of suicide since, as we are informed at the end of "Purgatory," she is shot dead by Israeli marksmen who wrongly suspect that the backpack of books she has carried into a cinema is a bomb (she gave patrons five minutes to leave while calling upon anybody who wanted "to die for peace" to join her). In Olga's film the African American figure performs an entirely reactionary function as an armed marine in white uniform fishing in the waters of an unspecified natural zone monitored by the military. Like the Asian American soldier seen quietly patrolling the wire fence, he says nothing. Indeed, like all blacks now in Godard's work, the marine is simply surplus to Godard's radical political and ethical requirements. Here, faceless, distant, and mute, he is positioned as the very index of Olga's cinematic imaginings inspired by the same suicidal delusions and illusions that allowed her to state during her final conversation with her uncle Ramos: "There will be total liberty when it's the same to live or die." For this version of paradise is presented as a blank and unremittingly bland nonplace where the young play amongst themselves in indiscriminate hushed tones and where all communication is by nonverbal language and gesticulation (for example, an anonymous man holds out an apple to Olga in a gesture of sharing, which she accepts). This is arguably a more accurate vision of hell than the film's opening ten minutes, for the world presented here appears lifeless and inert due to an almost total reduction of difference between sound and image. It is as if Olga wanted simply to do away with metaphor altogether and flatten everything out, literally in the case of the repeated, sweeping, lateral tracking shots and the title of the book being read by one young man, *Sans espoir de retour* (the French edition of *Street of No Return* [1954] by the Jewish-American writer, David Goodis),[26] but also symbolically with the sharing of an apple and its trite message of quasilove and reconciliation.

Figure 6.10. Olga's film-within-a-film in *Notre Musique* (2004).

However, "Paradise" offers no escape in death from the impossibility of life, and indeed Olga's fundamentally nondissymmetrical "subfilm" represents the result of her desperately confused approach to life and otherness. As such, it serves as a perfect foil to Godard's *über*-film of the same title which is decidedly *not* about the politics of representation but rather the finer processes of poetics, and which employs a distinctly Christian template (the trinity of "Hell," "Purgatory," and "Paradise" of deliberately uneven size) to move beyond simple binaries and underscore difference. Hence, Godard shows once again here that politics, ethics, and philosophy mean little without the aesthetic. For the ethical cannot function alone and is always relational precisely because it operates in relation to the aesthetic. Moreover, the poetic principle operates above and beyond the politics of reconciliation and the creation of new allies out of former enemies. Which is to say, if the only real freedom is aesthetic, the only true politics for Godard is a combination of poetics and aesthetics ethically defined.

For Laura Rascaroli, it is ethically important in narrative terms that Godard doesn't view Olga's film. Instead, "we" as embodied receiver have the last word;

the director only asks the questions.²⁷ It might be argued further that what Godard engineers in the closing moments of *Notre Musique*, when the last image of the film-within-a-film (Olga closing her eyes tearfully accompanied by her voice-over: "[I]t was a fine day. One could see far. But not as far as Olga had gone") segues directly into the final credit sequence, is really an opening up of Olga's private cinematic musings to an impersonal Third person or other (for the occasion, the viewer). In other words, the event of montage performs as a bridging device and connector for Godard in the formal interests of cinematic difference, in keeping with the ever-present Third in the film as we have defined it. Yet this gentle final triumph of form and metaphor is again at the expense of a true engagement with difference as otherness, for it plays out as an opposition articulated around aesthetic value and takes the form of a clear inversion along cultural/political lines: Olga's *Notre Musique* is a Jewish and nonwhite American concoction devoid of difference, whereas Godard's film of the same name is an Arab-inspired European ode to metaphor where there is no illusion of final deliverance, certainly not from metaphor. Which is to say, Olga's short, part of her wish for self-deliverance as "martyr" (the sheets she holds in her hands during the master class sequence proclaim: "And deliverance? And victory? That will be my martyrdom"), functions ultimately as a negative *mise en abyme* of Godard's feature film, a blend of documentary and fiction driven, as we have seen, by the aesthetic play of difference and *champ/contre-champ* through sound and image. Indeed, this final sealing of Olga as an inverted other is just one more element in the film's expanding series of negative reverse fields that include the Native Americans and Judith. For Olga does not simply "mirror" Godard, as Emmelhainz suggests.²⁸ Her climactic spoken words in the third person appear supernumerary to Godard's film in which they are wrapped and enshrouded. The formal gesture of bridging and inclusion is thus revealed as one of exclusion. Godard's editorial hand has the last word,²⁹ and in the process Jew and black alike are consigned and reduced to the same inferior status, that of the Same.

This movement is contagious, since in the very same process (and this is the real measure of Godard's rhetorical reach in *Notre Musique*) Olga is reduced to the same as Judith. They had originally seemed like opposites, of course, despite their physical resemblance which made them look like sisters. As Erin Schlumpf correctly states, each appeared haunted by the other, even though they never actually meet: Judith is drawn to the light, Olga towards darkness, the one mirroring and counterpointing the other (contemplation or action, reconciliation or suicide) (see Schlumpf 2014). Indeed, the melancholic Olga seemed an exact mirror image of Judith for she skirted the borders of filmic visibility and invisibility, arriving at one point out of long-shot and hazy nonfocus into the clarity of mid-shot by means of a focus-pull recalling that of Rachel in *Hélas pour moi*. Olga acknowledges at this moment in a voice-off a potential sameness within difference, although there's also the suggestion of a schizoid splitting of the self: "It's like an image but that would come from afar. They are two together, side by side. Beside her is me. I've never seen her, though I recognize myself there. But I don't remember anything at all of that. It must happen far from here, or later." However, by the end of

Notre Musique, which upholds on a purely structural level the principle of the Third, Godard has paradoxically conflated both female characters into one side of a binary opposition that pitches them negatively against the film's creator (Godard). They both occupy the same reverse field for they are both revealed as naïve and simplistic in their highly personal, solipsistic, and ultimately doomed approach to politics and images. They are, in a sense, as misguided and myopic as the idealistic terrorists of *La Chinoise*, although here Olga, consumed by guilt about her identity as an Israeli and a Jew, wishes to "kill terror" by killing herself, while Judith aims for political salvation by blithely attempting to bridge over, and blanket out, the ethically irremediable or *indélibile*. In short, they cannot join up the right dots between poetics and ethics and politics and so remain trapped together in a fatal double-bind.

Godard's formal creation of aesthetic otherness in *Notre Musique* may be said to trope over the film's formless mass of political otherness. Yet is it not a little too easy, even distasteful, for Godard deliberately to project two young female characters as a compound negative other and foil to the greater intelligence and cinematic method of the character "Jean-Luc Godard" who never meets or addresses them directly (he politely brushes Olga aside, casually though not maliciously, when she offers him towards the end a digital copy of her film as a gift, adding simply "Give it to Rusmir")? The fixed binary method of evaluation at work here, an extreme manifestation of the additional property of Godardian montage to offer a form of judgment, will be taken to its logical conclusion in the video *Vrai Faux Passeport* made shortly after where Godard reviews a series of images which he declares to be either "*bonus*" or "*malus*" (the film's deliberately clunky subtitle is: "Fiction documentaire sur des occasions de porter un jugement à propos de la façon de faire des films" ["Documentary fiction on the opportunities for passing judgment about the manner in which films are made"]). Moreover, in terms of the larger themes pursued in *Notre Musique*, Olga and Judith are figured ultimately as a negative Jewish projection by Godard. Indeed, in a film that creates a clear pecking order of others (Palestinians at the top, supported metaphorically by Native Americans from below), they may be said to occupy the bottom rung of "subothers," on a par with African Americans. Such is the warped reality of Godard's poetic practice of dissymmetry and of his lulling metaphorical invocation of "*our* night, *our* musique."

To return to the particular question I raised at the start concerning Godard's practice of the relativity of cinematic truth and the need to forgive: such concerted rhetorical appropriation and ultimate sacrifice of the other in *Notre Musique* is precisely what Godard might need to forgive himself for, rather than simply for appearing in the film as a lofty and at times wholly uningratiating figure devoid of genuine empathy or sensitivity. In fact, what absolves him a little of the guilt of misrepresenting and manipulating the other for aesthetic ends is that he also casts himself ethically in doubt by presenting himself as partially culpable for Olga's death. It is, of course, entirely hypothetical whether Olga would have saved herself if the great man had deigned to acknowledge her gift and watch her film. Yet it is precisely in this gap of doubt and uncertainty that Godard ultimately places his ethicoaesthetic project and radically puts it into question. For what is at stake here is not, as one critic has suggested, just another self-reflexive strategy to make visible diegetically the basic fact that directors decide the fates of their films' characters, and that Godard the director of *Notre Musique* and Godard the character of *Notre Musique* are one (see Schlumpf 2014). With this implicit but wholly palpable sense of self-indictment demanding that the viewer forgive and redeem him (or not), Godard acknowledges here both the limitations of his own method (and the life or death propositions it produces) and the primacy of the intersubjective encounter between film and viewer. Indeed, he is essentially offering himself up here as the reverse field of his own film, sealed by his act in the last moments of "Purgatory" of picking up the phone while gardening at home and finding himself unable even to remember the voice at the end of the line: that of the man he had met just months before in Sarajevo, Olga's uncle, Ramos García. The reason for Godard's sudden lapse of memory at this particular juncture, especially when the film had been so keen to show this character, the very model of the *Juif errant* with his rich cultural background, saying nothing during Godard's master class and thereby tacitly approving Godard's approach to Jewish/Palestinian history, is a matter for conjecture.

Where has *Notre Musique* ultimately taken us? For Emmelhainz, the film, by exposing the problems of a simple commemoration of the past and of "humane intervention (intellectual, political and by NGOs)," "vouches for art and for an ethics and politics of the *art of living together*" (Emmelhainz 2009: 422; original emphasis). Viewed in this vein, the film would seem very much a natural continuation of Godard's much earlier two-minute short, *Je vous salue, Sarajevo* (1993), a close survey, fragment by fragment, of a photograph of soldiers taken by the freelance photojournalist Ron Haviv during the first Serb rampage of Bosnian Muslims' houses in the town of Bijeljina, and which includes Godard's spoken words condemning the elimination of the exceptional, pluricultural "art" of living together (a reprise of the art versus culture formula of *JLG/JLG*). Yet after what we have just witnessed in *Notre Musique*, ought we to conclude instead that aesthetic value and allure do not go hand in hand with ethical commitment? For Godard's use of metaphor in *Notre Musique* is profoundly ambivalent. The new, fresh figures of radical otherness and difference (the Native Americans) in Godard's poetic firmament become simply part of his glittering arcs and poetic constellations of figure and metaphor in, *métaphore oblige*, a galaxy of black holes containing the ghosts of collapsed, exploded, or expunged others. What seems the irreducible, radical Other is, in fact, no more than another bridge and chain in Godard's highly self-reflexive, poetico-rhetorical scheme. The problematic nature of such an outcome is further compounded by his ambiguous statements in interviews about the film where he calculatedly set the cat among the pigeons by presenting himself as a "Jew of the cinema" ("Juif du cinéma"), his new chosen metaphor for the marginalized and persecuted artist. This has provided further ammunition to important American commentators like Richard Brody who view Godard as anti-Semitic not only on account of his formal *rapprochements* in *Ici et ailleurs* and *Notre Musique*, but also due to his permanent discourse on Hollywood as an industry founded by Jewish "gangsters" and developed by producers according to the principle that to make a film is to create debts, for Brody a slanderous allusion to the Jewish system of usury. Moreover, the Jews, for Godard, "are to blame for the fundamental flaw of society, its preference for text over images, its anticinematic prejudice" (Brody 2008: 559). Such racist thinking, according to Brody, allows Godard to elaborate the ugly paradox that the same Jewish people who were crucial for the development of cinema were also effectively responsible for its downfall due to the industry's effective repudiation of the image, leading ultimately to its "failure" to preempt the Holocaust.[30]

In France, certain prominent Jewish intellectuals like Bernard-Henri Lévy and Fleischer have used their personal knowledge of Godard to offer public judgments on his alleged anti-Semitism—favorable in the case of the former, guarded and mixed in the case of the latter, who identifies a "strange malaise" in Godard's wish to position himself as a "Jew of the cinema" while freely admitting he doesn't know what a Jew really is (as opposed, say, to a Catholic who is such because s/he goes to Mass). Indeed, for Fleischer, although Godard may not be an outright anti-Semite as such, there is always an "anti-Semitic temptation" in his work and commentary due to "discreet emphases" and sidelong "muffled recurrences" that prove revelatory in their sheer accumulation (what he calls Godard's "small music" with its "perverse tonality") (Fleischer 2011: 113). For Daniel Cohn-Bendit Godard has "contradictory feelings" and makes jokes about the Jews "like everyone" but is not a "militant anti-Semite," rather an anti-Zionist who believes that the Palestinians should be protected from Israel just as the Jews should have been protected from the Nazis (Cohn-Bendit 2012: 91–93). For Frodon, Godard possesses a fundamental general wish to be both the same and different, namely, the final image of him in *Notre Musique* tending his garden alone at home in Switzerland. In this way Godard hopes to avoid the fantasy and "psychosis" of origins that always come with the desire to be unique and have no *contre-champ* (Godard 2004c: 20). For Junji Hori, meanwhile, Godard's self-appellation as Jew does not imply he is willing to identify himself with the Jewish people. Rather, "[i]n the light of a specific sense of belonging among the Jews in the Diaspora, [Godard] seeks to act differently in terms of national, ethnic and cultural identity" (Hori 2014: 75). No one opinion is conclusive, of course, yet the fact that Godard is an avowed anti-Zionist who knowingly plugs into—and molds to his artistic advantage—a "refined" anti-Semitic discourse long prevalent in France and elsewhere in Europe appears irrefutable.[31]

Taken as a whole, the interweaving threads in *Notre Musique* (personal, historical, aesthetic, political, philosophical) showcase once again the march of metaphorization and the relentless drive to abstraction in Godard's work. Yet the continuous metaphorical relay of the other in an expanding process of reversal and transformation is also proposed here as the best, and perhaps *only*, aestheticopolitical option remaining now for Godard at the present political juncture. Indeed, the film appears to suggest that the very idea of claiming to let the other speak is both hubristic and patronizing and that a politics of alterity is ultimately a misplaced and impossible project. To expose this critical fact, and to put continually into question the different rhetorical processes and structures at stake, including those relating to personal authorial mastery, is in itself, Godard implies, a vital ethical imperative. The risk otherwise is of blindly entering the symmetries of fantasy and simply reproducing and freezing the other like the false, exoticizing, touristic image of "Red Indian" otherness fabricated by Godard's negative other, Judith. The eminent value of metaphoricity is that it is a continually moving and shifting process of relationality which allows us as spatial and historical beings to make sense of the world. However, as James Geary acutely observes, it is a lens that distorts in the very act of clarifying, for while it focuses our attention on a specific set of associated commonplaces it also narrows our view (Geary 2011: 147). *Notre Musique* never allows us to forget that a degree of collateral damage is always involved in any cinematic engagement with the real where a reverse field is always present and needs to be filled by contingent others. In fact, the one clear message of the film is that we need to create as many sites and bridges of difference as possible in order to ensure the flow and transfer of metaphor which always carries an important ethical demand—one that may not, or even cannot, be met.

For these reasons the two-page hybrid document, "Regardezvoir, Godard," published in *Libération* shortly after the release of *Notre Musique*, ought to be considered as yet another instance of Godard's on-going series of aesthetic responses to Sarajevo and Bosnia-Herzegovenia, though far from the last (in 2014 he contributed a short episode entitled *Le Pont des soupirs* [*The Bridge of Sighs*] to the omnibus film, *Bridges of Sarajevo*).[32] Godard invited the critic and journalist Gérard Lefort to co-produce what he called a "dialogue through visual commentary."[33] With the exception of one photograph selected and annotated by Godard himself, it was Lefort who chose the set of five news images and wrote extended captions. The assorted photographs, each slightly different in size and proportion, range from a picture of Ayrton Senna in 1986 to a view of Gomel near Chernobyl, and from desecrated Jewish graves at Herrilshelm to images of the American torture of Iraqi soldiers. In other words, another cycle of metaphors of otherness and difference is established here. Godard then voiced aloud his own comments in response, subsequently transcribed to complete a "correspondence." The meeting between the two was, we are informed, amicable and often drole, and Godard's reflexions are both personal and critical, cinematic and anecdotal. We have at the most simple and tangible level a putting into practice of Godard's theory of *champ/contre-champ* as a new configuration and formatting of text and image suggestive of a new form of human relations. Let us call it provisionally: the revelation of sameness within difference. This formal display of metaphor is aesthetically powerful, yet in the light of all that we have seen in this chapter it remains ethically and politically questionable since it is achieved once again at the expense of a fully engaged encounter with, and representation of, the ever-desired, yet always already missed, "real" other.

If it is the case, as Godard proposes in a conversation with Youssef Ishaghpour, that cinema is the twentieth century's metaphor and that "[i]ts reality is already metaphorical" (Godard and Ishaghpour 2005: 87), then it's also true that the ethically failing and imperfect formal processes of rhetoric and metaphor may, in the end, be all we have and provide our only claim on reality. Constructed inevitably around binaries and reverse fields, cinema remains necessarily deficient and offers no easy short-cuts to ethical redemption. This is not, of course, to excuse Godard for his cavalier use of the Native Americans, who pay the price for his thoroughly disabused wish to be politically "incorrect" and not supply anything resembling a conventional politics of representation. Rather, it is to acknowledge that the only cushion we have against the encroaching biopolitical void, and the only means of crossing the darkness, is ultimately to trust in metaphors with no guarantee of equality or reconciliation. Like the idea of political democracy presented in one fleeting voice-off by Godard in *Notre Musique* as the result of "our" failure to liberate ourselves completely, this is perhaps as good as it can be.

7

Entering the Desert
Giving Face in *Film socialisme* (2010)

> With digital, you no longer have a negative, only a positive. You've got only the axis of the good, not the bad.
>
> —J.-L. Godard

> —Don't speak about the invisible, show it.
>
> —J.-L. Godard, *Film socialisme*

Film socialisme, presented by Godard at the time of its release in 2010 as his "last film for the moment," offers the fascinating case of a filmmaker laying waste to his current method and style and attempting to redefine and recharge his practice. It is not simply that it was Godard's first theatrical release to be shot entirely on a digital format (and the 1.85 aspect ratio), or that the credits at the start were organized around a new set of terms: Textos, Tekhnos, Logos, Audios, Videos. With a title unanchored by any article, definite or indefinite, *Film socialisme* is a blistering, at times tempestuous, virtually nonnarrative magma of hybrid sounds and images. Despite familiar motifs and musical variations (Arvo Pärt, Giya Kancheli, Werner Pirchner, etc.) intensively montaged with film and television extracts around the general themes of European history, war and culture (in other words, the idioms of late Godard, though here with an added emphasis on the circulation of money and gold), the film seems to unfold more like an unprocessed dream or nightmare mash-up than an extension of the painterly compositions of his recent elegiac and often melancholic film essays. The onslaught of saturated, phosphorescent, hi-gloss HD exposures intercut with low-grade surveillance footage, mobile phone images, and badly degraded video, all pushed at times to pixellated distortion, is matched by the grave, portentous chords and strings of Pärt, Alfred Schnittke, and the contemporary Israeli composer Betty Olivero (*Neharót, Neharót*), which alternate with the piercing diegetic sounds of the wind and other ambient noise captured like spasms on cheap camera microphones often subject to fading. Undermining the digital image from within, Godard is, as it were, injecting a necessary dose of negativity into the digital medium which he regards as fundamentally compromised because immediately "positive," in direct contrast to analog cinema, which is based on the processing over time of exposed, "negative" raw stock—a process as much metaphysical as purely material. Moreover, far from simply voicing resistance to naïve notions of a united Europe and the encroaching uniformity of global art and culture, *Film socialisme* surges forward with a violent experimental drive and urgency, in particular in the first of its three "movements" set on a casino cruise ship (prime symbol of Western capitalism) and bearing the open-ended title "Des choses comme ça" ("Things like that"). The fact that the ship in question, the *Costa Concordia*, would later sink off the coast of Italy in 2012 adds further fire to the film's central argument about an increasingly mindless and decadent society out of control and adrift on the ocean of global corporate capital about to go into free-fall. The heat and rage of this section are only intensified by the sudden switching of gears in the slow (though far from quiet) second movement ("Notre Europe," "Our Europe") and the equally dramatic uprooting to Godard's more essayistic style in the third ("Nos humanités," "Our humanities"), which focuses explicitly on the history and representation of Egypt, Palestine, Odessa, Greece, Naples, and Barcelona.

Film socialisme picks up where Godard's anti-communitarian critique of institutional culture and politics in *Notre Musique* left off. From its opening image of two red parrots together accompanied by a high-pitched sync plop to its final frame of screen-text "NO COMMENT" (Godard's rebuke to the all-screen, red, FBI warning sticker, ACCESS DENIED, over which he types in white that "When the law is not just, justice takes precedence over the law"), the film mounts a searing attack on the idea of art as property, specifically the 2009 French Creation and Internet (Hadopi) law which aimed to regulate internet access and prevent illegal downloading.[1] Godard's creation for the internet of a series of six different trailers for the film exemplified his desire to subvert the current terms of film advertising and distribution. Only the first, running at over four and a half minutes, behaves like a conventional trailer with snippets of sequences and dialogue from the film played at normal speed. The other five, of varying tempos and length (the sixth lasts just over a minute), are all variations on the theme of the super-speeded-up trailer, and each, a beautiful oddity in its own right, is a different work of montage punctuated by the main captions of the film like "*Des choses*."[2] Within the film itself, Godard deconstructs conventional English subtitles with what he calls "Navajo English" whereby, as noted in the previous chapter, complete sentences are abstracted and compressed into their key words without verbs, resulting in some arresting portmanteaus ("nocrimes noblood," etc.) and wild-looking broken verse. As Andréa Picard rightly remarks, "Navajo English" subtitles function as "an aphoristic interpretation, adding an additional level of meaning to the already dense composition."[3]

The swirling mass of real historical references, imaginary connections, and invented legends in *Film socialisme* (some of which Godard spun out still further on the eve of the film's release in a two-hour video interview for the French magazine and website *Mediapart*)[4] testify to the long and complex clashings of civilizations brought together in the Mediterranean basin. Indeed, with its many dense and provocative audiovisual folds, loops, and tangles, the film requires careful unraveling and analysis, notably regarding Godard's re-presentation of Arab-Israeli relations and the Palestine question.[5] It is on one level a transhistorical spy story based around the historical figure of Richard Christmann (a Nazi spy and triple agent during World War II) and featuring a Russian major, a French investigator, a Mossad agent, and a Palestinian couple, all spying on each other on board the ship via social networking and Google. It is also a study of three different kinds of professions embodied by a journalist, economist, and philosopher (including the real Alain Badiou). Further, in its second, longer movement set in the French provinces and devoted to the Martin family (a reference to the Resistance network called "Famille Martin" that operated in the Colmar region), the film offers a sensitive portrait of the problems of communication and conflict between the generations (the sister and younger brother, Flo[rine] and Lucien, are derived from Balzac's *Les Illusions perdues* [1837–43]). Through the children there is a tangible sense here of utopian, even Marxist, promise, matched by the ship's detour to Odessa which, in artistic terms, represents for Godard a rare moment when cinema operated in sync with revolutionary history (included are images from Eisenstein's *Strike* [1925] and *Battleship Potemkin* [1925]). We thus see again, as Irmgard Emmelhainz has highlighted, how aesthetic concerns in Godard are directly mapped onto geopolitical concerns, for he is seeking out traces of the sensible across figurative language (Egypt), European painting (Naples), tragedy (Greece), revolutionary film (Odessa), and the area of aesthetico-political representation (Palestine) (see Emmelhainz 2014). Indeed, Godard seems to be calling here directly for a repoliticized Europe—a Europe inspired by Greek democracy and the French and October revolutions.

Film socialisme encourages us once again to ask how, and to what degree, the deep social, cultural, and political turmoil and malaise so graphically depicted by Godard is potentially offset and reversed by the aesthetic act of montage itself, which, as Nicole Brenez notes, reveals an exciting development in Godard's organizational methods.[6] For indeed the film provides yet another occasion for Godard to reformulate his poetic practice of montage of unexpected associations, differential equivalences, and asymmetrical analogies, this time in terms of "dissonance," as suggested in a cited phrase from the composer Nikolai Rimsky-Korsakov about musical dissonance relying on common notes. Keeping this new formal conceptualization firmly in mind, I would like to consider here the particular function and significance of another part of the project that appeared in tandem with the film's release in France and that has not yet been properly addressed: the book of the same title published by POL.[7] The spunky provocation of its back cover, which attributes a calculatedly offensive phrase "Dialogue, foutre!" ("Dialogue, fuck!") to Stendhal, complete with a date (November 26, 1834), would appear to be in the same subversive vein of the film, puncturing its own status as an advert or blurb for a book that carries the subtitle: "Dialogues avec visages auteurs" (literally, "Dialogues with author faces"). Yet this is perhaps just a literary tease, for upon entering the book one senses that the sound and fury of the film, its pushing of the limits of plasticity sometimes to audiovisual convulsion, has been flattened out and muted, as if Godard were perhaps beating a measured aesthetic retreat. The 108-page book certainly looks different from Godard's previous literary works, transforming the style of his texts for POL in a reduced format derived from his films of the 1990s and which he presented as "Phrases (sorties d'un film)." These took the form of a more or less uninterrupted poetic flow of short lines of text and dialogue distilled from the film in question (whether *JLG/JLG, For Ever Mozart, Allemagne année 90 neuf zéro, Les Enfants jouent à la Russie* or *Deux fois cinquante ans de cinéma français*), and they included dutifully at the end a list of the authors and singers invoked. By contrast, in its larger, more conventional book-size format, *Film socialisme* seems more prosaic, with all the lines of dialogue and small blocks of text standardized and justified (each line starts mechanically with a capital letter). There is no final list of references here, despite the fact that much of the film's dialogue is again typically a series of quotes. And, although a reasonably faithful transcription of what is uttered or heard in the film, the lines, lacking punctuation and indeed any indication of the character who speaks them, appear simply anonymous and make sense only if one has just seen the film. Moreover, there has been no attempt to translate the blocks of Russian, Spanish, Italian, Hebrew, Arabic, Greek, and German which are offered intact. In addition, many of the original typewritten captions are simply transposed onto the page as square frames of screen-text, including the entire sequence relating to the Martin family conveyed by white captions over a black screen.

As for the images of the film, they are conspicuous here by their total absence. There is no record, for instance, of any of the eight shots extracted from Jean-Daniel Pollet mesmeric poetic short *Méditerranée* (1963) (made with Volker Schlöndorff with a text by Philippe Sollers), one of which—that of the Mediterranean sea glimpsed behind barbed wire—is clearly suggestive within its new context of the fortress state in which most Palestinians are now forced to live. Nor are there any visual traces of the many other powerful films cited such as Youssef Chahine's *Adieu Bonaparte* (1985), *The Four Days of Naples* (Nanni Loy 1962), André Malraux's *Espoir: Sierra de Teruel* (1939–45), Michelangelo Antonioni's *Lo Sguardo di Michelangelo* (2003), Manoel de Oliveira's *A Talking Picture* (2003), Claude Lanzmann's *Tsahal* (1993), Udi Aloni's documentary *Local Angel* (2002), and, perhaps most surprising of all embedded within the collage of "Nos humanités," *Le Chant des Mariées* (*The Wedding Song*) (2008), a Franco-Tunisian film by Karin Albou set in 1942 in Nazi-occupied Tunis about an increasingly strained friendship between two young women, one Jewish, the other Muslim. What is new and wholly unexpected, however, and what fills the textual void of the book by opening up a completely new set of questions, are the black-and-white photographs and reproductions of paintings and engravings that punctuate the text at irregular intervals. These are not stills or frame-grabs, nor indeed simply reproductions of any of the famous photographs employed in the film such as that of the photographer Robert Capa on assignment during the Spanish Civil War. Instead, they appear to operate on a different level altogether for they are almost all portraits of writers and philosophers ranging from Shakespeare and Goethe to Jean Giraudoux and Paul Ricoeur, many of whom we have already encountered in this book. These are buttressed by musicians and singers from Paco Ibáñez to Joan Baez and a young Patti Smith (different from how she looks in the film), as well as by the odd political figure such as Otto von Bismarck. In this highly eclectic mix which also takes us out of the film's strictly European/Mediterranean visual context, there are, significantly, no filmmakers or actors except for Billy Wilder, although his function appears limited to the title of his 1964 film, *Kiss Me, Stupid*, presented in a frame of screen-text onto which his portrait overlaps and which is preceded by the word "Palestine" (p. 83).

Again, all the photographs and engravings of faces are left unidentified and without captions. Any semblance of an artwork is either physically obscured by another image or else reproduced in miniature to the point of indecipherability. This is the case with a barely visible and unrecognizable image on page 82 alongside a short passage on Abraham and Isaac, as well as on page 63 with its small, underexposed reproduction of a detail of Jacques-Louis David's *Le Serment du Jeu de Paume* (1791). This overlaps with an engraving of the Abbé Emmanuel-Joseph Sièyes (c. 1780) that complements a series of lines of text on the founding moment of the *Déclaration des Droits de l'Homme* (we recall Godard's explicit citing of Sièyes's 1789 warning pamphlet, *Qu'est-ce que le tiers état?*, during his engagement with Hitchcock in episode 4A of *Histoire(s) du cinéma*, *Le Contrôle de l'univers*). Here, however, the visual images are shorn of their painterly value. Indeed, the book has none of the haunting aesthetic beauty of the Gallimard art books derived from *Histoire(s)*, with their hybrid, electronically filtered color plates—strange, eerie, processed images of distilled energy removed from the noise and sizzle of the machine and covering the entire range of artificially modulated brightness, hue and contrast. Equally, they lack the bold, samizdat-style quality and originality of the roughly-hewn, high contrast black-and-white photocopies of film stills in the 1985 edition of *Introduction à une véritable histoire du cinéma*. Still less do they carry the suggestive power and cultural, historical, and political charge of the photographic images and stills employed by Godard in his longstanding practice of photomontage (notably the special three hundredth anniversary issue of *Cahiers du Cinéma* he edited in May 1979). Instead, the cheaply reproduced portrait images, functionally cropped like virtual mug-shots, appear, with few exceptions, to be no more than workaday, thumb-nail images for reference, as if Godard were simply acknowledging in perfunctory visual fashion his sources in *Film socialisme*—a technique one might regard as at best academic, at worst purely sentimental.

On the face of it, then, the book of *Film socialisme* marks a major visual loss, even impoverishment, for the film's dazzling palette of strident blocks of color has been both reversed and reduced by the uniform black and white of the largely pocket-sized photographs and assorted images. The impression of something inchoate or not fully processed is consolidated by the eleven pages of text that follow the dialogues. First, a two-page typewritten extract from what we must presume is an early script for the film, specifically about the real/mythical story relayed in the film's first movement about the lost gold doubloons, which left the Spanish Republic during the Spanish Civil War and ended up first in Russia, then in Germany and France, via the International Communist Party (in the film, which also refers to a 1946 article by Fernand Braudel entitled "Monnaies et civilisations. De l'or du Soudan à l'argent d'Amérique: un drame méditerranéen," the Christmann figure, Otto Goldberg (Jean-Marc Stehlé), is taking back gold to Cartagena via Moscow and Odessa). Here, though, "JLG" is himself part of the dense narrative in which he relates his own encounters following the war with Jacques Tati and the film-producer Louis Dolivet, along with asides to the communist political activist of the 1920s/30s Willi Münzenberg, the socialist politician Pierre Cot, and Orson Welles (the wartime intrigue of backstage wheeler-dealings is further evoked in the film by the presence of the real Robert ("Bob") Maloubier, a former French secret agent who worked for Churchill's "Special Operations Executive"). Moreover, Godard's trace is everywhere on these pages in the form of handwritten additions and crossings-out–a process of erasure and effacement that adds to the dense palimpsest of relations and memories of the period in question.

These two pages are followed immediately, without any signposting (there is no "list of contents"), by the reproduction of a nine-page handwritten letter to Godard by the philosopher and writer Jean-Paul Curnier, dated November 9, 2009. Curnier is the author notably of *Montrer l'invisible: Écrits sur l'image* (2009), and, as we saw in the previous chapter, figured briefly as himself in *Notre Musique* where he averred during one staged conversation that (Western) society was confronted more than ever with a sense of nothingness. His letter here is a more personal disquisition on the links between "film" and "socialism" following his enthusiastic response to Godard's plans for *Film socialisme* and in particular its title (in interviews Godard has even credited Curnier with devising the title due to having misread the header of the presentational brochure originally sent him). Curnier positively runs with these two terms as he explores the politics of poetry, community, and the *élan vital*; socialism and cinema as resources of the Unknown beyond communication and representation; invention and the fabrication of forms that subjugate reason and reorganize its means of judgment; and the need for unity in the face of solitude. Again, Godard does nothing here to edit or filter this highly individual critical response except to redact it in three places, thereby exacerbating the book's deliberately rough and raw feel. In short, with its emphasis on its own materiality and process, this book of images seems to take to a new level the minimalist, *art brut* style of the installations for *Voyage(s) en Utopie, Jean-Luc Godard, 1946–2006*, Godard's controversial exhibit in 2006 at the Centre Pompidou in Paris.

What is Godard doing exactly in the book of *Film socialisme*? The extreme leveling of images may appear simply a crude and counterproductive version of his democratic strategies of videographic superimposition which, as we saw earlier, maintain different elements in equal tension within the same frame. Yet I want to suggest that Godard, by moving through and across different media, from digital media to the classic printed page, with the same core textual material, is effectively recomposing and reinventing the very nature of his project. For not only does his particular use of text and image testify to a highly refined and subtle sense of graphic design, but also it reveals the book as yet another manifestation of the unique creative and connective processes made possible by the cinematic event, defined in episode 3B of *Histoire(s)* as the "fraternity of metaphors." By expanding the very boundaries of relationality and the poetic, *Film socialisme* the book, as I hope now to show, gives further concrete form to the possibility adumbrated throughout Godard's later work of a new poetics of cinematic being.

Let us look more closely at the faces. Some are more intimate and overt than others, and often the links and associations between face and related text are easily deduced. For example, Bergson is located next to a paragraph on matter and the spirit (p. 37), La Rochefoucauld alongside one of his famous maxims (p. 77), and Shakespeare with "To be or not to be." The American film critic Neal Gabler follows reference to Jewish influence in Hollywood, the beautiful image of a young Hannah Arendt sits below a passage about having friends not defined by either race or religion (p. 10), Braudel smiles between lines of text about duration and points of rupture (p. 89), and Bismarck gazes out left towards the text suggesting the continuity of German expansionism (p. 45). Further, Sophie and Hans Scholl, members of the nonviolent White Rose student resistance group in Nazi Germany, stand side by side in two small separate photographs illustrating the idea that "The dream of the State is to be alone/ The dream of individuals is to be together" (p. 62) ("Le rêve de l'État c'est d'être seul/ Le rêve des individus être deux [sic]"); Christa Wolf (author of the 1984 novel *Cassandra*) appears (p. 89) next to a reference to Cassandra; Samuel Beckett, author of the short story, *L'Image* (1959), poses with a cigarette (p. 58) next to the phrase "C'est fait j'ai fait l'image"; the historian and novelist Zoé Oldenbourg stares out blankly (p. 83) next to a passage on the Crusades and Jerusalem; and a young, striding Curzio Malaparte instigates a series of lines about American's "liberation as conquest" of Italy during World War II ("liberty costs dear") (pp. 90–91). Yet the levels of association are sometimes much more vague and oblique, and we have to take it on trust that the images of Charles Péguy (p. 28), Joseph Conrad (p. 55), Ossip Mandelstam (p. 57), the socialist activist René Dumont (p. 59), and George Sand (p. 65) are, like many others, somehow linked, if only tangentially, to the minimal lines of text they border. Goethe, for example, presented in iconic form (p. 15), rests above a single, apparently banal line in German. Beethoven stands alone within text (p. 68), but he's there surely because his *Pastoral Symphony* 6 and *Sonata Pathétique* for piano are heard around this point in the film.

The sense that these diverse and decontextualized portrait figures are more the flashes of a highly personal process of free association than the result of a concerted artistic strategy is accentuated by the fact that, despite first impressions, nothing is actually regular here. For on closer inspection the sizes and formats of the images (their depth, width, and length) are never guaranteed or programmed. Indeed, some are acutely elongated. Similarly, the profiles and expressions, whether frontal, side, upward, downward, or otherwise, are all very different. In addition, the layout comprising images, frames of screen-text, and lines of text is consistently changing, with the latter even acquiring different font sizes. What this produces are continually shifting volumes of blank space, between both the photographs themselves and the photographs and text. Hence, what at first appears a restricted palette of variables (text and image in gradations of black and grey) is actually a fluid process of experimentation and difference. Just as there is no one "right" trailer for the film, so, too, the book possesses no standard layout or design.

Yet patterns and rhythms do slowly begin to emerge which pass without comment and serve to foreground the power and mystery of the image. First, a number of faces are repeated, and the images covering different periods emphasize disparity in time and age. These include Bismarck, Braudel, Genet, William Faulkner, André Malraux, Claude Lévi-Strauss, Georges Bernanos, Denis de Rougemont, Shakespeare, the Italian singer Gabriella Ferri, and the actor and playwright Roland Dubillard. In the case of the latter, it is a matter of textual irony that the first image of a youngish Dubillard (p. 9), taken in his study, lies to the right of the line: "Once I encountered the void" ("J'ai rencontré une fois le néant"), followed by the words: "Well it [the void] is much thinner/ Than one thinks/ Jaffa 48" ("Eh bien il [le néant] est beaucoup plus mince/ Qu'on ne le croit/ Jaffa 48"). The second image (p. 26) is of a slightly older and heavier, more crumpled Dubillard, with a change to the text that reverses the passage of time as well as place: "Once in 1942 I encountered the void [. . .] Well it is much thinner/ Than one thinks/ Casablanca Algiers Cairo" ("Une fois en 1942 j'ai rencontré le néant [. . .] Eh bien il est beaucoup plus mince/ Qu'on ne le croit/ Casablanca Alger Le Caire"). Here, as elsewhere in the book, we are invited to make connections between the repeated human figures across time.

A typology of stylistic features can readily be established. I have already mentioned one: the odd overlappings of frames, both textual and visual, which replicate the Navajo portmanteau constructions in the film. But there are many others, notably the ironic juxtaposition of different cultures and generations. For example, the face of Heidegger staring out above that of Péguy (p. 28, again with varying sizes of image and croppings), while on the facing page is a single frame of screen-text that reads, "Abii ne viderem" ("I turned away so as not to see," a reference to Kancheli's 1995 work); Walter Benjamin as agonized modern Jewish intellectual almost leaning over the head of the dashing romantic poet Friedrich Hölderlin (p. 87); and the ageing novelist Claude Simon nestled gently above the French singer Barbara in her prime (p. 39). There are also the small concentrations of text and image that stage mismatchings and divergences. For instance (p. 47), Pirandello and Faulkner stare out directly towards the reader while wrapped visually around a passage about the Mother and the maternal blood-line—just four pages after the image of an older, sterner Faulkner looking down sideways to the right, introduces a short passage about the hatred caused by the paternal blood-line. The most complex and destabilizing connections, however, are those that play on one of the film's structuring dialectical oppositions: that between the Hebrew and Arab language and culture. For example (p. 25), to the left of an image of Lévi-Strauss as a young bearded anthropologist in the field lies a short untranslated phrase of Arabic in small font. Godard revisits this potentially charged interracial/intercultural configuration (p. 78) with the face of a young Genet smoking with, to his top-left, an epigraph about language and images from his confessional late work charting his experience with the Palestinians, *Un Captif amoureux* (1986).[8] To Genet's bottom left stands an oblong frame of screen-text containing a Hebrew phrase in black, superimposed over a phrase in white in Arabic (conveyed in the film as blood-red over white). What follows is a reference first to the start of photography in Palestine, then to the politics of language in the region as perceived in 1926 by the Kabbalah scholar Gershom Scholem (a figure whose propositions on tradition and the communicability of truth were explicitly cited at the beginning of *Hélas pour moi*).

Figures 7.1–2. Claude Lévi-Strauss and Jean Genet in the book of *Film socialisme* (2010).

The network of Arab/Hebrew associations is extended further on the following set of pages (pp. 80–81): an older Genet is pictured top left, while below him is the face of an older Lévi-Strauss, the two separated by a small square of German biblical script entitled "*Biblia Sacra*." Facing them on the opposite page is a strange assemblage of three images of faces of varying size: Rimsky-Korsakov, a young unidentified Palestinian in a checkered *keffiyeh* (similar to the image in *Ici et ailleurs*, reemployed in episode 4B of *Histoire(s)*, of a young *Fedayeen* woman patrolling a border fence in a refugee camp in Jordan), a page of Jewish scripture, as well as snippets of Arabic and Hebrew script. In this novel variant of text-image montage that disarticulates the original set of superimpositions and disperses the different elements across the page, no one face or race or culture predominates. Opposition has been remolded as difference, a process figured in the film by the sequence of overlapping male and female trapeze artists—an excerpt from Agnès Varda's *Les Plages d'Agnès* (*The Beaches of Agnes*) (2008) where they superimpose themselves mutually against the background of the Mediterranean to the sounds of both Hebrew and Arab chanting, a scene Godard brilliantly stop-starts. On the silent white page, the deconstructed montage appears all the more idiosyncratic for being so calm and understated.

Figures 7.3–4. Rimsky-Korsakov and an unidentified Palestinian in the book of *Film socialisme* (2010).

Finally, and most strikingly of all, are the concrete formations of images in series, usually at an angle and sometimes distributed across two pages. Two examples will suffice. First, the faces of Curnier and Dubillard looking right off-frame from separate and differently sized frames are lined up together diagonally. The eyelines are not exact, yet the approximation serves to reinforce the blank space now opened up on the page and draws out the void circulating self-reflexively in the text: "What's opening up in front of us is like an impossible/ (hi)story We're faced now with a kind of zero/ Once I encountered the void" (p. 9) ("Ce qui s'ouvre devant nous ressemble à une histoire/ impossible Nous voilà en face d'une sorte de zéro/ J'ai rencontré une fois le néant").

Figures 7.5–6. Jean-Paul Curnier and Roland Dubillard in the book of *Film socialisme* (2010).

In the book's last set of images (p. 92), three faces in varying size formats are lined up transversally across the page. Top right is an iconic heroic image of Malraux from the period of the Spanish Civil War; in the middle an elderly Ernst Busch alongside lyrics of his celebrated antifascist German song in support of the Spanish Republican cause; below left, a young de Rougemont (author of *Penser avec les mains* (1936), referenced extensively in later Godard). It might be tempting here to conceptualize the trio in purely historical terms as a demonstration of active political resistance, especially if one bears in mind that de Rougemont spent the war in the United States lecturing to raise money for the French Resistance. However, what stands out above all, due to the acute layout, is their shared mien and countenance—the way each man stares out directly and squarely towards the viewer as if in empathy and solidarity. The emphasis on the concrete and physical is followed up immediately (p. 94) with another archetypal image of Malraux gesticulating intensely with his hands in a late portrait as the engaged public intellectual—a neat visualization of de Rougemont's "thinking with one's hands." Hence, the photographs of the book *Film socialisme* tell new and different stories of association and connection, both by and in themselves and how they are positioned and configured on the page. To invoke the two captions that link together and subtend both the book and film, these material images are, both simply and profoundly, "Des choses" / "Comme ça" ("Things / Like that").

Figures 7.7–9. Ernst Busch, Denis de Rougemont, and André Malraux in the book of *Film socialisme* (2010).

What Godard is proposing here, therefore, are not dialogues from the film interspersed with authors' faces, but rather, in a decisive change of emphasis and direction, a series of *dialogues with* the faces of authors. Each face must be approached and appreciated on its own terms in relation to the other photographs/portraits and blocks of typewritten text and surrounding white spaces. An intersubjective space is created between text, face, author, and reader/viewer—a space of discovery and surprise that resolutely avoids the special prioritizing of art and painting which, as I've already indicated, is reduced here, quite literally, to the virtually unrecognizable. The result is a potentially all-inclusive and nonhierarchical network of new connections, alignments, and filiations. After the denial of access in the film, a new kind of immediate access and dialogue is provided, and it is summed up in the remarkable image of Sartre, the only photograph to be formally credited (to Bruno Barbey of Magnum Photos) and one of the few (almost) full-page images. Although it looks studio posed, it was, in fact, taken during one of the momentous debates at the Sorbonne during May 1968. Sartre is presented in side-profile and extreme close-up as a lone face in the darkness, looking out towards the preceding page of text that includes a chunk of classic Sartrean dialectical thought. His mouth is drawn out in a wry smile while his left hand cups his left ear in a theatrical gesture of listening to the other as a precondition for meaningful dialogue. Godard is revisiting here a hallowed moment of leftist debate and engagement as a means of reconsidering the whole notion of human dialogue and relations. We turn the page and find another (almost) full-page portrait, this time of Stendhal, author of the charged epigraph about dialogue on the back cover. Here he is looking out right of frame to the facing page with a benign half-smile. Two essential figures of freedom and individuality, two different ways of conceiving socialism and political resistance, are thus standing back to back, literally so, *recto verso*, across the centuries.

How might we define Godard's unexpected reinvestment in the photographic here? Roland-François Lack has incisively shown how the film of *Film socialisme*, preoccupied as it is with its own photographic form (photographs, the photographic apparatus, people taking photos, the stilling of the cinematographic image), extends Godard's previous work on the essential opposition and discontinuity between cinema and photography (see Lack 2012). Positing the film's "mimicry" of still photography since the camera barely moves throughout, at most reframing or shaking slightly, he argues that photography and its associated objects are presented as simply "'things here' (in Rossellini's phrase), there to be manipulated by cinema." Lack focuses in particular on Godard's engagement in the film with two images of Palestine which are also discussed by the Palestinian historian and poet Elias Sanbar in his 2004 book, *Les Palestiniens: la photographie d'une terre et de son peuple de 1839 à nos jours*. In fact, Sanbar is himself visible on screen as the title of his history of photography in Palestine is alluded to on the soundtrack, and the intricate conjunction of image, text, and idea produced continues Godard's work in *Notre Musique* on Palestinian history and iconography explored in chapter 6. A brief soundless sequence is initiated at 0.31:35 by the intertitle "PALESTINE" in which we first see a generic, picturesque, black-and-white landscape by the Beirut-based French photographer Félix Bonfils of the bay of Haifa with a palm tree in the foreground and a village on the hills in the distant background (dated c. 1880). This appears to be the same photograph, now the right way round, which thirty seconds earlier a young woman (almost certainly Louma Sanbar in an uncredited role) held up from the back in front of her while facing the camera and asking in Arabic: "Where are you, my beloved land?," before then passing it on to someone off-screen.⁹ It is immediately followed by Joss Dray's explicitly political image of an olive tree in Palestine, photographed in 1989—an image of a land without its people and a key visual motif in Sanbar's book. The screen goes black, followed quickly in turn by the blindfolded Christ (presented implicitly here as a Jewish victim) in Grünewald's painting *The Mocking of Christ* (1503–05), and then by the damning title "ACCESS DENIED." Henrik Gustafsson correctly observes that a number of readings are possible here: either that Palestine has no access to its territory or history, or that there is no longer an image to conjure of the people or the place. He writes: "In light of Sanbar's thesis that Palestine was obliterated by the image of the Holy Land, the century that separates the two photographs also evokes what hasn't changed between them: the notion of a Palestine as a place, not a people, as neither image evince [sic] human beings, only trees, adhering to the Zionist motto of a 'land without a people'" (Gustafsson 2014: 224). Gustafsson adds suggestively: "Maybe there is also another possible meaning: that Palestine is what we fail to imagine, belonging without a state" (ibid.).

Figures 7.10–11. Viewing the photograph of Haifa Bay from both sides in *Film socialisme* (2010).

The primacy of the cinematic, and specifically montage, over the photograph is, of course, a central theme in Godard, notably in *Histoire(s)* where it is shown that photography had to pass through painting in order to become cinema. In Godard's crucial move beyond ontology and cinema's photographic relation to reality, painting and film are connected by their pictorial qualities and also their capacity to judge. Yet removed from this particular aesthetic scheme, the photographs of the book *Film socialisme* seem to carry an alternative significance and value. Rather than functioning primarily as a (negative) index of the real, they perform instead as (positive) emblems of difference. They may look confusingly similar at times: is that Roman Jakobson on page 80 above mention of his linguistic lectures in New York, or rather Lévi-Strauss again? (Jakobson, a strange dead-ringer in his later years for Braudel, is, in fact, absent in the book.) But even when the figures are repeated it is never the same photograph because they are always from a different period and at a different age. Hence, to invoke the Bachelardian distinction currently favored by Godard between the implicit and explicit image (part of Bachelard's phenomenology of the imagination in *The Poetics of Space* (1958) and other works where the intimate intensity and salience of the poetic image, its "transsubjective" sonority of being, is revealed in its "reverberation" ("*retentissement*") rather than through rational discourse, causality and scientific knowledge):[10] while the individual faces may appear clear and explicit in their signification, the process by which they are arranged, and which foregrounds similarity through difference, renders their meaning more implicit, internal, and organic. We could perhaps make a link here with the practice of music in later Godard where, as I suggested in chapter 5, although the same piece of music may sound the same, each instance of its playing is different and unique, for we always hear it *as if for the first time*. Indeed, unlike a textual quote, music cannot be replaced by, or substituted for, anything else. It is, as it were, irreducible, untranslatable and nondeconstructible, and for this reason it exceeds the linguistic, discursive, and rhetorical, in particular the tricks of chiastic reversibility of which Godard is so fond. Music offers a valuable aesthetic model for Godard precisely because it enables him to step down from the cross of his chiastic thinking, imprinting itself in a much larger intersubjective and inclusive process, that of memory, which relies on the recognition and respect of difference within the totality of the whole, specifically between past and present.

Viewed in this expanded frame, the photographs in the book of *Film socialisme* capture some of the unlimited potential and resurgent mystery of the cinematic, despite (or perhaps paradoxically because of) the often very average, low-contrast quality of reproduction. For what is at issue is not the inherent "vertical" power and pathos of the unique photograph revealing, say, a Barthesian *punctum*, vehicle of irretrievable loss and noncatharsis, but rather a new kind of nonhierarchical, inclusive, and thoroughly materialist montage of images and text based around the commonalities and continuities of human expression. To return to the book's subtitle: *Dialogues avec visages auteurs*, we need to take the photographic here as the very mark of the figural, for the figurality of the portraits, and the dialogues thus formed between figures across different times, cultures, and generations, render secondary the indexical accuracy or otherwise of the photographs. Without captions and thus an explicit metadiscursive level, these images work in a realm beyond language at the level of affect and the poetic-like spark of recognition (we either "know" the face or we don't). Even if they can't be immediately identified (and it took this reader in some cases many long and fascinating hours trekking through Google Images), they each *give face* and invite comparison in their human expressions and the fundamentally generic ways in which they are formally organized and arranged.

The way Godard deploys photographs here can, in fact, be linked to what I identified earlier in the videographic montage of *Histoire(s)* as those horizontal moments of confluence, contiguity, conjunction, and coincidence that resist the vertical pull of his characteristic rhetorical and imaginary maneuvers. These constitute a counter-movement, a "minimal" moment of metonymy, whereby images are linked and molded together by contour, outline, gesture, silhouette, and profile. Such nondiscursive moments of association, contiguity, and conjunction trace the interrelations of human form at the level of shape and figure and are thus more basic and spontaneous approximations, at once material, proximate, local, instinctive, and intuitive. Such play of detail operates as if in silence since it is never directly commented on or integrated or rationalized as part of an argument or thesis. Indeed, throughout *Histoire(s)* the nonlinguistic resists any totalizing conceptualization or theorization and thus remains a pure affective and inclusive moment of seeing and feeling rather than one of interpretation. It might even appear sentimental and naïve in comparison with the dense, more aggressive intellectual processes and rhetorical formations initiated elsewhere in the work. For in *Histoire(s)*, as in the embodied images of the book *Film socialisme*, the figural is above all the human figure at its most concrete and literal, and the work's meaning ultimately lies somewhere between the figural and the awesome reach of Godard's sublime—part of what I call the inherent struggle in *Histoire(s)* between sense and the sensible, the latter operating as a kind of resistance to the logic of Godard's own rhetorical maneuvers by means of a collaboration of forms. In the words of Pierre Reverdy cited repeatedly in Godard's later work: "What is great is not the image but the emotion that it provokes [. . .] [This] is true because it is born outside of all imitation, all evocation and all resemblance" (from "L'Image" [1918]).

This is not to say, of course, that *Film socialisme* lacks rhetorical structures. Both film and text end with the dynamic call for action already cited about natural justice versus the law: "Quand la loi n'est pas juste, la justice passe avant la loi." This supremely chiastic phrase actually goes back to Godard's 1970s work for television, specifically *France tour détour deux enfants*, where it was similarly typewritten over the screen. The link between the two works runs much deeper, however. A series in twelve "movements," *France tour détour deux enfants* explored in intensive close-up and stop-start motion the human body (that of children) as the paradigm of representation and expression. The new video technology allowed Godard to exploit, almost like a painter, the image's capacity to create and disclose feelings and emotions beyond language. It is no surprise that this earlier work is echoed in the surprisingly tender second movement of *Film socialisme*, with its domestic family scenes conveyed in meditative long-takes and close-ups. For Godard is reengaging again directly with the place and status of children within the world of adults, one that now involves rights. Before, the young children Camille and Arnaud were questioned by the reporter Robert Linard and pitted by Godard against the "monsters" of the adult system. Thirty years on the boy Lucien and his older, almost adult sister Florine (whose face is highlighted at one point in slightly slowed motion) are fired by idealism and question their parents directly on the real meaning of *liberté, égalité, fraternité*. They have their own voice and agency, demand to be recognized as citizens, and consider even replacing their own mother in her campaign for local office. Like Hans and Sophie Scholl they also propose their own social program based in universal terms on art and society (i.e., not the state), which might just as easily be Godard's own: "Hold on to hope/ Be right when your government is wrong/ Learn to see before learning to read" (p. 67) ("Garder de l'espoir/ Avoir raison quand votre gouvernement a tort/ Apprendre à voir avant que d'apprendre à lire"). Florine reads Balzac's *Les Illusions perdues* and Lucien paints a Manet landscape and continually "performs" with his physical gestures to the classical and jazz music constantly forming inside his head and which we are made privy to (at one point he sucks loudly on a straw to the beats of modern jazz). To invoke the title of the 1990 short Godard made with Anne-Marie Miéville, *L'Enfance de l'art* (literally, The childhood of art) (an episode in the anthology film for UNICEF, *Comment vont les enfants?*), the hope here is perhaps of a new dawn in art that might potentially bring all arts together, like early silent cinema initially promised to do through montage. Could it also provide the possible grounds for a new way of conceiving Europe that does not simply reproduce the same tragic, fatal narratives and models from antiquity? We are subsequently told by means of a series of screen-texts that the Conseil d'État approved the children's right to seek election to the local council and that they are on the point of winning in their own name rather than that of their parents. The final outcome is left deliberately unclear, however. What is certain is that the book of *Film socialisme* develops and advances this extended theme of the cycle of human generations and the transmission of collective human traits and values through its visual focus on both the passing of time of the human figure and its insistency on continuity though difference.

For all these reasons, the book of *Film socialisme* might best be regarded as the second stage of the same project. It is as if the profound chaos and negativity of the new visual sphere confronted in the film were a necessary step towards the creation of new aesthetic thinking about history and time. We are not far away from Malraux's central idea, propounded in *Les Voix du silence* (1951) and the trilogy *La Métamorphose des Dieux*, of the transformative status of art which he defines as man's ambition over time to discover and reclaim what makes us human. Art, for Malraux, is a means of transcendence, an antidestiny, and thus a revolt against man's fate. It is no surprise, therefore, that Malraux comes eventually to the fore in the book since he is a key figure in Godard, especially in the opening key episodes of *Histoire(s)* where, over images of the Holocaust, Godard endorses Malraux's absolute belief in the resurrectional status of art: "[A]rt is what is reborn in what has been burnt." The second image of Malraux in the book, which is also its final image, runs alongside lines of text about Barcelona and "[a] kind of immense hope after the Occupation" (a clear allusion to Malraux's own film *Espoir* (*Sierra de Teruel*), released in France in 1945). This is also, typically, an ironic inversion of time since the particular photograph dates from Malraux's later period as an art historian when he was attempting to connect everything. What is new and crucial in the case of Godard's approach to the aesthetic in *Film socialisme* (book) is that he pursues it not through the history of art, but rather the usually demoted form of photography, and specifically the genre of portraiture.

As we have seen, by putting to one side standard photographic concerns of likeness and identity, accuracy and knowledge, Godard allows us to trace new types of human connection and kinship beyond strict family ties and blood-lines, both maternal and paternal (compare Lucien and Florine's wish to use the French word "*les parents*" in an expanded sense of humankind and fraternity). As a film, *Film socialisme* progressed deliberately from the material ("Des choses comme ça") via the specific ("Notre Europe") to something more universal ("Nos humanités"), and it was mapped out explicitly in terms of genre, with captions such as "Des animaux," "Des enfants," "Des paroles," "Des salauds," and "Des légendes." The book allows us to understand exactly this emphasis on humankind as a species, to be contrasted with—yet never predominant over—other forms of species. In fact, the film is also a veritable kinship bestiary of parrots, cats, Egyptian owl, camel, llama, and donkey, all of which are presented at some point in their own frame like the human faces in the book. By concentrating on ourselves as humans and on what makes us unique and different from other species and "things," we can perhaps establish potential new affinities and proximities with the world. As one voice-off early on puts it gnomically, encapsulating Godard's absolute commitment to comparing and (re)combining images and sounds while disqualifying any notion of hierarchy or the *sans pareil*: "one can compare only/ From the incomparable of the non-comparable" (p. 22) ("on ne peut comparer que/ De l'incomparable du pas comparable"). To take an instructive example from the film: while painting by numbers a Renoir landscape a donkey standing gently tied next to him, Lucien refers to his work-in-progress metaphorically in animal terms: "He passed by/ beautiful things, this animal" (p. 69) ("Il est passé à côté de/ Belles choses cet animal"). (This is, in fact, a phrase derived from the French early silent filmmaker Ferdinand Zecca [pictured in the book looking off-frame to the right] with reference to Shakespeare.) To trace the different features, physiognomies, shapes and patterns in the ever-surprising layout and structure of the book of *Film socialisme* is thus to experience not only the affective, intuitive capabilities of Godardian montage, but also the potentially limitless genealogies and universal "common notes" of the image.

    I would like to return finally to the quote from Genet that I alluded to earlier, since I think it encapsulates Godard's general approach in the book of *Film socialisme*: "Stock up all of language's images and help yourself to them, for they're in the desert where you must find them" (p. 78) ("Mettre à l'abri toutes les images du langage/ Et se servir d'elles/ Car elles sont dans le désert/ Où il faut aller les chercher"). Godard, who has consistently professed in dramatic terms that "Texts are death, Images are life," has responded to Genet's general call here for the liberation of all imagery by raiding the image banks and archives and providing us with new and unexpected visual mysteries freed from the standard constraints and ideological presuppositions of language and discourse. Unlike in his previous literary experiments he succeeds here in creating an artistic work in its own right where, in the wilderness of white pages and black print, one has to learn to *see* before learning to read. In this respect, his aims mirror closely those of Curnier for whom the image can serve as a way of thinking which established thought, because based on language, cannot recognize and attempts to domesticate. It is only natural that the hand of Curnier is so visible in the book, since for both Curnier and Godard images, even when stranded in the desert of new digital media and global communications, can, once reclaimed, bring us back to the world—the same world which words, with their false transparency, would seek to draw us away from. As Lucien puts it twice in the film while painting, "I'm welcoming a landscape from the past" ("J'accueille un paysage d'autrefois")—a twin emphasis on receptivity to history and artistic engagement with the world underlined at the end with the statement (over a panning shot of the Sagrada Família): "Better to say Barcelona will soon welcome us" ("Mieux vaut dire Barcelone nous accueille bientôt").

Godard encourages the reader and viewer of *Film socialisme* to emulate Lucien by actively harnessing the untapped potential of the archives, real and virtual, visual and audial. For the power of the imaginary has not yet been completely usurped by the forces of state-sanctioned culture, commodification, and spectacle. The extended story of *Film socialisme* is one of aesthetic transformation which recasts the cinematic event as the play of the visual and photographic within the space of the literary. By restoring critical and ethical power to the image by taking it out of its original format and context and opening it up to new kinds of relations between the human, nonhuman and aesthetic, Godard inspires us to engage in fresh, unauthorized forms of critical thinking and dialogue—part of our ethical obligation to our own collective humanity and creative freedom. Further, a general commitment to open access and to resolutely disrespecting the laws of property and propriety may help us to disrupt and reconfigure the social and cultural field, and so counter the depredations of neoliberal capitalism. Such shared, open, free exchange is visually evoked during the film in the extreme close-up of the face of an extraordinary Egyptian watch where there are no hands to tell the time since it operates according to natural light and the simple alternation of the "night of time" and the "day of time." Its pristine beauty escapes therefore the temporality and values of the prevailing Western aesthetic regime ruled by the marketplace. Far from being an incomprehensibility now accessible to all, as some critics initially dismissed the film, *Film socialisme*, when grasped as an aesthetic whole, represents both a new kind of figurative art and the potential seeds of a new and invigorating *Arte Povera* for contemporary times. The title of Godard's next feature? *Adieu au langage*.

8

Soft and Hard/Back to Back

Erotic Encounters between Voice and Image in the Zone

> Writing is an act of love. If it is not, it is only handwriting. It consists in obeying the driving force of plants and trees and in broadcasting sperm far around us.
>
> —J. Cocteau

> Can one say that in the cinema one writes in reverse.
>
> —J.-L. Godard

Godard's voracious appetite for literature appears insatiable. The later corpus in particular presents a vast and expanding network of textual and intertextual (re)grafting culled from the Western literary, poetic, dramatic, and philosophical traditions which Godard selectively plunders for quotes, from the New Testament, Greek mythology, and the classics, to French neoclassical theater, German romanticism and postromanticism, and European/American modernism. *JLG/JLG: autoportrait de décembre* even offers admiring glimpses of the book-lined shelves in Godard's private sanctuary, which the camera lovingly tracks, though whether all the works on display have actually been read by their owner is a matter for conjecture. Much time could certainly be spent listing and referencing all the sources in his films, even if in some cases like *Nouvelle Vague*, where the entire soundtrack appears to be derived from literary and philosophical texts, any attempt to identify each in turn risks looking futile (the credits, which lack any mention of Godard as author of the film, note simply that certain lines of dialogue spoken by Alain Delon and Roland Amstutz [the gardener Jules] were extracted from *Vous qui habitez le temps* [1989] by the Swiss playwright Valère Novarina). Yet far more crucial is the fact that, as Jonathan Rosenbaum notes, Godard's formal strategy towards literature has always been one of critical transformation rather than simple homage (Rosenbaum 1997: 8–11). Indeed, as we have seen throughout this book, a number of distinct textual approaches and maneuvers are staged and restaged: from the simple, almost throwaway and not always accurate quoting of one-liners and aphorisms, to shots of book covers within the frame, extended meditations around an entire text, the citing of lines of aesthetic theory as poetic manifesto, and the rhetorical troping on pretexts which can reenergize the original. To take just one example of the latter from episode 1A of *Histoire(s) du cinéma*: Robert Bresson's "[s]ans rien changer, que tout soit différent" ("without changing anything, let all be different") (from his seminal *Notes sur le cinématographe* [1975]) is recast as: "ne change rien pour que tout soit différent" ("change nothing for everything to be different"). The process of transmutation can also extend across media. Another phrase form Bresson recited by Godard in *Histoire(s)*, "Garde-toi une marge d'indéfini" ("Retain for yourself a margin of vagueness"), is punctuated differently in the book version to become: "Garde, toi/ une marge/ d'indéfini" ("Keep, yourself, a margin of vagueness") (Godard 1998a, vol. 1: 17). We have even witnessed Godard's self-ironic reference to his own methods of citationality with the deliberately "sub-Godardian" film-within-a-film at the end of *Notre Musique*.

Figure 8.1. Godard in his library in episode 1A of *Histoire(s) du cinéma* (1988–98).

Yet as we have also seen, this multiple intertextual, or hypertextual, process can sometimes take place below the radar. In *Notre Musique*, for instance, the explicit visualizing of the cover of a Folio edition of Julien Green's *Minuit* (1936) is not really essential to the film's progression (at most, as a novel of brooding melancholy that begins with a suicide and relates the boredom of its female protagonist, it complements Olga's profound desire to kill herself). Darwish's poem "The Last Speech of the Red Indian," however, is fundamental to the film's central theme of difference and identity, although it is never explicitly presented as such. The same applies to Broch's *The Death of Virgil* in *Soigne ta droite*, where it is extracted at length and often reworked and modified but never identified by name. It is as if these special intertexts had to remain clandestine in order to function as textual generators of the films they occupy. The principal difference, however, between an early Godard film like *Pierrot le fou* and a later work like *Histoire(s)*, which consistently inverts or corrects existing aesthetic axioms, is the increasing seriousness of Godard's intertextual approach.[1] When in *Pierrot le fou* Ferdinand (Jean-Paul Belmondo) read a volume of Élie Faure's *Histoire de l'art* (1919–21) to his daughter while sitting in a bathtub, it remained at the level of an intertextual joke, whereas in *Histoire(s)* Faure, like the Malraux of *Les Voix du silence* (1951), represents an entire tradition of Western thought and aesthetics which Godard wishes to engage with directly. In the same vein, when Hegel's *Elements of the Philosophy of Right* (1820) is excerpted in *Allemagne année 90 neuf zéro*, or when Edgar Allan Poe's *The Power of Words* (1850) appears in *Puissance de la parole*, the words are read aloud slowly and deliberately and demand the viewer's full consideration.

The central and defining paradox of Godard's textual method has been well formulated by Philippe Dubois: that while literary citation and borrowings have been the main sources of the voices heard in his films, writing for Godard always embodies the Law as opposed to the image which embodies desire (Dubois 2004: 232). Moreover, although Godard may claim that his number one enemy is the text (Scarpetta and Païni 1984–85: 5), and that texts, contrary to images, represent "death" (Bergala 1985: 146), thereby giving the firm impression, as Susan Sontag recognized as early as 1968, of "being engaged in an unending agon with the very fact of literature" (Sontag 2009a: 153), he also allows his actors very little leeway with the dialogue he rigorously imposes on them. This is all the more ironic in view of the fact that he and his fellow New Wave critics felt liberated from the terror of writing when they started making films because they were no longer "intimidated" by the specters of the great writers (Bergala 1998: 436). Of course, Godard's approach to the spoken and written word has always been willfully contradictory, ever since as the young critic "Hans Lucas" he attacked the deadly conception of cinema as the translation of a literary scenario. He realized that he could play instead with words through the mouths of others as well as inscribe them in bold color on the screen. It is with the same spirit of contradiction that he has increasingly allowed the spoken word to circulate profusely across different media, knowing it can only solidify into the mortal form of the published interview or reproduced fax.

In fact, since the early 1980s Godard has engaged with cinema from a determinedly literary perspective, experimenting self-consciously with a number of literary forms, including prefaces, introductions to books and catalogs, discursive scripts written for publication (the four possible scenarios for *Nouvelle Vague* included in "Vague nouvelle" [Godard 1990a]), the four-volume hybrid art book of *Histoire(s) du cinéma* for Gallimard, and the short books produced since 1996 for Éditions P.O.L. subtitled "Phrases (sorties d'un film)" which transcribe and distill poetically the spoken words and written phrases of certain films, in some cases with the title slightly altered (*JLG/JLG, For Ever Mozart, Allemagne neuf zéro, 2 x 50 ans de cinéma français, Les Enfants jouent à la Russie, Éloge de l'amour*). A representative example of his intensive literary method and approach is his preface to a 1987 edition of the collected memoirs of film producer Pierre Braunberger entitled *Cinémamémoire* (in Bergala 1998: 208–10). Written in the form of a personal letter, it is a compact blur of literary and filmic associations larded with intricate references to (among others) Poe, Virgil, Marivaux, Dumas, Gide, Giraudoux, Desnos, Picabia, Shakespeare, and philologist Georges Dumézil, as well as to assorted film and artistic figures such as Renoir, Raimu, Garbo, Dreyer, Carax, Lubitsch, Goya, Van Gogh, Beethoven, Matisse, Picasso (included also are the film theorists and historians Jean Mitry and Georges Sadoul). Playing on the two meanings of the word "*légende*" (legend, as in English, but also title or caption accompanying a photo), the preface pursues a Proustian narrative of redemption, using the labor of visual memory to transform lost time into time regained, and a mere name into cinematic legend.

Many of the texts and interviews published by Godard from the mid-1980s to the late 1990s, which constitute a vital component part of the developing project of *Histoire(s)*, operate in a similar fashion. For although employing a generally plain and unremarkable vocabulary, even when Godard is aiming at a philosophical level (questions such as "What comes before the name?," and: "What is that object we call history?"), they also demonstrate a distinctive rhetorical strategy, a kind of "humble sublime," since they function as the springboard for occasional bursts of individual brilliance, whether in the form of elaborate wordplay or of poetically sharp formulae and *bons mots*. Such moments of concision, paradox, contradiction, and inversion are all the more striking for Godard's often stuttered oral delivery, yet they afford him the fleeting chance to commune with the French language whose rhetorical clarity and incorruptible syntax he often alludes to approvingly.[2]

Godard has always been drawn, of course, to the genre of the philosophical dialogue with writers, intellectuals, and scientists. This ranges from recorded interviews to guest spots in his films, some clearly defined and respectful such as Brice Parain in *Vivre sa vie* and Juan Goytisolo, Mahmoud Darwish, and Jean-Paul Curnier in *Notre Musique*, others more ambiguous and ironic, even parodic, like Alain Badiou lecturing to an empty auditorium in *Film socialisme*. Indeed, Godard has continued to pursue an often awkward public dialogue with highly mediatized literary figures such as Philippe Sollers, with whom he was filmed in the early 1980s discussing the themes of incest and paternity in *Je vous salue, Marie*.[3] Such staged events are a means for Godard to mediate anxieties and desires regarding his own uncertain status as author, for he is both fascinated and horrified by the detached freedom of the writer. As early as 1966, in conversation with the contemporary French writer Jean-Marie Le Clézio for *L'Express*, he emphasized how, as a filmmaker, he feels constrained by the visible and what exists in the real, whereas a writer, a virtual demi-God, would appear to have complete license to create *ex nihilo* (see

Bergala 1985: 286–91). Raymond Bellour has rightly argued that Godard is the most writerly of filmmakers precisely because he takes cinema for life itself, even when everything in him rejects what that implies. "Life" here signifies both the reality that appears on the screen and the way of life that permits this reality to appear. In his exchange with Le Clézio Godard insists that as a filmmaker he doesn't make a distinction between life and art, whereas Le Clézio admits to a certain detachment from reality (what the writer calls "technique"), such that, according to Bellour, he is separated by the very power that guarantees him access to the entirety of the world (his writing, his language). Moreover, Godard displays a pragmatic ethics of cinema inspired by Rossellini, one that adapts to the given reality of things and approaches the cinematic image as an indivisible block of space-time. Bellour concludes that for Godard cinema represents life, whatever it may show, and despite the manipulations of montage to which images and sounds are increasingly subjected in his work. That is to say, Godard still assigns a clearly defined status to the image as an extension or emanation of life (see Bellour 1992: 222–23).

Yet Godard's sustained critical and aesthetic engagement with literature reflects far more than a personal "complex." A central feature of his intertextual method of the last thirty years or so is that those literary works with which he engages most are identified more by the names of their authors than by their titles. This accounts for the summary lists of cited authors provided at the back of the book version of *Histoire(s)* and of the "Phrases" volumes where no attempt is made to distinguish the textual origin of the works in question. In the case of *Film socialisme: Dialogues avec visages auteurs*, the lack of a list of authors is partially compensated for by the inclusion of photographs of writers. It is the author, not the particular work, that is most important for Godard, and his working approach to his chosen authors is to engage with them as individual "spirits." This is because literature is conceived of by Godard as essentially the voice of the individual against the state, operating largely outside the financial institutions, circuits, and systems of funding and distribution that bedevil cinema as a collective enterprise. It is, as he puts it, "a form of speech [*la parole*] of men one by one" (Bergala 1998: 439). Godard goes even further in this regard by referring to writers in concrete, personal terms as his "friends" (books are, after all, accessible and tactile, unlike "text" in the abstract), and the best of them also possess a "style" which he defines, endorsing Buffon's famous axiom "Style is the man himself," as "a place where the soul rests" (ibid.: 434). For these reasons literature provides Godard with both a refuge and a moral conscience. "Literature is a sanctuary," he asserts, "[i]t has deepened my understanding of the world. Books have told me things not said by living beings. Literature has interrogated the world. In this sense it has given me a lesson in artistic morality. I owe it my moral conscience" (ibid.: 439). Literature possesses real, moral "value" for Godard precisely because, unlike cinema which criminally failed to show the camps, it still managed in his view to engage with the Holocaust and provide some form of contact with the historical real. Yet Godard's sense of style in literature as inimitable and linked to the soul also explains why he sees no point in trying to adapt individual literary masterpieces to the screen, to be contrasted with the all-too-easy option of adapting merely "average" novels such as Beniamino Joppolo's *I Carabinieri* for *Les Carabiniers* (1963) and Alberto Moravia's *Il Disprezzo* (1954) for *Le Mépris* (though he confesses to having harbored a secret wish to film Faulkner's 1939 novel, *The Wild Palms*) (see Bergala 1998: 435). Moreover, it means that any cited line or passage in a Godard work carries potentially the trace of a "real" engagement with the author behind it, thereby making the whole process of citationality a highly invested, interpersonal performance.

How might we define this process theoretically, especially since Godard's understanding of literature is not only highly individualized but also clearly gendered? He remarks, for example, of the novels extracted in *Soigne ta droite* that they are "his mother" (Bergala and Toubiana 1988: 51), and has even suggested that literature is like a "godmother" to him. It was his mother, after all, who gave him as a gift for his fourteenth birthday a copy of André Gide's *Les Nourritures terrestres*, his first "discovery of the world of literature" (Bergala 1998: 432), although he attributes to his father his particular taste for German romanticism and the romantic modernists.[4] In his 1982 short, *Changer d'image*, Godard states that, unlike with images, "any text is a text to the beloved," gendered here specifically as female ("la bien-aimée") (the film's subtitle is *Lettre à la bien-aimée*). This naturally raises the question how essential are sex and gender to Godard's dealings with particular authors as "friends," and at what stage a primary need for literature transmutes into the workings of desire, opening up potentially new intersubjective spaces in Godard's work with the author as figure. One is reminded of the Barthesian reader trying to account for his attraction to particular writers in *Le Plaisir du texte* (1973): "*I desire* the author: I need his figure (which is neither his representation nor his projection), just as he needs mine (except to 'prattle')" (Barthes 1973: 39; original emphasis).

I wish to explore the precise nature of Godard's highly personal engagement with literature and the particular questions it raises about writing and desire by focusing on two figures of different sex who have arguably most marked his filmic practice. First, the late writer, dramatist, and filmmaker Marguerite Duras who summed up Godard as the "greatest catalyst in world cinema" (Duras 1987a: 67) and was already championing his work in the 1960s, notably *Deux ou trois choses que je sais d'elle*, awarded the Prix Marilyn Monroe du Cinéma in January 1967 by an all-female jury on which she sat. The two even appeared together along with Louis Malle and Anne Wiazemsky (though not in the same shot), on a program discussing Bresson's new film, *Au hasard Balthazar*, compered by Roger Stéphane and broadcast in February 1966. For Godard, Duras, who was allied briefly with the Nouveau Roman, incarnated the contemporary practice of literature as *écriture* in Barthes's sense of a morality of form. In fact, she was the only female writer to feature in the eclectic selection of classic and modern European writers written on the blackboard in *La Chinoise*, before being erased like all the others apart from Brecht as a suspect trace of the bourgeoisie. Many of the images of the sea, sky, balcony, open window, and beach at Trouville in Godard's work of the 1980s such as *Soigne ta droite* directly evoke those of Duras's films of the same period such as *Agatha et les lectures illimitées* (1981).

Figure 8.2. Guillaume (Jean-Pierre Léaud) erasing the literary canon in *La Chinoise* (1967).

The second determining figure for Godard is the multi-media artist Jean Cocteau who had already passed away in 1963 as Godard was establishing himself as a director but whose presence and influence have marked the entirety of his work (his name featured similarly on the blackboard in *La Chinoise*). According to film legend, when Godard first arrived in Paris in 1946 he proclaimed: "I shall be the Cocteau of the new generation" (cited in Astruc 1975: 123). Whether this statement is true or apocryphal, Godard has always acknowledged his immense debt to Cocteau as an exemplary *auteur* and film poet. In fact, Godard's work is starred with references to Cocteau. The end of *Le Petit Soldat* explicitly cites the novel *Thomas l'imposteur* (1923) (and, more obliquely, *Le Grand écart* [1923]), while the *Orphée*-imbued *Alphaville* is the first in a long line of effective remakes of *Orphée* (1950) that includes *Allemagne année 90 neuf zéro* and *Hélas pour moi*. Cocteau represents for Godard a model of creative longevity and survival, a fact powerfully emphasized in *King Lear* where we see photographs of Cocteau at different stages in his life. Moreover, just as Cocteau was perpetually in the act of reinventing himself and coming back into fashion (a process that perhaps explains his fondness for the myths and tropes of eternal return), so Godard's career has been one of continual molting and an increasing fascination with the themes of resurrection and redemption, most obviously in *Nouvelle Vague*. In addition, Godard shares with Cocteau a contradictory reverence for the art of the past, on the one hand distancing himself from the contemporary world and popular culture by citing and rewriting the classics, while on the other relying on modern images of the café, sports arena, hotel lobby, and so on. Further, since the 1970s Godard has progressively adopted Cocteau's method of bringing his own biography directly into his work. In his most autobiographical film, *JLG/JLG*, Godard even refers to his younger self by his childhood nickname "Jeannot," the name Cocteau attributed to his young lover and long-time collaborator, Jean Marais.

Godard gleefully included both Cocteau and Duras, along with Marcel Pagnol and Sacha Guitry, in his illustrious "Gang of Four," defined as writers who also became filmmakers and were often rejected as imposters and marginalized by the world of cinema. Duras was never very happy to find herself in bed with these figures, who were mainly men of the right (Cocteau and Guitry were both accused of collaboration with the Germans during World War II), and were often deemed aesthetically "light" (a badge of honor for Guitry who reveled in *esprit*, a source of daily turmoil for Cocteau). Godard even dared to suggest that Duras was their joint "offspring": "Your beautiful laugh when I told you that in the cinema you were the true daughter of Cocteau, Pagnol and Guitry" (Bergala 1985: 616). Yet Duras also recognized early on the important implications of Godard's engagement with her work and his projection of her as a female artist, particularly in the immediate wake of May 1968, when she was both an engaged writer (she co-founded the short-lived Student-Writers Action Committee at the Sorbonne) and a celebrated feminist, even if she quickly drew a skeptical distance from feminism and those whom she later disparagingly called "*femmes-écrivains*," preferring instead to be identified simply as a writer. Godard's more sustained textual encounter with Cocteau has involved Godard in the intimate and profound realms of desire and fantasy across multiple artistic fields. Yet in both cases Godard's intrinsically gendered and rhetorical interpersonal practice of cinema is brought dynamically to the fore. Before we can enter fully this highly charged literary and cinematic territory straddling the borders between the real and the imaginary where Godard also comes face to face with different forms of sexuality and desire, we will need first to trace briefly the history of Godard's general approach to language and narrative discourse and establish how the aesthetic relations between word and image evolved in his practice during the 1970s and early 1980s. This was a crucial, formative period for Godard during which he dramatically extended the terms and conditions of artistic exchange and dialogue across gender through his extensive collaboration with Anne-Marie Miéville.

Soft and Hard: Hard to Say

In his film-work of the 1950s and 1960s Godard identified narrative coherency as a prime target in his struggle against the fatigue of naturalistic film conventions. Indeed, to disrupt the happy functioning of a term like *histoire* by destabilizing the "natural" relationship between words and images was, for Godard, to focus his aggression on the narrative foundations upon which so much of the established social and political order is built. His practice was always, and it still remains, to encourage the different meanings of *histoire* ("story," "history," and, in certain circumstances, "matter" or "question") to coincide and interfere with each other. Yet during his militant phase covering approximately the period from *La Chinoise* to his break with the Dziga Vertov Group in 1973, Godard appeared to suffer an overdose of *histoire* in the leftist sense of the term, that is, of the transcendental narrative of revolution. By the mid-1970s, politics and history were ideological nightmares from which Godard dearly wanted to awake. In *Six fois deux: sur et sous la communication* and *France tour détour deux enfants*, he found a response to the problem of historical finality and the traumatic responsibility of storytelling by using a quasimathematical or serial organization of time. In both cases, French television had offered Godard a deal (what he would call an *affaire*) and supplied him with a certain quantity of air time and money to occupy and spend. The result: "six times two" fifty-minute slots, or twelve times twenty-six "movements," around France. Godard is openly ironic about the lack of a "story" in *France tour détour*. At the end of each movement, "HISTOIRE" is flashed onto the screen, and we cut away to the studio, where a talking head announces parodically: "I think it's now time for a story [*histoire*]."

In view of the expressed difficulty of becoming a subject, or rather of "projecting" oneself cinematically as a subject, historical or otherwise, how could Godard bring together his personal history and the impersonal nature of history and cinema? This is the question he tried to resolve in his Montreal lectures in 1978, which resulted in the book *Introduction à une véritable histoire du cinéma* (1980). The formal set-up was a business deal (another instance of an *"affaire,"* this time with Serge Losique, director of the Conservatoire d'art cinématographique) as well as a historiographical "projection." Structured as a succession of seven encounters or "voyages," each divided into two parts, between his own films of the 1960s and examples of classic cinema (notably Eisenstein, Rossellini, Hitchcock, and American directors of the 1950s) projected alongside each other in the auditorium, the public talks were meant to pave the way for a "true" video history of cinema composed of sounds and images rather than of texts. In retrospect they may be viewed as a first, rough version of the method of historical montage based on comparison that Godard would later develop in *Histoire(s)*. Crucially he opted for the spontaneity and irreproducibility of the oral in preference to the more daunting finality of the written word. Yet, written in time, the experiment opened up to the vagaries of chance, finance, travel, and other means of more or less reliable communication (plane, projector, tape). The process, which Godard described as a form of "public psychoanalysis" since he ranged freely from artistic methods and aesthetic preferences to political beliefs and personal/professional relationships, was suddenly curtailed due to a lack of funds with only seven of the planned ten voyages completed. Godard succinctly recounts the circumstances of this failure in a brief prefatory note to the volume effectively disavowing all that follows. The letter plays with the question of *histoire* and is an excellent illustration of Godard's highly deliberate and reflective literary style:

> On each trip I brought with me a little of my story [*un peu de mon histoire*] and plunged back into it at a rate of two of my films at the end of each month. But often the bathwater brought out something other than what my memory had recorded. The reason for this was that in

the morning we screened pieces of films from the history of cinema [*l'histoire du cinéma*] which back then were connected for me with what I was doing. And I commented on it all on the spot in front of three or four Canadians who were just as lost as I was in this history [*dans cette histoire*] [. . .] Then everything came to a halt [. . .] But just the same, he [Losique] was bold enough to break new ground, and *nobody's perfect*. (Godard 2014: xi).

Godard's letter thus signs over to a third person all responsibility for the constitution and authenticity of his text. Indeed, what is lacking in *Introduction à une véritable histoire du cinéma* is a concerted decision on his own part to assume not just the role of critic, but also the mantle of writer.

At this stage in Godard's career, his hope of reinvesting cinematically the literary and the linguistic appeared limited. In 1979, on page 3 of the three hundredth issue of *Cahiers du Cinéma* which he guest edited with a novel collage of texts, photographs, and stills, he acknowledged the impossibility of editing the journal on a regular basis. The question remained how to acquire and control through film the verbal power that "speaks things passionately into being," as Poe describes it in his poem "The Power of Words," the springboard for his later videowork, *Puissance de la parole*. Which is to say, how is one to find a pure form of thought uncontaminated by writing and ideology? Or, to put it in the terms we have been using, how can one finally speak one's own *histoire*? The answer would ultimately be found in the intricate folds of Godard's practice of videographic montage in *Histoire(s)*, as well as in the many satellite works that feed into and out of that mammoth project, where Godard exploits the different meanings of *histoire* to engage simultaneously with the history of cinema, history in general, and his own personal history as a filmmaker.

Yet already, during the mid-to-late 1970s, the idea of female storytellers had been gradually proposing itself to Godard as a potential way out of the narrative impasse. Sections 4A and 4B of *Six fois deux*, for instance, juxtapose a political image entitled "Pas d'histoire" ("No history"), where an Israeli soldier drags a Palestinian girl along the ground by the hair, with a picture of Miéville and the words: "A woman speaks about herself and 'silences' her words like a farmer sows his land. She says things no man can invent" (Bergala 1985: 395). Miéville occupies a central position in Godard's shift towards a new conception of what *histoire* might mean. The Sonimage studio/workshop they developed during the early 1970s, first in Paris, then Grenoble, finally Rolle, was romantically conceived as a combination of her "sound" and his "image." As Michael Witt observes, this represented "an attempt to live out a working practice in which the divisions of labor and of the sexes were dissolved in a reflection on the implications of finding pleasure in one's work whilst collaborating with a partner one loves (to love work, and work at love)" (Witt 1998: 10). The primary aim was clear: "to put talk of audio-visual decentralization into practice; work collaboratively; engage with television; and, through ownership of the necessary production equipment, take time to explore the technical and aesthetic potential of video as a compositional medium" (Witt 2001: 173).⁵ The pair had already made and edited together *Ici et ailleurs*, where Miéville is often heard on the soundtrack correcting his version and analysis of the unfinished *Jusqu'à la victoire*, as well as *Comment ça va* (1976) and *Numéro deux* where her voice extended itself via that of Sandrine to telling the man "a thing or two." *Six fois deux* and *France tour détour* were also fully joint collaborations, and Godard's subsequent return to commercial cinema with *Sauve qui peut* was co-written and co-edited by Miéville. Their most significant and groundbreaking work together from this period, however, was the fifty-two-minute video essay *Soft and Hard* for Channel 4 in 1985. Subtitled "Soft Talk on a Hard Subject between Two Friends," this was a wholly new kind of collaborative piece and artistic encounter for Godard configured explicitly in terms of gender, and it heralded the more intimate style of much of his later work.

The essay begins with a swift, self-reflexive deconstruction of the basic elements and binaries of narrative film (image versus sound, title versus voice-over, narrator versus character, speech versus music) through the establishing of a set of oppositions and equivalences between feminine and masculine: Miéville starts writing at her small desk while reading out in a voice-off a short story about a son writing a letter to his family; Godard sits at a larger desk while speaking in English on the phone to Channel 4 about securing the money for the video piece we are watching. In both cases, an implicit contrast is set up between the image (the shared domestic space) and the sound (the talk of dramas and deals taking place elsewhere). Miéville is filmed ironing while Godard pretends to play tennis in the sitting room. The dialogue is initially formalized in the masculine around the difference between feeling in control of one's identity ("all belonged to him [*tout lui appartenait*] [. . .] but it was only a beginning") and understanding the nature of personal identity ("working out to whom he belonged [*à qui il appartenait*]"). This opposition will unfold in the work as essentially the difference between Godard's male privilege and authoritative voice and Miéville's female need for validation and the space to explore her own perspective. Intercut throughout the entire extended opening sequence is an assortment of stills and photographs of mainly actresses from the history of the moving image: Lillian Gish lying by the water in W. D. Griffith's *Way Down East* (1920), Ingrid Bergman in Rossellini's *Joan of Arc at the Stake* (1954), stills from Miéville's own 1984 short *Le Livre de Marie*, Hitchcock's *Rear Window* (1954), a generic Hollywood gangster film, *Frankenstein* (1931) (the monster with the young Maris), as well as an on-set photograph of a Hollywood shoot and the contemporary image of a TV newsreader. Some of the images are held for longer than others and in some cases superimposed over each other at different speeds and rhythms. The effect is eclectic, spontaneous, and apparently random, emphasizing the formal play of difference and the unpredictable, just as on the soundtrack we hear a range of nondiegetic music ranging from modern free jazz to a rather schmaltzy, gentle muzak.

Figures 8.2–4. Godard and Anne-Marie Miéville in different domestic formations in *Soft and Hard* (1985).

With the basic set-up of a close study of a "film couple" now in place, *Soft and Hard* settles into a twenty-seven-minute still-frame frontal shot of Miéville and Godard with his back and side to the camera—a position and an angle that create the possibility for a new kind of dialogue with his interlocutor. For Bergala introducing the piece in the 2011 Intermedio DVD edition, *Soft and Hard* is like a home movie, the more fluid video format enabling for the first time in Godard's work a real and mutual dialogue with another in real time. The two friends relate the personal stories of their "coming to the image" as children, while many of the stills and photographs flashed up at the beginning are superimposed over their bodies, so creating a layering effect and play of montage in the future style of *Histoire(s)*. They are also separated by a white lamp in the left corner of the frame recalling the long centerpiece conversation in *Le Mépris* between Camille (Brigitte Bardot) and Paul (Michel Piccoli) in their temporary apartment in Cinecittà. Reworking the relations between dialogue/communication and power interrogated in *Ici et ailleurs*, the conversation turns to the theme of communication (its success and failure) and the place of the "subject" ("*sujet*"), here both the "topic" and the "self." Where before in the cinema the self was "projected," the couple reason, now in the era of the small screen it finds itself "subjugated" since television "projects us." This extends and develops the poetic passage they recited a little earlier about the search for a language in which the subject might engage with historical time. Time itself is made an issue in their very reading of the passage, since Godard begins reading it a few seconds before Miéville. This formal *décalage* means that her voice appears to be superimposed over his, creating an effect not so much of doubling but of a kind of chorus (or rather, since their words become harder to discern and disentangle, of an antiphony). Here are the key lines of the passage:

> We were still looking for the right path to our language [*le chemin vers notre parole*]. It was still the period of daily massacres in Beirut and already

the glorious era of flights to Venus and Mars. It was the moment that private televisions took over [. . .] It was also perhaps the time of the penultimate sessions of analysis and the last showings of cinema. In fact, we weren't really looking for the right path of our language [*le chemin de notre parole*], for we were speaking less and more quietly. There was no shortage of subjects of conversation. Or rather, there was. What wasn't lacking was objects. Piles of objects with their names, piles and piles of names. But subjects, true or false, had gone.

In a move that anticipates Godard's engagement with Heidegger and Hölderlin in *Allemagne année 90 neuf zéro* and *Histoire(s)*, the first line of the passage is a clear reference to Martin Heidegger's 1959 collection, *Unterwegs zur Sprache* (translated into French in 1969 as *Acheminement vers la parole*), which includes an essay entitled "A Dialogue on Language." This takes the form of a dialogue between "an Inquirer" ("I") and an imaginary Japanese friend which ranges loosely over aesthetics, philosophy, and cinema (specifically Akira Kurosawa's 1950 film *Rashomon*). According to Jerry White, Godard and Miéville follow both Heidegger's use of the philosophical dialogue and his desire to ruminate, however inconclusively, on the intersection between language, aesthetics, and knowledge (see White 2013: 128–35). For Heidegger, the act of "real" speaking involves a mutual exchange with another about something demonstrable and revelatory: "To speak to one another means: to say something, show something to one another, and to entrust one another mutually to what is shown. To speak with one another means: to tell of something jointly, to show to one another what that which is claimed in the speaking says in the speaking, and what it, of itself, brings to light" (Heidegger 1971: 122). In short: *"The essential being of language is Saying as Showing"* (ibid.: 123) (original italics). The desire to say and to show by communicating in poetry and in prose, in photographic realism and in high artifice, defines precisely Godard's project with Miéville, both here and elsewhere.[6]

The connection with the German tradition is further consolidated in *Soft and Hard* when Godard and Miéville present themselves wandering around a lake reading in turn from Broch's *The Death of Virgil* (in the 1955 French translation by Albert Kohn), although the text is never actually identified as such. The sequence seeks to integrate the visual images of peripheral landscape with a poetic text that is about that most modernist of preoccupations, the inadequacies of art. With book in hand Godard reads selected parts of a key passage about the "cruelty" and "pitiless" intoxication of art due to its "despairing attempt to build up the imperishable from things that perish, from words, from sounds, from stones, from colors, so that space, being formed, might outlast time" (Broch 1983: 122–23). He repeats twice a phrase about beauty being "accessible only to the glance." Then, as the clouds pass above her by the lake, Miéville takes over the reading—just one element in a montage of images that encompasses the screen-texts "Death and Life," "Hard Dream . . . Hard Stream" and "Soft and Hard," a shot of a small river, another screen-text "Two

Friends," and finally a return to the default interior sofa shot. For White, the vivid imagery of the Broch extract resonates with Godard and Miéville's desire to transform their preferred realm of beauty (the cinema) by immersing themselves in the remote periphery of Rolle. He adds persuasively that Broch's mode of address, a style of prose composed of long sentences and poetic digressions, corresponds formally to their own move from lyrical montages to extended dialogue in a single fixed-position shot. The question, however, of Godard's particular relationship to Broch as an agent of literature, and specifically of his approach to the Brochian notion elaborated in *The Death of Virgil* of the unity of a pure literary word beyond all understanding, language and speech, is left unexplored in *Soft and Hard*, to be taken up later by Godard in *Soigne ta droite* and ultimately, as we shall see, through his engagement with Duras and Cocteau.

As the conversation between Godard and Miéville progresses, she becomes more closely identified with the word, narrative, and talking cure, while he remains firmly allied to the image. He declares: "What I like about the image is that it's inaccessible, but that's what would appear to bother you. Must things always be shown?" In fact, the couple often seem out of sync with each other and disagree on certain topics more than they agree. Compare Godard's "characteristic irascible vulnerability" with Miéville's "somewhat brittle and, occasionally, confrontational style" (Grant 2004: 111). Further oppositions are drawn: he came to cinema late, while she as a young girl used to project images of her family onto the wall from photographic negatives. Yet Miéville also voices deep suspicion of the image, in particular the complacent self-evidence of its televisual "truth," and she declares that one of the hardest things in cinema is to film a true dialogue between two close people, taking as a case in point the "unconvincing" dialogue between the central couple in Godard's own *Détective*. In a spirit of respectful and constructive criticism, she suggests that Godard's conception of visual practice (to which she refers rather confusingly at one moment as "*ta parole*") might gain something from the fragility she perceives in cinema's "voice"—"this faint voice that might express itself."[7] What emerges from all this is Godard's sober recognition that although he derives much of his "apparent facility" from the mysterious power of cinema, something is still lacking in his art. It is either a little too easy or a little too hard. The couple concur, self-mockingly: "You ought to be a little serious, Jeannot." Given the way the oppositional terms balance out in the film, it can only be by forming a response to Miéville's *histoire* that Godard will find the necessary counterweight to his work with the image. Perhaps then, as she puts it rather curtly, he will finally be able to "make the grade" ("faire le poids") as an artist.[7] As Bellour rightly suggests, however, following her previous performances in *Ici et ailleurs* and *Numéro deux* (and also, we might add, in *Changer d'image* where she is heard on the soundtrack challenging Godard to explain further his approach to image-making), Miéville's voice in *Soft and Hard* offers to whosoever submits to it far more than simply masochism, since it provides "a renewed possibility of making an image, of placing his [Godard's] voice in the image, of reclaiming himself more as an image, as Godard has continually done" (Bellour 1992: 230).

It would be unwise, of course, to force the analysis of the material in *Soft and Hard* into too neat and progressive a story—Godard attempting to move from the image to the word, and, thanks to a maternal guide, from boyhood to maturity.[8] What is striking, however, is the significantly less antagonistic pose adopted here in relation to language, as well as the acknowledgment by Godard of a place for some kind of *histoire* within his work.[9] We can detect also the gradual emergence of a double narrative: the personal story of Godard alongside the impersonal history of film. For after forty-seven minutes the opening question of subjectivity as projection appears to be partially resolved when the set-up is suddenly dismantled, and the camera initiates a slow, uneven, discontinuous zoom towards a monitor lying on the floor showing television commercials. The latter segue, as if activated by the camera movement, into the opening tracking-shot credit sequence of *Le Mépris*. The camera then motions towards the adjacent blank, white wall, which becomes a screen onto which Godard projects the same sequence. In fact, the entire screen has now become a projection of *Le Mépris*. In keeping with the mood of the Broch text, the sound of the television is entirely dubbed over by the gentle strains and pathos of romantic orchestral music, although the sounds of birds outside in the garden can still be heard. We then catch sight of the silhouette of Godard and Miéville's outstretched arms and open hands from the left of the frame, first hers rising slowly (one more diagonally than the other), then his protruding downwards, thus sounding again the note of difference and *décalage* with which *Soft and Hard* began.

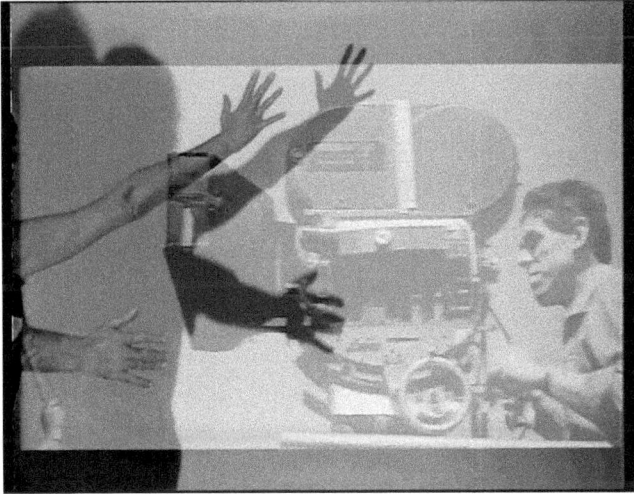

Figure 8.5. Superimposition as shared projection: replaying the start of *Le Mépris* at the end of *Soft and Hard* (1985).

The effect created by these different visual strata is of a live palimpsest whereby the original cinematic image (a bleached-out televisual image) is projected over a white wall, over which are inscribed in turn real arms and their shadows as they enter the cinematic frame. This breathtakingly simple performance of *ombres chinoises*, a set-piece of "soft" superimposition as shared projection over and through the cinema (here Godard's own), would appear to transcend and redeem the couple's highly melancholic meditation on the defining difference between the large and small screens in terms of projection. As Timothy Long well observes: "Both inside and outside the frame, an indexical trace of the body and a figure of symbolic transcendence (a camera eye or the angel Gabriel!), their shadows unite, for a brief moment, abstraction and figuration" (Long 2014: 212). Finally, as Coutard in the sequence from *Le Mépris* starts to turn the camera round towards the viewer, the projected image vanishes. The arms still remain in place before they too disappear into black via a quick fade. The voices of Godard and Miéville share one final question-and-answer exchange:

GODARD: "Where has all that gone? That project of growing and enlarging into subjects."

GODARD: "Where has it gone?" [in English]

MIÉVILLE: "It is hard to say." [in English]

GODARD: "Hard to say." [in English]

Hard to say, certainly, but still possible to show, even in a reduced, minimal form. The last word is precisely that of the Image, not the Word.

Duras/Godard: The Right Side and Inside Out

What happens, however, when the lines between a feminine voice and a masculine image are redrawn explicitly as an encounter between writing and cinema? Such is the significance of *Sauve qui peut*, where Godard as an agent of the Image engages directly with the Voice of literature, Duras. Let us be absolutely clear about the stakes of this encounter. For Godard, Duras, at that point still a relatively marginal *avant-garde* figure, represented the idea of literature as an expression of freedom, that is, of an entirely new, individual *parole* liberated from traditional narrative discourse and epistemological paradigms which she took delight in pulverizing in uncompromising and groundbreaking novels like *Le Ravisssement de Lol V. Stein* (1964). Indeed, her idiosyncratic, muscular use of language was deemed by some in the French literary Establishment as a direct attack on the rules of French grammar and syntax—the very rules Godard professes elsewhere to admire. Hence, Duras embodied for Godard a totally fresh and original poetics of language outside the phallocentric networks of discourse as power. Whereas before he was obliged to focus his aggression on the narrative foundations of Western society, now it seemed to him possible, at least on paper, to welcome a writer into his cinema in order to achieve a new and radical unity of word and image.

Godard initially enlisted Duras's active participation in *Sauve qui peut*, inviting her to come to Lausanne for a one-to-one interview that would feature in the film. The experience proved underwhelming for Duras, however, who, in her later account of the shoot, didn't take kindly to being interviewed by Godard in a schoolyard during break-time when they could barely hear themselves speak (see Duras 1987a: 47–48). In fact, the only trace of Duras's presence in *Sauve qui peut*, left uncredited, is a brief voice-off sequence, not always fully audible, where, as the protagonist and filmmaker Paul Godard (Godard's alter ego played by Jacques Dutronc) drives through central Lausanne with his daughter Cécile (Cécile Tanner), she is heard on the soundtrack describing matter-of-factly the madness and abjection involved in the act of writing: "[I]t is to disappear . . . to be behind something . . . suspicious, I would say almost immoral." In what appears a set of disconnected edited fragments she talks of the necessary silence created by the spoken word when one is reading a text properly. Finally, after opining that "the place of women, if one such exists," is connected to childhood, while men are simply childish, her voice is peremptorily cut.

Figure 8.6. Paul (Jacques Dutronc) driving his daughter Cécile (Cécile Tanner) while Marguerite Duras speaks on the soundtrack in *Sauve qui peut (la vie)* (1979).

We shall come back shortly to the particular erotic linking of abjection and the "behind" in Godard's aesthetics. For the moment let us consider further Duras's ambiguous role in the narrative of *Sauve qui peut*. When, twenty-four minutes into the film, Paul Godard arrives in a university classroom to introduce her to a class of film students, she is presented as unavailable.[10] She is apparently next door but "immobile." No reasons are given, but the clear suggestion is that she is incapacitated by drink (a condition not unfamiliar to Duras during the 1960s and 1970s as she would herself attest in works like *La Vie matérielle* [1987]). Yet if Duras remains invisible, her words are heard loud and clear, for the classroom sequence is prefaced by an extract from the soundtrack of her landmark 1977 film, *Le Camion* (*The Lorry*), playing on the classroom monitor in preparation for her visit. We hear some of her signature words from the film: "C'était tellement difficile . . . Tellement dur, tellement . . . C'est mieux comme ça" ("It was so difficult . . . So hard, so . . . It's better like that"). With Duras refusing to enter the classroom and speak, and therefore directly embodying the key theme of female refusal and resistance in *Le Camion* which revolves around the hitchhiker, "la dame du camion," who is never visualized and who shuns the normal rules of society and politics, Paul is reduced to reading a key statement from her 1977 book, *Les Lieux de Marguerite Duras*: her confession that she makes films simply to keep herself busy. In an appropriative gesture, he adds: "It's valid for me, too," concluding: "As for Duras, every time you see a passing lorry, think of it as a woman's word passing [*une parole de femme qui passe*]." Such easy endorsement, said partly out of frustration, has a clear misogynistic ring to it, evident also in the cursory way he treats the female instructor, Janine, who was counting on Duras's visit. Indeed, he will soon dismiss female speech as "just words," when, after the brief car sequence already mentioned, he encounters his writer-girlfriend and co-worker, Denise (Nathalie Baye), outside the TV studio where she had arranged to interview Duras for a program to be broadcast that evening. When Paul claims to have already taken Duras back to the airport because she wanted to leave early, Denise lashes out at "Paulot" in a violent and abusive rage, accusing him of always speaking for her on her behalf–another manifestation of the film's contagion of quotidian violence.

Duras, then, is presented as a source of tension and discord in the film: she sets the agenda and dictates proceedings without ever being visible. Like "la dame du camion," she is a free and autonomous spirit. It is *her* word. *Her* call. *Her* will. *Her* desire. This is the triumph of the Voice over the Image, one that renders almost irrelevant the neat academic formula written chiastically on the blackboard about cinema and video being like Cain and Abel ("CAÏN ET/ ABEL CINÉMA ET/ VIDÉO"). It reflects precisely that Godard and Duras represent polar opposites in their treatment of the relationship between text and image, a fact readily acknowledged by Duras herself when she suggests elsewhere that, at least up until *Sauve qui peut*, she and Godard experienced "reverse" problems in film (Duras 1987a: 47–48). Duras had, of course, approached cinema principally as an extension of her writing, even to the point of destroying it as a visual spectacle with an increasingly abstract, minimalist technique reducing images to merely *passe-partout* approximations.[11] Crucially, Duras proves always one step ahead of Godard in understanding the essential difference between herself as a writer making deliberately "amateur" films *contra* cinema and Godard as the supreme film *auteur* and iconophile. He eventually recognizes this himself in a letter he wrote to Duras during the shoot of *Détective* though never actually sent: "Can one say that in the cinema one writes in reverse. Yes. Your green eyes saw this before me" (Bergala 1985: 616). Yet the case remains that Duras felt entirely set up by Godard in *Sauve qui peut* and considered her reduced presence in the final edit as both a failed collaboration and unfinished business.

The scenario would be dramatically reversed eight years later in "Deux ou trois choses qu'ils se sont dites," a program for the series *Océaniques* broadcast on the mainstream channel FR3 on December 28, 1987. Billed as an early New Year's gift to the nation by two exceptional artists, it marked the release of their latest work: Godard's *Soigne ta droite* and Duras's novel, *Emily L.* (1987). Edited down to an hour from over two hours of recorded material, this "second take" of their missed encounter in *Sauve qui peut* (and as it turned out their last formal encounter together) represents arguably the realization of their longstanding project to make a film together. Once again it directly pitches Duras as the Voice of literature against Godard as the Image of cinema. Invited into the inner recesses of her private apartment in Paris for a nighttime chat, Godard, looking distinctly nervous with a scraggy one-day beard, willingly plays the role of an innocent abroad in alien territory, allowing Duras, armed in her by-now-standard uniform of polo and cardigan (a light-brown-and-black combination), to take immediate command of the interview. Disposing quickly of polite formalities, and with a wicked glint in her eye that seems to run across the frame of her thick, black glasses, she cuts straight to the chase. Capitalizing on his frank admission that he would never have succeeded as a writer, she coolly exposes the futility of his long-cherished ambition to write a novel: "There's something in the very principle of writing that on the one hand attracts you, but on the other scares you and becomes intolerable. Faced with writing, you're simply not up to it [*tu ne tiens pas le coup*]!."[12] Godard is put directly on the defensive by such abrasive language and all but capitulates when he states that perhaps he shouldn't have used words (or at least so many) in *Soigne ta droite*. She proceeds to point out his various complexes around language and writing as if she were his therapist ("You're impatient, with texts, with films, and even with others speaking"), and she instantly dismisses his quasiromantic fantasy that, unlike with writing, cinema might relieve him of the need to think since "it's the film that thinks." "Cut the drivel," she retorts, "the film doesn't think alone. Without you, there's no film."

Figure 8.7. Godard faces off against Marguerite Duras in "Deux ou trois choses qu'ils se sont dites" (1987).

What then ensues is a series of personal swipes and often bitchy ripostes, of blows and counterpunches, some clearly below the belt. Indeed, the tense sparring becomes a slugfest of put-downs between two old bruisers rather than a prize conversation between two elite intellectuals (Godard recognizes this later in the conversation when he remarks they have acted like two heavyweights ["*rochers*"] calling for a trainer). Her apparently innocent question whether he has read Kierkegaard, which elicits the answer, "[Y]es, in my youth," provokes her damning response that it was an age when he read. Godard appears completely out of his depth here and merely soft putty in Duras's hands. She even warns him at one point, as if scolding a child: "If you yawn, I'll cut it short!" (this knee-jerk remark was carefully omitted in the published transcription of the interview). Some serious themes are broached, notably the worth of Claude Lanzmann's 1985 documentary, *Shoah*: for Duras, Lanzmann showed the Holocaust (the graves, the survivors); for Godard, he showed nothing. Yet the tone remains largely self-absorbed, petulant, and petty. When Godard offers Duras a backhanded compliment for refusing him the rights to adapt *L'Amant*, she simply replies that he would not be able to follow the story anyway. She returns again to *Soigne ta droite* but only to stick the knife in, stating with no real justification or concrete proof that all one hears in the film is shouting, thus insinuating a case of verbal excess and logorrhea covering up the lack of a real subject. *Dur, dur!* Yet in pure passive-aggressive fashion, Duras also fishes narcissistically for his approval, asking him whether he doesn't agree with her that she can alone can capture in her novels those precious, revelatory "first moments" of classic music. Godard does attempt in the last stages to salvage something, if only a neat formulation about their relationship: "You're one of the few people I know who can be either my wrong side or my right side [. . .] I can listen to you." This falls on deaf ears, however, as Duras now takes over proceedings completely to deliver a long monologue on the difficult genesis of *Emily L.* Of course, she is partly obliged to do this because Godard reveals he hadn't actually read her novel and refrains from even asking any questions about it. Having gradually worn him down during fierce interrogation, Duras now cruises to the end stylishly on her own. Godard has become no more than a screen for her to project ever more dazzling ideas about her own work. In direct contrast to her disembodied and disfigured presence in *Sauve qui peut*, Duras's imperious voice always articulates the right word here. Such cool mastery of the other goes well beyond the sometimes difficult moments shared between Godard and Miéville in *Soft and Hard*. Indeed, Duras's calculated deployment of blunt expressions like "*tenir le coup*" completely surpasses Miéville's "*faire le poids*."

Yet Godard actually has the last word in the interview, and it's an honest, downbeat admission of disappointment and sadness at the way it unfolded. He intimates that Duras had stayed well within her comfort zone by playing her usual number, while he himself had proved unable to achieve what he's capable of (left undefined). In short, the encounter was conducted exclusively on her terms, and he had allowed this to happen. There's a realization here that not only did a mutually respectful dialogue with Duras not take place, but also that it probably never could, precisely because for her a conversation is always a dynamics of power and rivalry where there can only ever be one winner (the insurmountable power of the spoken Word). In their blistering *face à face* she incarnates the masculine HARD principle and he the feminine SOFT instance. This might seem entirely natural, in fact, since *Soigne ta droite*, like other Godard films of this period including *Soft and Hard*, valorizes "softness" ideologically in its love of the countryside and the beauty of nature, in sharp contrast to the political hardness of his earlier Maoist period. Significantly, at one point in the interview when Duras slyly refers to his film as *Soigne ta gauche* (a play on the Tati short *Soigne ton gauche* [*Keep Your Left Up*] [1936]), he states approvingly that she is always more political than he is—an indication perhaps that he actively sought to position her as Hard. In fact, Godard positively excels at "playing soft" in public as the shy, self-deprecating, artist-intellectual, all coy and evasive, in particular with female artists and intellectuals like Miéville and Duras. An encounter with Duras promised initially the almost perfect combination due to her skill at playing both the gentle "*marguerite*" ("daisy") (prompting Godard at the start to compliment her for knowing how to say such nice things about his film) and the tough, no-nonsense intellectual who could dismiss Sartre, as she does here, with the simple flick of a phrase (Sartre was simply a "transitive" political writer and so not authentic). To Duras's effortless sadism, Godard's ready masochism. Indeed, here and in other media performances of the 1980s, Duras gleefully oscillated between the public and private positions of passive desired object and active *voyeuse*, victim and aggressor. It was a sadomasochistic model of interpersonal relations she had already well rehearsed with her young interlocutor Gérard Depardieu in the "*chambre noire*" of *Le Camion*, a stunning exercise in authorial control and seduction recorded in Duras's own home where Depardieu is all but elided in the closing stages.

In short, having looked to Duras for the chance to experience the freedom of the spoken word, Godard ended up being wholly undermined and deflated by it. The potential for a positive and mutually enhancing friction between cinema and literature was ultimately canceled out by Duras's solo performance of raw aggression. Hence, "Deux ou trois choses qu'ils se sont dites" inverts the gendered terms of the axiom often employed by Godard (in particular in *Histoire(s)*) to explain the relations between cinema and the real: "Cinema authorizes Orpheus to look back without causing Eurydice's death." Here, in the "home" of writing, it is Orpheus as literature (i.e., Duras) who looks back and kills Eurydice as film (Godard). In an interview shortly after Duras's death in 1996, and still no doubt smarting from their unsatisfactory missed encounter, Godard summed up her achievement in a highly ambivalent manner. In his judgment she had pushed her luck too systematically with originality by trying out every style. On a personal level, too, "there was her avarice, her need for recognition" (Bergala 1998: 432). He then puts her firmly in her place: she was "a pure *littéraire*, in the best sense of the word" (ibid.: 423), one who had made one or two very good films with little money. Godard, it now turns out, had never really rated Duras's literary countercinema in works like *Le Camion* based on the spoken text and voices, leading him more than once to remark very patronizingly that if she could claim so easily there was nothing to making films other than the act of reading a text aloud, then she should at least make more of an effort. Ironically, and rather cheekily in the circumstances, Godard presents his books of *Phrases* as "close to some texts by Duras" (ibid.: 436), and in *For Ever Mozart* he will even include a standard phrase from Duras (unattributed) about an actor's need to let the imaginary of the text speak for itself rather than attempt to act it out.

Yet however limited and blocked their one-to-one encounters, the lasting value of Duras for Godard was precisely to allow him to formulate more clearly the specificity of cinema and its essential (positive) difference from writing. Moreover, while the poles of masculine and feminine were distorted, twisted, and reversed in their public relationship, a solid heterosexual structure still remained visibly intact. We have already witnessed in the context of music Godard's phobia towards male homosexual desire (notably in *Masculin Féminin* and *Sauve qui peut*), and it is the case that alternative forms of sexuality are rarely explored in his cinema. Even in *La Chinoise* Maoist precepts are used to attack the darling actors and *choux-fleurs* of the Comédie-Française, while in *Vladimir et Rosa* Godard and Gorin strike each other violently while disguised as macho policeman in leather uniforms and brandishing gigantic batons. Clearly intended as an image of disgust at authority and cinema, the latter appears to unfold as a virtual pastiche of soft gay porn (it goes without saying that all the instances of pornography cited in Godard's subsequent work such as *Histoire(s)* are unambiguously straight). As for Duras, she was steeped in a normative tradition of sexual difference and became obsessed in her later work with the "royalty" of heterosexual difference. For her, homosexuality represented the potential collapse of sexual difference since it was a "dominion," like death, accessible to no one except God. In her literary practice of *"écriture courante"* developed during the 1980s and 1990s in her work for Éditions de Minuit, she honed a style and process of intertextual difference featuring "Great Men" or intertextual Thirds. *Emily L.*, for example, engineers an intricate heterosexual cross-breeding of an Emily Dickinson poem ("There's a Certain Slant of Light") and a John Huston film (*The Night of the Iguana* (1964)) (see Williams 1997: 76–83). Yet at the same time Duras consciously fashioned an external margin to her *"écriture courante."* I have shown elsewhere how this exterior zone of "minor" "antiliterature," published largely with POL, had direct homosexual connotations, for Duras's highly rhetorical discursive strategies of reappropriation and sublimation established the male homosexual as an impossible element within her system, its "other face" (ibid.: 108–12). Younger gay writers in particular allowed Duras to project the indeterminate character or "image" of the textual process by fashioning an intertextual "face" to embody it, even if this face represented the very "nonface" of homosexual *vagabondage*. Duras, too, had a natural attraction for the chiasmus, yet her restless, chiastic tropings on the static "mirror-image" of gay desire, part of her rhetorical framing of sexual and textual difference, promoted the case for the "correct" (read: heterosexual) principle of desire and fixed membership of the heterosexual club (as opposed to the interchangeability of pleasure in homosexual practice, which she also acknowledged). Indeed, however "open" and nonbinding

Duras's intertexual chiasmus appeared, it still functioned characteristically as the most inward-pointing of all rhetorical figures, providing her work with a water-tight seal of textual and sexual identity that outlawed even further her chosen *tiers exclu* (ibid.: 107). The style and tone of her treatment of Godard in "Deux ou trois choses qu'ils se sont dites" recalls, in fact, her intertextual use of her younger gay male companion, Yann Andréa (or "Y.A. homosexuel"), loitering off-screen during the filming of the interview and with whom she shared the last sixteen years of her life. A simulation and "beastly" parody of the real (i.e., heterosexual) thing, Andréa came to represent both the sublime and abject other in Duras's later work, most obviously in films like *L'Homme atlantique* (1981), where his initial fleeting image is soon subsumed by black spacing punctuated only by the sounds of her spoken voice and the sea.[13]

This marks a crucial point of difference between Duras and Godard. For while a positive representation of homosexuality or nonnormative sexuality would also appear to be all but impossible in his cinema, Godard, for whom writers are fundamentally friends and allies, presents the strange and fascinating case of a straight filmmaker becoming *queer* during his encounters with gay literature. Indeed, textually speaking, he reveals himself as remarkably versatile and uninhibited. It's not just that he feels he "belongs" to a wider artistic network he can plug into and out of with ease, unlike in the House of Duras where he is offered no real creative room for maneuver and is promptly ejected once his time is up. Attuned to the sexual undercurrents and reverberations of literature, he displays a genuine familiarity and ease with gay male literary influence. Gay modernist writers like Cocteau, Proust, Gide, and Genet constitute an integral and intimate part of his personal symbolic of kindred souls. Proust and Gide, for example, are liberally cited throughout *Histoire(s)*, and we already noted in chapter 1 Godard's very knowing reference in episode 1B to Gide's young lover, Marc Allégret, a director who represented for the New Wave the very worst of the discredited *cinéma de papa* and whom he lacerated in a 1958 review for *Arts* in the form of an archly parodic apostrophe of love employing the ambiguous word "gentil" ("kind"/"nice"): "Marc Allégret! I love you very much! You're the sweetest of filmmakers") (Bergala 1985:150). The Genet of *Un Captif amoureux* (1986), dealing with the Palestinians, is much referenced by Godard in his later work, but so also are less well-known works like "L'atelier d'Alberto Giacometti" (1957) read by Julie Delpy in *Histoire(s)* 1A). Other cases of engagement with contemporary gay writing include Julien Green's *Frère François* (*God's Fool: the Life and Times of St Francis of Assisi*) (1983), a biography exploring the material life of the saint which the pregnant Marie reads aloud in *Je vous salue, Marie*. More recently, in his 2000 short, *De l'origine du XXIe siècle*, Godard incorporates the voice of the often graphically violent novelist and playwright Pierre Guyotat, author of the homoerotic 1967 book about wartime atrocity, *Tombeau pour cinq cent mille soldats*, as well as of the banned and for a long time censored 1971 novel *Eden, Eden, Eden*. The Guyotat we hear reading here from *Progénitures* (2000), however, while typically stretching lexical and grammatical sense with his unique, elliptical syntax and urban creole, is also unusually tender, offering phrases such as "ma chérie, sa joue roz' l'oreiller brodé d'or [sic]" (literally, "my beloved, her pink cheek the pillow embroidered in gold").

A particular bone of literary contention between Duras and Godard was Louis Aragon, a recurring point of reference for Godard ever since Aragon championed his unique method of cinematographic collage in the mid-1960s as that of a *"monteur"* and *"collagiste"* in the tradition of Lautréamont (see Aragon 1965 and Smith 2014) and proposed him as the new Delacroix capable of resolving the question "What is art?." The song performed by Anna Karina in *Bande à part* based on Aragon's poem "Les poètes" (1960) is replayed in episode 1A of *Histoire(s)*, and there are references to the poems "Les lilas et les roses" and "Elsa je t'aime" in *Histoire(s)* in 1A and 3A respectively. In fact, Godard had already used "Elsa je t'aime" (from the 1941 collection, *Le Crève-coeur*) in a voice-off sequence in his first feature *À Bout de souffle*, where Godard himself recites with a female voice, over the soundtrack of an American Western, the lines "Au biseau des baisers/ Les ans passent trop vite" ("With the sharp cut of kisses/ The years pass too quickly"), playing rhythmically and phonetically with the line "évite, évite, évite, les souvenirs brisés" by reading it out fast as: "et vite et vite et vite les souvenirs brisés" ("and quickly and quickly and quickly the broken memories"). An early photograph of Aragon the avant-garde dandy is also included in the book of *Film socialisme* (Godard 2010: 184), while in episode 3A of *Histoire(s)* a photograph of Aragon from the 1940s accompanies the superimposed extract from *Le Crève-coeur*. Godard's positive and productive engagement with Aragon is to be contrasted with Duras's withering dismissal of him in *Les Yeux verts* as an unreconstructed "communist writer" (an oxymoron in itself for Duras), and, by implication, as a man of questionable sexuality. Duras regarded Aragon as a total sham: not only did he never recant his die-hard communist beliefs (he occupied a major position in the PCF until his death), but also, immediately after the passing away of his wife and muse Elsa Triolet in 1970, he came out publicly as bisexual, appeared flamboyantly at Gay Liberation marches and parades, and enjoyed an "out" relationship with his young male lover and companion, Michel Larivière (as it happens, Aragon had always been open with Triolet about his sexuality and never sought to hide it).[14]

Another important and instructive case of gay male writing for Godard is that of the late film critic and theorist Serge Daney, a self-styled *ciné-fils* who, up until his tragic early death from AIDS in 1992, was pursuing a unique and radical project of gay French cinephilia.[15] Godard engaged with Daney as a writer and thinker of film rather than practitioner (he never made a film), and it was Daney who invited him to guest-edit the three hundredth issue of *Cahiers du Cinéma*. With his crystalline clarity and intelligence, intellectual boldness and originality, and open, capacious spirit, he was perhaps the only critic who could keep up with Godard as a live interlocutor, as evidenced by their brilliant long interview together recorded at Godard's house in Rolle in 1998 entitled "Godard fait des histoires" (transcribed and later included in Bergala 1998: 161–73), intended as a pedagogical dossier for *Histoire(s)* and extracted throughout episode 2A (*Seul le cinéma*) where it plays a central structuring role. The seriousness of this particular exchange is confirmed by the fact that it plays out in *Histoire(s)* literally in stereo: Daney dominates the right channel, Godard the left. Like Godard, Daney was passionate about tennis as a site of open encounter and exchange, and Godard's touching tribute to Daney following his death begins: "There it is. The dialogue is over. The exchange between the real and us has finished, the passer having passed [*le passeur ayant passé*]" (Bergala 1998: 252). Godard positions Daney and his exceptional "critical gaze" as arriving at the end of an illustrious line of French art critics whom he refers to intimately by their first names—Denis (Diderot), Charles (Baudelaire), Élie (Faure), André (Malraux). The same point is made even more emphatically a few years later in *Deux fois cinquante ans de cinéma français*, which offers a far more extensive roll-call of French art and film critics including Cocteau and culminating with Duras and Daney. Godard also directly invokes and embraces Daney's private life with a concrete allusion to an evening spent in a club near the Arc de Triomphe where Daney is imagined taking off his famous cap and becoming "free" in the heady atmosphere ("It's up to us now to accept and understand as we search in the heart of ourselves whether we also loved" [ibid]).

Daney was also linked with Duras, of course, and she referred to him in her own valedictory tribute as "le jeune Serge" ("the young Serge"), troping on Claude Chabrol's 1958 film, *Le beau Serge*, starring the late, openly gay actor Jean-Claude Brialy (see Duras 1993: 179–80). A year before his death, he publicly defended Duras against Jean-Jacques Annaud following the release of Annaud's highly commercial 1992 blockbuster adaptation of *L'Amant*, claiming it to be utterly crass and by the world's first "post-filmmaker." He had also commissioned her to edit the special June–July 1980 number of *Cahiers du Cinéma*, which he personally assisted on and which became *Les Yeux verts*. Yet for Duras, Daney was ultimately little more than an invisible (and uncredited) facilitator of her work. While she may claim in her tribute a deep personal friendship with him (they, too, had bonded around tennis and their "love" was "refracted through Bjorn Borg"), she nevertheless infantilizes him as a gangly and overtalkative, if brilliant, "adolescent." He was certainly never for her an active collaborator or *compagnon de route* in the way that he was for Godard.

The core of Godard's engagement with gay writing and cinema, and gay influence in general,[16] centers, however, around Cocteau, a figure about whom, as we might now expect, Duras remains decidedly ambivalent and suspicious, largely on account of the gay audience he attracts—the not so mysterious, undifferentiated "*ceux-là*" she refers to cryptically in *Les Yeux verts* ("I think Cocteau is beautiful but for others, not for me. As soon as *those people* speak about cinema, I know *they* love Cocteau" [Duras 1997a: 66; my emphasis]). Significantly, no mention of the key role of Cocteau in the casting and thematics of *Soigne ta droite* was made by either Duras or Godard in their filmed interview together. Things were perhaps better left unsaid, though Duras does acknowledge there in noncommittal fashion that Cocteau was "a charming man, a myth." It is to Cocteau then, and to Godard's full-scale immersion in a gay artist's personal imaginary, that we now turn.

Cocteau/Godard: Back to Back

The ethico-aesthetic project of Godard's later work, in particular films like *Nouvelle Vague* and *JLG/JLG*, clearly resembles that of late Cocteau in its chaste and somber tones, its explicit attention to love as friendship, and its extended speculations on what it is to be human (works like *La Difficulté d'être* [*The Difficulty of Being*] [1947]). Indeed, Godard's evolving self-portrait as an isolated film artisan communicating only with (usually deceased) writer-friends and filmmakers as he attempts desperately to create a dialogue with the other, draws some of its force directly from the ascetic model embodied by Cocteau, a character as "unique" and "alone" as the universe of cinema itself, whose only offspring was likewise his prolific work, yet who nonetheless succeeded in creating an extended (gay) family of friends, former lovers, and adopted sons.[17] Cocteau's investment in new forms of human kinship and affective relations was already recognized by Godard in one of his first formal encounters with Cocteau, the 1958 short *Charlotte et son Jules* dedicated to Cocteau, which engineers a number of symmetrical inversions of Cocteau's 1939 play *Le Bel Indifférent* concerning gender. In Cocteau it's a middle-age woman who tries in vain to hold on to a young male lover initially refusing to listen to her monologue, while in Godard's short Jean (Jean-Paul Belmondo) rages misogynistically against a woman who, he believes, still loves him. In fact, she no longer considers him her "*jules*" and had only come back to his apartment to retrieve her toothbrush while her new lover waits for her outside. Godard has replaced Belmondo's voice with his own, a method that recalls Cocteau's own ventriloquizing of his actors' voices, notably in *Orphée*.

Godard returns to the theme of the indifferent lover much later with *Armide* (1987), an episode in the compilation film *Aria*. This short is inspired by the opera of the same title by Jean-Baptiste Lully, a lyrical meditation on the knight Renaud who remains indifferent to the spells of the magician Armide. The film stands out in Godard's work for its male nudity in the form of a group of male bodybuilders pumping iron in the gym. Apparently lost in their own exclusive, solipsistic narcissism as they thrust their bodies in silence on the machines, they appear not to notice the presence of two young female spectators (Marion Peterson and Valérie Allain) who strip and pose provocatively beside them and even touch their bodies while fondling themselves and each other autoerotically. The desirous nubile women are effectively rejected by the men who look as if they might themselves be participating in a gay male porn scenario, except for the fact that they never engage in any type of contact with each other and stare only blankly off-screen. Out of sexual frustration the women begin to imagine fantasies of vengeance, at one point holding a knife to the back of one of the men, yet nothing comes of this, and they end up attributing the lack of reciprocal interest to their own insufficient physical charms. Hence, although a *mise-en-scène* of heterosexual pornography is clearly set in motion here and taken to phallic excess with the use of the knife and the men's heads bopping up and down, enjoyment itself is blocked and release denied. The bodybuilders eventually trot out of the gym in a quiet line, leaving the women to their exaggerated gestures and statufied poses recalling Cocteau films like *La Belle et la bête* (1946) and *L'Aigle à deux têtes* (*The Eagle with Two Heads*) (1948). For Peter Wollen, this bespeaks not simply a familiar heterosexual model of male resistance to, and annulment of, female desire (the man humiliates the woman who desires him and gratifies himself in her humiliation), but also perhaps, more generally, the only solution that Godard can now envisage to the eternal problem of destructive, and self-destructive, male sexuality (Wollen 1992: 190–91). Wollen rightly concludes that Godard is presenting here a world in which female desire, so threatening in his early work, is doomed to disappointment by male indifference, and that the film thus constitutes an "elaborate defense against adult or assertive femininity, against feminine 'hardness'" (ibid.: 189).

Figure 8.8. Tales of the gym: desire and frustration shared by Marion Peterson and Valérie Allain in *Armide* (1987).

Yet Wollen also poses here an important question regarding the men, asking whether the bodybuilders might not be transposed versions of *Orphée*'s motorcycle riders, and thus whether Godard is not reworking Cocteau's homosexual text to suit his own heterosexual dilemma (ibid.: 190). If so, as seems likely, this would prove, according to Wollen, that whenever Godard has recourse to Cocteau, the (homo) erotic aspect diminishes, for indeed the utterly respectable bodybuilders of *Armide* with their overdeveloped muscle have scarcely the same sensual impact and thrill as the roving angels of Death rigged out in black leather who carry the corpse of Cégeste through the mirror in their gloved hands. While I largely concur with Wollen's assessment of the loss of homoerotic charge from Cocteau's *Orphée* to Godard's *Armide*, this represents only part of the story. In the same article Wollen talks of Godard's highly involved critical piece, "Ignorés du Jury" (1958) (Bergala 1985: 152–55), a written defense of Jacques Demy's *Le Bel Indifférent* (1957), a very different adaptation of Cocteau's play from *Charlotte et son Jules* which Godard compares stylistically with yet another play by Cocteau on the same theme, *Renaud et Armide*, premiered in Paris in 1943. According to Wollen, Godard was doubtlessly aware of the transposition of gender between Cocteau's original gay treatment of the theme and Demy's manifestly heterosexual version. This would appear to confirm Wollen's theory that what interests Godard is above all the "heterosexualization" of Cocteau's universe, whether by Godard himself or by other filmmakers. Yet in "Ignorés du Jury" Godard also describes Cocteau and Demy very knowingly in the specific terms of "front" and "behind," as if they were part of an all-male relay of screens and "parade," a quintessential Coctelian term. He writes: "The screen on which *Le Bel Indifférent* is projected is the mirror *before* which [*devant lequel*] Cocteau paraded and *behind* which [*devant lequel*] Demy from now on hid" (Bergala 1985: 154; my emphasis). Such evocation of an intermale mirror has obvious associations with the sexual use of the two-way mirror in Cocteau's work, explicit in literary texts like *Le Livre blanc* (1928) and implicit in films like *Le Sang d'un Poète* and *Orphée*. Moreover, there is a subtle implication here of the repressed homosexuality of Demy, who in 1962 married filmmaker Agnès Varda (also featured in "Ignorés du Jury"). The cinematic screen fleshed out by Godard in his article should thus be regarded as inherently homosexual since it functions as a primary means of (re)projecting male fantasy.

We can better grasp the ramifications of Cocteau's gay mirror-screen, and Godard's particular fascination with it, if we consider a key passage in Godard's 1964 review of *Orphée*, where he lauds the film's unique linking of the biographical (*"le cinéma-vérité"*) and the legendary (*"le cinéma-mensonge"*); its interweaving of reality and dreams; and, above all, its exciting blend of documentary (Lumière) and fiction (Méliès). For Godard, Cocteau had a special talent for combining the real and the imaginary, and it served as a permanent source of inspiration for his own work. In the much later short *Changer d'image*, for example, the third-person male narrator on the soundtrack reports that the "idiot" (i.e., Godard), "after much reflecting in front of an old mirror given by the director of *La Belle et la bête*, thought it better to stay in shape [*garder la forme*, literally, maintain form]." (The identification with Cocteau is sealed by the narrator's description of the "idiot"/Godard as a "free figure skater" moving always chiastically "between the images of life and the life of images," an idea that corresponds exactly to Godard's view, expressed elsewhere, that "Cocteau executed free figures in the compulsory exercises" [Godard 2003].) In his review of *Orphée* Godard evokes the premiere of Truffaut's *Les 400 coups* at Cannes in 1959 when Cocteau was president of the jury and took Truffaut under his wing. Cocteau is portrayed as "le vieil ange Heurtebise" ("the old angel Heurtebise"), an allusion not only to the character in *Orphée* but also to his long 1925 poem of male passion, "L'Ange Heurtebise," which describes the at once spiritual and violent homoerotic fantasy of possession by a "heavy male sceptre," both a violent creative spirit and a young male lover. The poem includes the arresting lines: "The angel Heurtebise, with an unbelievable/ Brutality jumps on to me. Out of grace/ Do not jump so hard/ Bestial boy, flower of high/ Stature" ("L'ange Heurtebise, d'une brutalité/ Incroyable saute sur moi. De grâce/ Ne saute pas si fort,/ Garçon bestial, fleur de haute/ Stature"), as well as the famous refrain: "How ugly is the happiness one desires/ How beautiful is the pain one has" ("Qu'il est laid le bonheur qu'on veut/ Qu'il est beau le malheur qu'on a"). Godard writes: "He [Cocteau] guided him [Truffaut] across the spotlights and whispered to him [. . .] in front of my amazed, amateur eyes, it was the old angel Heurtebise, still in the center of the throng, who was protecting the young phantom of Vigo under his large, black Academician's wing" (Bergala 1985: 252–53). Godard is proposing here an intoxicating cocktail of connections and positions: Cocteau embodies the mighty angel Heurtebise who presents to the world a raw, new talent ("jeune voyou"), an avatar of Jean Vigo, the *auteur*-martyr of French cinema *par excellence*, while Godard himself as ravished spectator looks on in admiration and wonder. This accords with the active/passive axis that is made so powerful and dramatic in "L'Ange Heurtebise," but in reverse fashion: where before Cocteau the implied narrator succumbed to the eager and pitiless desires of Heurtebise (a reincarnation of Cocteau's companion/lover Raymond Radiguet who died tragically young in 1923), here in historical reality he directs the scene of seduction with consummate control.[18]

This primal scene in the story of the emerging New Wave is so fundamental to Godard that he will develop it still further in his later preface to the 1988 edition of Truffaut's correspondence, where he multiplies the male associations to include not only Truffaut but also his adolescent star Jean-Pierre Léaud in an intricate network of artistic and sexual relations encompassing Cocteau, Genet, and Pier Paolo Pasolini. The preface exemplifies Godard's graphic approach to writing as a form of collage: the title is composed of words handwritten by Godard which are then repeated in the closing lines ("François is perhaps dead. I'm perhaps living. Same difference, is it not."). Two specifically gay pairings are established: the writers Maurice Sachs and Genet who were both at different times part of Cocteau's circle (Sachs even became one of Cocteau's "adopted sons"), and Pasolini and the young actor Ninetto who played in real life the double role of son and lover.[19] It is as if, in a movement that recalls the erotic exchange of flowers between prisoners in Genet's erotic short, *Un Chant d'amour* (1950), Godard reconstitutes his own flower of homosexual petals only to pluck them out again, before resuscitating them in multiple inversions *ad infinitum*. He writes:

> Along the Croisette, a strange trio advanced amid the applause: an old bird with big wings already greying with age, a young tearaway straight out of a book by Jean Genet or Maurice Sachs, pale and erect, and holding by the hand an even younger boy, a fugitive from the early novels of René Fallet, who was going to become the French equivalent of Pasolini's Ninetto. Cocteau, Truffaut, Léaud. The angel Heurtebise uttered the passwords: lo-ok to the left, lo-ok to the right. Smile at *France-Soir* and France Roche! Wave to the Minister! Slow down! Accelerate! (Bergala 1998: 210–11).

Of course, the relations between Godard and Truffaut would eventually explode publicly in the early 1970s, and in this preface which he intends as a kind of posthumous reconciliation Godard harks back directly to their "quarrels." Crucially, he places their falling out in the context of another set of gay angels: Genet and Fassbinder (the latter's *Querelle* [1982] was an adaptation of Genet's *Querelle de*

Brest [1947]). The dyad is further completed by an allusion two paragraphs later to Frédéric and Sénécal in Flaubert's 1869 novel, *L'Éducation sentimentale*. Godard then underlines the fact that the origin of his dispute with Truffaut was of a mysterious nature, unarticulated and in a sense repressed:

> Why did I quarrel with François? Nothing like Genet's quarrel with Fassbinder. Something else. Which has fortunately renamed nameless. Dumb. Retarded. Happily so, while all the rest turned into signs, mortal decorations, Algeria, Vietnam, Hollywood—and our friendship, and our affection for the real. Sign, song and swansong [*Signe, et chant du signe*]. (ibid.: 11)

Employing his now standard trope of the cinematographic as the realm of the (in)visible and unsaid above language and discourse, Godard suggests here that what constituted the vital link and affinity between himself and Truffaut, and what allows him to write the preface even now after all these years, was their shared belief in the power of the screen at a time when the work was still a *thing* and not the *sign* of something, and before the screen itself became an object of pomp and rivalry. Godard deliberately strives for poetic effect here with the phrase "Signe, et chant du signe," a Baudelairean play on "*signe*" as a homonym of "*cygne*" ("swan") associating signification with death.

Taken as a whole, what this imaginary scene on the Croisette reveals is a series of artistic relations that could be interpreted in different fantasmatic ways, most obviously between the gay father (Cocteau), the son (Truffaut), and the grandson (Léaud) (it should be said no proof exists of actual or intended sexual relations either between Truffaut and Léaud, or between Truffaut and Cocteau with whom Truffaut enjoyed a special bond, even donating the profits from *Les 400 coups* to fund Cocteau's final film, *Le Testament d'Orphée* [1960]). Seen from this perspective, Godard is arguably wresting Cocteau back from the arms of his one-time peer and later rival, Truffaut. Yet Cocteau, who helped bring Godard and Truffaut together on account of their unconditional love for the cinema (and, of course, for Cocteau himself), figures also at the apex of another triangle where he embodies an avuncular figure at once protector and seducer—a sort of homosexual Virgil *vis-à-vis* Dante figured by Godard. By insisting so heavily on this primal male scene, Godard appears to make Cocteau even more gay in order precisely to remain faithful to Cocteau's unique artistic example and line of influence. We have here a prime instance of what Lawrence Schehr has defined as the "homotext," that is, a theorization both of homosexuality and of a different type of textuality and textual poetics (Schehr 1989: 35), in this case in the form of a dense paratext where homosexuality and homoeroticism serve as a vehicle for the inscription of desire. This process, of course, is already part of the "Zone," that enchanted masculine space in Cocteau's cinema and its literal and erotic *mise en abyme* which, as we shall now see, expands freely into the open, intertextual territory of Godard's own cinema and takes powerful, concrete form in *Histoire(s)* where Godard finally defines has status as a writer in exclusively filmic terms.

For a New Erotics of the Cinematic Encounter

Cocteau is omnipresent in *Histoire(s)*. Film extracts from *Le Testament d'Orphée* feature directly in episodes 1A and 1B, from *Orphée* in 1B, from *Le Sang d'un poète* in 2A, and from *La Belle et la bête* in 2B, 3B, and 4B. Photographs of Cocteau appear in 2A, 2B, and 4A, and he is cited textually in 2B and 3B. His voice is also heard in short extracts from *Le Testament* in 1A, 1B, and 3A, in the first case accompanied by a full-length photographic portrait. Finally, he is part of the montage of images and texts in 1A around the first name "Jean" encompassing Cocteau, Renoir, Vigo, and Epstein. It is, in fact, as a model of montage that Cocteau most directly imposes himself on Godard's cinematic consciousness. Godard puts it like this: "If one says reading a book that it's like Cocteau, it's not due to the sentence itself or the tone but rather to the shock of ideas. In his own way he loved montage, that is, the bringing together of distant things that create a shock because one hadn't thought that anything could come of such a linking" (Godard 2003). To gain an immediate sense of the scale of Godard's formal investment in Cocteau as a figure of montage in *Histoire(s)*, let us explore a sequence near the beginning of episode 2B, *Fatale Beauté*.

The sequence begins around four minutes in with an extract (minus sound) from *La Belle et la bête* of Belle entering the chateau of la Bête, followed by the famous 1926 photograph by Berenice Abbott of a young Cocteau in a trench coat firing a pistol at the camera. This violent image is flashed rapidly in order to honor its message: the unique modernist speed and pace of Cocteau. Godard then relates on the soundtrack Cocteau's own statement that he entered the cinema "fraudulently" ("en fraude"), that is, as an untrained amateur, but that "the die was cast" ("le rouge est mis"). This is an allusion to the 1953 documentary short *Le Rouge est mis* (1953) by Igor Barrère and Hubert Knopp for which Cocteau provided the commentary. At the same moment the words "the fatal moment will always arrive to distract us" ("toujours l'instant fatal viendra pour nous distraire"), the final line from Raymond Queneau's 1948 poem "L'Instant fatal," are printed over the screen in green lettering. The music heard is from the urgent first movement of Stravinsky's *Symphony in 3 Movements*. (In the initial version of episode 2B, as in the book version [Godard 1998a, vol. 2: 126–27], the screen text is in red, and Godard colorizes the black-and-white Cocteau photograph with a red spot to illustrate, perhaps a touch too literally, the line "Le rouge est mis.") What is striking here is that the film extract is conveyed as a series of discontinuous still-frame images producing an elliptical distillation of Belle's arrival. Yet precisely through the limitation of movement, Godard emphasizes the original balletic slow motion of Belle. Moreover, the images do not appear to be screenshots but rather rough and grainy photographs, as if they have been subjected to an entirely different technical process and suddenly resurfaced in a potent display of the kind of epiphanic wonders of the machine promoted by Cocteau. More than that: the original image has been flipped over and reversed, for the open windows and flowing curtains now stand on the left. This formal play and trickery *à la Cocteau* resonates perfectly with the cited line about Cocteau entering the world of cinema "fraudulently"—a line that can now be read as a self-reflexive remark by Godard about his own "fraudulent" intertextual misquoting of Cocteau as homage. It is significant that Godard achieves this maneuver with Cocteau at his most "gender bending" (the beast of *La Belle et la bête* is grammatically female [*la Bête*], wears male and female clothing, and transforms him/herself in the end to Prince Charming), and, moreover, within an episode of *Histoire(s)* dedicated to two women (the film critic and militant Michèle Firk and the actress Nicole Ladmiral who both took their own lives). Further, the fatalistic phrase "le rouge est mis," which can refer literally to "putting on rouge," is fully in keeping with the episode's focus on the "fatal beauty" of women in cinema, in particular Hollywood with its direct links to advertising and cosmetics and its postwar attraction to the garish effects of Technicolor (cinema's attempt, Godard explains, to repress the fact that it had extracted life from the real). Out of such artificiality and "falseness" a certain truth about cinema can, as here, be obtained, in the style of Cocteau himself who often quipped: "I'm a lie that always tells the truth."

Godard will reemploy the same extract from *La Belle et la bête* at the start of episode 3B (*Une Vague nouvelle*) but in a totally different manner. It now plays in its original form as a series of moving images superimposed over—and deftly interwoven with—a scene from Rossellini's *Paisà* (1946) where Harriet and partisan Massimo try to reach "the other side" (that is, the side of Florence still under fascist control). This set-piece of montage is propelled dynamically by the pulsating rhythms of Shostakovich's score for Kozintsev's *Hamlet* (1964). As Witt rightly observes, the interlinking of two films both made in 1946 sets the tone for the episode which focuses on the New Wave and its roots in Italian neorealism and "evokes the idea of the discovery of the world, of cinema, and of the world through cinema by the generation of children who grew up during the war" (Witt 2013: 156). Yet this new, dense, composite image of different cinematic styles, speeds, and rhythms is also a brilliant reinvention by Godard of Cocteau's film and throws into powerful relief its plastic qualities and textures, further amplified by the extract from *Paisà*, which suggests that the left side of the corridor of la Bête's castle has now been opened up to the outside, resulting in an expanded through-space of movement. Such an extraordinary hybrid sequence, which ends with Belle arriving in full frame to the words "Seul le cinéma" printed on the screen, offers a clear Coctelian message: that only cinema can pull off something so simple and yet so profound and beautiful. In fact, Godard will return again to *La Belle et la bête* a little later in the same episode with a still frame of an overhead shot of Belle leaving la Bête's dinner table accompanied by the caption: "After a certain point, return is no longer possible" ("À partir d'un certain point, il n'est plus de retour"). Thus does Godard follow through his encounters with Cocteau to their logical conclusion, from arrival to departure, always to insist, like Cocteau, that once having entered the world of cinema one can live nowhere else.

The most visibly dramatic instance of intertextual exchange between Godard and Cocteau in *Histoire(s)* occurs, however, in episode 1B, *Une histoire seule*. The meeting here between the two connects with the key scene from *Le Testament* where Cocteau as the Poet is pierced from behind by Minerva's javelin, an image already co-opted by Godard in episode 1A as part of his discourse on the various betrayals committed by the French nation and the world of cinema during World War II. In the early stages of 1B Godard refers to his own film *Soigne ta droite*, and specifically its use of François Périer who, he explains, also starred as Heurtebise in *Orphée* (as well, of course, as one of the judges in *Le Testament*). At the same moment we are shown an extract from the opening scene of *Orphée*: the riot at the Café des Poètes during which Heurtebise telephones the police. Godard states on the soundtrack: "I asked the actor who plays Death's chauffeur in Cocteau's film to say this line, and I called the film *Une place sur la terre* [the film's subtitle]."

How should we interpret the exchange of ideas and associations here between Godard and Cocteau via Heurtebise? In an important article on the role of the back and the behind in Godard, the film theorist Jean-Louis Leutrat focuses on Godard's use of *Le Testament d'Orphée* in connection with the key phrase repeated in *Soigne ta droite*: "but it's in the back that the light will stab the darkness" ("mais c'est dans le dos que la lumière va frapper la nuit"). As we noted in chapter 4, although the line might appear by association to be from Hermann Broch's 1945 novel, *The Death of Virgil*, cited at length throughout the film, this is not, in fact, the case. Nevertheless, it is germane to a whole set of connections featured at the end of episode 1B where Godard includes an extract of himself as the Prince/Idiot falling down an aircraft ramp in *Soigne ta droite* while carrying the reels of his own film. This climactic sequence of catastrophe alternates, as we saw, with the figure of the angel—in the initial version of *Histoire(s)* Paul Klee's *Forgetful Angel* (1939–40), in the final version a religious, iconic image—which can, of course, be linked back to Cocteau's young Angel Heurtebise. Yet despite his exclusive focus on the back and the *derrière* (the article is accompanied by a still from *Le Testament* where Cocteau walks past his own double with his new real-life partner Édouard Dermit at his side), Leutrat sees no homoerotic charge to Godard's solicitation of Cocteau. I think, however, on the contrary that Godard is willingly seduced by, and into, Cocteau's obsessive play with the behind, to the degree even that he will associate with Cocteau his vital, anonymous phrase on light striking darkness in the back. "*La nuit*" ("night") was, of course, Cocteau's preferred term for the unconscious or subconscious, and Godard may be viewed on one level as plunging here directly into Cocteau's nocturnal desires. It is a highly ambivalent artistic gesture, for Godard seems to identify with Cocteau as the passive victim, yet at the same time it is Godard, the new generation following the old as surely as night follows day, who, to put it frankly, "shafts" Cocteau by means of a sexual assault *à la Heurtebise*, since presumably the passive figure is not offering his consent. Or is he? Does the ever-haunting ghost of Cocteau perhaps want this all along—another manifestation of Cocteau's endless restaging of the creative will?

The question has no ready answer, of course. What is certain, however, is that Cocteau has inspired a sublime act on Godard's part—let us call it for the moment a "phallic act" of poetic will—since Godard is inserting his own invented phrase within Broch's passage and thereby simultaneously troping on Broch. In so doing, Godard becomes the author of a singular act of montage which constitutes his videographic signature in *Histoire(s)*. Visual identification and verbal aggression coexist in a double movement of desire that transports us inexorably to the consistently fertile Coctelian realm of anality, which, as I've argued elsewhere in a study of the homoeroticism of Cocteau's filmic style, provides, along with oral eroticism, for the "real," sustained erotic moments of his work due to reverse motion, framing and *mise-en-scène* (see Williams 2006b: 157–85). Indeed, Cocteau's promiscuous captivation by the male behind is part of his compulsion to look and take *a tergo*. This operates in contradistinction to the dazzling array of phallic shapes and forms and often whoppingly phallic instances of ascension and resurrection visible in Cocteau's cinema—all proof of its virility and poetic gloss, yet which serve in actual fact as little more than a customized ornamental frame for those other, more unusual and far more enticing filmic pleasures of reverse and slow motion produced internally within the camera and externally between male bodies, generating new images and sensations as if *for our eyes only*. Such heady moments offer glimpses of what may seem to some merely ugly and formless: grotesque and abject examples of an ambivalent, viscerally real, and even terrifying body, "monstrous" because it signifies nothing. It is a body not defined as an object of representation but rather as a zone of affective intensity. This mobile, anal, erotic zone reveals the full literal force of the Zone in *Orphée*, defined by Cocteau as both a "no man's land" and a "site of ruination of men's habits." Ironically, it is Cocteau's female characters who end up incarnating the phallic instance, precisely because they are not privy to the supplementary pleasures of desymbolization and undifferentiation enjoyed by the male protagonists.

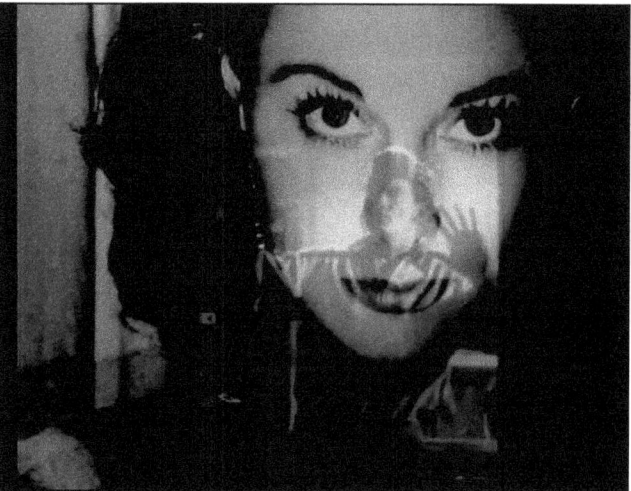

Figure 8.9. Superimposing *Orphée* over *Orphée* in *Histoire(s) du cinéma* (1988–98).

Godard is also interested in anal matters, of course, most graphically in *Numéro deux* with its scenes of troubled masculinity and (heterosexual) anal rape, as when Pierre sodomizes Sandrine. Similarly, in *Passion*, Isabelle (Isabelle Huppert) consents to being taken sexually by Jerzy (Jerzy Radziwilowicz), first from the front and then from the rear "without it leaving any traces," while François (Jean-François Stévenin) repeatedly commands, "Say your line" ("Dis ta phrase") to his female assistant, Sophie (Sophie Louachevsky), as he sodomizes her. Meanwhile, in *Sauve qui peut* the intricate Sadian *combinatoire* of sound and image is extended by assorted scenes of female prostitutes baring their behinds to male clients or even farm cattle while being instructed to speak. In fact, it is extremely difficult to find in Godard's increasingly brutal deconstructions of heterosexual love an instance of "normal" sexual relations involving frontal penetration that either endures or doesn't simply abort in frustrated male masturbation—a fate Joseph is reduced to in the shower after being rejected by Carmen in *Prénom Carmen*.[20] This raises the more general issue of male masochism in Godard's and Cocteau's work, where it is linked in both cases to the core challenges of artistic creation which trades in violence as an unavoidable reality. Godard being physically beaten by an anonymous male figure in *Changer d'image*, encasing himself in the videographic "superscription" of sexual/social blockage and abjection in *Numéro deux*, or having his voice and image violently obscured and mangled by the inhuman vibrations of the machine in *Histoire(s)*: these are just the most spectacular and piquant manifestations of a recurring theme in his work which features an array of personal figurations of self-exposure and self-erasure.[21] For Godard, as for Cocteau, the sublimating project of creating forms is derived precisely from a deep understanding of its anal lining or "depravation" (Cocteau)—the attraction, at once frightening and irresistible, for nondifferentiation which is anality's key formal feature. In *Histoire(s)* Godard taps directly into the prehistory and spatial hinterland of high moments of Coctelian resurrection. That is to say, he "takes" Cocteau just as the Poet's back is transfixed by Minerva's javelin and when, with blood oozing from his stomach around the reverse point of entry, we hear the repeated words: "How horrible! How, how horrible! How, how horrible!" ("Quelle horreur! Quelle, quelle horreur! Quelle, quelle horreur!").

What is remarkable, in fact, is how Godard is often content simply to repeat the most visible and erotic aspects of Cocteau's cinematic style. *King Lear*, for instance, imitates perfectly a classic moment of Coctelian reverse motion (tulips coming into being petal by petal), presented in the film as one of the very few visual signs and motifs to be salvaged from the recent dead past. This sequence of magical resurrection directly recalls the hibiscus petals coming to life in Cocteau's hands in the 1951 short *La Villa Santo-Sospir*, as well as in *Le Testament*. The resurrection of flowers in *King Lear* can be read as an utterly concrete demonstration of Cocteau's filmic process of "thinking through one's hands," an act championed by Godard in *Histoire(s)* with reference to Denis de Rougemont and to which he directly aspires through editing. Yet to replay an almost generic sequence from Cocteau and then reproject it is, for Godard, also to hand him back the flower and so participate in that magical exchange of objects by men (guns, gloves, etc.) which is such a distinguishing feature and constant of Cocteau's cinema. If the flower in transition represents the reversibility of time in *Le Testament*, it is also a supremely erotic object when stripped naked of its petals and resurrected into plenitude through reverse motion (twice in succession in *King Lear*).

Figures 8.10–11. Erotic hand-play in *King Lear* (1987) and episode 2A of *Histoire(s) du cinéma* (1988–98), where Jean Cocteau's *Le Sang d'un poète* (1932) is embedded into Godard's conversation with Serge Daney

Such is Godard's process of "zoning" Cocteau: plugging into him like an ever-reproducible object of the real that can be continually doubled, replayed, expanded and reversed in order to sustain and develop his own creative project. In *Histoire(s)* Godard constructs an intertextual and intersexual *no man's land* of inversion and reversal where, as in Cocteau's own filmic world, boundaries simply melt away. For like the Zone *Histoire(s)* can become, as here in 1B, a warm, porous, instinctual, and always seductive open space of different tempos, registers, and rhythms that generate spontaneous, transverse, *queer* assignations and trace intricate, erotic shapes and patterns complete with signature flourishes. Indeed, Godard's erotic, polymorphous play with Cocteau installs him as a guiding principle for his experimental practice, to the point that Cocteau becomes the privileged vehicle of sublimation in his work. More accurately, Cocteau functions for Godard as both sublime and abject, ideal and false, as suggested even by Godard's review of *Orphée* where he characterizes the film as "contraband poetry" ("poésie de contrebande") (a possible play on the French verb *"bander,"* slang for "to have a hard on"), and refers also to Cocteau's confession of cinematic "fraudulence" in *Le Rouge est mis*, which Godard expands with the phrase "à l'instant où le rouge s'allumait" (Bergala 1985: 252), literally "at the moment the red light was switched on" (for recording), but which also carries connotations of prostitution (the red light) and sexual tease (the French noun *"allumeur, -euse"*). Hence, Godard reaps the rich textual rewards of Cocteau's radical ambivalence—the fact that his work is always, as the title of one of his films highlights, an "eagle with two heads." Indeed, by taking Cocteau *from behind* in the shared, potential space of film and video, Godard forges a safe passage through and out of the tensions not simply of (gay) male sexuality, but also potentially of sexual desire *tout court*, although this would be for a separate discussion. Certainly it is a delicious irony that *Histoire(s)*, the nexus of Godard's hard-core historiographic project, possesses an extensive, soft, inner gay lining and rigging—not only Cocteau, of course, but also Daney.

The full measure and scale of Godard's erotic-aesthetic engagement with Cocteau in *Histoire(s)* can truly be gained by comparing it with the limited role reserved there for Duras who is never allowed to become an agent of open chiastic reversibility, functioning instead always as a fixed point of opposition. She remains the voice of controlled violence and manipulation, although ironically we never actually hear her voice in *Histoire(s)*. Indeed, in yet another instance of Godard's innate mistrust of any overidentification in cinema with raw reality, Duras ends up representing the very "voice of the real." In the case of episode 3A, for instance, Duras is linked directly to the ambiguities of wartime France which her work illustrates perfectly through the prolonged torture session of a suspected collaborator carried out by the narrator Thérèse, a member of the Resistance, in a key chapter from *La Douleur* (1985) entitled "Albert des Capitales." The brutal phrase from this account, printed on-screen: "Must just hit, how real it is, how right" ("Faut frapper, que c'est vrai, que c'est juste"), is accompanied by a photograph of Duras from the same period. Hence, although she is not directly identified by Godard in his voice-over (the only sounds we hear at this point are of Julien Carette's 1937 song, "Si tu veux, Marguerite"), the aligning of Duras with violence is unambiguous. She signifies the incontrovertible event of violence, both of war and of verbal language. To Cocteau's promise of masochistic play and poetics, Duras's all-too-real tales of sadistic torture and revenge.

Later in *Histoire(s)* Godard's intertextual relations with Duras become even more polarized. Nine minutes into episode 3B, and following visual and written reference to Cocteau's 1929 novel *Les Enfants terribles*, a classic black-and-white 1960s photograph of Duras is superimposed over the black-and-white image of a young Sacha Guitry, whose right arm appears stretched out over her head as if holding her down and, together with his left hand poised under her face, enveloping her—an effect made ever more emphatic by the interspotting of the two images (in the book of *Histoire(s)* the composite image is repeated twice on the same page [Godard 1998a, vol. 3: 110]). Meanwhile, on the soundtrack, we hear Miéville utter in quick-fire fashion Truffaut's loaded phrase "the art of cinema is to have pretty things done to pretty women," while typed on the screen are the words originally spoken by Marianne (Karina) to Pierrot (Belmondo) in *Pierrot le fou*: "You speak to me with words. And I look at you with feelings." Throughout this entire short sequence we hear Jeanne Moreau ruing her failing memory in her 1963 song, "J'ai la mémoire qui flanche." In this new ironic twist on sexual difference, Duras, while again rendered mute, is positioned on the side of unfeeling language, while Godard and Guitry, due to the configuration of the visual effect described, embody the visual gaze and therefore emotion. In the process, the underlying meaning of the phrase from *Pierrot le fou* is reversed: what was originally an attack on male insensitivity seems now to be an attack on the very power of female speech. A little later in the same episode, a screen-text of "Faust / Margue / rite" (white on black) leads directly to the same 1960s photograph of Duras in her prime superimposed and spotted over an image of Nicolas de Staël's *Nu Couché bleu* (1955) (or Godard's pastiche of it), as if she were sandwiched in the center of the painting between the two diagonal sides of the figure. A new sequence of words inverting Duras's first name ("Rite / Margue / France") is printed in red over the composite image of Duras and de Staël, forming with Duras's bleached out face and the white halo effect created around her head the three colors of the French *tricolore*. This composition provokes in turn the screen-text (also spotted): "Histoire de France."

Figures 8.12–13. Conflicted encounters with Marguerite Duras in episode 3B of *Histoire(s) du cinéma* (1988–98).

Thus does Duras always appear doomed in *Histoire(s)* merely to reflect the national context she operates in and the violence of her times (including that of her own writing). Indeed, there is an absolute qualitative difference between Durassian time and space (the programmed stand-offs with Godard and others conducted at her own pace in her private space) and the timeless, imaginary, open (non)spaces lovingly negotiated between Godard and Cocteau in the luxurious folds and curves of the Zone. Whereas Godard makes intertextual hay with Cocteau in a deviant, self-engendering erotics of reversal that achieves a genuine cross-fertilization of ideas and sensations, all appears cold, flat, and grimly predictable in his textual dealings with Duras.

In our analysis of three very different kinds of dialogue and encounter across language and literature—Godard-Miéville, Godard-Duras, Godard-Cocteau—we have observed both continuity and discontinuity. The way the collaboration between Miéville and Godard is formally staged and executed in some of their work together is not dissimilar from the powerfully gendered Duras model of heterosexual relations where Godard must invariably occupy the subservient role of Image to her supreme Voice. With Miéville, however, Godard can work in mutual respect, whatever their personal tensions, even to the extent that, when initially released, her twenty-eight-minute short, Le Livre de Marie, ran directly into the celluloid flesh of Je vous salue, Marie to form an organic whole. Yet with Duras Godard is always on the receiving end of her words because she has already formalized in advance the fixed terms of their antagonistic aesthetic relations. By contrast, in his intimate male-to-male zoning with Cocteau, which radically destabilizes and subverts the heterosexual dynamic, Cocteau embodies for Godard a utopian dream of literature and cinema through the inexhaustible (re)combinations and permutations of sound and image. Godard's exuberant, fully fledged engagement with Cocteau by mutual consent, exemplary in its formal inventiveness and commitment, has nothing to do with the double games, bluff, and subterfuge of Duras and the fixed rules of her negative, abject (gay) Outside where her others (Godard for the occasion) are locked in time and place, enjoy no agency, and are denied the pleasures of free movement and reversibility. Whereas for Duras the idea of the abject behind serves as the "real" basis for a self-declared "sacred" writing process, for Godard it remains a continually floating work-in-progress played out *as if for real* in his erotic, calligraphic art with Cocteau. Indeed, in the case of the ever-receptive Cocteau, there is always the desire for still further imaginary identification and inversion.

So loyal and giving is Cocteau a co-agent in Godard's erotico-aesthetic experimentation that the appearance in the final moments of Histoire(s) of a yellow rose superimposed over Godard's nose and mouth ("I was that man") reveals itself ultimately as far more than a "straight" poetic association with Borges, Coleridge, and Dante, as proposed above in chapter 3. I want to suggest by way of conclusion that another Borgesian flower is at stake during this solemn climax: the subject of a short tale entitled precisely "A Yellow Rose" (1960), which imagines the death of the seventeenth-century epic poet Giambattista Marino, inheritor of Homer and Dante. Here, a yellow rose placed by Marino's bedside on the eve of his death provokes in him a revelation: all the volumes in his library are not, after all, a mirror of the world as his poetic vanity had led him to believe, and the rose exists only in its own timelessness (Borges: "Marino saw the rose as Adam might have seen it in Paradise").[22] Bearing in mind that Marino was a writer of ambiguous love poetry and almost certainly gay, and that Godard, as we've seen, displays an acute sense of homosexual genealogy across the Western literary tradition from Virgil and Dante onwards, the superimposition of a flower over Godard's face, held in turn over an image of Van Gogh by another gay artist, Francis Bacon, may be said to render visible the deep oral and anal basis of Godard's total immersion in Coctelian matter. When Godard first arrived in Paris, his identification with Cocteau was crystalized by the act of holding a rose—an erotic gesture of artistic filiation and promise. The dangerous, exciting, sublimatory work of cinema remains always to be done, as much in Godard as in Cocteau. *En route!*

Coda

Cinema after Language

Words are ruins, they indicate the presence of what in reality is not there.
—J.-L. Godard, *Les Trois désastres*

I am [*suis*] a dog and this dog follows [*suit*] Godard.
—J.-L. Godard

As I was completing this book in the fall of 2014 Godard's new feature in 3D, *Adieu au langage* (*Goodbye to Language*), arrived at the London Film Festival following its successful premiere at Cannes, where it won the Jury Prize. It incorporates and expands elements of his first foray into 3D, *Les Trois désastres* (The three disasters), a seventeen-minute contribution to the 2013 portmanteau film *3X3D* that ruminated on the "dictatorship" and superficiality of digital despite its appearance of depth.[1] Structured in three parts, each beginning with a roll of the dice of fate and chance (the three "*dés*" of "*désastres*"), *Les Trois désastres* directly addressed the apparatus of 3D in a stunning set-piece sequence where the camera tracks forward towards a hand-made 3D camera composed of two digital, single-lens, reflex cameras bolted onto each other, one right-side up, the other upside-down, assembled on a stationary mount facing a large mirror. *Les Trois désastres* was firmly in the mold of Godard's late video-essay style, however, with obligatory references to twentieth-century disasters now seen through a stereoscopic lens (Hiroshima, for example, when people in 3D were flattened to the second plane as their vaporized bodies were blasted onto walls), as well as copious citings of the history of cinema (updated to include big-budget 3D films like *The Three Musketeers*, *Final Destination*

5, and the 2012 rerelease of *Titanic*) and ambiguous or mischievous references to art-house 3D experiments like Wim Wenders's *Pina* (2011) and Werner Herzog's *Cave of Forgotten Dreams* [2010]).[2] Complete with Godard's guiding voice-over, this was a measured and highly controlled, formalist study of makeshift 3D filmmaking as "Infinity and Zero."

By contrast, *Adieu au langage* is a scrappy, abrasive, freewheeling, fiery, experimental poem that physically assaults the viewer and mounts a visceral attack on the retina and optic nerve. The effect, magnified when projected, as at the festival, onto the giant screen of an IMAX theater with sensurround sound speakers, is one of sustained and unmediated shock, at once raw, primal, and anarchic, even hallucinatory. Godard takes 3D by the scruff of the neck and turns it inside out. In what is perhaps the first 3D home movie shot on a combination of smartphones, low-end amateur Go-Pro and Lumix devices, and Canon 5D Mark II camera, *Adieu au langage* destroys any illusion of "total cinema" that is so often associated with cinematic stereoscopic technology by engineering rupture and disorder at every level. Harking back to *La Chinoise* with its Brechtian imperative to challenge and subvert, this seventy-minute, Burroughs-like mash-up is an incandescent, exasperating, yet wholly exhilarating cinematic event. Such is the ferocious force and drive of Godard as aging Old Master exploding the medium in order to reinvent it.

Many of the trademark themes of late Godard are on display here: the breakdown in social relations and human communication, the increasing homogeneity of society and culture, global economic imbalance and the state's unregulated power and incapacity to acknowledge its own violence. These give rise to assorted philosphical axioms and aphorisms about individual freedom, difference, and strangeness culled from (among others) Freud, Dolto, Valéry, Benjamin, Blanchot, Badiou and Levinas. There are also repeated references to some of Godard's once favored others such as Native Americans (here the Apache tribe) and Africans. The backstory of one narrative thread involving the Democratic Republic of the Congo is framed by an allusion to V. S. Naipaul's *A Bend in the River* (1979) and the citing of the philosopher Jocelyn Benoist's provocative open question: "Is it possible to produce a concept about Africa?." The film declares itself "an essay of literary investigation," and many of the writers present in Godard's work of the last thirty-five years are duly referenced (Apollinaire, Cocteau, Hugo, Proust, Beckett, Sartre, Aragon, Céline, Chardonne, Borges, Green, and van Vogt). New, however, is the mention of the late French antitechnology philosopher Jacques Ellul (the table of contents of Ellul's 1945 essay "The Victory of Hitler?," cited throughout, is glimpsed ironically on a smartphone screen). Much of the music is also familiar, whether by Beethoven, Sibelius, Kancheli, Schoenberg, or Tchaikovsky (the portentous opening chords of *Slavic March*), yet several new ECM composers are featured, such as Dobrinka Tabakova (*Suite in Old Style Part II [for strings]*) and Valentin Silvestrov (*Holy God*). The same with the art references, which include Courbet (*The Origin of the World*), Monet, Duchamp, and de Staël (an art book about the latter is directly visible within the frame).

Figure C.1. Musical superimposition in *Adieu au langage* (2014).

On a structural level, too, *Adieu au langage* takes further the ideas of duplex construction, internal doubling, and asymmetry of characterization explored in *Nouvelle Vague*, *Hélas pour moi*, and *Notre Musique*. As David Bordwell has carefully shown, the film offers multiples of two: a prologue bookended by an epilogue; two opening parts entitled "1—Nature" and "2—Metaphor" which mirror each other; and two much longer sections which continue the sketched out stories (see Bordwell 2014).³ The two couples—Josette and Gédéon (Héloïse Godet and Kamel Abdelli) in the first half, Ivitch and Marcus (Zoé Bruneau and Richard Chevallier) in the second—appear visually similar, and almost every scene in the second part has its counterpart in the first (two nude scenes, two toilet scenes, two bloody sink scenes, two mirror scenes, two movie-on-TV scenes). This creates the impression of the same couple in duplicate: Marcus: "Look in the mirror, Ivitch. There are both of them." Ivitch: "You mean the four of them." Bordwell rightly suggests that we are free to see the characters either as couples running uncannily in synchronization, or as the same couple in two guises, or even as two stories in parallel universes (ibid.). For much is left typically vague, and we have to infer that the pair have been together for at least four years and that the man has stabbed his partner. They can barely relate to each other now in their thoroughly disabused, exhausted passion except via their solitary pet dog, a lurcher named Roxy Miéville, who effectively acts as "interpreter." Yet Godard eventually cracks open this neat 2x2 formation by resorting, as one might expect now, to an instance of the Third, here another couple. Towards the end a man is seen reading (the matching voice is Godard's) while another female figure writes in a journal. This couple is immediately paralleled by that of Percy Bysshe and Mary Shelley, poet and novelist, in a sudden, brief swerve to costume drama and historical reconstruction (the year is 1816 on the banks of Lake Geneva). It serves paradoxically to foreground the key Godardian question of whether, and how, the present can ignite the future through the sparks of human creativity and social transformation. While her husband reads from his poem "Hell" about revolution and the threat of despotism, Mary is depicted in the act of completing *Frankenstein*. In a voice-off Godard introduces a reading of the episode in her novel where the doctor asks whether, by not creating a companion for the monster (brought to life, we recall, by electricity), he has perhaps himself committed a vice.

The particular structure of *Adieu au langage* reveals yet again Godard's unstoppable push towards metaphor and poetic abstraction. It is not simply that the film is poised between "nature" and "metaphor" (Godard's official "long synopsis" for the film is precise: "A second film begins:/ the same as the first,/ and yet not./ From the human race we pass to/ metaphor"). The question of the vital difference between "a metaphor" and "an idea" is explicitly acknowledged by another character, a middle-aged professor called Davidson (Christian Grégori), and we hear twice a phrase about the Apache Indians calling the world "forest" because they viewed the world metaphorically and saw no point at all in distinguishing between the two. Again, Godard's message seems to be that one must not get bogged down in notions of reality, still less "super-reality" as promoted by 3D, but instead trust in our imagination (one of the film's opening lines warns: "Those lacking imagination take refuge in reality"). In *Adieu au langage* any naïve desire we may have for the supposed truer reality of 3D is systematically destroyed by Godard who transforms the real through ever greater abstraction which, like metaphor, is perhaps the closest we can ever get to it. For Blake Williams, this is also the function of the film's multiple emphases on poetic literature as an abstraction of syntax (notably Rilke and Dostoyevsky), on impressionism and Fauvism as abstractions of the pictorial (the dazzling chromatic palette of hypersaturated, phosphorescent colors and smudged yet radiant shots of landscapes through the car wind-screen), and on Reimann-like abstractions of space such as the recurring shot of a large white dot on a black screen (Williams 2014). The porous boundary between the concrete and abstract, the representational and figurative, which typically for Godard is conceived in musical terms (Reimann, we are told, "arrived at a landscape in which each point is transformed into music"), is further extended by the film's use of more associative, second-degree constructions of montage. Sometimes the associations are textural or pictorial (at one point Godard links the black *impasto* brushstrokes of a painting to images of mud and the moist streaks on Roxy's coat), but they can also proliferate to encompass images of the French revolution, crowds lined along the road during the Tour de France, or flowers in full bloom. In short, *Adieu au langage* is Godard's attempt through 3D image-making to harness metaphor as a passageway back into nature. Indeed, nature appears here as the ultimate metaphor, with cinema, in one choice phrase, standing as "the metaphor of reality."

Yet this is already starting to sound rather dry and academic, for on a purely plastic level *Adieu au langage* breathes fire into every frame with its blistering, modernist commitment to experimentation and innovation in the style of early DADA or the cinema of Stan Brakhage (notably *Dog Star Man* [1962–64]). Dispensing with the niceties of *mise en scène*, Godard fully exploits the potential of 3D to open up the cinematic field and release new vertical/horizontal planes and cubist volumes of space whereby different axes and surfaces diverge, collapse, swivel round, and fold back onto each other. Seven different cameras and frame rates were employed by Godard, who is concerned not merely with reproducing the standard 3D effects of objects moving towards the viewer head-on, but with generating clashing juxtapositions, overlays, and superimpositions of colors, titles, and subtitles, as well as disorienting deep-focus compositions that spill over the screen as illusions of depth emerge and recede.[4] Oblique, tilted angles and cockeyed, hand-held framing (much at Roxy's eye level) create the impression that figures and objects might slide out of the frame at any moment (at one point a car screeches to a halt *upside-down*). The technique of using dual cameras in parallel also allows Godard to split the 3D image, with an image and plane in one eye and another combination of the two in the other, thereby causing the image to bifurcate into two deviating and seemingly opposing camera pans. In one early scene, a female figure walks off-frame into a shot superimposed over the previous one, then returns to her original location as the striated images re-merge and compress. With multiple lines veering off and intersecting, sometimes in reverse, any sense of a fixed point of perspective (pinpointed in *Les Trois désastres* as the "sin" of Western visuality since it sought to conquer space and "caused memory to disappear") is nullified. Indeed, the apparent chaos of *Adieu au language*, intensified by warped and degraded 2D video images, is designed expressly to undermine the false smoothness and coherency of digital (one exquisitely composed crane shot over a parking lot happily includes the silhouette of the camera).

Figures C.2–3. Public and domestic superimpositions in *Adieu au langage* (2014).

The same is true of the stereophonic soundtrack. Sheets of sound, including crystalline curves of recited lines of dialogue, short, random stabs of music, and angular stabs of ambient noise, appear to dart and surge forward into earshot, whether from the left channel or the right, or both. The sound can be deafening, like the repeated, grinding chords of strings from Kancheli's *Abii Ne Viderem*. On one level, of course, 3D merely maximizes the peculiar quality of cinematic sound always to escape containment, for hearing is already a three-dimensional, spatial perception (we hear in all directions) and, like the 3D image, sound can penetrate into the spectator's space. Language is thus continually scattered and splintered, like the various visual permutations of the title *Adieu au langage* ("Ah dieu" ["Oh God"], "À Dieu" ["to God"], "Ô langage" ["Oh language"]). Indeed, there is a continuous rip-and-tear effect, often vertiginous, sometimes nauseous, for some of the sound effects literally are *shit*, as when the all-too-real sounds of Abdelli pooping on the toilet in the pose of Rodin's *The Thinker* plop scatalogically into the mix. Paradoxically, this process allows the soundtrack to recuperate a certain material purity, for, by cutting into the dense verbiage of human speech, the pulverized natural sound appears temporarily cleansed of the acculturated sediments of language and social discourse. Godard, who, as we have consistently seen, always starts formally from a position of *imagelessness*, appears here to be bidding a decisive farewell to the symbolic structures of articulation and communication, for in the extreme sonic and visual barrage created whereby each element surges forward into the lap of the viewer to be appreciated as a sensory event in itself, epiphanies of form are created in the immediate instant on their own terms.[5] Yet while Godard's fundamentalist belief in the revelatory power of both sound and image blazes throughout the film, language cannot be said to have simply disappeared. One still has to work through the negativity of acquired language and convention, and the film demands at every moment that we simultaneously listen, read, and process the dense audiovisual matter and verbal information.

The most crucial development and innovation in Godard's practice performed by *Adieu au langage* concerns, however, the particular position now accorded to the viewer due to the film's remarkable liberation of the spectatorial field. In Godard's historical work from *Histoire(s)* onwards, the use of archive images and film has occupied center-stage, yet here, where he devotes himself less to the afterimage of catastrophe than to the *bouleversement* of the preimage, such material is consigned intratextually to the back of the frame like mere décor. Extracts run without audible sound on a super-large, flat plasma screen and are barely noticed by the couple. Among the films playing are Artur Aristakisyan's *Ladoni* (*Palms*), Boris Barnet's *By the Bluest of Seas*, Jean-Pierre Melville's *Les Enfants terribles*, Howard Hawks's *Only Angels Have Wings*, Henry King's *The Snows of Kilimanjaro*, Fritz Lang's *Metropolis*, Rouben Mamoulian's *Dr. Jekyll and Mr. Hyde*, and Robert Siodmak's *Menschen am Sonntag* (*People on Sunday*). Sometimes the monitor simply broadcasts static.[6] What this means is that the foreground of the frame is now fully opened up to the viewer/listener, a strategy that makes impossible any complacency or passivity on our part for we are directly addressed and interpellated, most often aggressively, as images and sounds leap up from the screen and break into the traditional viewing cocoon. We are literally zapped between the eyes, yet at the same time transported physically into new parts of the frame whose sides are opened up visually and acoustically to a potentially limitless *hors champ*. This new spatially and emotionally expanded cinematic field marks the logical next step in Godard's ethicoaesthetic engagement with alterity, relationality and spectatorial affect. Using the terms defined earlier, we have now become Godard's primary chosen (human) other. Indeed, we *are* the other in the film, all the more so since the film's minimal characterization is made virtually irrelevant (in a statement derived from Sartre's preface to André Gorz's *The Traitor* (1957), Bruneau declares: "I hate characters. Ever since birth we're mistaken for another. We push him, we pull him, we force him to get in character"). There is no obvious distraction here either by a "major" star, or even by Godard himself. For this reason *Adieu au langage* is very different from an earlier film like *Numéro deux*, which shares a similar graphic emphasis on the *caca* of domestic life but where the dense, visual superimpositions and superscriptions requiring continual renegotiation are stacked intensively within the frame alongside the authorial presence of Godard.

To say we are directly implicated in the cross-fire of audio and visual matter of *Adieu au langage* is also to acknowledge that we are now invited by Godard to participate fully in the cinematic event and experience *as if from within* the sublime chiastic crossings of form that define his work. We even have the freedom to create our own reverse fields and *champ/contre-champs*, for montage can now potentially take place between our left and right eye and ear, according to how we choose to receive the distorted 3D effects. At stake is a new politics of projection and spectatorship, since in order to enjoy *Adieu au langage* in its full sweep and turbulence and submit to the sheer elation of its transgressive energy, we must view it with special glasses in a specially equipped theater. This means we cannot easily access the film in a reduced format via i-Phone or i-Pad. By insisting on the collective and immersive experience of a public screening, Godard arguably recaptures the egalitarian promise of silent cinema which he has always celebrated for its potential to initiate new thoughts, feelings, and sensations—a unique opportunity scandalously squandered by current big-budget, digital productions. Art may be politically powerless to transform the world in its material reality, but this type of intimate encounter with the viewer offers at least another means of aesthetic resistance.

Figure C.4. Roxy Miéville on the loose in *Adieu au langage* (2014).

Before the final credits arrive we hear the sounds of barking and a newborn baby crying, suggesting the possible birth of a new language in a natural cycle of renewal. It encourages us to consider where Godard's monster 3D creation might ultimately take him, and cinema. What will it spawn and give rise to now that the primary other in the relational field has become the viewer? Before we have the chance to speculate any further, *Adieu au langage* suddenly restarts and the "real" ending begins: Roxy wandering off into the distance, then, in the space of an edit, bounding back eagerly towards the camera and a figure located off-screen. The film thus insists finally on creative freedom, mystery, and yes, love, in the very image of its star canine who has ranged through water and vegetation for almost half its length, beholden to man's command, yet always alone and free to commune spontaneously with the natural world (compare Roxy with the more docile Arthur in *Je vous salue, Marie*, Joseph's only loyal companion but kept firmly on a lead). If it is the case, as we are informed via Derrida, that all animals are never "naked" because nudity doesn't exist in nature, and that what's "inside" is known only to animals (a quote from Rilke's eighth "Duino Elegy"), it is also true, as Jonathan Romney adroitly observes of the film, that "dogs are [. . .] one of the fundamental *metaphors* by which we represent nature to ourselves in our daily lives" (original emphasis).[7]

In a similar way, Godard, for whom the term "cinema" is always both a way of being and doing and a metaphor for the world, enables us to place into sharper perspective the much proclaimed "end of cinema." For in *Adieu au langage* he is not simply indicting a society on the verge of self-destruction with its own technological tools. Rather, the utopian gesture of making 3D a creative resource of new aesthetic rhythms, textures, and vibrations available to all constitutes, at this particularly gloomy juncture of late capitalist culture, a defiantly ethical and radical artistic act. Despite often appearances to the contrary, Godard is always focused on the essential duties and potential ends of cinema rather than on its final passing. It is also a beautiful fact that a completely new generation of younger viewers have been attracted to his recent experimentations with new technology, so much so that in the first week of its exclusive run at two cinemas in New York in October 2014, *Adieu au langage* scored the best pertheater-average of films opening in under five-hundred-seat cinemas across the United States (even more than was the case for *Film socialisme*, which enjoyed relative commercial success). Much could certainly be made of the sad irony that Godard's attempt at direct contact with his audience has once again been thwarted, in this case by the simple fact that most arthouse exhibitors are currently not equipped to screen films in the stereoscopic format.[8] Yet for those who have been fortunate to experience Godard's artistic experiment as intended, its electrifying force and radiance are profoundly moving and inspiring. Just as new forms of cinema generate new kinds of audience, so new kinds of spectatorship will stimulate in turn new forms of critical encounter. With *Adieu au langage*, Godard proves emphatically, and with galvanizing urgency, that in matters of art, all still remains possible.

Notes

Introduction

1. This and all translations from the original French are my own unless otherwise indicated.

2. The chapter "Godard," which explores the word/image relation and the idea of cinema as a form of proof and demonstration eschewing psychology, takes further some of the key ideas Sontag had aired in an earlier piece specifically on *Vivre sa Vie* (1962) and included in *Against Interpretation* (1966) (Sontag 2009b: 196–208).

3. The comment was made in an interview Godard gave with *Le Monde* on June 10, 2014.

4. Said highlights two particular features of late style: "catastrophe" (evident, for instance, in Beethoven's episodic, fragmentary music "riven with the absences and silences" that cannot simply be filled or ignored or explained away (Said 2007: 16)) and "a semiresistant artwork of considerable power" (ibid.: 136). These aspects will prove of particular importance to our understanding of aesthetic resistance in Godard, notably in chapter 2 where another figure considered by Said, Theodor Adorno, who himself ruminated at length on Beethoven's socially resistant late style of renunciation, will be discussed in the context of his dismissal of the culture industry and his fiendishly difficult prose that insists on antimonian oppositions and unresolved contradictions. Said describes Adorno in words that could just as well apply to late Godard, as "an untimely, scandalous, even catastrophic commentator on the present" (ibid.: 14), "hell-bent on remaining untimely and contrary in the Nietzschean sense" (ibid.: 92). Yet whereas for Adorno "lateness includes the idea that one cannot really go beyond lateness at all, cannot transcend or lift oneself out of lateness, but can only deepen the lateness. There is no transcendence or unity" (ibid.: 13), Godard, as we shall see, is often tempted to think and do precisely otherwise in the poetic heat of cinematic montage

5. See, for example, Bellour 1992, Temple and Williams 2000, Brenez et al. 2006, and Witt 2014. Also available is Scemama 2006, a fairly complete table of references in *Histoire(s)* by Céline Scemama, as well as her remarkable "score" of the work, a detailed *découpage* and largely accurate database of sources which can be accessed on-line at http://cri-image.univ-paris1.fr.

6. *Snakes&Funerals* (2012) (14 mins., digital video), directed by Emily Jeremiah, Gillian Wylde, and James S. Williams, formed part of the *Queer, The Space* project, collaboration between Royal Holloway, University of London, and Goldsmith's College London. It played in a continuous loop as the centerpiece of a site-specific installation exhibited at a public

showcase of the project in May 2012. The standard set up of projection was "deframed," for with the screen positioned at an angle, the projected image exceeded its assigned place and frontality and seeped into the surrounding white space peopled by outsize speakers. The film can be accessed via the link: http://framescinemajournal.com/article/snakes-and-funerals/.

7. Blanchot's original words in *L'Amitié* (1971) (48, 50–51), slightly modified by Godard and made specific to cinema, develop an idea about the artwork and the imaginary expressed earlier by Blanchot in *L'Espace littéraire* (1955), where he writes that the joy of the image derives from the fact that it constitutes a limit in relation to the indefinite.

8. Jacques Aumont's book *Amnésies* (1999), a series of astonishingly detailed close readings of *Histoire(s)*, is exemplary in its theoretical intensity yet makes no concession at all to the nonspecialist. This limits in my opinion the critical success of such a formidable yet forbidding volume, despite its many brilliant insights.

Chapter 1

1. See, for example, Reader 2004.
2. The Ben Barka affair also involved the cinema, for Ben Barka was lured to Paris by the publisher and former criminal Georges Figon to take part in a film project about decolonization called *Basta!* involving Georges Franju and Marguerite Duras.
3. See Rancière 2006: 143–53.
4. Jean-Paul Sartre's *L'Imaginaire* (1940), a phenomenological psychology of the imagination, addresses the phenomenological specificity of the image and its "negative" aesthetic of imagination with regard to perception.
5. See Martin's "*La Chinoise*, vers le matérialisme" (in Brenez et al. 2006: 63–67), which also presents material relating to the film's production, including notebooks of the shoot and lyrics of the title song. Althusser's original article can be found in Althusser 1996: 129–50.
6. On his return to France in 1966, Jeanson was commissioned by culture minister André Malraux to establish the new Maison de la Culture at Chalon-sur-Saône, which he headed until 1971. He later participated in experiments of open psychiatry, before becoming, in 1992, president of the newly formed Association Sarajevo to help the Bosnian people. He died in 2009.
7. See Brody 2008: 308.
8. See Morrey 2005: 54–61 for an incisive critique of the film's sexist gender lines, which underscores that the male characters are presented by Godard as far more convincing and "real" than their female counterparts.
9. See Bosetti 2007: 62–64. Godard would later admit in his extensive and fascinating postmortem interview in *Cahiers du Cinéma* in October 1967 entitled "Lutter sur deux fronts" that he had "the details" but not "the right structure" in *La Chinoise*. (Bergala 1985: 311). In the same interview he also regrets not having made the characters more explicitly like Chinese Red Guards, rather than Marxist-Leninists, as that would have avoided certain ambiguities (ibid.: 305). By contrast, in his important wide-ranging panel discussions at the University of Southern California in February 1968, Godard is at pains to defend the film, insisting, for instance, that "[w]e make a mistake in looking at any work of art as something that exists wholly in itself for all time" (Youngblood 1998: 48).
10. See in particular David Faroult, "Never more Godard. Le Groupe Dziga Vertov, l'auteur et la signature" (in Brenez et al. 2006: 120–26), and Michael Witt, "Godard dans la presse d'extrême-gauche" (ibid.: 165–74). See also Williams 2011 and *cinéma* 68 (1998) for

an introduction to the role cinema played during "*les événements*," including in relation to other visual and performing arts. Godard was, in fact, the first director to voice a commonly shared regret that cinema had somehow missed the events and arrived too late for its moment of destiny with revolutionary history. He declared at the Cannes Film Festival that year, which he helped with fellow directors to bring to a total halt: "There's not a single film showing the problems of workers or students today—we're late! We must show solidarity."

11. Godard probably contributed to twelve *ciné-tracts* in all (see select filmography). Another, entitled *Film-tract, No. 1968* and known as *Le Rouge* (16 mm, color, 2 min., 45 sec.), was made in collaboration with the artist Gérard Fromanger, based at the École des Beaux-Arts, and featured red paint bleeding slowly left across the screen first into white, then into blue, in an action painting of the French *tricolore*.

12. For a detailed analysis of *Jusqu'à la victoire* and its status within Godard's cinematic practice, see Faroult 2006.

13. Bosetti 2007: 71.

14. Brody 2008: 307.

15. Cited in MacCabe 1980: 75.

16. Reading *La Chinoise* against tradition and beyond enduring attachments to its symbolism and aura regarding revolution and leftist politics, Grace An suggests it has continued making itself (or unmaking itself) over time with its enduring capacity to fascinate, shock, and mystify. She argues persuasively that by effectively doing away with the past (whether by displaying the students' rejection of established thinkers, writers, and poets, or by undoing itself by the time it ends), *La Chinoise* accesses a different notion of the past against the pressures of memorialization and nostalgia that have interceded with our ongoing experience with the film. In this way, she concludes, the film may be said to resist its own future memorialization. See An 2014, which also places *La Chinoise* in the context both of the supremely self-indulgent nostalgia of Bernardo Bertolucci's *The Dreamers* (2003) and of Wiazemsky's own disidentification from the film in later interviews. We note that *La Chinoise* has continued to blaze brightly within Godard's future work. Fragments reappear in *Histoire(s)* as well as in Godard's collaborative short with Anne-Marie Miéville, *Dans le noir du temps* (2002), notably the moment when Kirilov first pretends to shoot himself, used to illustrate Godard's uncompromising account of the increasing violence and alienation of the twentieth century.

17. The potential risks of textual saturation in Godard's extreme practice of montage, whether in the form of book covers or the loquaciousness of characters, are considered by Christopher Pavsek, who argues that language often gets in the way of film thinking with images, especially in Godard's later work where a voice-over sometimes tells us how to read the image and dominates the image-track. See Pavsek 2013: 24–76. The specifically linguistic aspects of Godardian montage will be explored in chapters 2, 3, and 4.

18. Brenez et al. 2006: 92–93.

19. Godard 2014: 270. This excellent new English translation by Timothy Barnard restores missing original material and conversations not transcribed in the original French edition by Éditions Albatros, the illustrations of which are reproduced with translated captions.

20. See also Petit 1973 for an excellent account of Diop's short life by his close friend Marc Petit.

21. The play ran at the Théâtre de Poche in Montparnasse in November 1965 under the title *Métro Fantôme*. In the original play the black man's name, Clay, is symbolic of the putative malleability of black identity and manhood, as well as of integrationist and assimilationist ideologies within the black civil rights movement at this period. Godard does

not include in the short extracted scene Clay's additional statement that he would rather choose to pretend to be ignorant of racism than attempt to eradicate it by fighting with whites.

22. The song "Sympathy for the Devil" being recorded by The Rolling Stones in *One plus One* is, of course, heavily derived from black music. Indeed, as Elshaw notes, "[w]hite musicians were famous for going to Harlem and other Negro cultural centers literally to steal the black man's music, carrying it back across the color line into the Great White World and passing off the watered-down loot as their own original creations. Blacks, meanwhile, were ridiculed as *Negro* musicians playing inferior coon music" (Elshaw 1998; original italics). To demonstrate this point Godard intrudes upon the scenes in the junkyard by cutting back to another long take of The Rolling Stones rehearsing in the studio. In so doing Godard insists on the derivation of art, its political transformation, and importantly, the ramifications of imperialism co-opting art.

23. See Lelièvre 2013 for a useful introduction to the overall representation of Africa in *Film socialisme* in the light of Godard's earlier work. The specific link between hieroglyphs and black femininity is also made in *King Lear* in the scene immediately following Cordelia's death. A Taiwanese man waves incense and chants in a non-Western language (a probable purification ceremony), after which a black woman is seen placing herself in front of the camera and standing in a dance posture resembling a hieroglyph. The dim yellow lighting obscures and transforms her into an indecipherable and silent silhouette, making her appear as if etched on the screen (the scene is subtended by the word "shadow"). The black woman has thus been actively drawn into the narration but as a ritualized stereotype of the postcolonial other, the white man's mute shadow. Compare this act of decorative erasure with the moment in *La Chinoise* where an anecdote is told by Henri about the ancient Egyptians accompanied by images of Egyptian tombs. Here, the high status of Egyptian culture is explicitly recognized in terms of discourse, yet it is a very ambivalent gesture for the story of the experiment of Egyptian children who ended up simply bleating because all they heard growing up was the sound of sheep reveals that there is no innate or superior "language of the gods," and that, in fact, we are all socially conditioned. The clear socialist message being promoted here is that everything is constructed, and change is always possible.

24. We shall return to this key image in chapter 6.

25. There is, in fact, another black female figure in the first part of *Éloge de l'amour* set in Paris: a young African woman is sitting on a roadside bench talking to a young white man (possibly her boyfriend or partner), while directly behind them, back to back, sits Godard. The woman is the obverse of the strident African American assistant in the film's second part, yet the representation is ultimately no more positive since the couple can barely be heard due to the ambient sounds of traffic and appear almost silenced. These two equally ambivalent portrayals of the black African woman may be compared with that of the Arab figure of Djamila in *For Ever Mozart* (1996), played by Ghalya Lacroix. In many shots she looks to have white, European skin, even though on the train she speaks some Arabic and could perhaps be Turkish. Yet although initially presented on equal terms as part of the young trio of idealists traveling to war-torn Sarajevo to stage Alfred de Musset's *On ne badine pas avec l'amour* (she intends to play the role of Rosette driven to suicide by the machinations of romantic "life and death"), she soon recedes into the background by preparing dinner for her comrades as if she were the maid ("Rosette") of her "sister" Camille (Madeleine Assas) (who introduces herself as Albert Camus's granddaughter, so establishing in the film a clear white, European *pied noir* framework and tradition) and Jérôme (Frédéric Pierrot), who wishes to pursue a relationship with her. Djamila is last seen on the battlegrounds of Bosnia holding a copy of *Hasards de l'Arabie heureuse* (a translation of *Nine Days to Mukall:*

A Journey into the Arabian World (1953) by the American writer Frederic Prokosch), before she is eventually interrogated, tortured, raped as a Muslim (presumably by Serbs), and, we are led to assume, killed (by contrast, Camille and Jérôme are shown literally, and tragically, digging their own graves).

26. It was, in fact, a troubled project from the beginning. Diawara relates that Guerra and others became impatient with an increasingly isolated Godard who was spending far too much time theorizing and agonizing over *mise en scène* or which camera to use (Diawara 2003: 105–7). Diawara has recently argued that Abderrahmane Sissako's 2006 film *Bamako*, a formally experimental film that revolves around a trial of the debt policies of the IMF and World Bank in a courtyard in Bamako, is exactly the type of film Godard would have wanted to make when in Mozambique since it is a form of "anticinema" that produces an African image at once fresh, unpredictable, and impossible for dominant film discourse to repeat or appropriate. See Diawara 2010: 118–20.

27. It is significant that in his much later "video letter" posted on-line to the directors of the May 2014 Cannes Film Festival to "apologize" for not making it to the premiere of *Adieu au langage* (another highly public "failure" to deliver on a stated promise), Godard juxtaposed the same photograph of Bamberger and the young African boy with a particularly violent sequence of masochism from *Changer d'image*. The juxtaposition both foregrounds the sexual aggression inherent in the image and testifies to the special importance of this short as a delayed counterreaction by Godard to the abortive Mozambique project. See Godard 2014.

Chapter 2

1. "Il y a la culture/ qui est de la règle/ qui fait partie de la règle/ il y a l'exception/ qui est de l'art/ qui fait partie de l'art/ tous disent la règle/ cigarettes/ ordinateurs/ t-shirts/ télévision/ tourisme/ guerre [. . .]" (Godard 1996a: 16–17).

2. Here is one such example: "Art is Dostoyevsky, culture was watching my mother read. Later I discovered art in the books that she used to read" ("Une boucle bouclée": interview with Alain Bergala, in Bergala 1998: 23–24).

3. "Il est de la règle/ que vouloir/ la mort de l'exception/ non/ c'est/ non/ il est donc de la règle/ de l'Europe/ de la culture/ règle de l'Europe/de la culture que/ d'organiser la mort/ de l'art de vivre/ qui fleurissait/ encore à nos pieds" (Godard 1996a: 19–20).

4. "Jean-Luc Godard in conversation with Colin MacCabe" in Petrie 1992: 103. In the light of this statement the commercial selling in 1998 of the video box-set of *Histoire(s)*, which included interviews with Alain Bergala relayed in retail outlets in France such as FNAC to advertise the handsomely priced product, would appear a major contradiction and spectacular turnaround. Yet Godard has never denied "democratic" culture its positive, nourishing, pedagogical role. Indeed, from the very beginning of *Histoire(s)*, when he explained his aims for the project to Serge Daney, he has harboured a wish that all the material be available to the public and perform an educative function. See "Godard fait des histoires" in Bergala 1998: 161–73.

5. See Ang 1992: 27. Ang argues that the best way for Europe to disentangle itself from its hegemonic past is to become "post-European," a spirit epitomized by those "new ethnic" films made in Europe but not from Europe (e.g. Stephen Frears's *My Beautiful Launderette* [1985], Po-Chih Leong's *Ping Pong* [1986]) which "attempt to come to terms with the complexities of the present without resorting to idealized images of either the past or the future" (30). I will be arguing that Godard adopts a "trans-European" and "transaesthetic"

approach in *Histoire(s)*. For an excellent analysis of *Passion* that places the film in its European context while arguing for its postmodern status, see Jameson 1992.

6. Aumont 1999: 225. Aumont refers to the fundamentally documentary nature of these three national cinemas torn between two "postulations" of fiction, American and Russian.

7. Péguy began *Clio* in 1909, a year after he had refound his faith, and in it he dismisses the new schools of scientific-sociological enquiry. Yet running throughout the text is a profound sense of failure. The problem in writing ancient history, Péguy argues, is that the references are lacking, while for the writer of modern history there are simply too many. Moreover, if history runs parallel to the event, memory is central to it. Hence, the most delicate problem of aesthetics is essentially a problem of the very organization of memory. For a filmmaker like Godard, of course, the process of anamnesis unfolds a little differently since, as he often expresses it, cinema necessarily entails a forgetting of the real. However, if this forgetting is duly recorded, one can start to remember and potentially even (re)gain the lost real. Such is the immense aesthetic challenge of *Histoire(s)*.

8. See Spengler 1962.

9. De Rougemont 1936: 21. Godard rarely modifies the selected extracts except when he wishes to make the language more clear or accessible. The one important exception to this rule is that "x is a person/ a creative element/ an incalculable freedom" (Godard 1998a, vol. 4: 62). The original passage, located just before the end of the text, reads: "The only value that one can give to the x of the world's equation is that of a person. Yet since a person is a creative act, it introduces every time into the equation an irrational and incalculable element, an element of freedom" (245). Godard's dynamic fusion of ideas in this passage, which attributes directly to "a person" the qualities linked by de Rougemont to "an element" and thus itself performs the idea conveyed of creative freedom, is significant for the fact that it takes place under the letter x—a fact whose importance will become clear shortly when we discuss the chiastic dimension of Godard's self-reflexive montage.

10. "Le cinéma est fait pour penser l'impensable" in Bergala 1998: 296. Godard has just explained the complex sequence of association in *Allemagne* where, during discussion of a young girl beheaded during the war, a white rose arrives in the frame to the sounds of a typewriter. This requires historical knowledge of the White Rose student movement founded in Germany in 1942–43 by Hans and Sophie Scholl, who were arrested and killed for distributing typewritten anti-Nazi tracts.

11. The extended project of *Histoire(s)* constitutes in itself an exemplary Malrucian case of the transformation of forms across media. This 264-minute work, which began life as an experimental series of improvised talks and lectures Godard gave at the Conservatoire d'Art Cinématographique in Montreal in the late 1970s (subsequently transcribed and published in 1980 as *Introduction à une véritable histoire du cinéma*), was originally made as a video for Canal+, ARTE, and Gaumont. The opening two long episodes were broadcast on British and European television in 1988, and subsequent parts were screened at film festivals and museums as and when they were finished. It was not until 1998 that the film saw the light of day as a complete (and reedited) whole, released in France by Gaumont as a four-part VHS box-set and complemented at the same moment by a box-set of four hybrid art books by Gallimard, which Godard presented as a series of "archives" lifted directly from the video's "ultrasound scan" of History. Only the major voice-over passages and written texts are retained in their entirety in the volumes, and certain sequences of images are shuffled out of order or lack crucial elements. Moreover, the lists of films, writers, and photographers included at the back of each volume are incomplete and do not always observe the actual order of appearance. No attempt is made to identify the paintings and

other works of art—further evidence of Godard's essential wish to neutralize the power of painting. In fact, the book completes the major leveling process undertaken in the video by rendering equal in force all the various kinds of image featured. One could argue that this represents another stage in the process of sublimation of mourning and redeeming the real at work in the video, for the images have been liberated and as it were resurrected onto the page transhistorically, if only in the sense that they all bear the mark of their impersonal history and evolution in Godard's memory machine. Hence, the book marks a further stage in a continuing metamorphosis of forms, one that actually sacrifices the video of *Histoire(s)*, just as the latter "sacrificed" cinema in order to recuperate it as an instrument of thought. The project continued further with the release in 1999 of a remixed CD version of the soundtrack by ECM Records comprising a box-set of 5 CDs and transcriptions in French, German, and English. It was only in 2008, after many delays due to copyright issues, that the DVD of *Histoire(s)* was finally made available in its entirety to an English-speaking audience, although the optional subtitles are far from complete and appear at times extremely selective. The DVD remains largely unchanged from the 1998 video version which many had expected by this stage to be fully reedited, perhaps even digitally, by Godard, particularly in the light of his 2004 compilation of edited "highlights" transferred to 35 mm, *Moments choisis des Histoire(s) du cinéma*. Crucially for our discussion, the DVD refuses to conform to the expectations of "DVD culture": there are no tailor-made special features, no interviews with the director or actors, and no supplementary catalogue or essay. It is not even divided into commodified, user-friendly "chapters," an authorial decision by Godard not simply to avoid confusion with the nomenclature of *Histoire(s)* itself which was originally divided into eight "chapters," but also to oblige the viewer to experience the work as an organic whole without editorial guidance. In fact, the artisanal aspect of the presentation, further enhanced by the minimalist style of the packaging recalling the *art brut* installations of Godard's 2006 exhibit, *Voyage(s) en Utopie, Jean-Luc Godard, 1946–2006*, at the Centre Pompidou in Paris, serves to underline and guard intact the artistic status of *Histoire(s)* as a video rather than DVD. This is an uncompromising statement of faith by Godard in (analogical) art as opposed to preprogrammed (digital) culture, as well as in the intelligence of his audience. For a well-informed argument for considering *Voyage(s) en Utopie* as the final stage of the extended project of *Histoire(s)*, see Lundemo 2014.

12. See "Pour la Serbie" in Hugo 1940: 255–58.

13. For an excellent analysis of the political and discursive strategies adopted by Mitterrand and his minister for culture during the GATT talks, including the advocacy of European construction through cultural cohesion and the invocation of a European "spirit of resistance" and "consciousness," see Strode 2000. Strode argues convincingly that France, although calling for the protection of European cultural identity (vaguely defined) and "the universal idea of culture," seeks above all to utilize the opportunities of the European Union to bolster its own identity through policy making on visual culture.

14. See Derrida 1991. Derrida refers to "Notes sur la grandeur et décadence de l'Europe" and "La crise de l'esprit" in Valéry 1957. In the latter piece, Valéry asks: "Will Europe become what it is in reality, that is, a small head of the Asiatic continent? Or else will it remain what it appears to be, that is: the precious part of the terrestrial universe, the pearl in the sphere, the brain of a vast body?" (Valéry 1957: 995).

15. Malraux puts it a little differently in *Les Voix du silence*: drawing a specific link between the filmic succession of shots and the style of the Baroque, he argues that art became abstract once cinema arrived and proceeded to usurp art's function of portraying movement and fiction.

16. See Bataille 1955: 103.

17. See Sollers 1997: 42. Sollers talks of *Histoire(s)* in Heideggerian terms as "l'*Historial du cinéma*" and emphasizes its prophetic and apocalyptic tone, claiming that it is both a "practically funerary monument" (40) and a "Last Judgment" for the films extracted since Godard, like a "conductor of ghosts," is determining their guilt or innocence.

18. The film historian Bernard Eisenschitz, who identified for Gaumont (with Godard's assistance) most of the cited films and authors and contributed the lists available in the published art books, suggests that the image of Berlin shown at this point is from Joe May's silent 1929 film, *Asphalt*, produced by Erich Pommer for UFA. See Eisenschitz 1998: 54. Of course, it is not possible, nor perhaps even desirable, to identify all the sources while viewing *Histoire(s)*. Compare *Histoire(s)* in this regard with Godard's often neglected collaborative piece with Miéville, *The Old Place* (1998), commissioned by the Museum of Modern Art in New York, which has a similar elegiac sense of melancholy and mourning for the lost potential of art (among the titles of the fourteen chapters are "Les illusions perdues" and "Le vieux monde"). It, too, is preoccupied with themes of death, collapse, and noncommunication (including references to Valéry's 1941 collection, *Mélange*), and the glimpsed images culled from a wide range of media and sources (though ironically, and crucially, precious few from MoMA's extensive vaults of postwar abstraction) encompass beauty, horror, suffering, and everyday banality. As Margaret Flinn suggests, *The Old Place* should be viewed as a "resistant text" issuing a challenge to play the game of identifying the citations in the audio-visual assemblage (see Flinn 2014). I would argue further that, in both cases, what counts most for Godard in his elaboration of a moral aesthetics of figuration is that an intersubjective critical space is created which actively encourages the processes of human memory and obliges us to consider the value and significance of our own filmic and aesthetic associations.

19. Emily Brontë's poem beginning "The evening passes fast away" includes the words: "And where thy heart has suffered so/ Canst thou desire to dwell?/ Alas! the countless links are strong/ That bind us to our clay;/ The loving spirit lingers long,/ And would not pass away—." The poem, written in 1842–43, was commenced in Brussels a fortnight before Brontë returned home on account of the death of her aunt and foster mother. Again, in the spirit of *La Monnaie de l'Absolu*, art, resistant and pugnacious, is linked to a real journey induced by loss and pain.

20. The painting appears to be *Nu Couché Bleu* (1955), although this is almost certainly not the original but an imitation by Godard himself since he was not legally allowed by the de Staël family to reproduce any of the artist's paintings. What is perhaps more significant is the fact that the image was painted by de Staël in 1955 just before he killed himself. As such, it can be compared to another image favored by Godard in *Histoire(s)*, Van Gogh's *Wheatfield with Crows*, his very last picture, and also to Paul Klee's *Vergesslicher Engel* (*Forgetful Angel*), a key part of the initial 1989 version of the final sequence of episode 1B, drawn in 1939 just before Klee's death in 1940 from the rare debilitating disease of scleroderma. Godard is consistently drawn not only to the late period of artists, but also to traces of early personal tragedy, notably that of Novalis. For an excellent general introduction to the instances of art and painting in *Histoire(s)*, see Shafto 2006.

21. The first edition of *Gilles* in 1939 was censored, but the novel was reissued in complete form in 1942. It is a neohistorical, picaresque modernist novel in four parts, covering the years from 1917 to the Spanish Civil War.

22. See de Man 1979: 53.

23. In Warner 1998, Marina Warner has suggested that this image may actually be one of incestuous cannibalism since the buttocks suggest a female youth. If so, the image

may not be of Saturn at all but of Kronos incorporating one of his daughters. Warner bases her argument in part on a comparison with another image by Goya used in *La Monnaie de l'absolu*, the drawing *Saturn Devouring His Children*.

24. I will explore in detail in the following chapter the figure of the chiasmus in terms of the mechanical and inhuman as it operates in episode 2B of *Histoire(s)*.

25. See "*Histoire(s) du cinéma: à propos de cinéma et d'histoire*" in Bergala 1998: 403.

26. See Mondzain 1998: 97–98. Mondzain argues that the newly born America transferred its belief in incarnation and resurrection into a new regime, industry, and thus the uniqueness of cinema's initial gesture (notably in the work of Griffith) was soon destroyed by trade. For an extensive study of Godard's changing notion of cinema as preeminently a national cinema, see Witt 2000a.

27. In "Résistance de l'art" in Bergala 1998: 443–46, an interview that originally appeared in November 1997 in *Le Monde de l'Éducation*, Godard talks of his long interest in the period of the Occupation and the Resistance and argues that *Rome, Open City* was a film of resistance because of its value of resurrection. Godard does not, however, consider here the question of resistance in cinema as it informs his own film practice and particularly *Histoire(s)*.

28. "Une boucle bouclée" in Bergala 1998: 18: "'*L'État, c'est la pensée qui forme.*' Moi, je crois plus à une forme qui pense [. . .] C'est la forme qui pense, au cinéma. Dans le mauvais cinéma, c'est la pensée qui forme."

29. De Rougemont 1936: 243.

30. See "Le bon plaisir de Jean-Luc Godard" in Bergala 1998: 305–22 (318).

31. For an excellent analysis of the changes affecting nation-state sovereignty in the new "Greater Europe," see Bauman 1995, in particular "Europe of Nations, Europe of Tribes" (243–56). Bauman argues that the Wall offered an effective barrier to the spread of the privilege called "Europe" (245), but that now, with the idea of a supra-state and all-European institutions and agencies, what is left of the traditional sovereignty of nation-states (and especially of their contractual obligations towards their subjects) appears very easy, too easy, to hold and uphold, i.e. "a prize with no penalty attached; a right without duties, taking without giving, pleasure without responsibility" (248). Bauman signals the dangers today of an "endless fissiparousness of nationalisms" with ever new regional, linguistic and denominational differences being picked up by ever new prospective elites as distinctive identities powerful enough to justify a separate state, or quasi-state, formation (250). The forces of ethnicity (in Serbia, for instance) "are once more set loose, untamed and unanchored, free-floating and uncontrolled" (247), and states have become now "no more than transit stations in travel of goods and money administered by multi-national (i.e. non-national, trans-national) executives."

32. See Skoller 1999, where Skoller argues that Godard is interested in the space between the shots that holds them apart such that there is no chain of interlinked images to form a whole. The interstice is a form of thought, a virtuality that exists between nonlinking images. According to Skoller, *Allemagne* creates a distinction between knowledge and thought since thinking is defined by the virtual or what is unthought, and to think is to experiment and create (42).

33. Habermas 1994: 71. According to Habermas, world history has offered a unified Europe a "second chance," and "Europe must use one of its strengths, namely its potential for self-criticism, its power of self-transformation, in order to relativize itself far more radically *vis-à-vis* the others, the strangers, the misunderstood. That's the opposite of Eurocentrism" (96).

34. See "Jean-Luc Godard rencontre Régis Debray" in Bergala 1998: 423–43, where Godard claims that art has disappeared and that Picasso represented the end of one of the chapters of man's artistic creation as conceived by Malraux (423).

35. See Debray 1999: 103. The book was part of the new series Fondation Marc-Bloch, which advocated the state and nation as the only proper framework for democracy and the continuation of the republic. Interestingly, Debray also considers the case of Péguy and Hugo, referring to the latter's introduction to the guide of the 1867 Exposition Universelle entitled "Paris," where Hugo talks fancifully of Paris as being in the twentieth century the capital of a new nation in Europe eventually to be called simply "Humanity" (72).

36. The original reads: "Si une image, regardée à part, exprime nettement quelque chose, si elle comporte une interprétation, elle ne se transformera pas au contact d'autres images. Les autres images n'auront aucun pouvoir sur elle, et elle n'aura aucun pouvoir sur les autres images. Ni action, ni réaction" (Bresson 1995: 23). It goes without saying that for Godard there is never a single image, but rather relations of images and the movement between them. See Witt 2000b for an extensive analysis of Godard's terms of reference for montage.

37. See Bergala, "Une boucle bouclée," in Bergala 1998: 35.

38. For a fine discussion of the Kantian sublime in the context of history, see Lyotard 1989.

39. See Deleuze 1995: 234–35. Deleuze talks of Godardian montage as operating "between two actions, two affections, two perceptions, two visual images, two sound images, between sound and the visual: to show the indiscernible, i.e. the border" (235).

40. See Bellour 1990: 330–37. Bellour refers to Godard's use of video as a *"passeuse"* which offers an intermediate vision, an "intermedial" language.

41. See Silverman and Farocki 1998: 184. They also declare that in *Passion* Godard uses the trope of analogy but only to renounce it: "[T]here is nothing sublime about similarity; it is not the point where contraries meet, but the site of their disappearance" (185). I will argue differently that in *Histoire(s)* analogies of the human form are pursued, maintained, and even prioritized.

42. Episode 1A of *Histoire(s)*, *Nouvelle Vague*, and *Allemagne* are all punctuated by the slow, deep murmurings and mounting crescendos of Hindemith's symphony *Mathis der Maler* (Mathis the painter) (1933–34), notably the opening moments of the second and third movements, "Grablegung" and "Versuchung des heiligen Antonius." Inspired by the life of Matthias Grünewald and in particular his *Isenheim Altarpiece*, the symphony is linked in theme and style to Hindemith's later opera of the same name, in which an artist leads a rebellion against authority. Its ultimate message is one of faith in art rather than politics, and as such the music expresses exactly the type of artistic resistance currently cultivated by Godard. It is worth noting that performances of the opera were banned in Germany by the Nazis, a fate that also befell Hindemith's other spiritual, Christian works such as the 1923 song cycle, *Das Marienleben* (The life of Mary).

43. Godard: "ô quelle merveille que de regarder ce qu'on ne voit pas/ ô doux miracle de nos yeux aveugles'; Bernanos: 'ô merveille, qu'on puisse ainsi faire présent de ce qu'on ne possède pas soi-même, ô doux miracle de nos mains vides!" (Bernanos 1994: 200).

44. See Rancière 1999 where Rancière laments Godard's sacred belief in the image and its original vocation of presence subsequently destroyed by the "original sin" of nineteenth-century artifice and fiction. Placing the sequence in the particular context of Claude Lanzmann's *Shoah* (1985), Libby Saxon argues similarly that the many allusions to sacred music, texts, and images lend themselves to the image of Christian redemption (see Saxton 2008: 46–67). For Miriam Heywood, who provides a valuable overview of the main debates surrounding

Godard's treatment of the Holocaust, Godard's practice of montage of images is not "unethical" and indeed works against the Nazi policy of extermination by allowing the archival images to communicate with other images so that the horrors of the Holocaust might temporarily be exposed (see Heywood 2009). For Alan Wright, meanwhile, the multimedia presentation in the "Elizabeth Taylor at Auschwitz" sequence of a "fleeting glimpse of happiness and the deadly grip of terror within the same frame," by which Godard "attempts to document that which can only obtain expression at the extreme limits of comprehension," "produces an apparition of the Real, a sublime recognition of the impossibility of doing justice to reality" (Wright 2000: 54–55). As such, according to Wright, Godard's practice of montage constitutes a decisive updating of Benjamin's dialectical image for contemporary times (ibid.: 60). Perhaps the most affirmative reading of Godard's engagement with the Holocaust in *Histoire(s)*, however, is that by Max Silverman who focuses on an equally complex sequence of montage around the Holocaust in episode 4B (see Silverman 2013: 128–32). Defending Godard's formal *rapprochements* against charges either that he has simply assimilated the Holocaust into Christian iconography or, as has Céline Scemama asserts in Scemama 2014, that he has effectively allowed ideology to take over from thought by preventing cinema from relating history, Silverman argues that Godard's dynamic practice of montage, whereby superimposed and dissolved images become literally "palimpsests" since they leave behind their traces (ibid.: 131), "establishes a more relational, dialectical and open-ended structure rather than one that should be read simply in terms of an instrumentalist understanding of screen memory" (ibid.: 143). Silverman argues convincingly that if there is any epiphanous flash of light from the darkness during such moments in *Histoire(s)*, it is not the redemptive incarnation of a holy spirit but the infinite, interconnecting traces of the ghosts of the past which haunt the present. What is at stake, therefore, is a new understanding of the cinematic encounter in terms of the historical event and trauma. Silverman writes: "The missed encounter (like trauma itself) can be re-staged through the montage of cinematic images, not in order to re-enact the moment beyond representation (as in Lanzmann's *Shoah*) but to involve the spectator in a process of reading the event historically [. . .] Godard's montage [. . .] produces *a belated cinematic encounter* of truly startling, and often shocking, import, which propels us into a *new relationship with the event*" (ibid.: 128; my emphasis). Silverman concludes resoundingly that "[b]y placing the horror-stricken face of the Jewish victim of the Holocaust in a series of similar but different faces of horror, Godard shocks the Holocaust out of its framing within any preceding aesthetic (the negative sublime, Hollywood's sentimentalized piety, and so on) to propel it (vertically, paradigmatically, and dialectically) into history, or at least the history/histories of the cinema" (ibid.: 132). Finally, in a probing study exploring whether Godard goes beyond the standard ethical questions of rendering Holocaust horror visible and the (im)possibility of representing the Holocaust, Kriss Ravetto-Biagioli argues that *Histoire(s)* does not offer an image of the resurrection or redemption of the image so much as its reanimation or return. This is because, she suggests, the image that returns in *Histoire(s)* is one devoid of the image of resurrection, maintaining only its unsettling gesture. Ravetto-Biagioli concludes rightly that Godard creates a number of problems for those who wish to speak about moral imperatives or to use them for political purposes. See Ravetto-Biagioli 2014.

45. See Rancière 1999: 62.
46. See Godard and Ishaghpour 1999: 31.
47. Sollers 1997: 48.
48. See "Godard peintre" in Aumont 1989: 242. Aumont places Godard in the context of classicism where the body "expresses" and is the privileged site of feeling, of "passion."

Compare this with Angela Dalle Vacche's analysis of Godard's collage method in the much earlier *Pierrot le fou*, which argues that the film is animated by a logocentric impulse, and, more generally, that Godard's cinema tends towards abstraction and is actually iconophobic. Dalle Vacche claims specifically that Godard's use of collage and its ability to thrive on the boundary between word and image (thus creating semiotic permutation) marks an attempt to overcome the pain of sexual difference. See Dalle Vacche 1996: 107–34. What Aumont and Della Vacche do not disagree on, however, is the primary importance for Godard of the image's capacity to create and disclose feelings and emotions.

49. See Lyotard 1985: 11–18. For Lyotard, the function of art (as opposed to the ego) is to lift repression and reverse it: "[T]he forms forbid the fulfilment of desire, they prevent it from hallucinating itself and discharging itself into the lure of carrying the contents into effect, simply because these forms do not let us stay ignorant of themselves" (355). And: "Fantasy makes opposition out of difference; the poetic remakes difference out of *that* opposition" (357). It could surely be argued that the rich, poetic montage of *Histoire(s)*, which freely connects resurrected traces of the recorded past, epitomizes Lyotard's notion of art as difference and the lifting of repression.

50. A point of comparison in this regard might be Jean Louis Schefer's notion of the "enigmatic," "paradoxical body," which he opposes to doxical figuration in Western painting produced by perspectival and volumatic space. Godard has a similar suspicion of perspective, and his perception of the body is equally attached to the elements of time and memory. Yet Godard's presentation of the body in *La Monnaie de l'absolu* is from a specifically Christian perspective, whereas Schefer's is that of the pagan body which Christianity combats (Schefer is drawn to those films precisely which figure unformed, deformed, or freakish bodies). See Smith 1995, in particular "The Plague" (37–53) (on Uccello's *Deluge*) and "Cinema" (108–38).

51. See Eagleton 1990: 357. Much could be said of the resemblances in style between *Histoire(s)* and the Adorno of *Minima moralia*, including the shared method of intensive fragmentation and the use of epigramatic *aperçus*.

52. Adorno 1974: 247.

Chapter 3

1. Flusser 1996: 244. In a useful introduction to digital film in the historical context of the moving image, Lev Manovich shows how the manually constructed digital image actually marks a return to nineteenth-century precinematic practices where images were hand-painted and hand-animated. See Manovich 1997: 31.

2. Flusser 1996: 244.

3. Kroker 1992: 5.

4. See Sedgwick and Frank 1995: 515.

5. Ibid.: 517–18.

6. In the early 1980s, Godard stated: "Invention, or creation, is always an analogical thing. Maybe that will change. Digital interests me as a thing in itself, or as a technique, but not as a basis for creation. Otherwise the digital becomes the foundation and the analogical disappears" (cited in Bergala 1985: 604). Up until then Godard had used video more as a conceptual tool and a way of rehearsing ideas for his film-work, as in the case of the short video scenarios and "notes" for *Sauve qui peut (la vie)*, *Passion* and *Je vous salue, Marie*. For two fine accounts of Godard's entry into digital prior to *Histoire(s)* with the dazzling

twenty-five minute video short, *Puissance de la parole* (1988), made for France Télécom, see Bellour 1996 and Lundemo 2004.

7. See Beghin 1998.

8. See Meek 2010: 163–70.

9. See Shaviro 1993. Underpinning Shaviro's idea of masochistic excitement is Jean Laplanche's idea that fantasy, or the imaginary expression and fulfilment of a desire, is itself a sexual perturbation (*ébranlement*) intimately related in its origin to the emergence of the masochistic sexual drive. This psychic disturbance is essentially an experience of pleasure as pain, and thus already a form of masochistic sexual excitement.

10. Ibid.: 60.

11. The term "discomfited" (from the French "*défait*") is used by Godard himself to describe the contemporary weakness of men. See Bergala 1998: 620. Phil Powrie examines Godard's treatment of the figure of the weak male, notably in *Détective*, in Powrie 1987: 96–108.

12. We shall return to Cocteau in chapter 8 to consider the full implications of Godard's complex intertextual encounter with this pivotal artistic figure.

13. De Man 1979: 53.

14. This sudden recourse to the German philosophic and poetic tradition is typical in Godard's work, particularly in later films such as *Allemagne année 90 neuf zéro*, where he engages directly with Hegel's *Elements of the Philosophy of Right*. For reasons that will become clear shortly, it may also be compared with Deleuze and Guattari's return to Spinoza's ethics as a revelatory principle of romantic mysticism during their otherwise unlimited voyage into "desiring machines" and "bodies without organs" in Deleuze and Guattari 1987.

15. See Heidegger, "What Are Poets For?," in Hofstadter 1975: 94.

16. The sentence is reported by Luke in the Acts of the Apostles 16, 28. Alain Bergala argues persuasively that the sentence must be understood as a self-injunction by Godard, that is to say, as an imaginary summoning of Godard by those who expect him to save them from the limbo of Purgatory where they are suffering physically and erring spiritually: "[W]e are all still here expecting from you the Redemption." Bergala suggests that Godard believes they expect this from him alone since he has indeed wished to undertake such a mission. See Bergala 1999: 223. *Nous sommes tous encore ici* is also the title of a 1997 film by Anne-Marie Miéville staring Godard alongside Aurore Clément and Bernadette Lafont.

17. See Habib 2014: 226. Habib analyzes the chronicle of failure of *Voyage(s) en utopie* in terms of Godard's "performance" of failure, and explores the tension always between "utopia" and "failure"—"a movement that allegorizes both the 'grandeur' and the 'decadence' of Godard's 'petit commerce de cinéma' and the complexities of his museum performance" (Habib 2014: 229). Habib concludes correctly that one of the underlying principles governing Godard's work as a whole is "how a 'fidelity to failure' can open a 'new occasion, a new term of relation.' It is precisely what we witness between the failure of 'Collage(s) de France' and the expressive act that displays *Voyage(s) en utopie*, an expressive act of its impossibility, which performs cinema's utopian possibilities" (ibid.: 230). Des O'Rawe has written of *Voyage(s) en utopie* that is became like a construction site which deliberately denied a collective experience. Minimalist techniques were employed to break up and atomize space, and the image was radically deframed producing a scattering and disconnecting of objects. It was thus more like a "de-installation" that refused to "situate its own artefacts (and associations) into anything resembling a theme" (see O'Rawe 2011). Yet the result was precisely a reinvigoration of filmic practice stimulating fresh debates about both the possibilities and the limits of new

visual forms and the tools of multimedia. For a detailed account of the precise evolution and aesthetic stakes of this (anti)-exhibit, see Païni 2006, which includes images of the original model for the nine-room "Collages de France." For Godard's own video tour of this model before it was abandoned, see his intimate home movie short, *Reportage Amateur (maquette expo)* (2006), co-directed by Anne-Marie Miéville.

18. See Faroult and Williams 2006, which examines the genetic elements of the project, including a comparison of equivalent sequences extracted from Giraudoux's play, Godard's sixty-page screenplay, his documents of the shoot, and the final *découpage*.

19. See Morrey 2005: 214.

20. See, for example, Fieschi-Vivet 2000.

21. We note that the theme of redemption is already sounded at the start of the film where part of "Thesis II" of Walter Benjamin's *Theses on the Philosophy of History* (1940) (in its French translation) is read out in a voice-over: "[T]he past requires a redemption of which a tiny part may be found within our power [. . .] We have been awaited on earth."

22. See Guillory 1983: 169.

23. In a fascinating discussion of the figure of the angel of history, Bergala examines Godard's original use of Klee's depictions of angels in the particular context of Benjamin's *Theses on the Philosophy of History*, specifically "Thesis IX." There Benjamin interprets the central figure of another Klee painting, the 1920 watercolor entitled *Angelus Novus*, as the angel of history whose "face is turned towards the past" (Benjamin: "Where we perceive a chain of events, he sees one single catastrophe"), but who is also looking at human beings moving through time. In Benjamin's interpretation, the angel of history is irresistibly propelled into the future. Yet if history marks an attempt to make sense of the continual passage of time, it is defeated by the same force that makes it impossible to fulfill all our dreams of the future. Hence, time, progress and history are all forces that continually transform our lives but which we cannot halt or even adequately represent. See Bergala 1999: 221–49.

24. Other representations of angels in episode IB include the detail of the two faces (male and female) from *Tango of Archangel* (c. 1930) by Kees Van Dongen, and the detail of an angel leaning on the shoulder of a young man from Rembrandt's *The Dream of St Joseph* (1650). These extend the cohort of angels encountered in the first episode of *Histoire(s)*, notably by Giotto (including Godard's torquing of a *Noli me tangere* scene by Giotto that transforms Mary Magdalene into an angel, as discussed in chapter 2), and the detail of a work by Raphael of the Archangel Michael. But there are also, of course, the many angels announced textually in the titles and intertitles such as "L'ANGE," or else hidden in names such as "Langlois," thereby creating a rich web of metonymical associations.

25. Rilke 1978: 60.

26. See Weiskel 1976.

27. Merleau-Ponty 1962: 142.

28. "[S]i un homme / si/ un homme/ traversait/ le paradis/ en songe/ qu'il reçut une fleur/ comme prévue/ de son passage/ et qu'à son réveil/ il trouvât/ cette fleur/ dans ses mains/ que dire/ alors/ j'étais cet homme" (Godard 1998a, vol. 4: 306–11). The original line from Coleridge's *Anima Poetae* reads thus: "If a man could pass thro' Paradise in a Dream, & have a flower presented to him as a pledge that his Soul had really been there, & found the flower in his hand when he awoke–Aye! and what then?" In a compelling discussion of this exemplary transaesthetic sequence in Godard, which also brings together Dante and Van Gogh, in the context of Godard's identificatory gestures in *Histoire(s)*, Roland-François Lack points out that the accompanying frames from *JLG/JLG* and *Allemagne* undergo a

transformation. Specifically, the white rose, symbol of the short-lived White Rose student movement in WW2, becomes yellow, and in the process moves form the realm of history into that of eternity (see Lack 2004: 325–9). As for Bacon, he is a key painter for Godard throughout the later corpus. In *Puissance de la parole*, for example, his *Study from the Human Body* (1949) is flashed up and electronically reprogrammed at the beginning and end, while the falling *Figure in Movement* is used in conjunction with Ravel in the film's finale.

29. Godard 1980: 301.

30. See "Something like: 'Communication . . . without Communication,'" in Lyotard 1991: 108–18.

31. Ibid.: 110.

32. See "Heidegger/Merleau-Ponty: the chiasmus" in Fóti 1992: 37–8.

33. Flusser 1996: 245.

34. Bukatman 1993: 96.

35. For a wide-ranging definition of this concept within the theoretical field of the digital unconscious, see Monk 1998: 30–44.

36. See Bergala 1994: 25–27.

37. See Lyotard 1991: 176.

38. Connor 1997: 159.

39. Ibid.: 162.

Chapter 4

1. No direct dialogue or "traffic" between Godard and Agamben has actually taken place since. In fact, Agamben did not take part in the Round Table (chaired by Jean-Michel Frodon and in which Godard himself participated) that brought to a climax the series of debates on the first six completed episodes of *Histoire(s)* organized by the film historian Bernard Eisenschitz at Locarno in August 1995, which inspired the special supplement in *Le Monde*. Godard himself regarded the occasion as a lost opportunity for genuine dialogue between philosophers, historians, writers, and critics and never publicly responded to Agamben's article). A little later, Godard conceived of a possible dialogue with Agamben and other prominent European philosophers as part of his ambitious but never realized project of talks and debates entitled *Collage(s) de France* at the Centre Pompidou in Paris.

2. See Agamben 2000: 42–60.

3. See Deleuze 1992. Deleuze talked of the cut as an "irrational" interstice and of the new "law" of "false continuity." Agamben's account of Deleuze argues that the mythical rigidity of the image has been broken in Deleuze's "movement-images" and that, properly speaking, "there are no images but only gestures. Every image, in fact, is animated by an antinomic polarity: on the one hand, images are the reification and obliteration of a gesture (it is the *imago* as death mask or as symbol); on the other hand, they preserve the *dynamis* intact (as in Muybridge's snapshots or in any sports photograph)" (Agamben 2000: 54). The former is linked to the recollection seized by voluntary memory; while the latter is linked to image flashing in the epiphany of involuntary memory. Further, the latter refers always beyond itself to a whole of which it is a part, so that even the *Mona Lisa* could be seen as a fragment of a gesture or as a still of a lost film where it might regain its true meaning. Agamben concludes that "it is as if a silent innovation calling for the liberation of the image into gesture arose from the entire history of art" (ibid.: 55). See Witt 2001 for a fine account of the corporeal resistance and remarkable play of energy created in Godard's

video work with children, which places *France tour détour deux enfants* in the context of the embryonic first stage of early cinema (Marey, Muybridge).

4. Agamben's *Community to Come* (1993) contains a chapter (originally a preface for the Italian translation of Debord's *Commentaries on the Society of the Spectacle* [1988]) in which Agamben attempts to rescue Debord from the narrow perspectives that corral him into the confines of 1980s appropriation art and practices of *détournement*, but divorced from their context and ossified in postmodern visual art. As Christian McCrea argues, instead of placing Debord in a category such as the film-essay cliché, or historicizing him (predictably his fate in academia), Agamben sees the contemporary significance of Debord's intervention as "a manual for exodus" or "a weapon for resistance" (see McCrea 2009: 313–19).

5. Godard's poetics of cinema, which I shall refer to in my discussion of *Soigne ta droite* as the "music of the crystal," has clear resonances with Deleuze's philosophy of the "crystal-image," the cornerstone of his "time-image" inspired by Bergson, where the actual optical image crystallizes with its own virtual image. Because it is irreducible to the actual and virtual, as well as to the present and contemporaneous past, the "crystal-image" allows us, according to Deleuze, finally to "see" time (see Deleuze 1985: 92–128). However, despite the complex taxonomy he provides, the "crystal-image" is glimpsed in only a few exceptional films like Hitchcock's *Vertigo*. Hence, its status remains more abstract and purely theoretical than concrete and real. By contrast, Godard's "music of the crystal," derived, as we shall see, in preeminently aesthetic terms from Hermann Broch, is both revealed and instantiated in the alchemical heat and affect of cinematic montage and projection. It is precisely this at once concrete and absolute investment in the revelatory power of the cinematic event that differentiates Godard as an artist from Deleuze and Agamben as philosophers.

6. Agamben 2002a: 315.

7. Ibid.: 319.

8. Agamben 2000: 56.

9. Agamben 2002a: 317.

10. The exceptions are Delvaux 1988a (a short study of five fragments of the film published on its release, though strangely with no explicit mention of Broch) and Morgan 2013. See also Morrey 2005: 184–89 and Brody 2008: 480–89.

11. *King Lear* is littered with black-and-white photographs and stills of filmmakers, Cocteau, Bresson, Pasolini, Visconti, Lang, Tati, Pagnol, Rivette, Franju, Losey, Becker, Welles (an image from *The Merchant of Venice* [1969]), as well as reproductions of Giotto, Doré, Watteau, Renoir, da Vinci, Morisot, Manet, Van Gogh, Tex Avery, and others. They all function for William as forms of *aide-mémoire* and signs of the apparently lost artistic and cultural past. In one formal "experiment" by Pluggy in a darkened video studio with a bank of video monitors, we see projected on two monitors a juxtaposition of the central figure of Fuseli's *Lady Macbeth Sleepwalking* and the moment of the eyeball being razored from Buñuel/Dalí's 1929 *Un Chien andalou*, the latter alternating with clips from Disney's Goofy. This could almost be a student primer on the scopic drive, the "reality" of the image, and the violence of the cut. The film also includes demonstrations of reverse-motion photography à la Cocteau, and fragments of the soundtrack of the Russian version of *King Lear* (1969) by Grigori Kozinstev, played here as another "Professor" by the curator of the Cinémathèque Suisse, Freddy Buache. The philosopher Timothy Murray highlights Godard's postapocalyptic project and his stress on the recovery of cinematic history and montage now that perspective had been "abolished" and the vanishing point "erased." He talks of the distancing here and generally in late Godard from an art of resemblance for the sake of a cinema of affect. For Murray, the film champions in Deleuzian terms the idealism of pure

montage and the generative passions of the clash of its "incompossible" systems of analogue and digital representation. For it situates the new electronic meaning of cinema in relation to the contemplation of the radicality of silence and its impact on the law in Shakespeare: the doubled image, the silence of the break, and the gap of sequentiality sustain the rule of what Deleuze calls Godard's cinema of incommensurabilty. See Murray 2000: 178.

12. See Witt 1999 for an excellent introduction to Godard's continually evolving discourse on the end(s) of cinema.

13. One brief example will suffice: "When you say good-bye to someone, you feel like saying a little something, or making a sign, a gesture, returning the ball. But it's only in sport that one can communicate" (Bergala 1998: 126). Godard will later distill these world-weary thoughts in his 1991 poem, "La Paroisse morte" (The dead parish) (in Bergala 1998: 254).

14. Agamben 2000: 59–60.

15. Malraux is, of course, a key figure in later Godard precisely because of his humanist belief in the resurrectional status of art as a means of transcendence, or "antidestiny," and thus as a revolt against man's fate (the phrase "art is what is reborn in what has been burnt" is heard throughout *Histoire(s)*).

16. What is delivered in *King Lear* is a slightly revised version of the first part of Reverdy's prose poem: "The image is a pure creation of the soul. It cannot be born of the comparison but of a reconciliation of two realities that are more or less far apart. The more the connection between these two realities is distant and true, the stronger the image will be, the more it will have emotive power. Two realities that have no connection cannot be drawn together usefully. There is no creation of an image. One rarely obtains forces and power from this opposition. An image is not strong because it is brutal or fantastic, but because the association of ideas is distant and true. Analogy is a medium of creation. It is a resemblance of connections. The power or virtue of the created image depends on the nature of these connections. What is great is not the image but the emotion that it provokes. If the latter is great, one esteems the image at its measure. The emotion thus provoked is true because it is born outside of all imitation, all evocation and all resemblance."

17. See Saxton 2014 for an excellent account of the processes of cinematic montage and video superimposition in these two works which produce an energetics of gesture across form.

18. Murray 2010: 90.

19. Morgan unpacks a complex genealogy of political action and moral responsibility at the heart of the film's work on matters of aesthetics, linking the hands to Denis de Rougemont's key concept of "thinking with one's hands" ("penser avec les mains") promoted repeatedly in Godard's later work. See Morgan 2013.

20. See Morgan 2013: 45, 242.

21. Godard remarks briefly of the music in the film that it "expresses the spiritual" and "provides inspiration"; "there's nothing to understand, only to hear and take" (Bergala 1998: 123).

22. Agamben 2000: 79.

23. This is part of Godard's crucial idea of human beings projecting themselves onto something greater (the world, the cosmos), an instinct he regards as now extinguished in the West. See Morgan 2013: 206–12 for an excellent summary of Godard's evolving theory of projection and its different modalities in the later corpus, where the term involves the mode of exhibition and the different spaces and sizes in which images are seen (206). Cinema is always conceived by Godard according to the theatrical, Lumière model, that is, of a large public screen and collective experience. This is cinema as a projection of the world at a given time, and it is a fundamentally democratic and egalitarian, if not utopian, space

(everybody sees more or less the same thing simultaneously). Further, projection makes possible an open set of relations between viewer and screen: our experience in a theater is one of forming connections and associations (including historical) because we are reminded of films and events not explicitly contained within, or referred to by, the film being screened. The concept of projection becomes more complex and controversial when Godard applies it to the processes of history itself, for instance, with his notion of the law of stereo in *JLG/JLG* whereby Germany "projected" the Jews into an autonomous state (i.e., Germany generated out of itself the state of Israel), and Israel then "projected" the Palestinians. We shall explore the issues raised by Godard's formulation of Israeli-Palestinian relations in chapter 6.

24. Strangely, this passage from the French translation of the novel is absent from the American edition.

25. We noted in chapter 2 the mantra-like recurrence in Godard's later work of Bresson's key theory: "If an image looked at separately expresses something clearly, and if it presents an interpretation, it will not transform itself on contact with other images. Other images will have no power over it, and it will have no power over images. Neither action nor reaction" (Bresson 1995: 23).

26. Broch 1983: 481–82.

27. Contrast this positing of innocence within the framework of projection with Agamben's very short yet striking essay on cinematic illusion and fantasy, "The Most Beautiful Six Minutes in the History of Cinema," his reading of a silent sequence from Orson Welles's unfinished *Don Quixote* set in the 1950s. Agamben writes that the scene really is about the destroying of an illusion of child innocence in the form of a young girl Dulcie (Agamben suggests Dulcinea) who looks at Don Quixote "reprovingly" after he has slashed down the screen of a public movie theater in his effort to "save" a woman in distress projected suddenly in the image (a figure for his idealized Dulcinea whom he has never met). Agamben concludes: "But when they [our fantasies] prove in the end to be empty and unfulfilled, when they show the void from which they were made, then it is time to pay the price for their truth, to understand that Dulcinea—whom he saved—cannot love us." See Agamben 2007: 63–64. In Agamben, there exists no projection or nostalgic fantasy of an original purity or freedom in children that can be retrieved, relayed, or championed through the "decreating" powers of cinema. As Murray glosses, "the young girl we hope to save, Quixotic in our imaginings, can never love us; our imagination must be exposed as 'empty and unfulfilled' in order that we can begin to reconstruct a new form of image, a new poetics that denies imagination as a distortion of the here and now, as cinema so often does" (Murray 2010: 92). By contrast, in *Soigne ta droite*, despite having the French window slammed on her repeatedly, there is no reproach or recrimination in the face of the young girl. For Godard this is always the *aesthetic* challenge: to make love and mutual understanding (and redemption) possible. During such moments Godard takes the risks of essentialism and nostalgia and positively embraces them as a fundamentalist badge of courage and optimism against the odds. For Godard, any fantasy that might be provoked by the projected image is not the crucial aspect. As long as there is a projection at the macrolevel in the form of a public screening that brings people together, or at the microlevel in the form of an act of cinematic montage that brings together the distant and dissimilar, there is always reason for hope. For the record, Godard also references Welles's film in episode 1A of *Histoire(s)* with a still of Pancho Sanchez as one of an illustrious list of cinema history's unfinished films.

28. Robinson 1988: 22.

29. Agamben 2000: 79.

30. Habib 2001.

31. See Bachelard 1992: 103–11. I am indebted to Douglas Morrey for this reference. See Morrey 2005: 167.

32. Agamben 2000: 60.

Chapter 5

1. See *Godard/Jousse: Les écrans sonores de Jean-Luc Godard* (Paris: France Culture and Harmonia Mundi, 2000).

2. Godard's original plan for *Notre Musique* as a tribute to Eicher and his ECM family of musicians and composers never materialized. However, in the short "Projet de Film" that Godard initially wrote for *Notre Musique*, he raises particular issues about music that will preoccupy us in this chapter, namely music as a vehicle of hope able to speak to us in a way that television and the press no longer can, with honesty and fervor, and, more suggestively, music as constituting in itself an entire film. See Brenez et al. 2006: 410–11 which also includes my own brief interview with Eicher where he talks of his extensive collaboration with Godard in terms of affinity and intuition, emphasizing that decisions jointly taken are always artistic rather than analytical.

3. Exceptions to this critical norm include Delvaux 1988b, Jousse 1991, Aumont 1991, Jullier 2001 and Jullier 2004.

4. Cited in Bartoli 1997: 69.

5. For a succinct analysis of some of the strategies of fragmentation employed by Godard in his 1960s films, for example, preventing a melody from developing and randomly cutting into it to give it an analytical charge, see Aumont 1996: 265–69. See also Roustom 2014 for a useful account of Godard's use of Michel Legrand's multifaceted score for *Une femme est une femme*, Godard's brilliant reworking of the Hollywood musical which crystallized his disjunctive approach to music in the early corpus. Orlene Denice McMahon offers a far more critical assessment of Godard's "omnipotent" strategies towards the music he either borrowed or commissioned during this period, which she contrasts with the more complex and radical engagement with music by Left Bank group filmmakers such as Alain Resnais and Agnès Varda. See McMahon 2014.

6. Kancheli's orchestral work, *Abii ne viderem* (I turned away so as not to see) (1992–94), for example, provides a foundational structure for episode 4A. See Witt 2013: 198–208 for an excellent overview of the extensive use of music in *Histoire(s)*, which presents Godard expressly as a sound artist and sonic innovator and argues that this unique polyphonic work of sampling and orchestration of disparate sound materials (from music CDs to archival film soundtracks) might be more appropriately called "*Histoire(s) de la musique*." In ways that will connect with our own formal analysis of other works by Godard since the mid-1980s, Witt shows how the function of prerecorded music in *Histoire(s)* can sometimes shift very quickly (e.g., from underscoring an emotion articulated in the image to operating in counterpoint with it), how the sound level can jump dramatically from very loud to barely audible and *vice versa*, and how, like the image, sound can be manipulated through altered motion. Witt also highlights Godard's remarkable ear for the inherent musicality of the human voice, as evidenced by the multiple extracts of songs and the countless recordings of authors, actors, and filmmakers (from Paul Celan, Ezra Pound, and Fernand Braudel to Alain Cuny, Julie Delpy, Jean Renoir, and Alfred Hitchcock, among many others), and by the omnipresence of his own voice (including his method of saying different things through the two speakers at the same time as if there were two, three, or four of him). Episode 4A even includes

a reading of Paul Valéry's poem "Psaume sur une voix" in praise of the unique, expressive force of the voice, although Godard typically moves here between two different renditions of the same text.

7. See Alex Ross's fascinating article entitled "Ghost Sonata: What Happened to German Music?," which argues that German composers still fetishize and make a virtue out of ugly dissonance (the comfort of C major, for example, is taboo), so keen are they to forget the recent past, the fact, for example, that Hitler had Beethoven played in the camps (Ross 2003: 8). Compare with *For Ever Mozart*, where the section devoted to music takes pride of place at the end and the actual playing of Mozart by Les Jeunes de Fribourg is very limited. Indeed, the faint, muffled cello sounds of Darling quickly arrive with the final credits to function almost as a safety curtain.

8. See Bogue 2007: 69–89 for an interesting Deleuzian analysis of Godard's use of Beethoven's late string quartets in *Prénom Carmen*, which refers both to Deleuze's thoughts on the film in *Cinéma 2: L'image-temps* and to Beethoven's *Tagebuch* of 1812–18, cited directly and liberally in the film. According to Bogue, Godard "accepts Beethoven and allows the Quartets to serve as the milieu within which the film takes shape. If there is a dominant spirit to *Prénom Carmen*, it is that of the Beethoven score [. . .] *Prénom Carmen* is no tragedy, but if Nietzsche's spirit of tragedy is that of the artist-creator, and if that spirit is also the spirit of music, then this film, like tragedy, is born of the spirit of music" (Bogue 2007: 86). Bogue quotes Deleuze who talks of the combined use of sound and music forming "the power [*puissance*] of a single and self-same sonic continuum"—one that becomes a fourth dimension of the visual image, in which the sonic elements "rival one another, cover one another, traverse each other, cut into each other" (cited in Bogue 2007: 87). Yet Bogue emphasizes that *Prénom Carmen* "also makes use of Western tonal music in a way that links the film to the classic cinema, its quartet score functioning as does music in Nietzsche's conception of tragedy [. . .] What this suggests, finally, is that music provides common ground for the classic and modern cinema. Perhaps cinema as a whole, like tragedy, has one of its points of origin in the spirit of music—the generative ear latent in the eye" (ibid).

9. See Fox 2014 for an enlightening study of all aspects of the soundtrack in *Sauve qui peut*, from the use of Yared's theme music to an extract from an operatic aria (from Amilcare Ponchielli's dramatic opera, *La Gioconda* [1876]) and the diegetic musical passage in the closing tracking sequence. Fox draws upon Pierre Schaeffer's early essay on the relay arts to explore the idea of "acousmatic sound" in the film where the listening body and the process of listening come directly under the spotlight. See also Fox 2015 for a sustained analysis of what she terms "acoustic spectatorship" in Godard's 1980s film and video work.

10. David Wills takes direct issue with me on this particular point, stating that Godard's use of music from 1980 onwards is not premised on music as an ineffable mystery. Arguing that Godard is moving in *Éloge de l'amour* towards an outside of cinema and a "music-image," he remarks: "I would have that musical outside of cinema understood precisely as history ([*de*] *l'histoire*), in contrast to just a story (*une histoire*), according to the delineation that is consistently made explicit in *Éloge de l'amour*" (Wills 2010: 56). Connecting this process with the central theme in *Éloge* of a sovereign love that can never be represented ("which is where the film leads by means of Bataille, into a black screen that does not reduce simply to no image but rather tends towards a music-image" [ibid.]), Wills asserts: "As long as the image is relating to what is outside it, a 'crystal image' in Deleuze's terms, 'the indivisible unity of an actual image and "its" virtual image,' I would maintain that cinema is precisely prevented from falling, or leaping, via 'music' into the ineffable" (ibid.). Yet Wills also relies directly on the metaphors of *Notre Musique* in order to suggest a kind of "visual montage

of music, ceding the image to a type of sovereignty that exceeds it." He concludes: "[O]ur music [. . .] is understood also as the montage of our night, something seen beyond vision, something seen heard on the other side of the image" (ibid.: 61).

11. Cited in Douin 1994: 99–100.

12. See Aumont 1991: 47. Aumont interprets the end of *Sauve qui peut* as music's "revenge" after having been kept too much at a distance. This is a specifically feminine and maternal revenge, since Godard's alter ego will be eternally irritated by what he will hear finally as the music of his own death.

13. For a detailed and illuminating account of the complex interaction of the image-track and soundtrack in *Armide* which reveals a "chiasmatic design" of musical and visual motifs, see Latham 1998.

14. See Serrut 2011 for a comprehensive breakdown of all the instances and uses of sound and music in a selection of Godard's major films up to and including *Nouvelle Vague*.

15. Unlike Jullier who focuses on Godard's primary attraction for tonal music (in particular its ECM "postmodern" variant) as opposed to modernist atonal music (see Jullier 2004), I shall not be making any real distinction here between different forms of classical and modern music in Godard's work. Indeed, I will argue that what is crucial is not the particular music Godard chooses but rather how he uses it. On a related note, Jullier posits in the form of a rhetorical question that Godard chose ECM's melodic tracks, and edited and transposed them more spectacularly in order to highlight his own manipulation of them. The implication here of a deliberately soft musical backdrop to Godard's later work also lies behind the idea articulated by James Quandt that Godard's predilection for contemporary (ECM) composers like Pärt, Federico Mompou, and Hans Otte (whose felted, minimalist composition *Das Buch der Klänge* is employed at length in the 2000 video short, *De l'origine du XXIe siècle*) indicates a conservative sensibility in art and music (Quandt 2004: 420, endnote 8). Yet, as we shall see, if Godard were actually to engage with more avant-garde contemporary composers such as Luciano Berio (for example, his *Sinfonia* (1968–9) which takes the form of a complex collage in which spoken and sung texts in many languages are combined with a highly intricate orchestral score), this could potentially duplicate and cancel out the particular weft and warp of his own compound sound textures.

16. See Katherine Dieckmann's interview with Godard in Locke and Warren 1994: 121.

17. Ibid.: 120.

18. Ibid.: 121.

19. Ibid.

20. Michel Chion has celebrated *Je vous salue, Marie* as a film where Godard imposed the rule not to use more than two audio tracks at any given time, giving rise to what Chion terms very suggestively "sound shots" (Chion 2004: 42–44). Yet Chion offers a generally more negative appraisal of Godard's development of sound experimentation, highlighting the shortcomings of Godard's more explicit and complex work on music and sound using Dolby stereo. He states: "Neither in *Détective* nor *Soigne ta droite* does he [Godard] offer anything original in lapping and joining of sounds, by comparison to what he already achieved in monaural films; in addition, for *Nouvelle Vague* he has returned to his usual monophonic technique" (ibid.: 153). My following discussion of *Nouvelle Vague* aims to disprove Chion's sweeping judgment.

21. "La musique est la plus forte [. . .] c'est elle qui soutient tout" (Bergala 1998: 390).

22. Bartoli 1997: 76–77.

23. The sentence is almost certainly derived from a passage in a 1959 article by Michel Mourlet in *Cahiers du Cinéma* 98 entitled "Sur un art ignoré," where he writes:

"Since cinema is a gaze which is substituted for our own in order to give us a world that corresponds to our desires [*un regard qui se substitue au nôtre pour nous donner un monde accordé à nos désirs*], it settles on faces, on radiant or bruised but always beautiful bodies, on this glory or devastation which testifies to the same primordial nobility, on this chosen race that we recognize as our own, the ultimate projection of life towards God" (Mourlet 1959: 34). I am indebted to Jonathan Rosenbaum for this discovery. See Rosenbaum 1997.

24. See Swed 2000 (included in the promotional dossier for the 2000 CD box-set of *Histoire(s) du cinéma* containing reviews and interviews).

25. Paul Hindemith (1895–1963), hounded in Germany by the Nazis, was eventually forced into exile in the United States (via Switzerland): Béla Bartók (1881–1945) left Hungary in 1940 when the Horthy government aligned itself with the Nazis and died from leukemia in straitened circumstances in exile in the United States; Anton Webern (1883–1945) was shot dead by friendly fire in Mittersill at the end of the war; Dmitri Shostakovich (1906–75) was constrained for much of his life and career by a totalitarian regime.

26. See Godard's interview with Michèle Halberstadt (Halberstadt 2002), where Godard talks of cinema as essentially a lyrical art form. For an analysis of the lyrical in Godard's work, see Martin 2004.

27. This is the subtitle of Godard's very frank interview with Jean-Pierre Dufreigne around *Éloge de l'amour* in *L'Express*, May 4, 2001.

28. Kaja Silverman and Harun Farocki argue persuasively that since this gift cannot be possessed, it neither bankrupts the one who gives nor indebts the one who receives. The giver gladly gives, and the receiver gladly receives. They even propose *Nouvelle Vague* as Godard's account of heterosexuality at the end of the twentieth century. See Silverman and Farocki 1998: 197–227. Strangely, however, they barely mention the use and value of music in *Nouvelle Vague*, simply recording the fact that Godard uses only the initial nineteenth-century part of Schoenberg's *The Transfigured Night*. In a separate article, Silverman also describes *JLG/JLG* in terms of the gift, claiming that in this film existence is effectively defined as the giver, the world as the gift, and the author as the receiver. Godard, she suggests, will attempt to become the blank surface in which the world inscribes itself. See Silverman 2001.

29. See Žižek 1999, especially "The Politics of Truth, or, Alain Badiou as a Reader of St Paul" (127–70), and Žižek 2000, in particular "The Breakout" (143–60). Žižek bases his argument on his reading of Badiou 1988 and Badiou 1997. For Žižek, Badiou's four main "*génériques*" (love, art, science, politics) are ways of reinscribing the encounter with the Real Thing on to the symbolic texture. Interestingly, when Badiou writes specifically about *Histoire(s)* in Badiou 1998, he makes no attempt to relate his theories of the Truth-Event to Godard's actual work. We note in passing that Badiou appears as himself in the later *Film socialisme* but in the ironic form of a "nonevent": he lectures on "geometry as origin" (as the film's subtitles have it) to an empty theater on board the otherwise packed cruise liner.

30. Ibid.: 212.

31. Ibid.: 162.

32. Ibid.: 212.

33. "The Carrots are Cooked:" interview with Gideon Bachman (1983), cited in Sterritt 1998: 132.

34. "Jean-Luc Godard rencontre Régis Debray" in Bergala 1998: 429.

35. We recall that *Je vous salue, Marie* was heavily influenced by Dolto's reading of the Gospels in *L'Évangile au risque de la psychoanalyse* (1977), in particular the initial chapters which are directly cited in an early version of the script reproduced in Bergala 1985: 590–92. For a well-informed discussion of the links between Dolto's book and Godard's film, see

Laugier 1993 which argues that *Je vous salue, Marie* constitutes "a perplexed interrogation on the nature of Dolto's work" (30).

36. See Žižek 2001: 134–35.

37. See Guerin 2001:11. Guerin also makes the following highly suggestive statement: "There is no-one other [than Godard] to give actors this chance to know nothing of the story or mystery they are playing or figure in, yet still be sure of the art and beauty in the director's look and the period they are playing" (ibid.: 15).

38. See Taubin 2002: 52. Taubin observes correctly that if the images depend on variety and surprise (the framings are nearly always unexpected), there is rarely any cutting on movement, and each image retains its identity. We might add that the arresting black-and-white documentary views of Paris, which appear so free and spontaneous when intercut with black spacing, each acquire the status of a visual event and allow the viewer to see Paris as if for the first time.

39. This is not completely the case, however. The last thing we hear is a fragmented and slightly altered version of Edgar's opening voice-over text to the actress. What was: "and then again/ the first moment/ you remember the names/ no, no/ perhaps it wasn't said" (leading to: "and if we asked you/ that it was you/ that you had the choice . . ."), becomes in a solitary voiceover by Edgar: "if we asked you/ that it was you/ that you had the choice [. . .] and then, well,/ the first moment/ you remember the names/ perhaps/ it wasn't said/ perhaps it wasn't/ said." The last phrase is repeated altogether four times by Edgar and recited over the final instance of black spacing.

40. Compare this result with that of the contemporaneous short by Godard and Miéville, *Dans le noir du temps*, a contribution to the omnibus film *Ten Minutes Older: The Cello* (2002) and presented as the hypothetical ten final minutes of the world, each appearing with a title. The continuous playing of Pärt's slow, miniaturist composition for piano and cello, *Spiegel im Spiegel* (1978), one of the few cases where Godard makes primary or even exclusive use of a single preexisting work of music, or movement from such a work, like a film score (other examples include *Lettre à Freddy Buache, De l'origine du XXIe siècle,* and *Liberté et Patrie*), is interrupted only temporarily by a brief extract from a song by Miéville. Such blanket use of Pärt (specifically the ECM recording performed by Dietmar Schwalke and Alexander Malter which lasts just under nine minutes) has a smothering and chilling effect on the film as a whole, and it appears at first blush to chime very uncomfortably with the pathos of the image with its stuttering "last visions" and Godard's spoken plea for compassion. The musicologist Jürg Stenzl makes persuasive claims, however, for the consistent correspondences between the structure of the music and the "sectional articulation" of the images in his detailed technical reading of the short as the "filming of a musical form" whereby film and music reflect one another contrapuntally. He notes two basic features of the music: the internal unity of the evolving process creating the impression of a successively and imperceptibly evolving circular motion, "a motion rooted to the spot"; and the constantly changing nature of the deliberately limited musical material through octave transpositions in high and low registers, which opens up a "successively expanding tonal space" (Stenzl 2014: 20). He adds: "this 'global processuality' of *Spiegel im Spiegel*—a circular movement *in situ*—entails a continuous spatialization of the sound, thereby preventing the visual dynamism of the film from conflicting with musical staticity" (ibid.: 20–1). Stenzl concludes that "Godard's musico-pictorial montage is based on a masterly handling of time and motion within time—a mastery both cinematic and musical in nature [. . .] The correspondences between the pictorial quotations for the ten 'final minutes' and the structural divisions of the music used in the film are all rooted in a cyclical structure. The music appears ahistorical,

but in the Minute 4, 'Les dernières minutes de la mémoire,' it falls silent, faced with the 'ineradicable' ('L'imprescriptible') of the concentration camp images. It is restored to audibility at 'Les dernières minutes de l'amour' to coincide with the singing of Anne-Marie Miéville's chanson 'Dites-moi quand il est temps de partir, l'heure de mourir'" (ibid.: 24). It is precisely by falling silent and then returning to audibility, Stenzl suggests compellingly, "that music is able to generate the deep impact of this moment" (ibid.).

41. The quote in full from Bataille (which recurs in different forms throughout the film and is wrongly attributed to his 1957 novel, Le Bleu du ciel) reads as follows: "Nothing could be farther from the image of the loved one than that of the State whose reason is opposed to the sovereign value of love. The State does not have, or it has lost, the power to embrace before us the whole of the world, that totality of the universe which is given at once outside, in the loved one as object, and inside, in the lover as subject." Douglas Morrey has also underlined the significance of this quote in a fine discussion of history and resistance in Éloge, but the conclusions he draws for our understanding of love in the film are a little different. Morrey states that "love can only be known as a kind of grieving memory for a promise never fulfilled, whose trace remains in those indefinable alterations we notice in ourselves. In the same way, the total view of history is forever deferred by the work of history that is never finished, since it endlessly generates more history and thus more work, even as the effects of history begin to shape our lives. Love and history, then, bring us into contact with our necessary failure to attain them, and it is this painful consciousness of the limits of our thought that drives thought inexorably forwards." See Morrey 2003: 128. While Morrey is certainly right to make parallels between love and history in terms of an unattainable "absolute vision," I am suggesting in addition that the performance of music in Éloge (which Morrey does not explore) redefines history as memory and serves to transport love to a different level: that of the potential uniting of self and other through music which, with each successive note, is continually delivering on its promise.

Chapter 6

1. The tone of "Projet de film" is at once idealistic (music is placed defiantly above politics) and intimate (Shostakovitch, for instance, is referred to as "Tovaritch Chosta"). Yet Godard's text also falls squarely under literary influence with its allusion to Paul Claudel and a quote from Rilke, now a virtual commonplace in his work: "For Beauty's but nothing but beginning of Terror we're just able to bear." The twelve-line rhyming poem by Godard entitled "Le film," included in the press-book of Notre Musique, adopts a very different approach. It is not only about film in general but also directly political, addressing both the nature of the medium and its problematic status and value as a market and industry. Music, conveyed now in the plural ("Voici les musiques"), is to be regarded not simply in literal terms but also at a figurative and abstract level as a form of communality, understanding, and love. This idea is framed in terms of the "contre-champ," with Godard setting in play a set of interrelated aesthetic, ethical, and political themes: the morality of good and bad; reality and social relations; artistic freedom and responsibility in the cinema. Pitched at this higher, more universal level and unhampered by individual names, the poem has an ethereal, almost messianic feel ("Et vers le paradis voici l'achèvement/ Et voici notre amour et notre entendement"). In this passage from prose to poetry, we have moved from the concrete location and identity of music to the actuality of the present ("voici l'instant") and its beyond. See Williams 2006a which reproduces Godard's short prose piece "Projet de film"

and reveals that, as so often in Godard's work, the completed film marks only one stage of an organically developing project encompassing different media.

2. The particular importance of this sequence for Godard is emphasized by the fact that it also reappears in *Vrai faux passeport* (2006) and *Film socialisme*. While pursuing distinctly different artistic careers due to their individual backgrounds and chosen fields, the trajectories of Godard and Darwish from the early 1970s onwards followed a similar pattern. Both moved from direct political activism (the period of Darwish's "poetry of resistance" after joining the Communist Party in 1961 coincides roughly with the years of Godard's militant filmmaking) to a progressively more introspective, contemplative, and philosophical approach to their chosen medium.

3. See Witt 2005: 30. When Godard mentions two of the twentieth century's greatest physicists and uses the term "uncertainty," he is opening up still further the interpretative frame. Bohr's pupil Heisenberg went on to formulate the "Uncertainty Principle," which states that one cannot precisely determine both the momentum and the position of a particle at the same time. One of Bohr's theories which particularly influenced Heisenberg was the principle of correspondence between macrophysics and microphysics. It recalls the fundamental structural importance in this film of "correspondences" and also the "interactive" rather than merely passive role, in microphysics, of the scientific observer. Both of those theories may be linked, at least in the abstract, to Godard's cinema.

4. In his analysis of *The Old Place* Witt explores in detail the Benjaminian source for a poetic "constellation" linking past and present—a term used, like "flash," in a key reflection in *The Arcades Project* and also the "Theses on the Philosophy of History" where Benjamin develops the notion of "Jetztzeit" ("now-time" or the "here-and-now") to explain how an encounter with a work of art can suddenly explode the continuum of history." See Witt 2013: 183. The evocation of what Godard terms here an "ever-present landscape" offers for Witt a simultaneously optimistic and bleak vision of history. Indeed, the images clustered at this point in the film include archive images of Jewish children showing a camp number seared on their arms accompanied by the screen-text "Stars of David." We have already noted Godard's recurring use from *King Lear* onwards of Pierre Reverdy's poetics of *rapprochement* encapsulated in the proposition from "L'Image" (1918): "the reconciliation of two realities that are more or less far apart." This may also be compared with his use of Raymond Queneau's poem "L'explication des métaphores" (from the 1943 collection *Les Ziaux*), a key point of reference around the time of *Les Enfants jouent à la Russie* (1993), which includes the line "As thin as a hair, as vast as the dawn" (for Queneau an exemplary metaphor). The idea here that it is the relationship between the terms "hair" and "dawn" which creates the image consolidates Godard's core belief that an image implies a relationship. The specific links between metaphor and relationality in Godard's work have been explored by Leo Bersani in a discussion of what he calls the incongruous pairings or "couplings" in *Passion*—between, for example, the gestures of work and the gestures of love, and a woman feeling abandoned by a man and Christ on the cross asking his Father why he has abandoned him. "In each case," Bersani writes, "we have an analogy without similitude or, at most, one in which the likeness between terms is faint, remote, incongruous" (Bersani 2015: 65). Bersani argues that such analogies are fundamentally different from Proustian metaphors in which two terms are presented as having a common essence: "The singularity of Godard's similitudes is the insignificance or even the irrelevance of likeness itself to an irreducibly incongruous repetition (of two kinds of traces or two examples of abandonment) or to a comparison of terms (such as the thematic yoking together of love and work in *Passion*)" (ibid.: 65–66). Hence, Bersani claims, Godard allows us to rethink "alikeness" by shattering

the grounds on which we are accustomed to granting epistemological authority for analogic thinking. For Bersani, this implied movement of dissimilar terms toward one another is radical and affirmative since it exposes the potential for potentiality and points to a productively relational, rather than intrinsically oppositional, presence in the world. Bersani's bold reading is extremely suggestive yet it takes place outside any concrete consideration of history or politics. What happens when Godard formalizes his metaphorical and relational thinking into a theory of dissymmetrical *rapprochement* and then applies it to one of the most complex and contested areas of world politics, namely Middle East relations, will be the central and urgent question of this chapter.

5. Strangely Barr makes no mention of the figure of the Palestinians in his reading of *Notre Musique*, which thus remains incomplete. I will be arguing here that the Palestinian question constitutes the implicit crux of the film.

6. Other instances of the always-present Third in *Notre Musique* encompass both the human and the inanimate. James Clark notes, for example, that in the final one-on-one dialogue scene in the film between Cumier and "C. Maillard" in the bar, we see only two pairs of hands and yet three glasses on a table in a subtly striking yet balanced composition (the trio of glasses run along the central vertical axis, while the hands, notebook, and ashtray define the central horizontal line). Godard is heard in a voice-off at the start of the sequence talking briefly about the nature of democracy but is not visually present. Could it be, Clark suggests, "that the third glass is for *you* [i.e., the viewer]—an invitation to pick up the thread of his characters' argument and continue developing it for yourself?" See Clark 2005.

7. Slavoj Žižek has claimed that such a solution is far too neat, since far from being reducible to the symmetric domain of equality and distributive justice, politics is the very "impossible" link between this domain and that of (theological) ethics, which cuts across the symmetry of equal relations, distorting and displacing them. In his *Ethics and Infinity*, Levinas emphasizes how what appears as the most natural should become the most questionable—like Spinoza's notion that every entity naturally strives for its self-perseverance, for the full assertion of its being and its immanent powers: do I have (the right) to be? Is it not that by insisting in being, I deprive others of their place, I ultimately kill them? What one should fully acknowledge and endorse, argues Žižek, is that Levinas's stance is radically antibiopolitical: the Levinasian ethics is the absolute opposite of today's biopolitics with its emphasis on regulating life and deploying its potentials. For Levinas, ethics is not about life, but about something more than life. It is at this level that Levinas locates the gap that separates Judaism and Christianity—Judaism's fundamental ethical task is that of how "to be without being a murderer." Žižek sees a problem here, however, suggesting that although Levinas asserts this asymmetry as universal (every one of us is in the position of primordial responsibility towards others), this asymmetry ends up effectively privileging one particular group which assumes responsibility for all others, which embodies in a privileged way this responsibility, and directly stands for it—in this case, Jews–"so that, again, one is ironically tempted to speak of the 'Jewish man's (ethical) burden.'" See Žižek 2005a. Žižek develops some of these ideas further in Žižek 2005b where he proposes the idea of "excess" to rehabilitate a positive sense of the inhuman and so challenge the influence of Levinas on contemporary ethical thought.

8. Wright is drawing directly on Irène Heidelberger-Leonard's study of Améry's philosophy. Améry's philosophy may be linked with that of the "*imprescriptible*" and the 1971 book of the same name by the French Jewish philosopher and musicologist Vladimir Jankélévitch (directly evoked in *Éloge de l'amour*), which insists on no pardon or forgiveness for Nazi crimes.

9. See Emmelhainz 2009 for a brilliant contextualizing doctoral study of *Notre Musique*, at once formal, historical, theoretical, and political, in terms of leftist ideology and the changing nature of political engagement with what was once considered the Third World other due to the increased mediatization of politics since the 1970s and new attitudes to Third World subjects now figured as "terrorists" or "victims" incapable of determining themselves politically or developing economically (ii). For reasons that will become clearer later in the chapter, her major point of cinematic reference is Godard and Miéville's *Ici et ailleurs*. Her conclusion is that reconciliation and rehabilitation represent the reverse-shot of a world of violent ethnic strife evidencing the futility of the politicization of forgiveness. However, her essential claim that *Notre musique* is proposing the beautiful as the only thing that can "cover" the memories of catastrophe, and that the aestheticopolitical task is to regulate the distance between the viewer and the screen on condition of a "belief in images, faith and the desire to see as our links to the world" (424) (in other words, a call for the "exception" of art), would appear to be undermined by her misreading of a key statement by Godard in *Notre Musique* (filtered via Céline) that we shall come to a little later in our discussion. She appears to mistranslate "the field of the text has already integrated [*recouvert*, literally "covered up"] that of vision" as: "'the text as having been re-covered by the image'" (422), which makes the image the subject of the act of "re-covering," with a suggestion also of recovery. Such ambiguity complicates still further the overall title of Emmelhainz's thesis, "Before Our Eyes: Les mots, non les choses. Jean-Luc Godard's *Ici et ailleurs* (1970–4) and *Notre Musique* (2004)," a title that on the face of it is wholly inappropriate since for Godard it is always a matter of "les choses, non les mots." Fortunately, this troubling point of confusion does not jeopardize the overall success of her complex and well-detailed argument.

10. Péqueux, who in 1995 was also put in charge of rebuilding six other bridges spanning the Neretva River, wanted to reconstruct the Mostar bridge (commissioned by Suleiman the Magnificent and built in 1566 by the Ottoman architect Hayyedin with 456 blocks of stone) as closely as possible to the original by reviving and teaching Muslim and Croat masons Ottoman techniques. Ironically, having been retrieved one by one from the river and individually numbered, the original stones were never actually used and Péqueux was summarily dismissed from his position and replaced by a Croat who made a bridge like any other, constructed out of local stone clad to make it look authentic. The blocks of the original bridge are now located in a spot the inhabitants of Mostar call "the cemetery of stones." The bridge finally reopened on July 23, 2004 (after *Notre Musique* was completed) and serves again as one of the few conduits of social and cultural exchange in what remains an ethnically divided town.

11. Darwish 2000: 289. The poem was also adapted for the stage December 2004 as *Masques blancs, Peaux Rouges* at the Théâtre de la Digue in Toulouse.

12. The speech in question is almost certainly Chief Seattle's moving treaty oration of 1854 to the newly arrived governor of the Washington Territory, heard by as many as one thousand Suquamish tribespeople on the banks of the Whulge. It contains a message of the enduring mark placed on the earth by generations of Suquamish, never to be erased by future history. No speech given by a Native American has been so widely quoted. Current research, however, is now casting doubt on the authenticity of the speech which exists in three different versions.

13. See Darwish 2003a. Darwish's collection of poems entitled *Murale* is imbued with melancholic anguish and yearning, yet the work skirts the realm of death the better to glorify life. Like the closing stages of *Histoire(s)*, the included poems insist as much on the possibilities of reversal and transformation, of eternity reconquered and the comfort

of resurrection, as they do on the forces of the unseen and the unknowable. See Darwish 2003b. An extensive comparative study could, in fact, be made of the formal techniques uniting Darwish and Godard, for instance, their shared preference for the rhythms of reversal, paradox, irony, and oxymoron (e.g., Darwish's bittersweet invocation of the "present-absent," Israel's label for internal Palestinian refugees whose lands it wanted to confiscate when the State was established), their common attraction for generative metaphors, and their equivalent rhetorical strategies (anaphora in the case of Darwish, chiasmus for Godard). Indeed, entire passages of Ibrahim Muhawi's excellent introduction to Darwish's poetics in the English edition of Darwish's 1995 collection *Une Mémoire pour l'oubli* could just as easily be applied to Godard's filmic practice in *Notre Musique*, for *champ/contre-champ* boils down, as we are seeing, to creating new associations, correspondences, and lines of difference, as well as still further metaphors. Muhawi has summed up Darwish's poetic method brilliantly as an attempt to create "a pure gesture in which writing itself becomes the dominant metaphor," resulting in "a multivocal text that resembles a broken mirror, reassembled to present the viewer with vying possibilities of clarity and fracture [. . .] Suspended between wholeness and fracture, the text, like Palestine, is a crossroads of competing meanings" (Darwish 1995: xxvi–xxvii).

14. We note in passing that Goytisolo had also published his 1988 "Journal Palestinien Juin 1988" in volume 29 of *Revue d'Études Palestiniennes*, the journal edited by Sanbar.

15. See Sanbar 2004a. The degree of mutual respect and theoretical convergence between Godard and Sanbar was illustrated when they appeared together following the release of *Notre Musique* at the Centre Culturel Le Volcan in Le Havre, which also hosted a photographic exhibit about Palestine organized by Sanbar. The topics of discussion included cinema, Israel and Palestine, *champ/contre-champ*, fiction and documentary. Sanbar expressed there his full admiration for Godard's film, in particular its fluid, liminal and nomadic status, and its foregrounding of an entire range of displaced people in transit and exile from their native land. For a transcription of the conversation held on November 5, 2004, see Godard 2004d.

16. In his theoretical introduction to the book entitled "Hors du lieu, hors du temps," which Godard himself considers of major importance to students of film, Sanbar presents his work of historical anthropology as "a subjective reflection on the *image* of the Palestinians" (original emphasis)–a task that proved all the more difficult for the very fact that the Palestinians did not really "exist," and indeed became "invisible" at key moments of their history. Sanbar also quotes Godard's interview with Alain Bergala (in Bergala 1998: 9–41) where Godard conceives of the image as a postcard composed invariably of three temporal elements (present, future, and past), and insists on the image as a process of montage. For Sanbar, who endorses Godard's notion of thinking in and through the "chains of images" in montage (Sanbar 2004a: 10–11), the technique of *champ/contre-champ* is Godard's "concept-couple" (ibid.: 12).

17. See Sanbar 2004a: 346.

18. Ibid.: 132.

19. See Sanbar 2004b: 145.

20. It perhaps goes without saying that Sarajevo serves also for Godard as a metaphor for cinema itself. He reasons thus: "Places like Sarajevo, Bosnia, or Palestine [. . .] which are, for the film-maker, places of exile with which he aligns himself are also a little bit of a metaphor for what the cinema has become for me, French cinema at least: a country still heavily dependent on subsidies, that can't survive by itself, that is under attack by the various forms of organized crime, that is drifting into prostitution. Cinema is an occupied

country with a governor, like the Roman governor of Palestine. Palestine, Sarajevo, the current cinema, these are all places of exile which is good for me because I've always felt profoundly exiled, because of family wars and cultural wars" (Godard 2005: 37).

21. Godard thinks now that this term was used by the Jewish prisoners themselves, suggesting in a 2005 interview that for the Jews the Muslim was a hereditary enemy who would not try to survive, whereas Judaism must survive irrespective of all difficulties. See Witt 2005: 30. For an excellent overview of Godard's treatment of the figure of the *Muselmann*, see Hori 2014. For Hori, Godard's continuous reflection on the term since the 1970s, when he adopted an avowed pro-Palestinian, anti-Zionist position, has tempered its sharp ideological overtones, turning it into "the emblem of an unfortunate repetition of history in a larger context." Citing Godard's statement in 1995 that Sarajevo as well as Beirut started in the camps when the Nazis called all-but-dead Jews *Muselmänner* ("People don't make a comparison"), Hori suggests that the term "designates a primal scene of repetitive calamities that Muslims have suffered in Lebanon, in Algeria, in Sarajevo" (Hori 2014: 74). According to Hori, this illustrates how Godard always highlights the repetitive aspects of historical events, regardless of their accuracy or preciseness: "His [Godard's] interest in history is less on events themselves than on how they are connected to each other, i.e. how to make a comparison (or montage) between several histories [. . .] Godard calls attention to the potential relations between Jews in camps and Muslims in Palestine or Sarajevo by making them collide from the (meta-)vantage point where he no longer manifestly supports the Palestinian cause" (ibid.: 75).

22. Interestingly, *Ici et ailleurs* also includes a sequence about "crossing," literally the crossing between life and death, when the Palestinian soldiers talk about how to cross a river without being spotted by the enemy. In a further example of continuity with *Notre Musique*, it ends with a personal statement by Godard and Miéville about how to see properly: "Learn to see here, in order to hear elsewhere. Learn to hear yourself speak to see what others do."

23. As Emmelhainz notes, the documentaries that have been made of Palestinians are characterized by oral testimonies that show people bearing witness to, and denouncing, the injustices. Hence, "[d]ocumentary is a form of expression that claims to be "bare" filmed records of events, allegedly repressing judgment and subjectivity" (Emmelhainz 2009: 656).

24. In *Notre musique* and elsewhere in his later work, Godard powerfully refuses any ethical call to bear immediate witness to interminable catastrophe that would seek to put all the emphasis on affect. This issue is addressed directly in Curnier's diatribe against the prevailing discourses of victimhood and witnessing during which he expresses his disgust with the intolerable public expression of misery that attempts to mobilize empathy and pity as political emotions: "That's why we give the floor to victims, and invite them all to express themselves as victims," he states, adding: "The world is today split in two, between those who line up to voice their misery and those for whom this public display provides a daily dose of moral comfort to their domination."

25. Narboni states that in the particular case of *Notre Musique*, Olga's suicide-attack tactic was clearly inspired by a recent Chechen terror attack in a Moscow theater using not books but stones, and which Godard crudely appropriated to pursue the idea of suicide. Speaking publicly after the film's premiere at the 2004 Cannes film festival, Chantal Akerman went further and claimed that the very idea that armed Israelis would simply gun down a Jew on the stage of a movie theater was itself anti-Semitic on Godard's part, since it implied that Israel was guilty of blind criminal violence. In his own later account of the production of *Morceaux de conversations avec Jean-Luc Godard*, Fleischer remarks that the fact that the plot-line of Olga's suicide revolves around books, so dear to the Jews, adds further insult to

injury and is a sign of Godard's "romantic perversity" (Fleisher 2011: 98). He also relates that during a break in filming Godard claimed to Narboni there was a parallel between Palestinian suicide attacks and the Jewish experience of the Holocaust, in that both represented a form of "sacrifice." For Fleischer, this "absurd" and "aberrant" remark exemplifies Godard's longstanding idea that European Jews went like lambs to the slaughter of the gas chambers in order ultimately to make possible the future state of Israel. Fleischer swiftly exposes the facile nature of this comparison between the forced and wholesale massacre of European Jews with the fate of individual Palestinians who choose to blow themselves up. See ibid.: 105.

26. We recall that in *Tout va bien* Jacques (Yves Montand) attributes his move into the more "honest" world of commercials to his realization, upon being asked to direct a film based on a Goodis detective novel, that he couldn't see himself making something "so stupid."

27. See Rascaroli 2009. Exploring *Notre Musique* as an "essay film" and Godard's shifting self-positioning as spectator, receiver, and "mirror," Rascaroli emphasizes the role of performance in the creation of the right conditions for a negotiation between director and audience.

28. Emmelhainz argues that Olga, who, like Godard, sees her books in her pocket as "friends," literally embodies the question of the image in the film: she struggles to remain a body, resists becoming a figure, and tests the image as mimesis. Indeed, she enacts the relationship between image and text as mimesis during Godard's master class, where she sits flipping over her lap title cards that are screen-texts in which her thoughts are written. See Emmelhainz 2009: 732.

29. Godard had played with a similar structure in *Éloge de l'amour*, but there Edgar's unfinished and impossible multiform "project" on Simone Weil is directly redeemed by the beauty of the final sequence where Edgar returns to Paris conveyed in dazzling, saturated, primary colors, his aesthetic project now actualized, as it were, by Godard's own creative powers. Nothing of this kind happens in *Notre Musique* where we see only Olga's sad and flat video piece which stands as entirely separate and distinct from the rest of Godard's film.

30. Brody sums up *Notre Musique* very negatively as a film of "ethnic politics, unambiguous rhetoric, and intellectual demagogy" which plays out as "a diatribe under the guise of reflection, a work of vituperative prejudice disguised as calm reflection, a work of venom dressed up as a masque" (Brody 2008: 623). He highlights in particular the moment in the master class when Godard states that "those who keep books are only accountants" while referring to "the tables of the Law, the Holy Scriptures, the people of the book." For Brody, "[t]he charge that the 'people of the book' are 'the accountants' whose insensitive and self-interested record of history causes it to be understood wrongly bears the unmistakable overtone of rhetoric against the Jewish demons of legend, one classic and the other modern: the Jewish usurer and the Jewish media" (ibid.: 621). For these reasons, *Notre Musique* typifies a work of "prewar prejudices adorned with postwar resentments—and, like much else in the history of anti-Semitism, with personal frustrations" (ibid.: 622). The debate in America around Godard's putative anti-Semitism came to a head at the time of Godard's honorary Hollywood Oscar for lifetime achievement in November 2010. Godard did not attend the ceremony in Los Angeles which was preceded in the weeks before by a number of articles in the mainstream U.S. media, most notably by Patrick Goldstein and James Rainey in the *Los Angeles Times* of November 2, 2010, which asked: "Jean-Luc Godard and his honorary Oscar: does it matter if he's an anti-Semite?" An earlier article by Tom Tugend appeared on October 6, 2010, in the Los Angeles-based *Jewish Journal* entitled "Is Jean-Luc Godard an anti-Semite?."

31. See Darmon 2011 for a valuable overview of the key lines of this ongoing debate in France which also draws on anecdotal evidence, for example, Godard once describing the producer Pierre Braunberger and early supporter of the Nouvelle Vague as a "sale Juif" ("filthy Jew"), or noting of Jean-Pierre Gorin, who requested some back pay: "Ah, it's always the same, Jews call you when they hear a cash register opening."

32. One of thirteen contributions to *Bridges of Sarajevo* produced by Obala Art Center Sarajevo and French Cinétévé, *Le Pont des soupirs* has been promoted in publicity material by its artistic director Jean-Michel Frodon, Godard's key interlocutor around *Notre Musique*, as a "sound and image incantation [that] evokes the way in which Sarajevo haunts the century and our imaginations, unveiling both its issues and impasses."

33. See Godard and Lafort 2004.

Chapter 7

1. In one of a number of interviews Godard gave at the time of the film's release where he talked directly about the Hadopi law, he characteristically made a distinction between "rights" and "duties," which, as we shall see, bears directly on his portrayal of the children in the Martin family. He stated: "I'm against Hadopi, of course. There's no intellectual property. I'm against estates, for example. That the children of an artist might enjoy the rights of their parents' body of work until they come of age, why not? But after that, I don't see it as automatic that Ravel's children get their hands on the rights for the *Boléro* [. . .] To be honest, authors' rights [*le droit d'auteur*] aren't possible. An author has no right. I have no right. I have only duties" (Godard 2010c).

2. The second trailer, for example, carried no music at all and offered instead a compressed soundtrack of screeching, inaudible sounds as if magnified static. Other trailers included intact the fragments of music, notably the first part of Arvo Pärt's *In Principio Erat Verbum* (2009) entitled "In Principio."

3. See Picard 2010. See also Bréan 2011, which focuses specifically on the reception at Cannes of Godard's Navajo subtitles.

4. See Godard 2010b.

5. See Mas and Pisani 2010 for an excellent compendium of the film's historical and cultural references.

6. See Brenez 2010, which argues that Godard is returning here once again to his revolutionary roots. This view is echoed in Pavsek 2013: 55–77, which argues that *Film socialisme* is calling in utopian terms for a return to "socialism as origin" and, by virtue of its special reference to a Valéry quote which translates into German as "a smile that supersedes [*congédie*] the universe," for a "positive supersession" of capitalism (77). Amy Taubin, however, considers the film to be more about the failure of language and meaning due to the kinetic montage of the cruise section created through abrupt juxtapositions, straight cuts, and little overlapping sound. Despite the visual pyrotechnics of the first section and odd scenes of rare tenderness (when, in the second section, for instance, Lucien clasps his mother with illuminated arms as in a Georges de la Tour painting), the mood, she argues, is ominous and despairing, resulting in an "enigmatic, painful, off-putting, ravishing" film (Taubin 2010: 46).

7. One exception is O'Rawe 2010. However, O'Rawe presents the book simply as a continuation of Godard's earlier work for POL and does not explore it on its own terms or in any real depth.

8. This reference to Genet arrives in the film over images of an expedition through Mauritania by Godard's own great uncle, Théodore Monod. A celebrated naturalist and explorer, Monod was also an activist and self-declared "Christian anarchist." Godard is effectively proposing him here as a figure of political resistance.

9. As Lack observes, this is, and isn't, the same image. The photograph shown first from behind is the colorized version with a blue tint produced in 1887 by Swiss image manipulators. The second instance of the image is a black-and-white version, but not, in fact, the original sepia version by Bonfils. In full keeping with the digitized processes traced throughout the film, it is another technologically manipulated version. See Lack 2012. Lack talks also here of Godard acknowledging the image-making process of cinema as an art of mutation. As we are seeing with the passage from film to book, such mutation is relentless in the expanded aesthetic project of *Film socialisme* and supposes no unique or "authentic" origin.

10. See Bachelard 1964: xi–xviii.

Chapter 8

1. For a valuable introduction to Godard's intertextual method in his early work, see Kline 2002: 184–221 (on *À bout de souffle* and *Pierrot le fou*) and Lack 2011 (on *À bout de souffle*).

2. Godard (1990c, for example), referring to Antoine de Rivarol, talks of French syntax, including that of French film, as being "incorruptible" (40).

3. See Jean-Paul Fargier's 1984 recording of the conversation, *L'Entretien*, which took place at the Maison de la Culture de Reims. One of Godard's declared starting points for *For Ever Mozart* (1996) was an article by Sollers in *Le Monde* on May 20, 1994, entitled "Profond Marivaux," in which he attacked Susan Sontag for mounting a production of Beckett's *Waiting for Godot* in Sarajevo in 1993, suggesting she should have put on a Marivaux comedy instead, *Le Triomphe de l'amour* (see Sollers 1993). In *For Ever Mozart* Godard has his lead character, Camille (Madeleine Assas), a philosophy professor, read Sollers's article (visually glimpsed at the start) and attempt to do just that. However, Camille is unable to find Marivaux at her local bookshop and settles instead for a play by Alfred de Musset, *On ne badine pas avec l'amour* (*One Does Not Trifle with Love*). It might be justifiably argued that with *For Ever Mozart*, an unsparing response to the war in Bosnia which culminates with a performance of Mozart, Godard shares some of Sontag's radical and ethical hope for the survival of the human spirit and its eternal regeneration.

4. Kathleen Rowe argues that Godard is a twentieth-century heir to the romantic movement, a fact that helps to explain his ambivalence towards women, his retreat from politics, his representation of himself as an anti-hero of sorts, and his stance of ironic detachment evident in most of his work. See Rowe 1990–51.

5. The Sonimage experiment ended in 1979, although the company of the same name continued to operate until 1981.

6. White shows how Heidegger's concern in "A Dialogue on Language" with "a beholding that is itself invisible and bears itself to encounter emptiness" matches Godard and Miéville's interest here in the unseen and those instances where representation fails. Miéville talks of an image of an egg apparently still, but inside which all sorts of things are happening invisibly. According to White, the entire video thus marks an attempt to reconcile the gap inherent in representation and engage in a communication where two people are speaking to and with each other. See White 2013: 135. The sense of an ongoing dialogue

between the two continues also in Miéville's own work. In her 1997 *Nous sommes tous encore ici*, for example, Godard delivers from memory a monologue from Hannah Arendt's *The Origins of Totalitarianism* (1951).

7. Miéville can also represent the musical instance. In a discussion of *Notre Musique*, Godard states that it was Miéville who noticed that one particular shot of the film (already referred to in chapter 6)—a close-up of the delicate feet of the Native American woman descending the hotel's marble staircase, where one foot is placed in front of the other with the tip of the front foot touching the next step inscribed with a thick, black, horizontal line—directly evokes a stave of music (see Frodon 2004b: 21). We note, too, that it is Miéville in *Ici et ailleurs* who draws attention to the style and context of the performance of the young Arab girl reciting Darwish's poem "Je résisterai." Hence, Miéville arguably consolidates the aesthetic legacy of Godard's own mother, who, as we noted in chapter 5, embodied the culture of music in Godard's childhood and established it as an essentially female instance.

8. Beginning with *Soft and Hard*, Godard's childhood assumes an increasingly important role in his work, most strongly in *JLG/JLG*. The theme can also be found in Godard's reflections on the history of cinema, for example when he describes cinema as "the childhood of art."

9. The dynamics of "soft and hard" between Godard and Miéville are markedly reduced in their other joint collaborations such as *The Old Place* and *Deux fois cinquante ans de cinéma français* (1995), a historical piece produced for the British Film Institute to commemorate the centenary of cinema. The latter plays out more as a shared commentary, particularly in the long closing sequence of homages to French directors and film critics, which is far more gentle and "respectful" in pace and style then *Histoire(s)*, even to the point of appearing subdued.

10. See Lyon 1982 for an excellent feminist account of *Sauve qui peut* and Duras's role in it.

11. For a comprehensive discussion of Duras's film work, which highlights the importance of montage as a conscious rhetorical and erotic strategy, see Williams 1997, in particular "Le système D.: *Le camion*" (25–46) and "Every Which Way but Loose: Duras and the Erotic Crimes of Montage" (47–66).

12. See Cléder 2012 for an interesting account of the Duras-Godard relation in the more general critical context of the relations between literature and cinema, including Duras's own notion of cinematographic writing and "l'image écrite" ("the written image").

13. See Williams 1997: 139–59 where I argue that Andréa lay at the core of Duras's reinvention of the collaborative form, indeed all form, as "sexual cure," to be understood as the rhetorical appropriation of the other against the threat of homosexual undifferentiation. When she was not simply co-opting gay writing and influence for her own particular rhetorical purposes through a strategy of pseudo-identification, Duras's general approach to gay writers was essentially to negate them. Her particular hostility towards Roland Barthes as a weak and timid writer, capable at most of an irenic fingering of intertextual detail, was based on the untenable and risibly homophobic idea that a male writer who has never "touched" a woman's body is a contradiction in terms (Duras 1987b: 41). In one notorious interview a matter of months after her *dialogue de sourds* with Godard and entitled "Duras est SEXY!," she confronted the out-gay Pierre Bergé, at the time managing director of Yves Saint Laurent (he was a former lover of the fashion designer) and soon-to-be head of the official Comité Jean Cocteau. Bergé offered Duras a rich smorgasbord of gay French writers including Genet, Aragon, and Violette Leduc. She was not impressed by any (Genet was

singled out in particular for the "bluff" of his sexual exhibitionism) and instead repeated her long-held admiration for de Lafayette and Racine. Two of the three photographs by Alain Duplantier for the interview picture her in monochrome close-up as forbiddingly Hard. In the third and final color image, however, she offers herself in the foreground as ideally Soft, the precocious daughter of Bergé who remains consigned to the shadowed area behind her, his paternal, corporate hand resting awkwardly atop her left shoulder. In the specific case of gay cinema, Duras devotes a long article to Charles Laughton's *The Night of the Hunter* (1955) in *Les Yeux verts*, but this soon becomes an elaborate exercise in imaginary reconstruction and "correction." Duras will not enter such profoundly alien territory on equal terms, however much she may claim to admire it. See Williams 1997: 88–90.

14. It is notable that Godard endorses without any questions Marcel Sacotte's *Où en est la prostitution* (1959), one of the main pretexts of *Vivre sa vie* extracted at length in the film. With its highly heterosexist presuppositions, Sacotte's study betrays a phobic attitude to the very idea of male prostitutes, mentioned only once in the entire book with palpable disgust. If Godard uses the book simply as a work of reference not worthy of his creative, intertextual investment, it is precisely because Sacotte does not represent the world of literature but rather a popular form of sociology in vogue at the time that could also drift into cod psychology.

15. For an appreciation of this project, see Williams 2004.

16. Godard's specific approach to gay cinema other than Cocteau would require a separate discussion. As we shall see shortly, he takes pleasure in referencing filmmakers like Pasolini and Demy in his writing, and later works like *King Lear* and *Histoire(s)* teem with references to Pasolini (notably *The Gospel according to St Matthew* and *Teorema*), Visconti, Eisenstein, and Demy. Yet Godard also displays a keen awareness of contemporary gay cinema. In one interview from 1989, "Week-end avec Godard," he refers favorably to *Encore* (*Once More*) (1988), the first mainstream French film about the AIDS epidemic by an out-gay director, Paul Vecchiali. Godard makes a point of liking the film because it was universally detested—evidence of his common desire to identify with the *artiste maudit* (the reproduced version in Bergala 1988 even includes on p. 178 a half-page still from the film of the male protagonist embracing another man). More recently, Godard has singled out the work of another rare out-gay contemporary French director, Alain Guiraudie, in particular his extended short *Ce vieux rêve qui bouge* (2001), due in major part to its story of class relations in a workplace setting and its central theme of the relations between manual labor and desire.

17. I explore these key themes in Cocteau's cinema at length in Williams 2006b: 136–56.

18. An earlier version of the scene had, in fact, already taken place in 1949, when, during the first Festival du Cinéma Maudit at Biarritz which he presided over, Cocteau ensured with a simple nod and wink that the young and uncouth Truffaut, Godard, and Rivette pass through a cordon of suspicious security men into his inner artistic sanctum.

19. Godard's linking of Truffaut and Genet here can be explained in part by the great interest Truffaut took in Genet's work. Returning to Paris in July 1951 after his desertion from military service, Truffaut wished to meet Genet with whom he had already entered into correspondence. The Pasolini-Ninetto pairing is also invoked in Godard's preface to Pierre Braunberger's correspondence referred to earlier, where he links the pair to Gide and Allégret (specifically the latter's 1929 silent film *Papoul ou L'Agadadza* for which Gide wrote the script). Godard claims that he only rediscovered the same "half-biblical" and "half-profoundly ordinary" tone of Gide in the work of Pasolini "with, or without Ninetto" (Bergala 1988: 209). Godard is clearly implying here a pan-European gay sensibility that he seems fully equipped to recognize, though he does not take the idea any further. See

Amy de la Bretèque 1994 for a useful introduction to the Cocteau-Pasolini connection. We note in passing that Allégret was a source of great sexual tension and jealousy between Cocteau and Gide during the late 1920s, to the point they refused to speak to each other for nearly twenty years.

20. See Loshitzky 1995: 165–67 for a general discussion of anality, incest, and paedophilia in this particular period of Godard's work.

21. See Silverman 2001 which reexamines the issues of Godard's supposed masochism created by such figurations, concluding that "it is Godard's very phenomenological idea that the artist is not properly a creator, but rather the site where words and visual forms inscribe or install themselves" (24). Making particular reference to *JLG/JLG* where Godard asserts: "Now I have to sacrifice myself so that through me the word 'love' means something, so that love exists on earth," Silverman proposes the general notion of Godard as "author-receiver." She also suggests rightly that if Godard links his cinematic project to painting over and against literature by producing self-portraits, this necessarily entails an interrogation of painting itself.

22. As Roland-François Lack notes, Borges is, of course, troping here on Dante, specifically *Paradiso* xxx and xxxi, where the traveler through Paradise is shown a white and yellow rose as the preliminary to a vision of the divine splendor. Lack concludes rightly that "Godard is more modest, troping only on Borges: *Histoire(s)* is a human, not a divine comedy." See Lack 2004: 326.

Coda

1. *3X3D* (b/w and color, 70 mins), comprising three short films by Godard, Peter Greenaway, and Edgar Pêra, was commissioned by the Portuguese city of Guimarães (European Capital of Culture in 2012) and first screened at the Cannes Film Festival in 2013.

2. *Les Trois désastres* also includes extracts from Antonioni's *Red Desert*, Bergman's *Prison*, Welles's *The Lady from Shanghai*, a clip of Eisenstein in conversation, as well as, from Godard's own work, the Wittgenstein sequence in *JLG/JLG* and the windswept audition scene in *For Ever Mozart*.

3. Bordwell proposes three multiple "draft-narratives." The narrative possibilities of the digital medium have been considered by the film theorist Garrett Stewart who argues that new film technology is leading to a "postfilmic" kind of cinema at the intersection of new intermedial sites where new forms of temporality—"framed" "*digitime*" and the "*timespace-image*" defined as the implosion of spatial and temporal categories into a fantastic zone (where, for example, the plane of the past can be morphed by retraversal and transformed, rather than just remembered) (Stewart 2007: 286)—offer the potential for very different kinds of narrative plotting and a new consciousness in, and of, images (ibid.: 1–19).

4. Godard maintains the contrastive sense of depth in other ways, too, for, as Bordwell notes, the low resolution of some of the images avoids harsh contours, while the "blown-out softness" can enhance volume (see Bordwell 2014).

5. Christopher Pavsek speculated in 2013, ahead of *Adieu au langage*, that it was "as if his [Godard's] fantasy is to transcend the gulf between language and things and to escape the constitutive lack that the signifier introduces into subjectivity" (Pavsek 2013: 63). Subsequent accounts of *Adieu au langage* have emphasized the film as visual metaphor versus the impossibility of language to articulate the disintegration of reality (see Ishaghpour 2014), and also its status as a stirring song of struggle (see Bourgois 2014) (the film includes

at the end an excerpt from Pino Masi's revolutionary song "La violenza" heard elsewhere in Godard's work, notably *Lotte in Italia* and *Histoire(s) du cinéma*).

6. We note that Godard recently disposed of most of his book and video archive at Rolle.

7. Romney 2014. This highly personal account of the experience of viewing *Adieu au langage* draws on Ted Fendt's detailed list of texts and films cited or alluded to in the film. See Fendt 2014.

8. The result was a limited run in the United States, while in the United Kingdom the film was not released theatrically by StudioCanal at all, and went straight to home video. Only on Blu-ray, however, can it be viewed as a 3D film.

Works Cited

Adorno, T. (1974), *Minima Moralia: Reflections on a Damaged Life* (London: New Left Books).
Agamben, G. (1993[1990]), *The Coming Community* (Minneapolis: University of Minnesota Press). trans. M. Hardt.
—— (1995), "Face au cinéma et à l'Histoire: à propos de Jean-Luc Godard, *Le Monde* (Supplément Livres): 6 October, I, x–xi.
—— (2000 [1996]), *Means without End: Notes on Politics* (Theory out of Bounds) (Minneapolis: University of Minnesota Press), trans. V. Binetti and C. Casarino. Includes "Notes on Gesture" (42–60).
—— (2002a), "Difference and Repetition: On Guy Debord's films" [1995], trans. B. Holmes, in T. McDonough (ed.), *Guy Debord and the Situationists International* (Cambridge MA: MIT Press), 313–20.
—— (2002b), *Remnants of Auschwitz* (New York: Zone Books).
—— (2007 [2005]), *Profanations* (New York: Zone Books).
Ahmed, S. (2004), *The Cultural Politics of Emotion* (New York: Routledge, 2004).
Althusser, L. (1996 [1965]), *Pour Marx* (Paris: La Découverte).
Améry, J. (1998 [1966]), *At the Mind's Limits: Contemplations by a Survivor on Auschwitz and Its Realities* (Bloomington: Indiana University Press), trans. S. P. Rosenfeld and S. Rosenfeld.
Amy de la Bretèque, F. (1994), "La descendance de Jean Cocteau au cinéma, ou les enfants d'*Orphée*," in C. Rolot and P. Caizergues (eds.), *Le Cinéma de Jean Cocteau* (Montpellier: Université Paul Valéry), 59–72.
An, G. (2014), "*La Chinoise* . . . et après?: Aging against Tradition," in T. Conley and T. J. Kline (eds.), *A Companion to Jean-Luc Godard* (Chichester: John Wiley and Sons), 282–95.
Ang, I. "Hegemony-in-Trouble: Nostalgia and the Ideology of the Impossible in European Cinema," in Petrie 1992: 21–31.
Aragon, L. (1965), "Qu'est-ce que l'art, Jean-Luc Godard?," *Lettres Françaises* 1096 (September 9): 1, 8.
—— (1980), *Le Crève-coeur/Le nouveau Crève-coeur* (Paris: Gallimard).
—— (2000 [1928]), *Le Con d'Irène* (Paris: Mercure de France).
Arendt, H. (2004 [1951]), *The Origins of Totalitarianism* (New York: Schocken).
Astruc, A. (1975), *La Tête la première* (Paris: Olivier Orban).
Aumont, J. (1989), *L'Oeil interminable: Cinéma et peinture* (Paris: Séguier).

—— (1991), "Lumière de la musique," in "Numéro Spécial: Godard—Trente ans depuis," *Cahiers du Cinéma*: 46–48.
—— (1996), *À quoi pensent les films* (Paris: Séguier).
—— (1999), *Amnésies: fictions du cinéma d'après Jean-Luc Godard* (Paris: POL).
Bachelard, G. (1964 [1958]), *The Poetics of Space* (Boston: Beacon Press), trans. M. Jolas.
—— (1992 [1931]), *L'Intuition de l'instant* (Paris: Stock).
Badiou. A. (1988), *L'être et l'événement* (Paris: Seuil).
—— (1997), *Saint Paul. La Fondation de l'universalisme* (Paris: PUF).
—— (1998), "Le plus-de-voir," *Art Press* hors-série (November): 86–91.
Baross, Z. (2009), "Jean-Luc Godard," in F. Colman (ed.), *Film, Theory and Philosophy: The Key Thinkers* (Durham UK: Acumen).
Barr, B. (2010), "Shot and Counter-shot: Presence, Obscurity, and the Breakdown of Discourse in Godard's *Notre Musique*," *Journal of French and Francophone Philosophy* 18:2: 65–85.
Barthes, R. (1973), *Le Plaisir du texte* (Paris: Seuil).
—— (1980), *La Chambre claire: Notes sur la photographie* (Paris: Éditions de l'Étoile/Gallimard "Seuil").
Bartoli, C. (1997), "'Le regard intérieur" ("Interior View," included in the booklet to the CD of *Nouvelle Vague* (Munich: ECM Records).
Bataille, G. (1995), *Manet: Biographical and Critical Study* (New York: Skira), trans. A. Wainhouse and J. Emmons.
Baudelaire, C. (1972 [1861]), *Les Fleurs du Mal* (Paris: Gallimard).
Bauman, Z. (1995), *A Life in Fragments: Essays in Postmodern Morality* (Oxford: Blackwell).
Beckett, S. (1988), *L'Image* (Paris: Minuit).
Beghin, C. (1998), "Invention de l'animation," *Art Press* Hors-Série (November): 52–57.
Bellour, R. (1990), *L'Entre-images: photo, cinéma, vidéo* (Paris: La Différence).
—— (1992), "(Not) just another film-maker," in R. Bellour (with M. L. Bandy) (ed.), (1992), *Jean-Luc Godard: Son+Image 1974–1991* (New York: MoMA), 215–31.
—— (1996), "The Double Helix," in T. Druckrey (ed.), *Electronic Culture: Technology and Visual Representation* (New York: Aperture), 173–99.
Bergala, A. (ed.) (1985), *Jean-Luc Godard par Jean-Luc Godard* vol. 1 (Paris: Cahiers du Cinéma/Éditions de l'Étoile).
—— (1994), "*Hélas pour moi*, ou du présent comme passé légèrement corrigé," *Cinémathèque* 5: 19–27.
—— (ed.) (1998), *Jean-Luc Godard par Jean-Luc Godard* vol. 2. Paris: Cahiers du Cinéma/Éditions de l'Étoile.
—— (1999), *Nul mieux que Godard* (Paris: Cahiers du Cinéma).
—— (2006), *Godard au travail: les années 60* (Paris: Cahiers du Cinéma).
——, and S. Toubiana (1988), "L'art de (dé)montrer": interview with J.-L. Godard, *Cahiers du Cinéma* 403: 50–57.
Bernanos, G. (1994 [1936]), *Journal d'un curé de campagne* (Paris: Pocket).
Bersani, L. (2015), *Thoughts and Things* (Chicago and London: University of Chicago Press).
Blanchot, M. (1955), *L'Espace littéraire* (Paris: Gallimard).
—— (1971), *L'Amitié* (Paris: Gallimard).
Bogue, R. (2007), *Deleuze's Way: Essays in Transverse Ethics and Aesthetics* (Aldershot: Ashgate).

Bordwell, D. (2014). *"Adieu au langage: 2 + 2 x 3D."* www.davidbordwell.net/blog/2014/09/07/adieu-au-langage-2-2-x-3d.
Bosetti, L. (2007), "Terror on Two Fronts: Godard and Lacan on 1968," *Nottingham French Studies* 46:3: 62–72.
Bourgois, G. (2014), "Les Chants de Roxy," *Trafic* 92: 19–27.
Bréan, S. (2011), "Godard English Cannes: The Reception of *Film Socialisme*'s 'Navajo English' subtitles." *Senses of Cinema* 60. http://sensesofcinema.com/2011/feature-articles/godardenglishcannes-the-reception-of-film-socialismes-%E2%80%9Cnavajo-english%E2%80%9D-subtitles/. Pp. 12.
Brenez, N. (2010), "Liberté, fraternité, prodigalité," *Cahiers du Cinéma* 657: 26–27.
———, and D. Faroult, M. Temple, J. S. Williams, and M. Witt (2006) (eds.), *Jean-Luc Godard. Documents* (Paris: Centre Pompidou).
Bresson, R. (1995 [1975]), *Notes sur le cinématographe* (Paris: Folio).
Broch, H. *La Mort de Virgile* (Paris: Gallimard, 1955 [1945]), trans. A. Kohn. *The Death of Virgil* (San Francisco: North Point, 1983 [1945]), trans. J. S. Untermeyer.
Brody, R. (2008), *Everything Is Cinema: The Working Life of Jean-Luc Godard* (London: Faber and Faber).
Bukatman, S. (1993) "Cybersubjectivity and Cinematic Being," in C. Sharrett (ed.), *Crisis Cinema: The Apocalyptic Idea in Postmodern Narrative Film* (Washington DC: Maisonneuve), 75–103.
Cerisuelo, M. (1989), *Jean-Luc Godard* (Paris: Lherminier/Quatre Vents).
Chion, M. (1994 [1990]), *Audio-Vision: Sound on Screen* (New York: Columbia University Press).
Clark, J. (2005), Review of DVD of *Notre Musique*, July 31. http://jclarkmedia.com/film/filmreviewnotremusique.html.
Cléder, J. (2012), "Anatomie d'un modèle: Duras/Godard—Cinéma/Littérature," *Revue critique de fixxion française contemporaine*. http://www.revue-critique-de-fixxion-francaise-contemporaine.org/rcffc/article/view/fx07.02/746.
Cohn-Bendit, D. (2012), "Mon ami Godard," in J.-L. Godard and M. Ophuls, *Dialogues sur le cinéma* (Lormont: Le bord de l'eau), 85–97.
Conley, T., and T. J. Kline (2014) (eds.), *A Companion to Jean-Luc Godard* (Chichester UK: John Wiley and Sons), 456–87.
cinéma 68 (1988). Special Issue Hors-Série of *Cahiers du Cinéma*.
Connor, S. (1997), "Feel the Noise: Excess, Affect and the *Acoustic*," in G. Hoffman and A. Homung (eds.), *Emotion in Postmodernism* (Heidelberg: Universitätsverlag C. Winter), 147–62.
Curnier, J.-P. (2009), *Montrer l'invisible: Écrits sur l'image* (Paris: Éditions Jacqueline Chambon).
Dall'Asta, M. (2004), "The (Im)possible History," in M. Temple, J. S. Williams, and M. Witt (eds.), *For Ever Godard* (London: Black Dog), 350–63.
Dalle Vacche, A. (1996), *Cinema and Painting: How Art Is Used in Film* (London: Athlone).
Daly, F., and A. Martin (2002), "Godard: Adult Concepts?," *RealTime* 50. http://www.realtimearts.net/article/issue50/6830.
Darmon, M. (2011), *La Question juive de Jean-Luc Godard* (Paris: Le temps qu'il fait).
Darwish, M. (1995), *A Memory for Forgetfulness: August, Beirut, 1982*, trans. with an introduction by I. Muhawi (Berkeley and London: University of California Press).
——— (2000), *La Terre nous est étroite, et autres poèmes 1966–1999* (Paris: Gallimard).

—— (2002), *La Palestine comme métaphore. Entretiens traduits de l'arabe par Elias Sanbar et de l'hébreu par Simone Britton* (Arles: Actes Sud-Babel).
—— (2003a), *Unfortunately, It Was Paradise: Selected Poems*. Trans. and ed. by Munir Akash and Carolyn Forché (with S. Antoon and A. El-Zein) (Berkeley and London: University of California Press).
—— (2003b), *Murale* (Arles: Actes Sud). Trans. from Arabic by E. Sanbar.
De Baecque, A. (2010), *Godard: Biographie* (Paris: Grasset).
—— (2012), *Camera Historica: The Century in Cinema* (New York: Columbia University Press). Trans. N. Vinsonneau and J. Magidoff.
Debray, R. (1992), *Vie et mort de l'image: Une histoire du regard en Occident* (Paris: Gallimard).
—— (1999), *Le Code et le glaive: après l'Europe, la nation?* (Paris: Albin Michel).
Deleuze, G. (1985), *Cinéma 2: L'image-temps* (Paris: Éditions de Minuit).
—— (1992), "Three Questions about *Six Fois Deux*," in R. Bellour with M. L. Bandy (eds.), *Jean-Luc Godard: Son+Image* (New York: Museum of Modern Art, 1992), 35–41 (originally appeared in *Cahiers du Cinéma* 271 [1976]).
—— (1995), *Cinéma 2: L'image-temps* (Paris: Minuit).
——, and E. Sanbar (1982), "Les Indiens de Palestine," *Libération*, 8–9 May.
——, and F. Guattari (1987), *A Thousand Plateaus*, trans. B. Massumi (Minneapolis: University of Minnesota Press).
De Man, Paul (1979), *Allegories of Reading: Figural Language in Rousseau, Nietzsche, Rilke, and Proust* (New Haven: Yale University Press).
Delvaux, C. (1988a), "Tirer son plan et puis le voir: cinq fragments sur *Soigne ta droite* de Jean-Luc Godard," *Revue belge du cinéma* 22–23: 190–205.
—— (1988b), "Godard musicien," *Revue belge du cinéma* 22–23: 51–53.
De Rougemont, D. (1936), *Penser avec les mains* (Paris: Albin Michel).
Derrida, J. (1991), *L'Autre cap: mémoires, réponses et responsabilités* (Paris: Minuit).
——, and A. Dufourmantelle (2000 [1997]), *Of Hospitality: Anne Dufourmantelle invites Jacques Derrida to Respond* (Stanford: Stanford University Press), trans. Rachel Bowlby.
Diawara, M. (2003), "Sonimage in Mozambique," in G. James and F. Zeyfang (eds.), *The TVideo Politics of Jean-Luc Godard* (Berlin: B. Books), 92–121.
—— (2010), *African Film: New forms of Aesthetics and Politics* (Prestel, 2010).
Dienst, R. (2000), "The Imaginary Element: Life + Cinema," in D. Wills (ed.), *Jean-Luc Godard's* Pierrot le fou (Cambridge: Cambridge University Press), 23–42.
Dixon, W. W. (1997), *The Films of Jean-Luc Godard* (Albany: SUNY Press).
Dolto, F. (1977), *L'Évangile au risque de la psychoanalyse* (Paris: Seuil "Points").
Douin, J.-L. (1994), *Jean-Luc Godard* (Paris: Rivages).
—— (2010), *Jean-Luc Godard: Dictionnaire des passions* (Paris: Stock).
Drabinski, J. E. (2008), *Godard between Identity and Difference* (New York: Continuum).
Dubois, P. (2004), "The Written Screen: JLG and Writing as the Accursed Share," in M. Temple, J. S. Williams and M. Witt (eds.), *For Ever Godard* (London: Black Dog), 231–47.
Duras, M. (1987a), *Le Camion: suivi de entretien avec Michelle Porte* (Paris: Les Éditions de Minuit, 1977).
—— (1987a), *Les Yeux verts* (Paris: Éditions de l'Étoile/Cahiers du Cinéma).
—— (1987b), *La Vie matérielle* (Paris: POL).
—— (1993), *Le Monde extérieur: Outside II* (Paris: POL).
Eagleton, T. (1990), *The Ideology of the Aesthetic* (Oxford: Blackwell).

Eisenchitz, B. (1998), "Une machine à montrer l'invisible: Conversation avec Bernard Eisenchitz à propos des *Histoire(s) du Cinéma*: Conversation avec Bernard Eisenchitz à propos des *Histoire(s) du Cinéma*," *Cahiers du Cinéma* 529: 52–56.

Elsaesser, T., and H. Malte (2000), *Film Theory: An Introduction through the Senses* (New York and London: Routledge).

Elshaw, G. (1998), "The Depiction of Late 1960's Counter Culture in Jean-Luc Godard's *One Plus One/Sympathy for the Devil*" (part two). http://elshaw.tripod.com/jlg/One_Plus_One2.htm.

Emmelhainz, I. (2009), "Before Our Eyes: Les mots, non les choses. Jean-Luc Godard's *Ici et Ailleurs* (1970–4) and *Notre Musique* (2004)." PhD dissertation, University of Toronto. https://tspace.library.utoronto.ca/bitstream/1807/19317/1/Emmelhainz_Irmgard_200906_PhD_Dissertation.pdf.

——— (2014), "Jean-Luc Godard: To Liberate Things from the Name that We Have Imposed on Them (*Film . . .*) to Announce Dissonances Parting from a Note in Common (*Socialisme*)," in T. Conley and T. J. Kline (eds.), *A Companion to Jean-Luc Godard* (Chichester UK: John Wiley and Sons), 527–45.

Fairfax, D. (2010), "Birth (of the Image) of a Nation: Jean-Luc Godard in Mozambique," *Acta Univ. Sapientiae, Film and Media Studies* 3: 55–67.

Faroult, D. (2006), "Du *vertovisme* du Groupe Dziga Vertov: À propos d'un manifeste méconnu et d'un film inachevé (*Jusqu'à la victoire*)," in N. Brenez, D. Faroult, M. Temple, J. S. Williams and M. Witt (eds.), *Jean-Luc Godard. Documents* (Paris: Centre Pompidou): 134–38.

———, and J. S. Williams (2006), "*Hélas pour moi*: éléments génétiques," in N. Brenez, D. Faroult, M. Temple, J. S. Williams, and M. Witt (eds.), *Jean-Luc Godard. Documents* (Paris: Centre Pompidou), 362–68.

Faure, E. (1923–30), *History of Art*, 5 vols. (London: John Lane), trans. W. Pach.

Fendt, T. (2014), "*Adieu au langage—Goodbye to Language*: A Works Cited." *Mubi.com*. 12 October. https://mubi.com/notebook/posts/adieu-au-langage-goodbye-to-language-a-works-cited.

Fieschi-Vivet, L. (2000), "Investigation of a Mystery: Cinema and the Sacred in *Hélas pour moi*," in M. Temple and J. S. Williams (eds.), *The Cinema Alone: Essays on the Work of Jean-Luc Godard, 1985–2000* (Amsterdam: Amsterdam University Press), 189–206.

Fleischer, A. (2011), *Réponse du muet au parlant: En retour à Jean-Luc Godard* (Paris: Seuil).

Flinn, M. C. (2014), "*The Old Place*, Space of Legends," in T. Conley and T. J. Kline (eds.), *A Companion to Jean-Luc Godard* (Chichester UK: John Wiley and Sons), 504–13.

Flusser, V. (1996), "Digital apparition," in T. Druckrey (ed.), *Electronic Culture: Technology and Visual Representation* (New York: Aperture), 242–45.

Fóti, V. M. (1992), *Heidegger and the Poets: Poiesis/Sophia/Techne* (New Jersey: Humanities).

Fox, A. (2014), "Constructing Voices in Jean-Luc Godard's *Sauve qui peut (la vie)* (1979)," *Studies in French Cinema* 14:1: 19–32.

——— (2015), "Acoustic Spectatorship: The 1980s Film and Video Work of Jean-Luc Godard." Ph.D. dissertation, University of London.

Frodon, J.-M. (2004a), "Jean-Luc Godard: Parmi nous," *Cahiers du Cinéma* 590: 16–19.

——— (2004b), "Juste une conversation": interview with J.-L. Godard, *Cahiers du Cinéma* 590: 20–22.

Geary, J. (2011), *I Is an Other: The Secret Life of Metaphor and How It Shapes the Way We See the World* (New York: HarperCollins).

Genet, J. (1986), *Un captif amoureux* (Paris: Gallimard).
Godard, J.-L. (1966), "La Question": interview with M. Delahaye, *Cahiers du Cinéma* 178: 26–35, 67–71.
——— (1972), *Godard on Godard* (New York: Viking), ed. J. Narboni and T. Milne.
——— (1979), *Cahiers du Cinéma* 300 (May), special issue edited by Godard.
——— (1984), *L'Entretien*: filmed interview with P. Sollers, 74 mins., video, col., dir. J.-P. Fargier, transcribed and published as "Jean-Luc Godard-Philippe Sollers 'L'entretien,'" *Art Press* 88: 4–9.
——— (1985 [1980]), *Introduction à une véritable histoire du cinéma* (Paris: Albatros). Trans. by T. Barnard as *Introduction to a True History of Cinema and Television* (Montreal: Caboose, 2014), with an introduction by M. Witt.
——— (1987), "Deux ou trois choses qu'ils se sont dites": filmed interview with M. Duras, *Océaniques*, FR3, December 28, transcribed and included in Bergala, *Godard par Godard* vol. 2: 140–47.
——— (1990a), "Nouvelle Vague" (découpage intégral), *L'Avant-scène cinéma* 396–97.
——— (1990b), "Conférence-débat à la Fémis du 26 avril 1989," *Confrontations*: 15–23.
——— (1990c), "Vague nouvelle," *Cahiers du Cinéma* 431–32: 40–43.
——— (1996a), *JLG/JLG: Phrases* (Paris: POL).
——— (1996b), *For Ever Mozart: Phrases* (Paris: POL).
——— (1997), "Résistance(s)": interview with J. G. Perrault, *Le Monde de l'Éducation* (November): 52–55.
——— (1998a), *Histoire(s) du cinéma*, 4 vols. (Paris: Gallimard-Gaumont).
——— (1998b), *Allemagne neuf zéro: Phrases* (Paris: POL).
——— (1998c), *Les Enfants jouent à la Russie: Phrases* (Paris: POL).
——— (2001), *Éloge de l'amour: Phrases* (Paris: POL).
——— (2003), "Un patineur," *Télérama* Hors-Série ("Cocteau, le poète aux cent visages"): 7.
——— (2004a), "À Sarajevo, le 'juif du cinéma' cultive l'optimisme": interview with J. Mandelbaum and T. Sotinel, *Le Monde*, May 13.
——— (2004b), "Godard parle": interview with S. Kaganski and J.-M. Lalanne, *Les Inrockuptibles* 5–11 May: 31–39.
——— (2004c), "Juste une conversation": interview with J.-M. Frodon (on *Notre Musique*), *Cahiers du Cinéma* 590: 20–22.
——— (2004d), "La troisième image": interview with C. Kantcheff and E. Sanbar, *Politis* 826 (November 18).
——— (2005), "Occupational Hazards": interview with F. Bonnaud," *Film Comment* 41:1: 37 + 40–1.
——— (2010a), *Film socialisme: Dialogues avec visages auteurs* (Paris: POL).
——— (2010b), "Avec Godard, en liberté": interview with Edwy Plenel, Ludovic Lamant, and Sylvain Bourmeau, *Médiapart* May 10. http://www.mediapart.fr/dossier/culture-idees/godard.
——— (2010c), "Le droit d'auteur? Un auteur n'a que des devoirs": interview with J.-M. Lalanne, *Les Inrockuptibles* May 18. http://blogs.lesinrocks.com/cannes2010/2010/05/18/le-droit-dauteur-un-auteur-na-que-des-devoirs-jean-luc-godard/.
Godard, J.-L., and Y. Ishaghpour (1999), "Archéologie du cinéma et mémoire du siècle," Dialogue 1, *Trafic* 29: 16–35.
——— (2005 [2000]), *Cinema* (Oxford and New York: Berg), trans. J. Howe.

——— (2006), *De l'origine du XXIe siècle, The Old Place, Liberté et Patrie, Je vous salue, Sarajevo* (Munich: ECM Records "ECM Cinema 5001") (an illustrated transcription in French, English, and German of the soundtracks, including a short essay by M. Althen ("The Lives of the Images") and a DVD containing all 4 films).
———, and G. Lefort (2004), "Regardezvoir, Godard," *Libération*, May 12: 38–39.
———, and A.-M. Miéville, *2 x 50 ans de cinéma français: Phrases* (Paris: POL).
———, and M. Ophuls (2011), *Dialogues sur le cinéma* (Lormont: Bord de l'eau).
Goytisolo, J. (1997), *La Forêt de l'écriture* (Paris: Fayard), trans. A. Ben Salem.
Grant, C. (2004), "Home-movies: The Curious Cinematic Collaboration of Anne-Marie Miéville and Jean-Luc Godard," in M. Temple, J. S. Williams, and M. Witt (eds.), *For Ever Godard* (London: Black Dog), 100–17.
Guerin, M. A. (2001), "L'amour enfui," *Trafic* 39: 1–15.
Guillory, J. (1983), *Poetic Authority: Spenser, Milton, and Literary History* (New York: Columbia University Press).
Gustafsson, H. (2014), "Remnants of Palestine, or, Archaeology after Auschwitz," in H. Gustafsson and S. Grønstad (eds.), *Cinema and Agamben: Ethics, Biopolitics and the Moving Image* (New York and London: Bloomsbury), 207–32.
Habermas, J. (1994), *The Past as Future* (Interviews with M. Hailer) (Lincoln: University of Nebraska Press).
Habib, A. (2001), "Before and After: Origins and Death in the Work of Jean-Luc Godard," *Senses of Cinema* 16. http://sensesofcinema.com/2001/16/godard_habib/.
——— (2014), "Godard's Utopia(s) or the Performance of Failure," in D. Morrey, C. Stojanova, and N. Côté (eds.), *The Legacies of Jean-Luc Godard* (Waterloo ON: Wilfrid Laurier), 217–236,
Halberstadt, M. (2002), "The Artistic Act Is an Act of Resistance," *Enthusiasm* 5: 2–7.
Heidelberger-Leonard, I. (2010), *The Philosopher of Auschwitz: Jean Améry and Living with the Holocaust* (London: I. B. Tauris).
Heidegger, M. (1971 [1959]), *On the Way to Language* (New York: Harper and Row), trans. P. D. Hertz.
Heywood, M. (2009), "Holocaust and Image: Debates Surrounding Jean-Luc Godard's *Histoire(s) du cinéma* (1988–98)," *Studies in French Cinema* 9:3: 273–83.
——— (2012), *Modernist Visions: Marcel Proust's À la recherche du temps perdu and Jean-Luc Godard's Histoire(s) du cinéma* (Bern: Peter Lang AG).
Hickey, D. (2009), *The Invisible Dragon: Essays on Beauty* (Chicago and London: University of Chicago Press).
Hofstadter, A. (1975) (ed.), *Martin Heidegger, Poetry, Language, Thought* (New York and London: Harper and Row).
Hori, J. (2014), "Godard, Spielberg, the *Muselmann*, and the Concentration Camps," in D. Morrey, C. Stojanova and N. Côté (eds.), *The Legacies of Jean-Luc Godard* (Waterloo ON: Wilfrid Laurier), 67–79.
Hugo, V. (1940), *Actes et Paroles* vol. 3: "Depuis L'exil 1870–1885 'Mes Fils'" (Paris: Albin Michel "L'imprimerie nationale").
Ishaghpour, Y. (2014), "Image du monde disloqué: *Adieu au langage* de Jean-Luc Godard," *Trafic* 92: 10–18.
Jameson, F. (1992), "High-tech Collectives in Late Godard," in *The Geopolitical Aesthetic: Cinema and Space in the World System* (Bloomington: Indiana University Press).
Jankélévitch, V. (1961), *La musique et l'ineffable* (Paris: Librairie Armand Colin).

Jousse, T. (1991), "Godard à l'oreille," in *Cahiers du Cinéma* "Numéro Spécial Godard—Trente ans depuis": 40–45.
Jullier, L. (2001), "Bande-son: attention travaux," in G. Delavaud, J.-P. Esquenazi and M.-F. Grange (eds.), *Godard et le métier d'artiste* (Paris: L'Harmattan).
—— (2004), "JLG/ECM," in M. Temple, J. S. Williams and M. Witt (eds.), *For Ever Godard* (London: Black Dog), 272–87.
Kawin, B. F. (1978), *Mindscreen: Bergman, Godard, and First-person Film* (Princeton NJ: Princeton University Press).
Kline, T. J. (2002), *Screening the Text: Intertextuality in New Wave French Cinema* (Baltimore MD: Johns Hopkins University Press).
Kroker, A. (1992), *The Possessed Individual: Technology and the French Postmodern* (New York: St. Martin's).
Lack, R.-F. (2004), "'Sa Voix,'" in M. Temple, J. S. Williams and M. Witt (eds.), *For Ever Godard* (London: Black Dog), 312–29.
—— (2011), "À bout de souffle: les intertextes d'un plan," in J.-L. Leutrat (ed.), *Cinéma et littérature: le grand jeu 2* (Le Havre: De l'incidence), 467–78.
—— (2012), "A Photograph and a Camera: Two Objects in *Film Socialisme*," *Vertigo* 30. http://www.closeupfilmcentre.com/vertigo_magazine/issue-30-spring-2012-godard-is/a-photograph-and-a-camera-two-objects-in-film-socialisme/.
Latham, E. (1998), "Physical Motifs and Concentric Amplification in Godard/Lully's *Armide*," *Indiana Theory Review* 19: 55–85.
Laugier, S. (1993), "The Holy Family," in M. Locke and C. Warren (eds.), *Jean-Luc Godard's* Hail Mary: *Women and the Sacred in Film* (Carbondale: Southern Illinois University Press), 27–38.
Lelièvre, S. (2013), "Africa and Cinema in the Mirror of Godard's *Film Socialisme*," *Journal of African Cinemas* 5:1: 123–27.
Leutrat, J.-L. (1990), *Des traces qui nous ressemblent:* Passion *de Jean-Luc Godard* (Seyssel: Éditions Comp'Act).
—— (1994), "*Histoire(s) du cinéma*, ou comment devenir maître d'un souvenir," *Cinémathèque* 5: 28–39.
—— (2001), "'Mais c'est dans le dos que la lumière va frapper la nuit,'" *Vertigo* 22: 93–102.
Levinas, E. (1979), *Totality and Infinity* (The Hague: Martinus Nijhoff).
—— (1991), *Entre nous: Essais sur le penser-à-l'autre* (Paris: Bernard Grasset).
Liandrat, S., and J.-L. Leutrat (2005), *Godard simple comme bonjour* (Paris: L'Harmattan).
Locke, M., and C. Warren (eds.) (1993), *Jean-Luc Godard's* Hail Mary: *Women and the Sacred in Film* (Carbondale: Southern Illinois University Press).
Long, T. (2014), "'A Place of Active Judgement': Parametric Narration in the Work of Jean-Luc Godard and Ian Wallace," in D. Morrey, C. Stojanova, and N. Côté (eds.), *The Legacies of Jean-Luc Godard* (Waterloo ON: Wilfrid Laurier University Press), 197–215.
Loshitzky, Y. (1995), *The Radical Faces of Godard and Bertolucci* (Detroit: Wayne State University Press).
Lundemo, T. (2004), "The Dissected Image: The Movement of the Video," in J. Fullerton and J. Olsson (eds.), *Allegories of Communication: Intermedial Concerns from Cinema to the Digital* (Rome: John Libbey).
—— (2014), "Godard the Historiographer: From *Histoire(s) du cinéma* to the Beaubourg Exhibition," in T. Conley and T. J. Kline (eds.), *A Companion to Jean-Luc Godard* (Chichester UK: John Wiley and Sons), 408–533.

Lyotard, J.-F. (1985), *Discours, Figure* (Paris: Klincksieck).
––––––– (1989), "The Sign of History" in A. Benjamin (ed.), *The Lyotard Reader* (Oxford: Blackwell).
––––––– (1991 [1988]), *The Inhuman: Reflections on Time*, trans. G. Bennington and R. Bowlby (Cambridge: Polity).
Lyon, E. (1982), "La passion, c'est pas ça," *camera obscura* 8–9–10: 7–10.
MacCabe, C. (1980) (with L. Mulvey and M. Eaton), *Godard: Images, Sounds, Politics* (London: BFI/Indiana University Press).
––––––– (2003), *Godard: A Portrait of the Artist at 70* (London: Bloomsbury).
Malraux, A. (1946), *Esquisse d'une psychologie du cinéma* (Paris: Gallimard).
––––––– (1952), *Les Voix du silence* (Paris: Gallimard).
––––––– (1957–1976), *La Métamorphose des dieux*, 3 vols. (Paris: Gallimard).
––––––– (1996 [1974]), *Lazare* (Gallimard).
Manovich, L. (1997), "What Is Digital Cinema?," *BLIMP* 37: 30–38.
Martin, A. (2004), "Recital: Three Lyrical Interludes in Godard," in M. Temple, J. S. Williams, and M. Witt (eds.), *For Ever Godard* (London: Black Dog), 252–71.
Mas, A., and M. Pisani (2010), "10: *Film Socialisme*," *Independencia*, June 1. http://www.independencia.fr/indp/10_FILM_SOCIALISME_JLG.html#.
McCrea, C. (2009), "Giorgio Agamben," in F. Colman (ed.), *Film, Theory and Philosophy: The Key Thinkers* (Durham UK: Acumen), 349–57.
McMahon, O. D. (2014), *Listening to the French New Wave: The Film Music and Composers of Postwar French Art Cinema* (Bern: Peter Lang).
Meek, A. (2010), *Trauma and Media: Theories, Histories, and Images* (New York and London: Routledge).
Merleau-Ponty, M. (1962 [1945]), *The Phenomenology of Perception*, trans. C. Smith (New York and London: Routledge).
Minh-ha, T. T. (1989), *Woman, Native, Other: Writing Postcoloniality and Feminism.* (Bloomington: Indiana University Press).
Mondzain, M.-J. (1998), "Histoire et passion," *Art Press* Hors-Série—"Guide pour *Histoire(s) du cinéma*" (November): 91–98.
Monk, J. (1998), "The digital unconscious," in J. Wood (ed.), *The Virtual Embodied: Presence/Practice/Technology* (New York and London: Routledge), 30–44.
Morgan, D. (2013), *Late Godard and the Possibilities of Cinema* (Berkeley: University of California Press).
Morrey, D. (2003), "History of Resistance/Resistance of History: Godard's *Éloge de l'amour* (2001)," *Studies in French Cinema* 3:2: 121–30.
––––––– (2005), *Jean-Luc Godard* (Manchester: Manchester University Press).
–––––––, C. Stojanova, and N. Côté (eds.) (2014), *The Legacies of Jean-Luc Godard* (Waterloo ON: Wilfrid Laurier University Press).
Mourlet, M. (1959), "*Sur un art ignoré*," *Cahiers du Cinéma* 98: 23–37.
Murray, A. (2010), *Giorgio Agamben* (London and New York: Routledge).
Murray, T. (2000), "The Crisis of Cinema in the Age of New World Memory: The Baroque Performance of *King Lear*," in M. Temple and J. S. Williams (eds.), *The Cinema Alone: Essays on the Work of Jean-Luc Godard, 1985–2000* (Amsterdam: Amsterdam University Press), 159–78.
Némirovsky, I. (2005 [1930]), *Le Bal* (Paris: Hachette Éducation).
O'Rawe, D. (2010) "The Fraternity of Metaphors," *Kinema* (Fall). http://www.kinema.uwaterloo.ca/article.php?id=475&feature.

——— (2011), "Towards a Poetics of the Cinematographic Frame," *Journal of Aesthetics and Culture* 3:1. http://www.aestheticsandculture.net/index.php/jac/article/view/5378.
Païni, D. (2006), "D'Après JLG . . . ," in N. Brenez, D. Faroult, M. Temple, J. S. Williams, and M. Witt (eds.), *Jean-Luc Godard. Documents* (Paris: Centre Pompidou), 420–26.
Pavsek, C. (2013), *The Utopia of Film: Cinema and Its Futures in Godard, Kluge, and Tahimik* (New York: Columbia University Press).
Péguy, C. (1932), *Clio: Dialogue de l'histoire et de l'âme païenne* (Paris: Gallimard).
Petit, M. (1973), "In Memoriam Omar Diop," *Les Temps Modernes* 323 bis (July).
Petrie, D. (1992) (ed.), *Screening Europe: Image and Identity in Contemporary European Cinema* (London: British Film Institute).
Picard, A. (2010), "Spotlight/Film Socialisme (Jean-Luc Godard)," *Cinema Scope* 43. http://www.cinema-scope.com/wordpress/web-archive-2/issue-43/spotlight-film-socialisme-jean-luc-godard.
Powrie, P. (1987), *French Cinema in the 1980s: Nostalgia and the Crisis of Masculinity* (Oxford: Clarendon).
Quandt, J. (2004), "Projecting Godard: Here and Elsewhere," in M. Temple, J. S. Williams, and M. Witt (eds.), *For Ever Godard* (London: Black Dog), 126–39.
Rancière, J. (1999), "La sainte et l'héritière: à propos des *Histoire(s) du cinéma*," *Cahiers du Cinéma* 537: 58–61.
——— (2006 [2001]), *Film Fables* (London and New York: Berg).
——— (2011), *Les Écarts du cinéma* (Paris: La Fabrique).
Rascaroli, L. (2009), "Performance in and of the Essay film: Jean-Luc Godard plays Jean-Luc Godard in *Notre Musique* (2004)," *Studies in French Cinema* 9:1: 49–61.
Ravetto-Biagioli, K. (2014), "*Noli me tangere*: Jean-Luc Godard's *Histoire(s) du cinéma*," in T. Conley and T. J. Kline (eds.), *A Companion to Jean-Luc Godard* (Chichester UK: John Wiley and Sons), 456–87.
Reader, K. (2004), "Godard and Asynchrony," in M. Temple, J. S. Williams, and M. Witt (eds.), *For Ever Godard* (London: Black Dog), 83–89.
Reverdy, P. (1975), *Nord-sud, Self Defence et autres écrits sur l'art et la poésie (1917–1926)* (Paris: Flammarion).
Rilke, R. M. (1978 [1964]), *Rilke: Selected Poems*, trans. J. B. Leishman (Harmondsworth: Penguin).
Robinson, M. (1988), "Resurrected Images: Godard's *King Lear*," *Performing Arts Journal* 31: 20–25.
Rohdie, S. (2010), "Some Things You Never Learn": interview with D. Williams. *Screening the Past*. http://tlweb.latrobe.edu.au/humanities/screeningthepast/28/sam-rohdie-interview.html.
——— (2012), *Intersections: Writings on Cinema* (Manchester: Manchester University Press).
Romney, J. (2014), "Film of the Week: *Goodbye to Language*." October 29. http://www.filmcomment.com/blog/c/jonathan-romney.
Rosenbaum, J. (1997), "Bande-annonce pour les *Histoire(s) du cinéma*," *Trafic* 21: 5–18.
Ross, A. (2003), "Ghost Sonata: What Happened to German Music?," *The New Yorker*, March 24: 64–71.
Roud, R. (1967), *Godard: Number One* (New York: Martin Secker and Warburg) (republished by the BFI in 2010 with a foreword by M. Temple).
Roustom, K. (2014), "Michel Legrand Scores *Une femme est une femme*," in T. Conley and T. J. Kline (2014) (eds.), *A Companion to Jean-Luc Godard* (Chichester UK: John Wiley and Sons), 71–88.

Rowe, K. K. (1990), "Romanticism, Sexuality and the Canon," *Journal of Film and Video* 42:1: 49–65.
Said, E. W. (1991), *Musical Elaborations* (New York: Columbia University Press).
—— (2007 [2006]), *On Late Style: Music and Literature against the Grain* (New York and London: Bloomsbury).
Sanbar, E. (2004a), *Les Palestiniens. La photographie d'une terre et de son peuple de 1839 à nos jours* (Lucon: Hazan).
—— (2004b), *Figures du Palestinien. identité des origines, identité de devenir* (Paris: Gallimard).
——, and G. Deleuze (1982), "Les Indiens de Palestine," *Libération*, 8–9 May.
Saxton, L. (2008), *Haunted Images: Film, Ethics, Testimony and the Holocaust* (London: Wallflower).
—— (2014), "Passion, Agamben and the Gestures of Work," in H. Gustafsson and S. Grønstad (eds.), *Cinema and Agamben: Ethics, Biopolitics and the Moving Image* (New York and London: Bloomsbury), 55–70.
Scarpetta, G., and D. Païni (1984–85), "La curiosité du sujet": interview with J.-L. Godard, *Art press* Hors-Série 4: 4–18.
Scemama, C. (1986), Histoire(s) du cinéma *de Jean-Luc Godard: La force faible d'un art* (Paris: L'Harmattan).
—— (2014), "Jean-Luc Godard's *Histoire(s) du cinéma* Brings the Dead Back to the Screen," in D. Morrey, C. Stojanova and N. Côté (eds.), *The Legacies of Jean-Luc Godard* (Waterloo ON: Wilfrid Laurier), 99–124.
Schehr, L. R. (1989), "The Homotext of Tournier's *Les Météores*," *SubStance* 58: 35–50.
Schlumpf, E. (2014), "*Notre Musique*: Juste une conversation," in T. Conley and T. J. Kline (eds.), *A Companion to Jean-Luc Godard* (Chichester UK: John Wiley and Sons), 515–26.
Sedgwick, E. K., and A. Frank (1995), "Shame in the cybernetic fold: reading Silvan Tomkins," *Critical Inquiry* 21: 496–522.
Serrut, L. A. (2011), *Jean-Luc Godard, cinéaste acousticien* (Paris: L'Harmattan).
Shafto, S. (2006), "On Painting and History in Godard's *Histoire(s) du cinéma*," *Senses of Cinema* 40 (July 31). www.sensesofcinema.com/2006/40/histoires-du-cinema
Shaviro, S. (1993), *The Cinematic Body* (Minneapolis MN: University of Minnesota Press).
Silverman, K. (2001), "The Author as Receiver," *October* 96: 17–34.
——, and H. Farocki (1998), *Speaking about Godard* (New York: New York University Press).
SOMA (San Francisco) (2003), 17:1.
Silverman, M. (2013), *Palimpsestic Memory: The Holocaust and Colonialism in French and Francophone Fiction and Film* (New York and Oxford: Berghahn).
Skoller, J. (1999), "Reinventing Time, Or The continuing Adventures of Lemmy Caution in Godard's *Allemagne neuf zéro*," *Film Quarterly* 3:3: 35–42.
Smith, D. (2014), "(Dé)collage—Bazin, Godard, Aragon," in T. Conley and T. J. Kline (eds.), *The Godard Companion* (Chichester UK: John Wiley and Sons).
Smith, P. (1995) (ed.), *The Enigmatic Body: Essays on the Arts by Jean Louis Schefer*, trans. P. Smith (Cambridge: Cambridge University Press).
Sollers, P. (1994), "Profond Marivaux," *Le Monde*, 20 May.
—— (1997), "Il y a des fantômes plein l'écran . . .": interview with A. de Baecque and S. Toubiana, *Cahiers du Cinéma* 253: 39–48.
Sontag, S. (2009a), *Styles of Radical Will* (Penguin).
—— (2009b), *Against Interpretation, and Other Essays* (Penguin).

Spengler, O. (1962 [1923]), *The Decline of the West* (New York: Alfred A. Knopf).
Stam, R. (1992), *Reflexivity in film and literature: from Don Quixote to Jean-Luc Godard* (New York: Columbia University Press).
Stenzl, J. (2010), *Jean-Luc Godard—musicien* (Munich: Text + Kritik).
—— (2014), "Jean-Luc Godard: *Dans le noir du temps* (2002)—the filming of a Musical Form," in D. Morrey, C. Stojanova and N. Côté (eds.), *The Legacies of Jean-Luc Godard* (Waterloo ON: Wilfrid Laurier University Press), 15–35.
Sterritt, D. (1998) (ed.), *Jean-Luc Godard: Interviews* (Jackson MS: University of Mississippi Press),
—— (1999), *The Films of Jean-Luc Godard: Seeing the Invisible* (Cambridge UK: Cambridge University Press).
—— (2000), "Speaking and Writing about Godard: A Response to Nochimson and Sutton," *Film-Philosophy* 4:8 (March). http://www.film-philosophy.com/vol4-2000/n8sterritt.
Stewart, G., (2007), *Framed Time: Toward a Postfilmic Cinema* (Chicago: Chicago University Press).
Strode, L. (2000), "France and EU Policy-Making on Visual Culture—New Opportunities for National Identity?," in E. Ezra and S. Harris (eds.), *France in Focus: Film and National Identity* (Oxford: Berg), 61–75.
Swed, M. (2000), "Sharing Sound Theories on Filmmaking," *LA Times*, 6 August, 50, 52.
Taubin, A. (2002), "In the Shadow of Memory," *Film Comment* 38:1 (Jan–Feb): 50–2.
—— (2010), "Wiping the Slate Clean," *Film Comment* (September): 44–6.
Temple, M., and J. S. Williams (eds.), (2000), *The Cinema Alone: Essays on the work of Jean-Luc Godard 1985–2000* (Amsterdam University Press).
——, and J. S. Williams and M. Witt (eds.) (2004), *For Ever Godard* (London: Black Dog).
Valéry, P. (1941), *Mélange* (Paris: Gallimard).
—— (1957), *Essais quasi politiques. Oeuvres*, vol. 1 (Paris: Bibliothèque de la Pléiade).
Warner, M. (1998), *No Go the Bogeyman: Scaring, Lulling, and Making Mock* (London: Chatto and Windus).
Wajcman, G. (1999), "'Saint Paul' Godard contre 'Moïse' Lanzmann, le match," *L'Infini* 65: 121–7.
Weiskel, T. (1976), *The Romantic Sublime: Studies in the Structure and the Psychology of Transcendence* (Baltimore MD: Johns Hopkins University Press).
White, J. (2013), *Two Bicycles: The Work of Jean-Luc Godard and Anne-Marie Miéville* (Waterloo ON: Wilfrid Laurier University Press).
Williams, B. (2014), "Cannes 2014/Adieu au langage (Jean-Luc Godard, France)," *Cinema Scope* 59. http://cinema-scope.com/spotlight/adieu-au-langage-jean-luc-godard-france/.
Williams, J. S. (1997), *The Erotics of Passage: Pleasure, Politics, and Form in the Later Work of Marguerite Duras* (Liverpool and New York: Liverpool University Press/St. Martin's).
—— (2004), "The Exercise Was Beneficial, Monsieur Daney," in M. Temple and M. Witt (eds.), *The French Cinema Book* (London: BFI), 265–72.
—— (2006a), "Présentation" (on *Notre Musique*), in Brenez et al., *Jean-Luc Godard. Documents* (Paris: Centre Pompidou, 2006), 406–09.
—— (2006b), *Jean Cocteau* (Manchester: Manchester University Press).
—— (2011), "Performing the Revolution," in J. Jackson, A.-L. Milne, and J. S. Williams (eds.), *May 68: Rethinking France's Last Revolution* (Basingstoke: Palgrave Macmillan), 281–97.

——, E. Jeremiah, and G. Wylde (2012), "Snakes and Funerals," *Frames Cinema Journal* 1. http://framescinemajournal.com/article/snakes-and-funerals/. Pp. 1–3.
—— (2013), *Space and Being in Contemporary French Cinema* (Manchester: Manchester University Press).
Wills, D. (2000) (ed.), *Jean-Luc Godard's* Pierrot le fou (Cambridge University Press).
—— (2010), "The Audible Life of the Image," *Journal of French and Francophone Philosophy* 18:2: 43–64.
Witt, M. (1998), "On Communication: The Work of Anne-Marie Miéville and Jean-Luc Godard as 'Sonimage' from 1973 to 1979." PhD dissertation, University of Bath.
—— (1999), "The Death(s) of Cinema according to Godard," *Screen* 40:3: 331–46.
—— (2000a), "Qu'était ce que le cinéma, Jean-Luc Godard? An Analysis of the Cinema(s) at Work in and around Godard's *Histoire(s) du Cinéma*," in E. Ezra and S. Harris (eds.), *France in Focus: Film and National Identity* (Oxford: Berg), 23–41.
—— (2000b), "Montage, My Beautiful Care, or Histories of the Cinematograph," in M. Temple and J. S. Williams (eds.), *The Cinema Alone: Essays on the Work of Jean-Luc Godard 1985–2000* (Amsterdam: Amsterdam University Press), 33–50.
—— (2001), "Going through the Motions: Unconscious Optics and Corporal Resistance in Miéville and Godard's *France/tour/détour/deux/enfants*," in A. Hughes and J. S. Williams (eds.), *Gender and French Cinema* (Oxford and New York: Berg), 171–94.
—— (2005), "The Godard Interview: 'I, a Man of the Image,'" *Sight and Sound* (June): 28–30.
—— (2014), "Archaeology of *Histoire(s) du cinéma*," in J.-L. Godard, *Introduction to a True History of Cinema and Television* (Montreal: Caboose), trans. T. Barnard, xi–lxix.
Wollen, P., (1992), "L'Éternel retour," in R. Bellour (ed.) (with M. L. Bandy), *Jean-Luc Godard: Son+Image 1974–1991* (New York: MoMA), 187–95.
—— (2013), *Jean-Luc Godard, Cinema Historian* (Bloomington: Indiana University Press).
Wright, A. (2000), "Elizabeth Taylor at Auschwitz: JLG and the Real Object of Montage," in M. Temple and J. S. Williams (eds.), *The Cinema Alone: Essays on the Work of Jean-Luc Godard, 1985–2000* (Amsterdam: Amsterdam University Press), 51–61.
—— (2012), "JLG/Jean Améry," *Screening the Past*. http://www.screeningthepast.com/2012/12/jlgjean-amery/. Pp. 1–12.
Youngblood, G. (1998), "Jean-Luc Godard: No Difference between Life and Cinema," in D. Sterritt (ed.), *Jean-Luc Godard: Interviews* (Jackson: Mississippi University Press), 9–49.
Žižek, S. (1999), *The Ticklish Subject: The Absent Centre of Political Ontology* (London and New York: Verso).
—— (2000), *The Fragile Absolute—or, Why Is the Christian Legacy Worth Fighting For?* (London and New York: Verso).
—— (2001), *The Fright of Real Tears: Krzysztof Kieślowski. between Theory and Post-Theory* (London: BFI).
—— (2005a [1997]), "Smashing the Other's Face." http://www.lacan.com/zizsmash.htm.
—— (2005b), "Neighbors and Other Monsters: A Plea for Ethical Violence," in K. Reinhard, E. R. Santner, and S. Žižek, *The Neighbor: Three Inquiries in Political Theology* (Chicago: University of Chicago Press).
—— (2008), *Violence: Six Sideways Reflections* (London: Profile Books).

Select Filmography/Discography

For a complete filmography including all Godard's shorter films and video works, preparatory video notes, music videos, sketches, filmed "open letters" and homages, commercials, trailers, festival pieces, works in other media, and initial versions of films and recorded interviews, see Michael Witt, *Jean-Luc Godard, Cinema Historian* (Indiana University Press, 2013).

Opération "béton," 1955, 35 mm, b/w, 20 min.
Une femme coquette, 1956, 16 mm, b/w, 10 min.
Tous les garçons s'appellent Patrick, aka *Charlotte et Véronique* (*All the Boys are Called Patrick*), 1957, 35 mm, b/w, 21 min.
Une histoire d'eau (*A Story of Water*) (co-dir. François Truffaut), 1958, 35 mm, b/w, 18 min.
Charlotte et son Jules (*Charlotte and Her Boyfriend*), 1958, 35 mm, b/w, 20 min.
À Bout de souffle (*Breathless*), 1960, 35 mm, b/w, 90 min.
Le Petit Soldat (*The Little Soldier*), 1960, 35 mm, b/w, 88 min [banned until 1963].
Une femme est une femme (*A Woman Is a Woman*), 1961, 35 mm, color, 84 min.
La Paresse (episode in *Les Sept péchés capitaux*), 1962, 35 mm, b/w, 15 min.
Vivre sa vie. Film en douze tableaux (*My Life to Live*), 1962, 35 mm, b/w, 85 min.
Le Nouveau Monde (*The New World*) (episode in *RoGoPaG*), 1962, 35 mm, b/w, 20 min.
Les Carabiniers, 1963, 35 mm, b/w, 80 min.
Le Grand escroc (*The Great Swindle*) (episode in *Les Plus belles escroqueries du monde*), 1963, 35 mm, b/w, 25 min.
Le Mépris (*Contempt*), 1963, 35 mm, color, 105 min.
Bande à part (*Band of Outsiders*), 1964, 35 mm, b/w, 95 min.
Une femme mariée: Fragments d'un film tourné en 1964, 1964, 35 mm, b/w, 98 min.
Montparnasse-Levallois: Un action film (episode in *Paris vu par . . .*), 1965, 16 mm, color, 18 min.
Alphaville, une étrange aventure de Lemmy Caution (*Alphaville, a Strange Adventure of Lemmy Caution*), 1965, 35 mm, b/w, 98 min.
Pierrot le fou, 1965, 35 mm, color, 110 min.
Masculin Féminin: Quinze faits précis (*Masculine, Feminine: in 15 Acts*), 1966, 35 mm, b/w, 110 min.
Made in USA, 1966, 35 mm, color, 90 min.
Deux ou trois choses que je sais d'elle (*Two or Three Things I Know about Her*), 1966, 35 mm, color, 90 min.

Anticipation, aka *L'Amour en l'an 2000* (*Love through the Centuries*) (episode in *Le Plus vieux métier du monde*), 1967, 35 mm, color, 20 min.
La Chinoise, 1967, 35 mm, color, 95 min.
Caméra-œil (*Camera-Eye*) (episode in *Loin du Vietnam*), 1967, 16 mm, color, 15 min.
L'Amour (episode in *Vangelo 70*, aka *La contestation*, aka *Amore et rabbia*), 1967, 35 mm, color, 26 min.
Week-end (*Weekend*), 1967, 35 mm, color, 95 min.
Le Gai savoir (*The Joy of Knowledge*), 1968, 35 mm, color, 95 min [first distributed in 1969].
Ciné-tracts (those made by Godard or in collaboration: 7, 8, 9, 10, 11, 12, 13, 14, 15, 16, 23, 40), 1968, 16 mm, b/w, 2–4 mins.
Film-tract No. 1968, aka *Le Rouge* (dir. Gérard Fromanger, technician Jean-Luc Godard), 1968, 16 mm, color, 2 min. 45.
Un film comme les autres (*A Film Like Any Other*), 1968, 16 mm, color and b/w, 100 min.
One American Movie, aka *One A.M.*, 1968, 16 mm, unfinished [a 90-minute compilation of the footage shot for *One A.M.*, and of a film being shot on the making of *One A.M.*, was edited by the cameraman D.A. Pennebaker and released as *One P.M.* in 1971].
One plus One, 1968, 35 mm, color, 99 min.
British Sounds, aka *See You at Mao* (co-dir. Jean-Henri Roger), 1969, 16 mm, color, 52 min.
Pravda (co-dir. Jean-Henri Roger), 1969, 16 mm, color, 58 min.
Vent d'est (*Wind from the East*), Dziga Vertov Group, 1969, 16 mm, color, 100 min.
Lotte in Italia (*Struggles in Italy*), Dziga Vertov Group, 1970, 16mm, color, 60 min.
Vladimir et Rosa (*Vladimir and Rosa*), Dziga Vertov Group, 1970, 16 mm, color, 96 min.
Tout va bien (*All's Well*) (co-dir. Jean-Pierre Gorin), 1972, 35 mm, color, 95 min.
Letter to Jane: An Investigation about a Still (co-dir. Jean-Pierre Gorin), 1972, 16 mm, color, 52 min.
Ici et ailleurs (*Here and Elsewhere*) (co-dir. Anne-Marie Miéville (co.dir Jean-Pierre Gorin for the *Jusqu'à la victoire* material), 1974, 16 mm, color, 53 min.
Numéro deux (*Number Two*), 1975, 35 mm and video, color, 88 min.
Comment ça va (*How Is It Going?*) (co-dir. Anne-Marie Miéville), 1976, 16 mm and video, 78 min.
Six fois deux: Sur et sous la communication (co-dir. Anne-Marie Miéville), 1978, video, color, 12-episode television series, 12 x 50 min.
France tour détour deux enfants (co-dir. Anne-Marie Miéville), 1979, video, color, 12-episode television series, 12 x 25 min.
Scénario de Sauve qui peut (la vie). Quelques remarques sur la réalisation et la production du film, 1979, video, color, 21 min.
Sauve qui peut (la vie) (*Every Man for Himself*, aka *Slow Motion*), 1979, 35 mm, color, 87 min.
Lettre à Freddy Buache: À propos d'un court-métrage sur la ville de Lausanne (*Letter to Freddy Buache: About a short film on the town of Lausanne*), 1981, video transferred to 35 mm, color, 11 min.
Passion, le travail et l'amour: Introduction à un scénario, aka *Troisième état du scénario du film Passion*, 1981, video, color, 30 min.
Passion, 1982, 35 mm, color, 87 min.
Scénario du film Passion, 1982, video, color, 53 min.
Changer d'image, aka *Lettre à la bien-aimée* (*Change of Image*) (episode in *Le changement à plus d'un titre*), 1982, video, color, 9 min. 50 sec.
Prénom Carmen (*First Name: Carmen*), 1983, 35 mm, color, 83 min.

Petites notes à propos du film Je vous salue, Marie, 1983, video, color, 20 min.
Je vous salue, Marie (Hail Mary), 1985, 35 mm, color, 78 min.
Détective, 1985, 35 mm, color, 95 min.
Soft and Hard: Soft Talk on a Hard Subject between Two Friends (co-dir. Anne-Marie Miéville), 1985, video, color, 52 min.
Grandeur et décadence d'un petit commerce de cinéma, aka *Chantons en chœur*, 1985, video and 35 mm, color, 91 min [a telefilm broadcast in the "Série Noire" series on TF1 in May 1986].
Meetin' WA, aka *Meeting Woody Allen*, 1986, video, color, 26 min.
Armide (episode in *Aria*), 1987, 35 mm, color, 12 min.
Soigne ta droite: Une place sur la terre (Keep Your Right Up: A Place on Earth), 1987, 35 mm, color, 81 min.
King Lear, 1987, 35mm, color, 90 min.
On s'est tous défilé, 1987, video, color, 13 min.
Puissance de la parole, 1988, video, color, 25 min.
Le Dernier Mot (episode in *Les Français vus par . . .*), 1988, video, color, 12 min.
Le Rapport Darty (co-dir. Anne-Marie Miéville), 1989, video, color, 50 min.
Histoire(s) du cinéma—initial versions of episodes 1A, *Toutes les histoires* (All the [hi]stories) (51 min), and 1B: *Une histoire seule* (A solitary [hi]story) (42 min), 1989, video, color [first broadcast on Canal Plus in May 1989].
Nouvelle Vague (New Wave), 1990, 35 mm, color, 89 min.
L'Enfance de l'art (The Childhood of Art) (episode in *Comment vont les enfants?*) (co-dir. Anne-Marie Miéville), 1991, 35 mm, color, 8 min.
Allemagne année 90 neuf zéro (Germany Year 90 Nine Zero), 1991, 35 mm, color, 62 min.
Pour Thomas Wainggai (episode in the series *Écrire contre l'oubli*) (co-dir. Anne-Marie Miéville), 1991, 35 mm, color, 3 min. (broadcast in December 1991 on all French television channels except TF1).
Les Enfants jouent à la Russie (The Kids Play Russian), 1993, video, color, 58 min.
Hélas pour moi (Oh, Woe Is Me), 1993, 35mm, color, 84 min.
Je vous salue, Sarajevo, 1993, video, color, 2 min. 24 sec.
JLG/JLG: autoportrait de décembre (JLG/JLG: December Self-Portrait), 1995, 35 mm, color, 56 min.
Deux fois cinquante ans de cinéma français (2 x 50 Years of French Cinema) (co-dir. Anne-Marie Miéville), 1995, video, color, 49 min.
For Ever Mozart, 1996, 35 mm, color, 80 min.
Adieu au TNS (Farewell to the Théâtre National de Strasbourg), 1996, video, color, 7 min.
Histoire(s) du cinéma, 1998, video (VHS), color, 264 min (4-part box set by Gaumont). 8 episodes: 1A: *Toutes les histoires* (All the [hi]stories); 1B: *Une histoire seule* (A solitary [hi]story); 2A: *Seul le cinéma* (The cinema alone); 2B: *Fatale Beauté* (Fatal Beauty); 3A: *La Monnaie de l'absolu* (Aftermath of the absolute); 3B: *Une Vague nouvelle* (A new wave); 4A: *Le Contrôle de l'univers* (The control of the universe); 4B: *Les Signes parmi nous* (The signs in our midst).
The Old Place: Small Notes Regarding the Arts at Fall of 20th Century (co-dir. Anne-Marie Miéville), 1998, video, color, 47 min.
De l'origine du XXIe siècle, 2000, video, color, 15 min.
Éloge de l'amour (In Praise of Love), 2001, 35 mm and digital video, b/w and color, 94 min.
Dans le noir du temps (episode in *Ten Minutes Older: The Cello*) (co-dir. Anne-Marie Miéville), 2002, video, color, 10 min.

Liberté et Patrie (co-dir. Anne-Marie Miéville), 2002, video, color, 22 min.
Moments choisis des Histoire(s) du cinéma, 2004, video transferred to 35 mm, color, 64 min.
Notre Musique (*Our Music*), 2004, 35 mm, color, 80 min.
Prière pour refusniks, 2004, video, color, 7 min.
Prière (2) pour refusniks, 2004, video, color, 3 min. 30 sec.
Reportage amateur (maquette expo) (Amateur report [exhibition model]) (co-dir. Anne-Marie Miéville), 2006, video, color, 47 min.
Vrai Faux Passeport: Fiction documentaire sur des occasions de porter un jugement à propos de la façon de faire des films (True False Passport: Documentary fiction on the opportunities for passing judgment about the manner in which films are made), 2006, video, b/w and color, 55 min.
Ecce homo, 2006, video, b/w and color, 2 min.
Histoire(s) du cinéma, 2007, video (DVD), color. Box set of 4 DVDs by Gaumont.
Film socialisme (directorial committee: Jean-Luc Godard, Fabrice Aragno, Jean-Paul Battaggia, Paul Grivas), 2010, HD video, color, 102 min.
Les Trois désastres (The three disasters) (episode in *3X3D*), 2013, 35 mm, HD video 3D, b/w and color, 16 min. 52 sec.
Adieu au langage (*Goodbye to Language*), 2014, 35 mm, HD video 3D, b/w and color, 67 min.
Le Pont des soupirs (*The Bridge of Sighs*) (episode in *Bridges of Sarajevo*), 2014, video, color, 8 min.

Select Discography

Nouvelle Vague (CD) (Munich: ECM Records "New Series" 1600, 1997).
Histoires(s) du cinéma (CD) (Munich: ECM Records "New Series" 1706, 1999). Box set of five CDs and four multilingual art books.
Godard/Jousse: Les écrans sonores de Jean-Luc Godard (CD) (France Culture and Harmonia Mundi, 2000).
Jean-Luc Godard—Histoire(s) de Musique (CD) (Universal France, 2007).

Index

Page numbers in **bold** refer to figures

3D films, 247–48; *Adieu au langage*, 247, 248–54, **249**, **251**, **253**, 259n27; *Les Trois désastres*, 247–48
3X3D, 247, 289n1

À Bout de souffle, 230
A Place in the Sun, 75–76, **76**, 136
A Talking Picture, 192
Abbott, Berenice, 237
Abdelli, Kamel, 249, 252
Action Directe, 32
Adieu au langage, 247, 289–90n5; backstory, 248; chiasmus in, 253; ending, 254; experimentation and innovation, 250–54; final sequence, 254; and metaphor, 250; point of view, 252–53; release, 290n8; soundtrack, 251–52; structure, 249–50; superimpositions, **251**, 251; themes, 248; use of music, 248, **249**, 251–52; video, letter, 259n27
Adieu Bonaparte, 192
Adler, Sarah, 152, 162–64, **165**, 166, 170–71, **171**, 174, 183
Adorno, Theodor, 53, 71, 80, 255n4
aesthetics: and ethics, 2, 8–13, 16; and politics, 15–16; and terrorism, 28–29 *passim*
Africa, Godard and, 45–51, **47**, **50**
African Americans, 43–44, **44**, 180
Agamben, Giorgio, 105–7, 108, 110, 115–16, 121–22, 123, 124, 175, 269–70n3, 269n1, 270n4, 270n5, 272n27
Agatha et les lectures illimitées, 212
Aguilar, George, 153–54, 161–62, **162**, **163**

Ahmed, Sara, 9
Akerman, Chantal, 283–84n25
Algerian War, 25, 26, 32
Ali, Tariq, 40
Allain, Valérie, 233, **233**
Allégret, Marc, 49, 229, 288–89n19
Allemagne année 90 neuf zéro, 55, 56, 60–61, 72, 73, 130, 143, 209, 213, 219, 260n10, 263n32, 264n42, 267n14, 268–69n28; use of music, 264n42
Allen, Woody, 120
Amstutz, Roland, 207
Alphaville, 213
Althusser, Louis, 22, 24, 256n5
Amarcord, 68
American culture and values, 44, 54, 60–61
Améry, Jean, 167, 280n8
Andréa, Yann, 229, 287–88n13
An, Grace, 257n16
Ang, Ien, 54, 259–60n5
Angelopoulos, Theo, 55
angels, 98, 268n23, 268n24
Annaud, Jean-Jacques, 231
anti-Semitism, 185, 284n30, 285n31
Antonioni, Michelangelo, 289n2
Apollinaire, Guillaume, 248
Aragon, Louis, 26, 64, 68, 230, 248, 287–88n13
Arendt, Hannah, 163, 195, 286–87n6
Argerich, Martha, 66
Arletty, 65
Armide, 131, 232–24, **233**, 275n13
Asphalt, 262n18
Assas, Madeleine, 258–59n25

Astor, Junie, 64
Astruc, Alexandre, 213
Au hasard Balthazar, 212
Aumont, Jacques, 55, 79, 131, 256n8, 265–66n48, 275n12
Auschwitz, 63, 71, 75, 77; *see also* the Holocaust
Avery, Tex, 270–71n11

Bach, Johann Sabastian, 58, 77, 91, 95, 128, 129, 130, 133–35, 136, 137, 140, 142, 144
Bachelard, Gaston, 124, 201–2
Bacon, Francis, 55, 245, 268–69n28
Badiou, Alain, 22, 34, 146–47, 191, 210, 248, 276n29
Baecque, Antoine de, 57, 179
Baez, Joan, 193
Balibar, Étienne, 22
Balzac, Honoré de, 191, 203
Bamako, 259n26
Bamberger, Jean-Pierre, 48, 259n27
Bande à part, 230
Barbara, 196
Barbey, Bruno, 200
Barbie, Klaus, 113
Bardot, Brigitte, 218
Baross, Zsuzsa, 7
Barr, Burlin, 166, 280n5
Barrère, Igor, 237
Barthes, Roland, 202, 212, 287n13
Bartók, Béla, 58, 129, 145, 276n25
Bartoli, Claire, 138
Bataille, Georges, 62–63, 148, 150, 274n10, 278n41
Battleship Potemkin, 118
Baudelaire, Charles, 6, 124, 153, 159, 231, 236
Bauman, Zygmunt, 263n31
Baye, Nathalie, 224
Bazin, André, 68, 116
Beausson-Diagne, Nadège, 42
Beckett, Samuel, 49, 119, 195, 248, 286n3
Beethoven, Ludwig van, 74, 128, **129**, 129, 132, 136, 143, 195, 248, 210, 255n4, 274n7, 274n8
Beghin, Cyril, 84
Bellour, Raymond, 12, 72, 211, 220

Ben Barka, Mehdi, 21, 256n2
Benjamin, Walter, 79, 106, 157, 196, 248, 265n42, 268n21, 268n23, 279–80n4
Benoist, Jocelyn, 248
Bergala, Alain, 9, 56, 71, 103, 218, 259n4, 267n16, 268n23, 282n16
Bergé, Pierre, 287n13
Bergounioux, Pierre, 152
Bergé, Pierre, 287–88n13
Bergson, Henri, 85, 98, 195, 270n5
Berio, Luciano, 275n15
Bernanos, Georges, 76, 140, 196
Bersani, Leo, 279–80n4
Berto, Juliet, 22
Bertolucci, Bernardo, 257n16
Bicycle Thieves, 68
Binoche, Juliette, 65, 77
Bird of Paradise, 66
Birds, The, 62
Birnbaum, Antonia, 152
Birth of a Nation, The, 173
Bitter Rice, 68
Bjørnstad, Ketil, 129, 147, 149, 152
Black God, White Devil, 49
black other, the, 37–38, 257–58n21, 258n23, 258n25; agency, 39; black femininity, 258n23, 258n25; function of, 41–42, 43–44; the immigrant, 38–39, **39**; the prophet, 42, **44**; the revolutionary, 39–40, **40**; and violence, 41, 43; visibility, 42, 43, 45; the worker, 40–42
black power, 39–40, **40**
Blake, William, 57
Blanchot, Maurice, 13, 248
Bogue, Ronald, 274n8
Bohr, Niels, 279n3
Bonfils, Félix, 200
Bordwell, David, 249, 289n3, 289n4
Borges, Jorge Luis, 100, 245, 248, 289n22
Bosetti, Luca, 29, 31
Bosnian War, 55, 59, 151–52, 155, 159, 164, 166, 168, 169, 281n10, 286n3
Boulez, Pierre, 127
Bouvet, Jean-Christophe, 152
Brahem, Anoaur, 152
Brakhage, Stan, 250
Brass, Ferlyn, 153–54, 161–62, **163**
Braudel, Fernand, 194, 195, 196, 201, 273n6

Braunberger, Pierre, 210, 285n31
Brecht, Bertolt, 24
Brenez, Nicole, 191, 285n6
Bresson, Robert, 1–2, 67, 74, 119, 208, 270–71n11, 272n25
Brialy, Jean-Claude, 231
British Sounds, 31, 40–41
Broch, Hermann, 109, 114, 116–17, 120, 209, 219–20, 239, 240, 270n5
Brody, Richard, 3, 31, 46, 184–85, 284n30
Bronte, Emily, 262n19
Bruneau, Zoé, 249, 253
Bryars, Gavin, 130
Buache, Freddy, 270–71n11
Bukatman, Scott, 102
Busch, Ernst, 199, **199**
By the Bluest of Seas, 88, 252

Cage, John, 136
Cahiers du Cinéma, 26, 61–62, 172, 230, 231, 256n9, 275–76n23; no. 300 (May 1979), 45–46, 193, 216, 230
Caméra-oeil, 15–16
Camus, Albert, 29
Camp, Cécile, 44
Capa, Robert, 193
Captain Blood, 49
Captain Horatio Hornblower, 62, 66
Carax, Leos, 137, 210
Cardoso, Margarida, 46
Carette, Julien, 69–70, 243
Casarès, Maria, 91, 93, 97, 112, **240**
Cave of Forgotten Dreams, 248
Ce vieux rêve qui bouge, 288n16
Celan, Paul, 273n6
Céline, Louis-Ferdinand, 175, 248
Centre Pompidou, 94, 178, 261n11, 269n1
Cerisuelo, Marc, 7
champ/contre-champ, **156**, 164, 170, 174, 179, 182, 186, 253, 282n13, 282n16; montage elements as, 155–60
Changer d'image, 14, 46–48, **47**, 50, 51, 131, 212, 220, 234, 241, 259n27
Channes, Claude, 20
Chardonne, Jacques, 248
Charlotte et son Jules, 232
Chevallier, Richard, 249
Cheyenne Autumn, 173

chiasmus, 10, 24, 123, 260n9, 261–62n13; in Adieu au langage, 253; Duras and, 224, 228–29, 243; in Éloge de l'amour, 147, 149–52; figuration, 101–3; in Film socialisme (book), 202–3; formations, 15, 117; in Histoire(s) du cinéma, 69–70, 70, 74, 77, 79, 90, **93**, 93–94, 97–98, 101–3; in La Chinoise, 16, 48; and metaphor, 282n13; and music, 130–31, 133, 275n13; in Notre Musique, 160; in Nouvelle Vague, 138–41; and reversal, 66; and silence, 114; in Soigne ta droite, 109; see also montage
Chichin, Fred, 111, **111**, 113; see also Les Rita Mitsouko
Chion, Michel, 275n20
Chirac, Jacques, 108
Christmann, Richard, 191
cinema: affective responses to, 86; aims, 105; decline of, 77; function, 16; Godard's view of, 271–72n23; invention of, 94; as national renewal, 67–72, **70**; power of, 123; power of transfiguration, 102–3; resistance in, 68; as silent dialogue, 10; status, 63–64; virtual otherness, 13
Cinémathèque Française, 29
Cinematic Event, the, 18, 133; music as, 144–48
Cissé, Souleymane, 48
Clark, James, 280n6
Claudel, Paul, 278n1
Clay, Cassius, 40
Cleaver, Eldridge, 39, 40
Cléder, Jean, 287n12
Clément, René, 142
Clift, Montgomery, 75
Clouzot, Henri-Georges, 157
Cocciante, Riccardo, 68
Cocteau, Jean, 71, 89, 207, 213–14, 229, 232–45, 244, 248, 270–71n11, 287n13, 288n18, 288–89n19, 288n16, 288n18; Godard and, 231, 232–36, 245–46; Godard's use of, 236–45; La Belle et la bête, 233, 237–38; L'Aigle à deux têtes, 233; Le Sang d'un poète, 241, **242**; Le Testament d'Orphée, 237, 239, 241–42; Orphée, 232, 233, 234–35, 237, 239,

Cocteau, Jean (*continued*)
    240, **240**, 242; presence in *Histoire(s) du cinéma*, 237–40, **240**, 242–43, 246
Cohen, Leonard, 89, 92, 136
Cohn-Bendit, Daniel, 23, 185
Coleridge, Samuel, 100, 245, 268–69n28
Collage(s) de France, archéologie du cinéma d'après JLG, 94, 178, 267–68n17, 269n1
Comment ça va, 217
Connor, Steven, 103
Conrad, Joseph, 195
Coppola, Francis Ford, 55
Corot, Jean-Baptiste-Camille, 62
Cot, Pierre, 194
Côte, Nicole, 3
Courbet, Gustave, 248
Coutard, Raoul, 24, **221**, 222
Cronenberg, David, 86
Cuny, Alain, 64–65, **65**, 273–74n6
Curnier, Jean-Paul, 152, 194, **198**, 198, 205, 210, 283n24
Cutts, Graham, 49

Dabashi, Hamid, 176
DADA, 250
Dalle Vacche, Angela, 266n48
Daly, Fergus, 10
Daney, Serge, 230–31, **242**, 243, 259n4
Daniels, Danny, 39
Dans le noir du temps, 257n16, 277–78n40
Dante, 68, 141, 236, 245, 268–69n28, 289n22
Darget, Chantal, 39, **39**
Darling, David, 127, 129, 137, 147, 149, 152, 279n2
Darmon, Maurice, 285n31
Darrieux, Danièle, 64
Darwish, Mahmoud, 152–53, 168–73, **171**, 209, 210, 279n2, 281–82n13, 287n7
David, Jacques-Louis, 193
de Baecque, Antoine, 3, 15, 57, 83
de Bruijn, Lex, 23, **24**
de Gaulle, Charles, 33, 65, 73
de Lafayette, Madame, 287–88n13
De l'origine du XXIe siècle, 229, 277–78n40
de Man, Paul, 90
de Marivaux, Pierre, 286n3

de Musset, Alfred, 258–59n25, 286n3
de Rivarol, Antoine, 286n2
de Rougemont, Denis, 55–56, 71–72, 77, 196, **199**, 199, 241, 260n9, 271n19
de Santis, Giuseppe, 68
de Sica, Vittorio, 68
de Staël, Nicolas, 55, 65, 77, 244, 248, 262n20
da Vinci, Leonardo, 62, 270–71n11
de La Tour, Georges, 285n6
Déa, Marie, 64–65, 273n6
Debord, Guy, 29, 67, 105–6, 107, 123, 270n4
Debray, Régis, 73–74, 264n35
Del Rio, Dolores, 66
Delacroix, Eugène, 54, 59
Delair, Suzy, 64
Delannoy, van Jean, 89
Delerue, Georges, 7, 128
Deleuze, Gilles, 72, 106, 179, 264n39, 267n14, 269–70n3, 270n5, 270–71n11, 274n8
Delon, Alain, 138, **140**, 141, 142, 207–8
Delpy, Julie, 137, 229, 273n6
Demy, Jacques, 233–34, 288n16
Depardieu, Gérard, 95, 227
Dermit, Édouard, 239
Derrida, Jacques, 60, 254, 261n14
desire, 231–36, **233**, 233–34, 243; *see also* sexuality and sexual difference
Détective, 136–37
Deux fois cinquante ans de cinéma français, 79, 287n9
Deux ou trois choses que je sais d'elle, 21, 39, 54, 212
"Deux ou trois choses qu'ils se sont dites," **225**, 225–27
Diawara, Manthia, 45, 259n26
Dickinson, Emily, 228
Diderot, Denis, 231
Dieckmann, Katherine, 134–35
Dienst, Richard, 88
Dieu, Nade, 180–83
digital technology, 4, 83–88, 266–67n6, 266n1; and editing, 84, **87**, 87–88; *see also* montage
Dixon, Wheeler Winston, 7
Diop, Omar, **35**, 35–38, 44, 48

Doherty, William, **44**
Dolivet, Louis, 194
Dolto, Françoise, 147, 248, 276–77n35, 276n35
Domahidy, Mathias, 42
Don Quixote, 272n27
Doré, Gustave, 270–71n11
Dostoyevsky, Fyodor, 23, 164
Douin, Jean-Luc, 7
Dr. Jekyll and Mr. Hyde, 252
Dreyer, Carl Theodor, 36, 210
Drabinski, John E., 7
Dreamers, The, 257n16
Drieu La Rochelle, Pierre, 65
Dubillard, Roland, 196, 198, **198**
Dubois, Philippe, 209
Duchamp, Marcel, 248
Duel in the Sun, 89–90, **90**
Duhamel, Antoine, 128
Dumas, Alexandre, 210
Dumézil, Georges, 210
Dumont, René, 195
Duplantier, Alain, 288n13
Duras, Marguerite, 70, 212, 214, 222–31, **225**, 243–45, **244**, 256n2; and chiasmus, 224, 228–29, 243; "Deux ou trois choses qu'ils se sont dites," **225**, 225–27; Godard and, 245–46, 287n12; presence in *Histoire(s) du cinéma*, 243–45, **244**; and *Sauve qui peut (la vie)*, 222–24, **223**; and sexual difference, 228–31, 287–88n13; status, 222
Dürer, Albrecht, 72
Dutronc, Jacques, 50, **223**, 223
Dvořák, Antonín, 128, 129, 133–34, 140, 142, 144
Dymon, Frankie, 39–40, **40**
Dziga Vertov Group, 11, 29–32, 34, 128

Eicher, Manfred, 127, 152, 273n2
Eine, Simon, 163
Eisenschitz, Bernard, 262n18, 269n1
Eisenstein, Sergei, 288n16
El Greco, 59
Ellul, Jacques, 248
Éloge de l'amour, 10, 274–75n10, 278n41, 284n29; black other in, 43–44, **44**, 258n25; chiasmus in, 147, 149–52; historical element, 149; structure, 149; use of music, 133, 148–50, **150**
Elshaw, Gary, 39, 258n22
Emmelhainz, Irmgard, 166–67, 169, 176, 182, 184, 281n9, 283n23, 284n28
Encore, 288n16
Espoir: Sierra de Teruel, 192, 204
Estates General of Cinema, 29
ethics, 123–24; ethical responsibility, 167–68, 280n7; ethical subject, the, 165–66; and aesthetics, 2, 8–13, 16
Europe and European culture, 54–57, 261n13, 263n31, 263n33 *passim*

Fairfax, Daniel, 46
Family Jewels, 107
Fargier, Jean-Paul, 286n3
Farocki, Harun, 7, 75, 264n41, 276n28
Faroult, David, 256n10, 268n18
Fassbinder, Rainer Werner, 235–36
Fatale Beauté (episode 2B of *Histoire(s) du cinéma*), 58, 237–38
Faulkner, William, 65, 196, 212
Faure, Élie, 128, 130, 147, 209, 231
Fauré, Gabriel, 130
Feldman, Valentin, 137
Fellini, Federico, 68
Fendt, Ted, 290n7
Ferrat, Jean, 36
Ferré, Léo, 130
Ferri, Gabriella, 196
Figon, Georges, 256n2
Film socialisme (film), 4, 6, 97, 173, 189–91, 204–5, 210, 254, 258n23, 276n29, 279n2, 285n6, 286n9; aesthetic transformation, 206; black other in, 42; central argument, 190; cruise ship movement, 190; Lucien, 205–6; montage elements, 189; Navajo English subtitles, 161, 190, 285n3; opening sequence, 190; second trailer, 285n2; structure, 191; title, 189; trailers, 190; use of music, 190
Film socialisme (book), 191–206, 285n7, 286n9; absence of film images, 192; aesthetic transformation, 206; aims, 194–95; Arab/Hebrew associations, 196–97; back cover epigraph, 191–92; bay of Haifa, 200–1, **201**; chiasmus in,

Film socialisme (book) *(continued)*
  202–3; dialectical oppositions, 196–97; photographs and images, 192–93, 201–3; portrait figures, 195–201, **197, 198, 199**; rhetorical structures, 203–4; status, 204; structure, 205; subtitle, 202; text, 192, 193–94
Film-tract No. 1968 (*Le Rouge*), 128, 257n11
Firk, Michèle, 238
Flaherty, Robert, 48
Flaubert, Gustave, 236
Fleischer, Alain, 176, 185, 283–84n25
Flinn, Margaret, 262n18
Flynn, Errol, 49
Flusser, Vilém, 83
focus pulls, 113–14, **114**
Fonda, Jane, 32
For Ever Mozart, 54–57, 72, 80, 128, 144, 258–59n25, 274n7, 286n3, 289n2
Fort Apache, 160
Fóti, Véronique, 101
Four Days of Naples, The, 192
Fox, Albertine, 274n9
France tour détour deux enfants, 203–4, 215, 217
Francesca, Piero della, 70, **70**
Franju, Georges, 270–71n11
Frank, Adam, 84
Frankenstein, 217
Freud, Sigmund, 248
Frodon, Jean-Michel, 185, 269n1, 285n32
Fromanger, Gérard, 128, 257n11
Fuseli, Henry, 59, 270–71n11

Gabler, Neal, 195
Gabin, Jean, 64
Garbo Greta, 210
García, Ramos, **154**, 158
Gardner, Ava, 92
Garrel, Philippe, 55
Gauguin, Paul, 89, 91
Geary, James, 186
Gégauff, Paul, 128
Genet, Jean, 196, 197, **197**, 205, 229, 235, 235–36, 286n8, 287–88n13, 288–89n19
Gentileschi, Artemisia, 58, 66
Germany Year Zero, 27, 59, 68

Gide, André, 49, 210, 212, 229, 288–89n19
Giger, Paul, 137
Giordano, Domiziana, 138, **140**
Giotto, 72, 75–77, **76, 98, 136**, 268n24, 270n11
Giraudoux, Jean, 24, 95, 193
Giscard d'Estaing, Valéry, 33
Glucksmann, André, 33
Godard, Jean-Luc, 20; anti-Semitism, 185, 284n30, 285n31; artistic method, 122; biographies, 3; cinematic self, **100**, 100–1; and Cocteau, 231, 232–45, 245–46; comparison with Malraux, 57; on digital technology, 266–67n6; and Duras, 222–31, **225**, 245–46, 287n12; encounter with Africa, 45–51, **47, 50**; engagement with literature, 207–14, **208, 213**; fall, 97–98, 103; and gay cinema, 288n16; and gay literature, 229–31, 287–88n13; historical project, 5; late, 4; literary method, 209–10; literary style, 214–16; Montreal lectures, 215; Mozambique experiment, 45–48, 259n26, 259n27; on music, 271n21; on musical movement, 134–35; narcissism, 158; in *Notre Musique*, 152–53, **154**, 155, 155–60; open letter to Malraux, 21; *Orphée* review, 234–35, 242; on the Palestinians, 174; on Renoir, 12; self-performance, 11–12, 94–97, 155–60, 184, 216–22, **218**; and sexual difference, 228–31; status, 4–5, 18; sublime, 75–77, 79; transformation into Maoist filmmaker, 29–32; view of cinema, 271–72n23; working method and approach 36; writings, 192, 225
Godet, Héloïse, 249
Goethe, Johann, 27, 73, 193, 195
Goldstein, Patrick, 284n30
Goodis, David, 181
Gorin, Jean-Pierre, 22, 29, 30–31, 32, 228, 285n31
Gorz, André, 253
Goya, Francisco de, 54, 58, 59, 61, 62, 77–78, 210, 263n23
Goytisolo, Juan, 152, 172, 210, 282n14
Grant, Cary, 155–56, **156**

Great Dictator, The, 145
Green, Julien, 208, 229, 248
Greenaway, Peter, 289n1
Grégori, Christian, 250
Grünewald, Matthias, 59, 60, 78, 201, 264n42
Guattari, Félix, 267n14
Guégan, Gérard, 20
Guerin, Marie Anne, 149, 277n37
Guerra, Ruy, 45
Guillory, John, 97
Guiraudie, Alain, 288n16
Guitry, Sacha, 214, 243, **244**
Gustafsson, Henrik, 173, 201
Gutiérrez, Léticia, 153–54, 161–62, **162**, **163**
Guyotat, Pierre, 229–30

Habermas, Jürgen, 73, 263n33
Habib, André, 94, 124, 267n17
Hadopi (Creation and Internet) law, 190, 285n1
Haïdara, Eye, 42
Hamlet, 238
Hartmann, Karl Amadeus, 149
Hartog, Simon, 36
Haskil, Clara, 66, 67
Hawks and Sparrows, 71
Hegel, Georg Wilhelm Friedrich, 209, 267n14
Heidegger, Martin, 91, 112, 196, 219, 286n6
Heisenberg, Werner, 157, 279n3
Hélas pour moi, 14, 54, 94–97, **97**, 143, 182, 213, 249
Hessling, Catherine, 64
Heywood, Miriam, 264–65n42
Hickey, Dave, 9
Hindemith, Paul, 58, 75, 129–30, 133, 137, 138–39, 144–45, 147, 148, 264n42, 276n25; *Trauermusik*, 137, 139–43
His Girl Friday, 155–56, **156**
Histoire(s) du cinéma, 2, 4, 7, 11, 17, 55–81, 122, 260–61n11, 262n17; aesthetic strategy, 80; Africa sequence, 50, **50**; Agamben and, 105–7; aims, 63–64; angels, 98, 268n23, 268n24; and art, 266n49; book, 57, 193, 209–10, 260–61n11; CD, 261n11; chiasmus in, 69–70, 70, 74, 77, 79, 90, **93**, 93–94, 97–98, 101–3; Christian dimension, 75–76, 98, 147–48, 264–65n42; Cocteau's presence, 237–40, **240**, 242–43, 246; debates, 269n1; and digital technology, 84–88, **85**, **87**; Duras's presence, 243–45, **244**; DVD, 261n11; episode 1A (*Toutes les histoires*), 75–78, **76**, **78**, **85**, 87, 88, 98, 103, 208, **208**, 229, 230, 264n42, 272n27; episode 1B (*Une histoire seule*), 58, **87**, 87, 88, 89, 94, 98, 99, 238–39; episode 2A (*Seul le cinéma*), 94, 97–98, 230–31, **242**; episode 2B, 237–38; episode 3A (*La Monnaie de l'absolu*), 56–81, 230; episode 3B (*Une Vague nouvelle*), 57, 61–62, 69, 238, 243–45, **245**; episode 4A (*Le Contrôle de l'univers*), 55–56, 60, 66, 72, 273–74n6; episode 4B (*Les Signes parmi nous*), 55, **100**, 100, 265n42; and Europe, 58–61; and European art and culture, 56–57; fall and catastrophe trope, 103; Godard's self-portrait, **100**, 100–1; intertitles, 84–85; montage elements, 58–61, **59**, 74–78, 86, 98, 105–7, 136, 202–3; on the nature of humanity and human relations, 99–104; point of view, 252; and resistance, 79–81; and the romantic sublime, 99, 100; soundtracks, 103, 128, 129–30; structure, 71; tensions of, 64; themes, 57–58; trans-European approach, 259–60n5; treatment of art, 61–64, **63**; use of music, 58, 144, 146–48, 264n42, 273–74n6; video box-set, 1998, 259n4; war imagery, 55
Hitchcock, Alfred, 66, 85–86, 89, 92, 270n5, 273–74n6
Hitler, Adolf, **178**, 178–79
Hölderlin, Friedrich, 196, 219
Hollande, François, 3
Holliger, Heinz, 58, 129, 137, 152
Hollywood, 50, 62
Holocaust, the, 55, 57, 67, 69, 80, 86, 113, 167, 175, 185, 204, 211, 226, 264–65n42, 283–84n25; *see also* Auschwitz
Homer, 170, 245
homosexuality, 131, 228–31, 234–36, 240–41, 288–89n19

Hondo, Med, 38, **39**
Honegger, Arthur, 129, 136, 147
Hori, Junji, 185, 283n21
Hôtel Terminus: The Life and Times of Klaus Barbie, 113
Hugo, Victor, 55, 57, 58, 60, 248
Huppert, Isabelle, 241

I Was a Male War Bride, 156
Ici et ailleurs, 30–31, 174, 175, **178**, 178–79, 184, 217, 218, 220, 281n9, 283n22, 287n7
"Ignorés du Jury," 233–34
India Song, 94
Introduction à une véritable histoire du cinéma, 35, 193, 215–16, 260–61n11
Ishaghpour, Youssef, 77, 186
Italian neorealism, 72–73, 78, 238

Jakobson, Roman, 201
Jankélévitch, Vladimir, 280n8
Jarrett, Keith, 58, 147, 152
Jaubert, Maurice, 149
Je vous salue, Marie, 3, 95, **129**, 133–36, 210, 245, 254, 266–67n6, 276–77n35; Joseph learning to love Marie sequence, **134**, 134; opening sequence, 133; sound shots, 275n20; use of music, 132–33, 139, 142, 145
Je vous salue, Sarajevo, 184
Jeanson, Francis, 15, **25**, 25–27, 37, 256n6
Jews, 184–85, 283–84n25, 283n21, 285n31; and Palestinians, 175–79, **176**, **178**
JLG/JLG: autoportrait de décembre, 5, 18, 53–54, 143, 148, 175, 207, 213, 232, 268–69n28, 271–72n23, 276n28, 287n8, 289n2, 289n21
Joan of Arc at the Stake, 217
Jones, Clifton, 39
Jones, Jennifer, 89
Jones, LeRoi, 38, 39, 40, 257–58n21
Joppolo, Beniamino, 212
Jousse, Thierry, 127
Jullier, Laurent, 147, 275n15
Jusqu'à la victoire, 30, 37, 48, 172, 174, 217

Kancheli, Giya, 129, 148, 189, 196, 248, 251, 273–74n6

Kandinsky, Wassily, 65
Karina, Anna, 21, 67, 135, 230, 243
Keaton, Buster, 107
King Lear (Godard), 11–12, 14, 94, 107, 108, 109, 213, 242, 270–71n11, 271n16, 279–80n4; and black femininity, 258n23; eroticism, 241–42, **242**; music, 137; white horse sequence, 120–22, **121**
King Lear (Kozintsev), 270–71n11
Kiss Me, Stupid, 193
Klee, Paul, 98, 239, 262n20, 268n23
Kline, T. Jefferson, 286n1
Knaifel, Alexander, 152
Knopp, Hubert, 237
Kramer, Rony, 153, **154**
Kroker, Arthur, 83–84
Kurtág, György, 152
Kuxa Kanema, 46

La Belle et la bête, 233, 234, 237–38
La Rochefoucauld, François de, 195
Labourdette, Élina, 67
Labro, Philippe, 21
La Chinoise, 15–16, 20, 183, 212, 228, 257n16; aesthetic terrorism, 28–29; aims, 20; the apartment space, 23; background, 21–22; Brody's reading of, 31; chiasmus in, 16, 48; construction, 24; Diop, **35**, 35–38, 48; editing, 24; ethical question, 34–38; final frame, 27; final title card, 34; Godard on, 15, 20, 26, 37; Guillaume, 27–29, **28**, 40, **213**; impact, 33–34; intentions, 19; major characters, 22–23; and Malraux, 21–22; montage elements, 16, 23–24, **24**; opening, 23; political intentions, 35, 258n23; problems with, 20; reality, 24; shooting, 24; soundtrack, 24, 128; structure, 256n9; terrorism, 25–29, 32–34; theme song, 20; title, 15; title song, 35; Véronique, 25–29, 32, 48; Véronique and Guillaume, 27–28, **28**; Véronique and Jeanson, 15, **25**, 25–27; Véronique's assassination attempt, 25; and violence, 19–38
Ladoni (Palms), 252
Lady from Shanghai, The, 289n2
Laemmle, Carl, 66

La Grande Illusion, 70
La Monnaie de l'absolu (episode 3A of Histoire(s) du cinéma), 17, 56–81, 230, 266n50; bridges, 64, 67; Christian dimension, 70–71; editorial maneuvers, 67; and Europe, 58–61; final sequence, 67–72, **70**, 79; inversion and reversal, 66; Italian film sequence, 68–69; montage elements, **59**, 61–62, 64–66, **65**, **70**, 70–71, 74–75, 77–79; opening sequence, 58–61, **59**; resistance in, 67–68, 80; Second World War sequence, 64–67, **65**; self-corrections, 66; soundtrack, 68; structure, 71–72; themes, 57–58; train sequence, 64–66, **65**, 72; treatment of art, 61–64, **63**, 72; turning point, 71; use of music, 58; visual conflagration, 59; voice-over, 62
Langdon, Harry, 107
La Religieuse, 21
La Vénus aveugle, 65
Lacan, Jacques, 29, 146
Lack, Roland-François, 200, 268–69n28, 286n9, 289n22
Lacroix, Ghalya, 258–59n25
Ladmiral, Nicole, 238
L'Aigle à deux têtes, 233
Lamumba, Patrice, 39
Lang, Fritz, 7, 270–71n11
Langlois, Henri, 29
Lanzmann, Claude, 226, 264n42
Laplanche, Jean, 267n9
La Règle du jeu, 145
La Strada, 68
Last Stage, The, 68
La Terra Trema, 68
Latham, Edward D., 275n13
Lautréamont, Comte de, 109, 230
La Villa Santo-Sospir, 137, 241
Leacock, Richard, 40
Le beau Serge, 231
Le Bel Indifférent, 233–34
Le Camion, 224, 227
Le Clézio, Jean-Marie, 210–11
Le Cercle Rouge, 112
Le Chant des Mariées, 192
Le Contrôle de l'univers, 71
Le Corbeau, 157

Le Dernier mot, 137
"Le dernier rêve d'un producteur," 45
Le Livre de Marie, 217, 245
Le Pen, Marine, 3
Le Petit Soldat, 213
Le Pont des soupirs, 186, 285n32
Le Rapport Darty, 129
Le Rouge est mis, 237, 242
Le Sang d'un poète, 234, 241, **242**
Le Signe du lion, 132
Le Testament d'Orphée, 236, 237, 239, 241–42
Leacock, Richard, 40
Léaud, Jean-Pierre, 23, **24**, **28**, **213**, 234, 236
Leduc, Violette, 287n13
Lefort, Gérard, 186
Legrand, Michel, 273n5
Leiris, Michel, 49
L'Enfance de l'art, 204
L'Éternel Retour, 89
Lenin, Vladimir Ilich, 19
Les 400 coups, 234, 236
Les Dames du Bois de Boulogne, 67
Les Enfants jouent à la Russie, 279–80n4
Les Enfants terribles, 252
Les Plages d'Agnès, 197
Les Rita Mitsouko, 111, **111**, 112, 115, 130
Les Signes parmi nous (episode 4B of Histoire(s) du cinéma), 55, 74
Les Trois désastres, 247–48, 289n2
Les Visiteurs du soir, 65
Lettre à Freddy Buache, 94, 131, **132**, 277–78n40
Leutrat, Jean-Louis, 7, 239
Levi, Primo, 175
Levinas, Emmanuel, 8, 164–66, 248, 280n7
Lévi-Strauss, Claude, 196–97, **197**, 201
Lévy, Bernard-Henri, 33, 185
Lewis, Jerry, 107
L'Homme atlantique, 229
Liandrat-Guigues, Suzanne, 7
Liberté et Patrie, 79
Linhart, Robert, 22
Liszt, Franz, 58
literature: Duras as voice of, 222–28; gay, 229–31, 287–88n13; Godard's engagement with, 207–14, **208**, **213**; intertextual approach, 209, 211 passim

Local Angel, 192
Loin du Vietnam, 15–16
Locke, Maryel, 7
Long, Timothy, 222
Lo Sguardo di Michelangelo, 192
Losey, Joseph, 270–71n11
Loshitzy, Yosefa, 289n20
Losique, Serge, 215
Lotte in Italia, 30
Lubitsch, Ernst, 210
Lubtchansky, William, 139
Lully, Jean-Baptiste, 131
Lumière, Auguste, 36, 234
Lyon, Elizabeth, 10
Lyotard, Jean-François, 79, 103, 266n49

MacCabe, Colin, 3, 19, 46
Macherey, Pierre, 22
McCrea, Christian, 270n4
McMahon, Orlene Denice, 273n5
Made in USA, 21, 27
Malaparte, Curzio, 195
Malcolm X, 39
Malle, Louis, 22, 212
Malmsten, Birger, 91
Maloubier, Robert, 194
Malraux, André, 15, 21, 29, 57, 62, 109, 149–50, 196, **199**, 199, 204, 209, 231, 261n15, 271n15
Mandelstam, Osip, 67–68, 195
Manet, Édouard, 57, 62–63, **63**, 72, 270–71n11
Mann, Thomas, 73
Manovich, Lee, 266n1
Marais, Jean, 89, 213, **240**
Marino, Giambattista, 245
Martin, Adrian, 24, 256n5
Masculin Féminin, 21, 131, 228; black other in, 38–39, **39**, 43
Mas, Arthur, 285n5
Masi, Pino, 290n5
Masliah, Laurence, 95
Mason, James, 92
Matisse, Henri, 210
May '68, 15, 19, 19–38, 29, 33–34, 37, 256–57n10
Mayo, Virginia, 66
Mayakovsky, Vladimir, 34
Méditerranée, 192

Meek, Allen, 86
Meir, Golda, **178**, 178–79
Méliès, Georges, 36, 234
Menschen am Sonntag (People on Sunday), 252
Merchant of Venice, The, 270–71n11
Merleau-Ponty, Maurice, 101–2
metaphor: and *Adieu au langage*, 250; and chiasmus, 282n13; connecting, 17; and montage, 151; music as, 150; Native Americans as, 168–75, 179; in *Notre Musique*, 151–55, 184; prostitution as, 2; and *Soigne ta droite*, 109
Metropolis, 252
Miéville, Anne-Marie, 5, 9, 31, 45, 46, 79, 127, 156–57, 204, 216–22, **218**, 226, 244, 245–46, 277–78n40, 281n9, 283n22, 287n7
Minh-ha, Trinh. T., 8–9
Mitry, Jean, 210
Mitterrand, François, 58, 108
Moi, un noir, 36–37
Mompou, Federico, 275n15
Mondzain, Marie-José, 69, 263n26
Monet, Claude, 59, 78, 248
Monk, Meredith, 137, 152
Monod, Théodore, 286n8
montage, 5, 6, 10–11, 13, 16, 18, 97, 144, 201, 264n39, 265n42, 282n16; Agamben and, 105–7; as *champ/contre-champ* 155–60; *champ/contre-champ*, **156**; editorial maneuvers, 67; exchangeablity of terms, 157; *Film socialisme*, 189; *Histoire(s) du cinéma*, 74–78, 86, 98, 105–7, 136, 202–3; inversion and reversal, 66, 74; *La Chinoise*, 23–24, **24**; *La Monnaie de l'absolu*, 61–62, 64–65, **65**, 70, 70–71, 74–75, 77–79; and metaphor, 151; poetics of, 66–67; power of, 121–22, 123; *Soigne ta droite*, 118; textual saturation, 257n17; *Toutes les histoires*, 98, 103; *Une histoire seule*, 89–90, **90**, 91–93, **93**; see also *rapprochement*
"Montage, mon beau souci," 61–62
Montand, Yves, 32, 284n26
Moravia, Alberto, 212
Morceaux de conversations avec Jean-Luc Godard, 176, 178, 283–84n25
Moreau, Jeanne, 243

Morgan, Daniel, 113, 271n19, 271–72n23
Morisot, Berthe, 270–71n11
Morrey, Douglas, 3, 7, 95, 256n8, 273n31, 278n41
Mostar bridge, 151–52, 154–55, 162, 164–65, **165**, 167–68, 173–74, 281n10
Mourlet, Michel, 275–76n23
Mozambique, 45–48, **50**, 174, 259n26, 259n27
Mozart, Wolfgang Amadeus, 9, 78, 128, 136, 144, 147, 274n7
Munk, Andrzej, 68, 77–78
Münzenberg, Willi, 194
Murnau, F.W., 78
Murray, Alex, 2712n27
Murray, Timothy, 270–71n11, 272n27
music, 58, 115, 202, 258n22; and chiasmus, 130–31, 133, 275n13; as the Cinematic Event, 133, 144–48; fragmentation, 273n5; intercutting, 134; as metaphor, 150; movement, 134–36, 139–41; thematic approach, 131–32; use in *Adieu au langage*, 248, **249**, 251–52; use in *Allemagne année, 90 neuf zéro*, 143, 264n42; use in *Dans le noir du temps*, 277–78n40; use in *Détective*, 136–37; use in *Éloge de l'amour*, 133, 148–50, **150**; use in *Film socialisme*, 190; use in *For Ever Mozart*, 144; use in *Hélas pour moi*, 143; use in *Histoire(s) du cinéma*, 135, 144, 146–48, 264n42, 273–74n6; use in *Je vous salue, Marie*, 132–33, 133–36, 139, 142, 145; use in *JLG/JLG: autoportrait de décembre*, 143, 148; use in *King Lear*, 137; use in *Notre Musique*, 274–75n10; use in *Nouvelle Vague*, 132–33, 137–43, 144, 145, 264n42; use in *Passion*, 145; use in *Prénom Carmen*, 274n8; use in *Week-end*, 145; use of, 127–33, **129**, **132**; Wills on, 274–75n10
Mussolini, Benito, 49
Musy, François, 128
Muybridge, Eadweard, 120, 121, 269n3

Naipaul, V.S., 248
Nana, 64
Napoléon, 62
Narboni, Jean, 178–79, 283–84n25
national renewal, cinema as, 67–72, **70**

Native Americans, 153–54, 160–63, **162**, **163**, 179–80, 183, 187, 248, 281n12; as metaphor, 168–75, 179
Némirovsky, Irène, 64, **65**
Night of the Hunter, The, 287–88n13
Nimr, Sonia, 176
Ninetto (Davoli), 235
Nizan, Paul, 22
Nosferatu, **78**
Notre Musique, 6, 14, 151–87, 210, 249, 273n2, 281n9, 283n24, 287n7; aesthetic processes, 174; African American marine, 180; assessments, 184–87; Bosnia-Herzegovina, 151–52, 155; Brody on, 284n30; *champ/contre-champ*, 155–60, **156**, 164, 170, 174, 179, 182, 281n13; chiasmus in, 160; Christian template, 181; closing moments, 182; and difference, 159; engagement with literature, 208–9; film-within-a-film sequence, 153, 180–83, **181**; Godard in, 152–53, **154**, 155, 155–60, 184; "Hell," 153, 160; Jews and Palestinians, 175–79, **176**, **178**; Judith, 162–66, **165**, 170–72, **171**, 182, 183, 186; key issues, 171–75; master class sequence, 155, 155–60, 175; metaphor, 151–55, 184; Mostar bridge, 151–52, 154–55, 162, 164–65, **165**, 167–68, 173–74; Native Americans, 153–54, 160–63, **162**, **163**, 179–80, 183, 281n12; Native Americans as metaphor, 168–75, 179; Olga 180–83, **181**, 209, 283–84n25, 284n28, 284n29; opening voice-over, 166–67; and otherness, 159, 160–63, **162**, **163**, 165; "Paradise," 153, 180–83; point of view, 157, 165–66, 182, 280n6; political context, 155; "Projet de film," 152, 273n2, 278n1; "Purgatory," 153; release, 282n15; soundtrack, 152; structure, 153, 284n29; "The Last Speech of the Red Indian," 168–69, 281n12; title, 152; use of music, 274–75n10; writers and artists featured, 152–53
Nous sommes tous encore ici, 127, 27n16
Nouvelle Vague, 7, 54, 95, 213, 232, 249, 264n42, 275n20, 276n28; chiasmus in, 138–41; Elena's rescue sequence, 139–41, **140**; final words, 139; hands embracing shot, **141**, 141; location, 137; opening

Nouvelle Vague (continued)
  sequence, 138; poetic passages, 141–42; press conference, 9–10; soundtrack, 128, 207–8; structure, 138; use of music, 132–33, 137–43, **144**, **145**, 264n42
Novak, Kim, 92
Novarina, Valère, 208
Nuit et brouillard, 175
Numéro deux, 84, 130, 217, 220, 241, 253

Old Place, The, 9, 79, 156–57, 262n18, 279–80n4, 287n9
Oldenbourg, Zoé, 195
Olivero, Betty, 190
Only Angels Have Wings, 252
On s'est tous défilé, 136
One A.M. (One American Movie), 40
One plus One, 39–40, **40**, 43, 161
Ophuls, Marcel, 113
O'Rawe, Des, 267–68n17, 285n7
Orphée, 89, 232, 233, 234–35, 237, 239, **240**, 240, 242
other, the, 252–53; black, 37–38, 38–44, **39**, **40**, **44**; speaking for, 34–38
otherness, 8–13, 37–38; and *Notre Musique*, 159, 160–63, **162**, **163**, 165
Otte, Hans, 152, 153, 275n15
Ovid, 68

Pagnol, Marcel, 214, 270–71n11
Païni, Dominique, 177–78
Paisà, 68, 238
Palestinians, 191, 282n13, 282n16, 283n22, 284n25; and Jews, 175–79, **176**, **178**; Native Americans as metaphor, 168–75, 179
Pandora and the Flying Dutchman, 92–93, 94, 98
Parain, Brice, 210
Pärt, Arvo, 129, 147, 152, 189, 190, 275n15, 277–78n40, 285n2
Pasażerka (Passenger), 68, 77, **78**
Pasolini, Pier Paolo, 68, 70–71, **70**, 79, 235, 270–71n11, 288n16, 288–89n19
Passion, 6, 9, 11–12, **44**, 54, 75, 86, 110, 128–29, 130–31, 137, 145, 161, 241, 264n41, 266–77n6, 279–80n4
Passion of Joan of Arc, The, 36

Pavsek, Christopher, 257n17, 285n6, 289–90n5
Peck, Gregory, 89
Péguy, Charles, 55, 195, 196, 260n7, 264n35
Pennebaker, D.A., 40
Péqueux, Gilles, 152, 281n10
Pêra, Edgar, 289n1
Périer, François, 108, 109, 112–13, 115, 116–17, **117**, 239
Pétain, Philippe, 65
Peterson, Marion, 233, **233**
Picabia, Francis, 210
Picard, Andréa, 190
Picasso, Pablo, 55, **78**, 210
Piccoli, Michel, 218
Pierrot, Frédéric, 258–59n25
Pierrot le fou, 11, 14, 21, 40, 67, 88, 128, 209, 243, 266n48
Pina, 248
Pinter, Harold, 24
Pirandello, Luigi, 196
Pirchner, Werner, 137, 189
Pisani, Martial, 285n5
Plein Soleil, 142
Poe, Edgar Allan, 36, 209, 210, 216
Pollet, Jean-Daniel, 192
Pommer, Erich, 66, 262n18
Pompidou, Georges, 33
Pound, Ezra, 273n6
Powrie, Phil, 267n11
Prat Quartet, 129, **129**
Préjean, Albert, 64
Prénom Carmen, 11–12, 85, 99, 128, **129**, 129, 130, 136, 241, 274n8
Prison 91, 92, 98, 289n2
Probst, Jacques, 47
Prokosch, Frederic, 258–59n25
Proust, Marcel, 229, 248
Psycho, 89
Pucccini, Giacomo, 58
Puissance de la parole, 136, 216, 209, 266–67n6, 268–69n28
Putzulu, Bruno, 149, **150**

Quai des Brumes, 64
Quandt, James, 275n15
Queneau, Raymond, 237, 279–80n4

Racine, Jean, 27, 109, 160, 287–88n13
Radziwilowicz, Jerzy, 161, 241
Raimu (Jules Muraire), 210
Rainey, James, 284n30
Ramuz, Charles Ferdinand, 91, 94
Rancière, Jacques, 22, 76–77, 179–80, 264n42
Raphael, 268n24
rapprochement, 10, 152, 157, 161–62, 168, 175, 177, 265n44, 279–80n4; *see also* montage
Rascaroli, Laura, 181–82, 284n27
Rashomon, 219
Ravel, Maurice, 128, 131, **132**, 136, 137, 268–69n28
Ravetto-Biagioli, Kriss, 265n42
Rear Window, 217
reconciliation, 166–67, 169, 183–84
Red Desert, 289n2
"Regardezvoir, Godard," 186
Rembrandt (Harmenszoon van Rijn), 54, 77–78, **78**, 103, 130–31, 268n24
Renoir, Auguste, 65, 270–71n11
Renoir, Jean, 12, 64, 70, 71, 149, 210, 273–74n6
Reportage Amateur (maquette expo), 267–68n17
resistance: films, 68; and *Histoire(s) du cinéma*, 79–81; in *La Monnaie de l'absolu*, 67–68, 80; Native Americans and, 160–61; French Resistance, 65, 67, 68, 191
Reverdy, Pierre, 109, 203, 271n16, 279–80n4
Ricoeur, Paul, 193
Rilke, Rainer Maria, 99, 101, 254, 278n1
Rimsky-Korsakov, Nikolai, 191, 197, **198**
Ringer, Catherine, 91, 92, **111**, 11; *see also* Les Rita Misouko
Rivette, Jacques, 21, 28, 270n11, 288n18
Robinson, Marc, 120
Rocha, Glauber, 49
Rode, Thierry, **134**, 134
Rodin, Auguste, 252
Roger, Jean-Henri, 31, 43
Rohdie, Sam, 4, 85
Rohmer, Éric, 132
The Rolling Stones, 258n22
Romance, Viviane, 65
Rome, Open City, 68–69, 72, 88, 263n27

Romney, Jonathan, 254
Rosenbaum, Jonathan, 208, 276n23
Ross, Alex, 274n7
Rossellini, Roberto, 27, 57, 59, 68–69, 71, 72, 200, 211
Rouch, Jean, 36–37
Roud, Richard, 7
Roussel, Myriem, 133, **134**
Rowe, Kathleen, 286n4
Roy, Claude, 67
Russell, Rosalind, 155–56, **156**

Sachs, Maurice, 235
Sacotte, Marcel, 288n14
Sadoul, Georges, 210
Said, Edward, 4, 144, 255n4
Saluzzi, Dino, 137, 138
Sanbar, Elias, 172–73, 177, 179, 200–1, 282n15, 282n16
Sand, George, 195
Sarajevo, 162–66, 172, 282–83n20, 285n32, 286n3
Sarkozy, Nicolas, 20
Sarris, Andrew, 174
Sartre, Jean-Paul, 26, 30, 200, 248, 256n4
Sauve qui peut (la vie), 5, 7, 50, 128, 130, 131, 217, 222–24, **223**, 228, 241, 266–67n6, 274n9, 275n12
Saxton, Libby, 264n42, 271n17
Scemama, Céline, 255n5, 265n42
Scénario du film Passion, 86, 100–1, 102, 110
Schaeffer, Pierre, 274n9
Schefer, Jean Louis, 266n50
Schehr, Lawrence, 236
Schiller, Friedrich, 73
Schlöndorff, Volker, 192
Schlumpf, Erin, 182
Schnittke, Alfred, 190
Schoenberg, Arnold, 129, 137, 149, 248, 276n28
Scholem, Gershom, 197
Schubert, Franz, 128, 136
Schumann, Robert, 58, 131
Schygulla, Hanna, 161
Searchers, The, 67, 173
Second World War, 55, 60, 64–67, **65**, 144, 149, 155, 194, 214, 239

Sedgwick, Eve Kosofsky, 84
Seim, Trygve, 152
Séméniako, Michel, 22
Senghor, Léopold Sédar, 35
Senso, 68
Serrut, Louis-Albert, 275n14
Seul le cinéma (episode 2A of *Histoire(s) du cinéma*), 230–31; Godard's fall, 94, 97–98, 103
sexuality and sexual difference, 14, 228–31, 244–45, 287–88n1; *see also* desire
Shakespeare, William, 24, 120, 137, 193, 195, 196, 205, 210, 270–71n11
Shaviro, Steven, 86–87, 88
Shelley, Mary, 249–50
Shelley, Percy Bysshe, 195
Shoah, 173, 226, 264–65n44, 264n42
Shostakovich, Dmitri, 129, 145, 238, 276n25, 278n1
Sibelius, Jean, 248, 152
Silverman, Kaja, 7, 276n28, 289n21
Silverman, Max, 49, 75, 264n41, 265n44
Silvestrov, Valentin, 248
Simon, Claude, 196
Sissako, Abderrahmane, 259n26
Six fois deux, 41, 179, 215, 216–17, 217
Skoller, Jeffrey, 73, 263n32
Smith, Patti, 193
Snakes&Funerals, 7, 255–56n4
Snows of Kilimanjaro, The, 252
Sofsky, Wolfgang, 152
Soft and Hard, 5, 79, 216–22, **218**, **221**, 226, 287n8, 287n9
Soigne ta droite, 5–6, 11, 14, 44, 107–10, 109, **110**, **111**, 116–17, 122, 212, 220, 225, 226, 239, 270n5, 272n27; chiasmus in, 109; cinematic gestures, 112, 115–16; closing sequence, **123**; exclusion image, 119; final sequence, 119–20; the Idiot/Prince, 108, **110**, 112, 124, 239; the Idiot/Prince's completed film, 116; literary sources, 109; and metaphor, 109; montage elements, 118; music, 115–16; narrative direction, 112; opening sequence, 112–13; progression, 116–20; projection scenes, 116–18, **117**; soundtrack, 113, 114, 130; structure,

108, 111; train episode, 115; use of focus pulls, 113–14, **114**; voice-over, 108, 112
Soigne ton gauche, 107, 227
Sollers, Philippe, 64, 192, 210, 262n17, 286n3
Son nom de Venise dans Calcutta désert, 94
Sonimage, 216, 286n5
Sontag, Susan, 1–3, 4–5, 8, 28, 209, 286n3
Soul in a White Room, 36
soundtracks 6; *Adieu au langage*, 251–52; *Histoire(s) du cinéma*, 103, 128, 129–30; *La Chinoise*, 24, 128; *La Monnaie de l'absolu* (episode 3A of *Histoire(s) du cinéma*), 68; *Notre Musique*, 152; *Nouvelle Vague*, 128, 207–8; *Soigne ta droite*, 113, 114, 130; *Une histoire seule* (episode 1B of *Histoire(s) du cinéma*), 89; *see also* music
Spanish Civil War, 55, 194, 199
Spengler, Oswald, 55
Spielberg, Steven, 43, 148
Stanko, Tomasz, 152
Stehlé, Jean-Marc, 194
Stendhal (Marie-Henri Beyle), 191, 200
Stenzl, Jürg, 277–78n40
Sterritt, David, 7
Stévenin, Jean-François, 241
Stevens, George, 75–76, 78, 136
Stewart, Garrett, 289n3
Stewart, James, 92
Stockhausen, Karlheinz, 24, 128
Stojanova, Christina, 3
Stravinsky, Igor, 237
Streisand, Barbara, 136
Strike, 191
Stromboli, 68
Svedlund, Doris, 91
Swed, Mark, 144, 276n24
Swindlers, The, 68
Sylvie et les fantômes, 68

Tabakova, Dobrinka, 248
Tanner, Cécile, **223**, 223
Tati, Jacques, 107, 194, 270–71n11
Tanner, Cécile, 223, **223**
Taubin, Amy, 149, 277n38, 285n6
Tautin, Gilles, 32

Taylor, Elizabeth, 75–76, **76**, 98, 265n44
Tchaikovsky, Pytor Ilyich, 248, 152
Teorema, 68
terrorism, 22, 32; aesthetic, 28–29; dangers of, 29; French revolutionary, 32–34; *La Chinoise* and, 25–29; worth of, 29
Thalberg, Irving, 85
Thiele, Wilhelm, 64
Tomkins, Silvan, 84
Tout va bien, 32, 39, 42, 284n26
Toutes les histoires (episode 1A of *Histoire(s) du cinéma*), 75–78, **76**, **78**, 85, 88, 208, **208**; Anna Karina song, 230; montage, 98, 103; opening sequence, 87
Touvier, Catherine, 6
Triolet, Elsa, 230
Truffaut, François, 234–36, 243, 288n18, 288–89n19, 288n18
Tsahal, 173, 192
Tugend, Tom, 284n30
Two Pennyworth of Hope, 91

Uccello, Paolo, 59, 266n50
UFA, 64, 262n18
Umberto D., 68
Un Chant d'amour, 235
Un Chien andalou, 91, 270–71n11
Une femme est une femme, 273n5
Une histoire seule (episode 1B of *Histoire(s) du cinéma*), 48–49, 87, **87**, 88, 229, 238–39; closing stages, 90–92, **93**, 98–99; intertitles, 89; inversions, 93–94; last image, 92; montage, 89–90, **90**, 91–93, **93**; opening sequence, 89–90, **90**; soundtrack, 89
Une Vague nouvelle (episode 3B of *Histoire(s) du cinéma*), 57, 69, 238, 243–45, **244**
Union des étudiants communistes (UEC), 22
Union des jeunesses communistes marxistes-léninistes (UJCML), 22
Universal Pictures, 62

"Vague nouvelle," 209
Valéry, Paul, 60, 248, 261n14, 262n18, 273–74n6

Van Dongen, Kees, 268n24
Van Gogh, Vincent, 210, 245, 262n20, 268–69n28
Van Parys, Georges, 149
van Vogt, A.E., 248
Vecchiali, Paul, 288n16
Velázquez, Diego, 59, 72
Vent d'est, 30
Verley, Bernard, 95
Vermeer, Jan, 62
Vertigo, 92, 93, 94, 97, 98, 98, 102, 103, 270n5
Vidor, King, 155–56
Vietnam War, 21
Vigo, Jean, 71, 90, 149, 235
Villeret, Jacques, 111, **119**
violence: black other and, 41, 43; Godard's ambivalence towards, 32; in *La Chinoise*, 19–38; political, 32; validity of, 29; Žižek on, 33–34
Virgil, 209, 236, 248
Visconti, Luchino, 68, 270–71n11, 288n16
Vitali, Élisabeth, 42
Viva Maria!, 22
Vivaldi, Antonio, 128
Vivre sa vie, 36, 210, 288n14; camera-as-pendulum scene, 6, 135
Vladimir et Rosa, 31, 228
Voyage au Congo, 48–49
Voyage(s) en Utopie, Jean-Luc Godard, 1946–2006, 94, 194, 260–61n11, 267–68n17
Vrai Faux Passeport, 183, 279n2

Warhol, Andy, 36
Warner, Marina, 262–63n23
Warren, Charles, 7
Watteau, Jean-Antoine, 9, 270–71n11
Way Down East, 217
Webern, Anton, 130, 145, 276n25
Week-end, 41, 128, 145
Weil, Simone, 86, 148, 284n29
Weiskel, Thomas, 99
Welles, Orson, 194, 270–71n11, 272n27
White, Jerry, 219, 220, 286–87n6
White Rose Group, 195, 203, 260n10, 268–69n28

White Shadow, The, 49
White Shadows of the South Seas, 48
Wiazemsky, Anne, 22, **25**, 25–29, **28**, 32, 37, 40, 212
Wilder, Billy, 193
Williams, Blake, 57, 250
Wills, David, 274–75n10
Witt, Michael, 5, 15, 175, 177, 216–17, 238, 269–70n3, 273–74n6, 279–80n4
Wittgenstein, Ludwig, 147
Wolf, Christa, 195
Wollen, Peter, 233–34

Woolf, Virginia, 120
Wright, Alan, 167, 265n44, 280n8

Yared, Gabriel, 128, 130, 274n9
Yeelen, 48

Zecca, Ferdinand, 205
Žižek, Slavoj, 33–34, 146–47, 148, 276n29, 280n7
Zola, Émile, 64
Zoya, 161
Zulu, 160